T5-AGR-376

PHILIP HENRY WICKSTEED

A Corner of the Study. Childrey

PHILIP HENRY WICKSTEED

HIS LIFE AND WORK

BY

C. H. HERFORD, Litt.D., F.B.A.

Honorary Professor of English Literature
in the University of Manchester

With
Foreword and Appreciation
by
JOSEPH H. WICKSTEED

LONDON & TORONTO
J. M. DENT & SONS LTD.

Printed in Great Britain at
The Temple Press, Letchworth, Herts
First Published in 1931

PUBLISHER'S NOTE

The proofs of this volume were passed for press by Dr. Herford himself. After his death, however, certain modifications were submitted to the publishers, and these have been made on pages 54, 58, 62, 70, 129, 136, 167, 180, 205, 209, 225, 250, 263, 277, and 307.

ERRATA

Page 17, line 14, *for* Flammau *read* Fammau
,, 22, note, *for* Saunderson *read* Sanderson
,, 25, line 31, *for* ἁβρὼς *read* ἁβρῶς
,, 28, ,, 31, insert comma after neighbours
,, 72, note, *delete* J.
,, 153, line 22, *for De Monarchia read Monarchia*
,, 154, note 2, *for* acknowledge *read* acknowledging
,, 177, line 12, *omit* "
,, 282, ,, 4 from foot, *delete* comma *after* however
,, 297, ,, 26, *delete* comma *after* as
,, 297, ,, 28, *for* had been *read* and had been
,, 299, ,, 7, *for* give *read* gives
,, 300, ,, 19, *for* Alfred Vossler *read* Karl Vossler

CONTENTS

LIST OF ILLUSTRATIONS

FOREWORD

by JOSEPH H. WICKSTEED

Charles Harold Herford, the author of this biographical study of my father, died when the book was almost through the press. It was a labour of love, undertaken some two years before his death, and carried through with undaunted courage despite failing eyesight and private sorrow.

There was something inevitable in the association of the two men, which this book has now made permanent. Both may be said to have derived from the same source of seventeenth-century culture, that, for nearly two hundred years, flowed parallel to the main current of English scholarship, to remain almost unmingled with it. With the opening of the older universities to Nonconformists in 1871 a gradual merging took place ; and Herford's two latest biographies, one of my father's oldest friend, Estlin Carpenter,[1] and the present one of my father himself, are capable of being read as part of a rich tributary stream's discharge into the main current of English academic thought and learning.

One of the gains incidental to the loss of those centuries of comparative isolation was a closer association with continental scholarship, which has always made some amends for the deprivation that Nonconformists suffered by exclusion from the public

[1] Clarendon Press, 1928.

schools and universities of their mother-country. As a young man my father studied in Leiden under the great Dutch scholars of that day, and Herford served a similar apprenticeship in Germany.[1] Both men, throughout their lives, read freely and deeply in the literatures of Western and Southern Europe, and turned their critical insight from their own to other literatures, almost unconscious of a passage.

Yet, notwithstanding this breadth of outlook, it may well be that the general English reader will be conscious, in the early chapters of this book, of a strange limitedness, even insignificance, in the setting. To those of us who know them from inside, there is nothing insignificant in the Nonconformist backwaters where power was developed for the later fertilization of the great plain of twentieth-century thought. But to those who know them only from outside it will not always be given to see the dissenting pulpit, and a ministerial study trespassed on by the schoolroom, if not the nursery, in "the light that never was on sea or land."

For Philip Wicksteed's children and their associates, the drab streets of Camden Town and the classical stucco of a tabernacle in the neighbourhood of Regent's Park were never far from fairyland, and were lit by occasional gleams of eternity, no less heavenly in origin than those that had, a century earlier, lit the region of Soho for William Blake. With no deliberate intention of hiding its light, the extreme left of English Nonconformity had been taught by many generations of enforced obscurity to keep in its shell

[1] Being some years the junior man he had previously enjoyed a distinguished career at the university of Cambridge, by then "opened."

and to rely on the sufficiency of its own spiritual illumination. But the rugged shell was lined with pearl, and, if one may again steal a sentence minted for other use by Wordsworth, "its exterior semblance did belie its soul's immensity."

Though kindred spirits in so many ways, Herford and Wicksteed had a characteristic difference. Regarded as men of letters, both were pre-eminent in their quality of humanity; but Herford loved literature for its own sake, and seemed able to charm the human voice from every book upon his shelves. For my father, many shelves remained silent, for he never *possessed* any literature, except when he himself was possessed *by* the mind or minds that fathered it. Herford made the books speak like men or sing like angels; Wicksteed made the men who wrote the books live and walk in speech with us. So while Herford had a wider and subtler appreciation of that "more varied and elaborate" voice,

> Those trumpet tones of harmony that shake
> Our shores in England.

and of other literatures across the seas, my father made "the antiquated earth beat like the heart of man."

A reference will be found on page 129 to a letter from Miss Wilhelmina Kuenen to myself, in which she says that to explain a man of such apparently discursive intellect as my father it would be necessary "to show . . . that he was doing one thing all his life."

I think it needs pointing out, in this connection, that though my father had so keen a zest in the subtleties and profundities of the pure intellect, and was so assiduous in the verification of his data, the task he set himself and never deserted, was not primarily an intellectual one. From his youth he was "a dedicated spirit," moved by inner prophetic impulsion to the ministry of Religion. He used the intellect to liberate the spirit of man; but both mind and spirit he saw as dependent on the common needs of earth. Vital as it seemed to him to explore the basic philosophy, in the Greek mind, of Europe's prophetic poetry, his task of spiritual liberation could not be finally discharged till he had set himself, like Wordsworth, to "inspect the basis of the social pile," and to discover the economic conditions which alone can liberate the bodily powers that underlie the higher life.

It was a task not for a peripatetic scholar, but for an intellectual knight-errant. He neither sought nor expected academic recognition or honours. Such things "must follow . . . if they come at all." That he should, in point of fact, have so pursued his quest as to be hailed as a master by a few eminent minds in every one of the fields upon which his militant ardour led him to trespass, was justification greater than he dared to hope.

I need only add here that the chapter by Professor Lionel Robbins, on the significance of my father's contribution in Economics, was invited by the biographer as a necessary complement to his own estimate of a widely varied achievement in Criticism—and in supplement of his biographical portrait, he welcomed, with characteristic generosity, the "Appreciation" which follows.

J. H. W.

June 1931.

APPRECIATION OF PHILIP WICKSTEED

by JOSEPH H. WICKSTEED

My father was fond of quoting (from where or whom I cannot remember) that the heroic age was the age when the great men did the same things as the lesser men, but did them better. This, at all events, was something like my father himself. If, at his country home, he dug an asparagus bed, it would be something which compelled the respect of the gardener, if not quite like what the gardener would have dug. If he sailed a little open boat for a long day through fifty miles of islands along the Norwegian coast, he would finish with a heroic, and generally successful, plea with the chief peasant of the village for quarters, and with his wife for a meal; for they recognized a large humanity expressed in their own terms.

For many years, he returned again and again to Norway, and especially to the Hardanger Fjord, until every place on the map had its associations with "triumph and delight, with hope and fear." Each day was the fragment of an epic, the marriage of a dream with the reality of the wild rocks and waters; a dream betrayed as such only when some incident for a moment broke the spell. If the sound of his own tongue on the lips of a native was a gentle shock, the offer of a tow into his destination by a friendly motor-boat was an artistic assault. Both alike brought him back fatally to the civilization he was bent on escaping. But a long day's struggle at the oars against the wind and waters, roused the blood of the Northman which his red hair and blue eyes still witnessed in him. Icelandic sagas spoke to him in the waterfalls and ice-fields of the land, and in the old Norse speech of a peasantry still fighting the gods and demons of the land throughout the year for bread.

But there were things belonging to his own age which, even among the hills and waters of Norway, he accepted whole-heartedly, for they aided him in intimacy with the elements. He taught us all to find our way through the intricacies of the coastal inlets and islands, or across the unpeopled highlands, by map and compass, until we bettered him at his own game, and to his mingled chagrin and delight repeatedly guided him to his goal against his "worser" judgment. He was once alone, and lost, for forty hours on the mountains without food or shelter. But such experiences neither alarmed nor much disconcerted him. For he had little fear of death, and certainly not an exaggerated idea of his importance in the world; and, for the rest, it had to be very good company, as he often said, to be better than his own.

It was characteristic of him that his admittedly poor sense of direction did not deter him from attempting things that seemed to demand some natural or acquired facility. In point of fact he had very few facilities, and to himself, I feel sure, seemed to possess scarcely more than the common human endowment. This, at all events, was what he put his trust in. Such outstanding powers as were undoubtedly his, although they were exercised to the full, like all his faculties, can hardly be said to have been cultivated at all. His unfailing zest and diligence enabled him to read many languages, but he never laboured to acquire finish in speaking them. He often wrote with ease and fluency as well as mastery, and his unforgettable conversation flowed, at its best, unchecked like a spring from its native source; but its arresting character, apart from the sheer breadth of zestful knowledge it revealed, was due to its vigour and spontaneity rather than to a polished refinement of expression. His rare memory for verse and prose made his quotations on every occasion delightful in themselves, and in their appositeness and humour. As a small grandchild returning from Childrey reported: "Whenever anybody says anything, grandpapa says a piece of poetry." His lecturing at its best combined these three faculties, the literary, the conversational, and the illustrative, so perfectly and yet so naturally, that many of us will look back to certain utterances of his as among the most memorable experiences of our lives.

He was master equally of the short address and the long one, and filled his allotted time as an artist fills his canvas. Asked to speak to an audience at Toynbee Hall for ten minutes on "Literature," he replied that the subject was too limited for so short a time, but he would speak on "Literature and Life," which he did to the enlargement of both, in exactly ten minutes. On another occasion he stepped on to the stage of a provincial theatre where a large audience was gathered to hear a speaker, who had missed his train. My father, although unknown to the great majority, held them spellbound for an hour, on a subject entirely different from the one they had come to hear.

But the fact remains that, even on such occasions, his art was essentially simple. There was no magic of voice, or gesture, or vocabulary, few dramatic or descriptive passages, and no worked-up emotion. Magnetism, humour, and learning there certainly were, but all subdued to the main end of presenting a structure of luminous thought, directed ultimately to some vital issue, and made lucid and enduring by consummately chosen illustrations of independent beauty or significance. At the conclusion, his audience found themselves resting on a summit reached by means of no magic carpet, but with all the exhilaration of an ascent, achieved in the footsteps of a guide, who knew and loved the ground he trod. As he moved towards his goal, it was almost as though what St. Augustine calls the din of speech subsided, and one shared for a spell the angelic privilege of pure intellectual motion undisturbed by utterance

He had an innate power of lifting simple things to great magnitude, due perhaps to an integrity of vision, which, if it did not enable him to see the whole of life the whole time, made it appear to be rediscovered in every part. The Greek tragedians, the Bible, Virgil, or Shakespeare, spoke as he read or quoted them, not themselves only, but—

> the memory of all books which lay
> Their sure foundations in the heart of man.

Even to lose one's way with him in a midnight adventure on the fells or fjords was to discover that one never could miss Mother Earth.

Pistol's brag, "the world 's mine oyster," might have been made in somewhat more modest, and more pregnant, form by my father; for the whole world was the other lobe of his mind and heart. Like the limpet that clings to the rocks, but with incomparably greater agility, he held fast to this world and never let it go. With him "the discerning intellect of Man" was ever "wedded to this goodly Universe in love and holy passion."

His love of Earth, his reverence for the things of Earth, and his deep human need of Earth were the foundations of all his philosophy and all his practice. It was also in a strange sense the foundation of a unique gift of companionship. If he used Earth as his other valve it was not the naked or unpeopled earth. Though his delight was in sun and wind and rain; in lake and river; in mountain, rock, and valley; in forest and meadow and all wild things, the fine flower of Earth was his own kind, and to be his companion for a long day anywhere was to find oneself a thing required in the economy of his mental and spiritual life. For the moment, one became his Earth, a thing as it were, taken for granted, as the second chamber of his mind and heart. Enoch, we are told, walked "with God and was not." Philip Wicksteed, like Shakespeare's mistress, walked "on the ground" and yet in his company personality seemed to disappear in the common mind of which we all partake. Many years ago at a Quaker wedding I remember him describing marriage as a "ladder set up on the Earth, the *top* of which reaches to Heaven." It described not only his own marriage, but everything else in his life. It was because his higher mind reached and rested on the top that he shrank with horror from anything that made the footing of the ladder a sham, or a snare, or any kind of slippery slope.

It is necessary to insist on the earthly foundations of his thought and life, because he has been described as one of the angelic doctors, a modern saint, and so forth. It may be so; and perhaps that is inevitably the only part of him that will survive. But his foundations were elsewhere. For those of us who knew him intimately, he was a man less possible to get into a stained-glass window than very much more ordinary people. The basis of his character was a healthy animal vigour. Instinctively he was a fighter,[1] and in moments of excitement he reverted to type, sometimes to his great mortification when he realized what it had betrayed him into. For twinned, as is so often the case, with his zest for hard blows, given and taken, was a vein of tenderness which never ceased to grow as he grew older. In his later years, he was rarely surprised into combat, except by his zeal for pure truth, or his deep and universal compassion. Perhaps both the zeal and the compassion made him a bad controversialist. Vigorous, even violent, assertion was sometimes allowed to take the place of impartial discussion. I have heard him pour out a torrent of feeling eloquence that moved, and even inspired, his opponents, leaving them silenced, but wholly unconvinced. And yet, even in these moments, any one who could stand up to him, and ply him with genuine doubts, or difficulties, was sure of carrying away some profound reflection that made the whole subject seem enlarged.

A characteristic, which many of his friends found even more perplexing, was his almost complete silence regarding his own views on those deep matters in which he was for ever expounding the views of his masters. It sometimes appeared as though he only

[1] *Vide* the admirable caricature, p. 130, for which I have ventured to supply a motto.

valued his own intellect as a means of discovering what seemed true to men in past ages. The solution of the problem is partly to be found in a parable he delighted to point out, in the perplexed countryman's apology for misdirecting a traveller: "If I wanted to go there myself, I should not start from here." My father, in attempting to understand any mind, began by trying to realize where that mind started. Every age, he believed, proceeded to think upon certain basic assumptions: Aristotle had his; the minds of the Middle Ages had theirs, and we had ours. "I have been trying to discover," I once naïvely admitted, "why our assumptions really are more reliable than theirs." "Well, that," he said quietly, but with unusual finality, "you will not be able to do."

He measured the minds of his masters not by their assumptions, but by the significance of the thought based on those assumptions. Small minds think even true things insignificantly. But Anselm, explaining that the Fall of Adam and Eve was due, not to the desire for knowledge, which was right, but to the attempt to win knowledge through wrong or premature action, had discovered a truth of deep and universal significance independent of the historicity of the story itself.

His attitude was essentially the same towards his disciples as towards his masters. He sought to help them from where they stood. It seldom seemed relevant to tell them where he stood, as it was so unlikely to be the same spot. To represent him, therefore, as only concerned with the minds of the past would be singularly wide of the mark. He was continually helping both the wise and the simple with their own immediate and present-day problems, moral, intellectual, and spiritual, and not least in the hourly crises which arose for us all during the war.

This same attitude again was carried by him into his rare speculations as to the future. He was content to leave to posterity the starting point of its own thought, but he felt he knew something of its goal. "I am not sure," he remarked to me at Oxford, some forty years ago, "whether the religion of the future will be strongly Theistic. But it will have to embrace things that only Theism has hitherto reached."

He was very conscious of the spiritual value of negations, and that great moments in the history of religion have, characteristically, if not inevitably, coincided with the rejection of beliefs hitherto held necessary to faith. And those who have the very legitimate desire to know what was his own basis, must be prepared to find it even simpler than they might expect. If St. Francis demonstrated how slender are the material possessions necessary for the life of the soul, the whole tendency of Philip Wicksteed's thought was to show how unexacting the spiritual life is, as to the amount, or the precise character, of the basis of dogma it demands. The one supremely important thing was that beliefs should be believed. Past ages, so far as they attracted him away from his own, did so not because of the contents of their creeds, which were often profoundly opposed to his own, but because their creeds were their real creeds. This gave them the strength necessary to sustain superstructures of universal and undying significance.

I am satisfied that he himself had for many years looked forward to no personal survival, except such as might exist in his work and the love and affection of his friends. In the last few days of his life, the personal importance of this belief, or want of belief, seemed to increase rather than diminish. He never spoke as though death were to be more feared than sleep, but he spoke with deep feeling of the oneness of body and soul.

I do not think there was anything incongruous to himself in the holding of such views, and being the exponent of the world's greatest utterance on life after death. The significance of Dante's *Comedy* was for him necessarily based on the spiritual experiences we meet in the present life, and the Catholic doctrine of the ultimate reunion of body and soul, though he did not believe it, was far less repugnant to him than the idea of the life of the spirit entirely apart from the body. He built his heaven upon the things we know here and now, and the spiritual possibilities of our bodily life were facts deep in his own experience.

Again, as an exponent of the Bible, though he saw in it the record of a continuous advance in the conception of God, it would be difficult to say in what sense he himself believed in the God, either of the Old, or of the New Testament. He certainly considered there was something in the nature of things akin to the moral and intellectual constitution of Man, and that, in our best living, we mysteriously approach that reality. But this is still a long way from the belief in an All-guiding, and All-sustaining, Providence moved by human prayer, such as the Theism of the Bible seems almost everywhere to postulate. Prayer was never, for him, the attempt to move God uswards, but the attempt to move ourselves Godwards. Yet difficult as his Theism was to define, difficult as he often found it to justify, he found it still more impossible to reject. The sense of God's presence was integral to his mind, and in all his highest moments it was, I believe, the very element on which he soared.

Some men only recognize their spiritual home when love of truth has made them exiles. I do not think my father ever felt exiled, but it may well have been that his freedom saved his faith. Just as his detachment from the actual creeds of his masters unquestionably helped him to interpret them, so I think his own freedom to doubt and to examine his faith, at once enlarged his sympathies and helped to confirm, if not to define, his creed.

Yet it must not be supposed that this intellectual detachment was attained without cost. Perhaps it did not weaken, it may even have strengthened, his personal faith, and it surely enabled him to discover and expound many faiths that were not his. But though he could show the goodness and the beauty of the beliefs of others, he could not show the truth even of his own.

This was the reason, I think, for his failure as a preacher, as compared with his outstanding success as an interpreter. But it gave a far deeper stimulus to the minds of those whom he most influenced. As they could not get their creed from him, they had to find it for themselves, and it became their own as no belief adopted from another could ever have been. All who came to him for light must bring some joy or vision with them, if they would get the best he had to give. That it was different from his vision made no difference to him. For he walked with us, not as an instructor pointing the way, but as a fellow pilgrim by our side.

Near Bergen, Norway

At Childrey

Emerson says somewhere that the function of genius is to reach the whole way from God, or pure truth, to the minds and hearts of the common people. Philip Wicksteed inspired us to believe that each of us had it in him to reach the whole way from the common mind and heart to pure truth.

I think it may be said that his essential message was, that heaven can be reached only from earth—each man's particular earth—but that earth can be interpreted only from heaven. He laboured, therefore, to bring the noblest thought of all the ages into our common lives, as the basis of all the noblest there can ever come to be.

Thus many have undertaken to expound the philosophy of Aristotle, the theology of Aquinas, the poetry of Dante; Philip Wicksteed attempted to show the significance of the philosophy, the theology, the poetry of these great minds for you and me here to-day.

And the burden of his economic message was that every man's daily and hourly conduct, the choices he makes of good and evil in his momentary wisdom or folly, hold the secret of all the complex drama of exchange, which is slowly and fitfully, but inevitably, welding mankind into a single society, and which, truly understood, is the only road to the healing of Earth's woes.

He made the great familiar and always he made the familiar great. In his company the gods descended to walk with us, that we might know our common Earth for the street we must still tread, and must still pave, to heaven.

JOSEPH H. WICKSTEED.

January 1931.

PHILIP HENRY WICKSTEED

by

C. H. HERFORD

TO THE
MEMORY OF MY WIFE

Wicksteed's books elucidate the mighty synthesis of human knowledge which Aristotle and Aquinas constructed for their times and which is to be redone in our day in order that civilization may grow conscious of its goal, and man may direct the potentialities of his nature in a world made peaceful therefor till again he lives in Eternity, while he carries out the tasks dictated by the illusions of Time.

J. H. WEATHERALL.

PREFACE

PHILIP HENRY WICKSTEED was a man who deeply and lastingly impressed a large number of minds, from the simplest to the most eminent, yet won no corresponding recognition in the general mind of contemporary England. He occupied none of the points of vantage which catch the eye and secure the *monstrarier digito* more easily than many kinds of solid service. He made no attempt to enter the avenues which often lead less remarkable men to wide reputations. Through the greater part of his working years he trod the unpretending paths of the Extension Lecturer and the Unitarian minister. You met him at any time in those years, correcting exercises in third-class carriages, on his way to lecture at Leicester or Bradford, or tramping in all weathers from Camden Town to his chapel in Marylebone. Qualified hearers recognized that he had important things to say; but a wider reputation was discounted by the fact that these were addressed to wholly different audiences, and concerned seemingly unrelated provinces of reality. You cannot in the modern world say even important things which belong to widely different regions of the universe of science, art, industry, commerce, without someone murmuring "sciolist," and another quoting Dryden's *Zimri*:

> A man so various that he seem'd to be
> Not one but all mankind's epitome.

Yet no descriptions could be more grotesquely untrue of Philip Wicksteed. A massive and powerful unity pervaded his life. His "variousness" was the expression of a nature too full and rich to be stirred to vital thought and utterance in only one of the provinces into which we choose to divide our experience. He saw, as we all do, a world resting upon imperious physical needs, and less imperious, but not less vital, spiritual needs. We do not accuse ourselves of distracting versatility when we return from a concert to supper, or after a day spent in earning "bread and butter" "unbend our minds," like Sarah Battle after the business of whist, over a book. For most of us the problems which underlie these antitheses remain implicit, the clues unpursued. The higher kind of versatility is the temper which refuses to leave them so.

But even when versatility is not the mark of a mind which "spreads" easily because it is soft and compliant, like butter, but of one that like a rich and generous liquor overflows, there are apt to be differences of stress or of ardour in the different pursuits. This, however, hardly touches cases like that of an illustrious contemporary, who after disturbing the outlook of New Testament scholarship, wrote a great book on Bach, to find his life-work incomplete until he had mastered medicine and gone out as a medical missionary to the negroes of the Congo. No one appraises the work of Albert Schweitzer in any one of these fields less highly because of his achievements in the others; nor does any one, either, regard him as a modern Pico de la Mirandola or Admirable Crichton, a brilliant virtuoso who exhibited his mastery of many instruments to the eyes of an astonished world. We recognize in him, rather, the gradual integration of a life-purpose, a man "fulfilling himself in many ways."

And that phrase rightly describes, on his humbler plane, the work of Philip Wicksteed. Parade was the last thing, unless it was profit, that he thought of. Few of those who hung upon his words as he led them, with Dante, through the glories of the Empyrean, suspected that at home he might be busy with the application of the Jevonian curves to the "higgling of the market" and the theory of rent. Regions, poles apart to most apprehensions were united, for him, by a perfectly clear nexus, the needs, spiritual and material, of man; and in both fields he had urgent and important things to say. To explain this inner nexus is a leading purpose of this book. It is hoped that the account which is offered in the later chapters of Wicksteed's work as an organic whole may do something to further this purpose.

But it is hoped also that some sections of these chapters may serve as introductions to the more abstruse portions of Wicksteed's work, both in the Dantesque and in the Economic field. The *Reactions between Dogma and Philosophy* (1920), in which the first group culminates, is a study, at once reverent and critical, of the origins of the accepted philosophy of Catholicism, only possible to one who was at once a master of Thomism, and completely detached from St. Thomas's faith; a book in which a great Catholic scholar could find "real spiritual support," which yet delineated with the clarity of scientific detachment the flaws and failures incident to St. Thomas's task. This, perhaps the greatest of Wicksteed's books, stands entirely alone in the scholarship of our day, and could probably have been written by no other man. For such a book the introduction here attempted, however imperfect, will hardly be superfluous.

But the more technical of Wicksteed's Economic books, though bearing such disarming titles as "Alphabet" and "Common Sense," stand in even greater need of the commentator. And the writer may express with less reserve his hope that the sections on these books contributed by Professor Lionel Robbins may do something to rectify the still very imperfect recognition among the educated public of Wicksteed's significance in this field. Among professed economists his reputation has always been high, and, like Bentham, he is even better known on the Continent and in America than at home. "It would be difficult," writes Mr. Robbins, "to find a really important work in pure economics during the last twenty years which does not contain some reference to his work or some trace of his influence"; and he holds that this influence, most conspicuous precisely among the younger men, is likely to increase rather than diminish.

Yet the man was even more remarkable than his books. It is hoped that the biographical chapters may do something more than give the human setting of his published work, and may do something to preserve for a while among those who did not know him the image of a personality the memory of which remains so precious and so fragrant for those who did. Or rather, let us refuse to associate a memory so radiant, so animating as his, with words suggestive of the quiescence of the faded scroll. Let us think of him, not as buried in any tomb, however sacred, nor as commemorated in any literary record, however articulate, but as of those who

> In the never idle workshop of nature,
> In the eternal movement
> Will find themselves again.

It remains to acknowledge the help which has been abundantly received by the writer. His indebtedness for an important contribution of Mr. Lionel Robbins, Professor of Political Economy in the University of London, has already been mentioned. Reminiscences, and other material, acknowledged in their place, have been given him by Mr. E. I. Fripp, Mr. F. M. Cornford, Mr. H. R. Beeton, Mrs. R. Roscoe, Mrs. R. Garnett, Miss H. Wainwright, Miss C. Sharpe, Mr. H. V. Herford, and by the Wicksteed family.

Letters have been lent by many of the above, and also by Mr. Thomas Wicksteed, Miss Alice Lucas, Miss Emilie Knappert, Rev. J. Lloyd Thomas, Rev. J. H. Weatherall, Miss M. Reynolds, Mr. W. J. Jupp, Mr. J. M. Connell, and Miss Hilda Hargrove. The Registrar of the University Extension Board in the University of London kindly supplied a list of Wicksteed's lecture courses for that body and the syllabuses of several courses.

To the librarian of Manchester College for frequent help; and to Miss Elsie Ball, without the aid of whose sifting and ordering hand and eye, this book would have been far more imperfect than it is.

C. H. HERFORD.

1930.

CHAPTER I

CHILDHOOD AND BOYHOOD

Leeds—Hafod—London: University College School—University Hall

I

"It is no use regretting Philip's vehement ways," his mother would say of the subject of this book, as a boy; "he has the blood of two martyrs in his veins. He will always insist on what he thinks true, whatever the consequences." Philip Henry Wicksteed was, in fact, descended, through his mother, from John Rogers, the first Protestant sent to the stake under Mary; and, through his father's mother, from the Puritan divine, commemorated in his own name, who in the milder purgatorial shades of the seventeenth century, suffered ejection for his faith. His father used to say, we are told, "that you could never gauge the real force that was in a man till you saw whether he could perpetuate his character in his posterity." The saying may be hazardous; for genius is apt to leave its posterity exhausted as by a concentrated output of racial energy. But it is much more often justified where "the real force that is in a man" is not of the kind that breaks out in sudden and astonishing explosions, but of that which is laid up in solid, balanced, and well integrated powers of mind and character. Men and women of this type have never been rare in England; they are the stamina, if we dare not say the staple, of the English people; and the chronicles of English family history disclose often enough a sequence of the type continuous, with little change, through several generations. So it was for two hundred years with the posterity of Philip Henry. It produced, says the subject of this memoir pleasantly, "neither a man of genius nor a rascal." But he added that neither term must be too strictly defined if the statement is to be perfectly accurate; and some who read these lines will question whether one-half of it did not come near to being belied in the person of Philip Henry Wicksteed himself.

His forbears, when they first distinctly emerge, are found living in that north-west midland district between the Pennines and the foothills of Wales, of which the old city of Shrewsbury is the natural capital. It is the country of the Darwins and the Wedgwoods, family stocks cognate with the Wicksteeds and the descendants of Philip Henry, both in solid character and in religious independence. About the beginning of the nineteenth century, John Wicksteed, son of a breeches-maker in Chester, began business as a starch manufacturer in Shrewsbury. He was a noticeable man, of a "tone of mind" not common in Shrewsbury town. He had been through the Grammar School at Chester; knew William Hazlitt, son of the Unitarian minister at Wem, ten miles north of Shrewsbury, and had perhaps, like young Hazlitt, heard Coleridge preach in the Shrewsbury Unitarian chapel at the close of 1798.[1] In after years Hazlitt, no facile praiser, spoke warmly of this friend of his boyhood. But he was not John Wicksteed's only link with the literary world. He had spent some time in London and attracted the

[1] Was he caught up into the ardour of young Hazlitt's hero-worship for Coleridge? Coleridge had, in 1797, hailed the philosopher Hartley as "wisest of men." John Wicksteed, like Coleridge himself, called a son by Hartley's name.

interest there of the literary circle in which the Aikins and the Barbaulds were conspicuous figures. His later history suggests that with John Wicksteed's talent and fascination was associated a sanguine, perhaps dangerously sanguine, temperament. In John Wicksteed we seem to discern a nature rich in possibilities which it was for a later generation to unfold. It was this noticeable man, who in the last years of the eighteenth century married one of the direct descendants of Philip Henry—Bithia Swanwick, of Wem. Their first home was a roomy house and garden in Shrewsbury known as "The College." Here, and in a country house some two miles out of the town, the elder members of their numerous family were born.

One of the elder of these, at once arrests attention. For before his tragic death, at twenty-four, Joseph Hartley Wicksteed had shown definite signs of infringing the family law of exemption from "genius," faithfully observed as far as we know by his mother's kin. In this brilliant young man, the vein of poetry, of natural fascination, which we surmise in his father, becomes clear and unmistakable. "He was a man," says his nephew Philip, "of rare intellectual and poetic gifts, a fine scholar and a fascinating companion. . . ." In 1824, when he had studied at Glasgow with no small distinction, he was drowned while bathing in Loch Katrine. Of the promise thus tragically frustrated no direct memorial remains; but the elusive figure of Joseph Hartley Wicksteed is enshrined, like Arthur Hallam's, in the passionate adoration of one to whom he too was "more than brother." It was indeed his own brother, nearly seven years younger than himself, and still a Shrewsbury schoolboy at his death. To this boy, says Philip, his elder brother was "almost a deity. They would go long walks together, Joe often reciting poetry, and kindling an admiration and enthusiasm [for it] in his brother's heart second only to his own. . . ." To this brother "Joe was the impersonation of poetry, the presiding deity, as it were, of romance and heroism and aspiration, and yet at the same time a fellow-worshipper with himself at the shrine. On bright July mornings," related the younger brother many years after his death, "I would stand by his side translating, in schoolboy guise, those beautiful episodes in the Georgics, or the fiery speeches of the Aeneid, and he with his arm round my neck, inducing as it were on my words, in his own deep mellow voice, the rich, fervid, feeling version of genius; and then we would wander forth into the groves of that finely-wooded county in which it was our fortune to dwell, or on the banks of its fair winding river—and whether the bard was in his hand or in his mind, it was alike poetry and happiness to me." The joys and sorrows of a long and busy life scarcely overlaid, in the younger brother, this "deep grief of his soul." "For twenty years," he would tell his children, "no day ever passed without his consciously dwelling upon his brother's memory. Night after night he prayed (but always in vain) to be allowed to see him in dreamland; and his children learnt to listen with a wondering grief and sympathy to the story which still filled their father's eyes with tears, and to repeat fragments of his poetry, which seemed to link their homespun lives with the distant world of genius and glory."[1]

One of the children who grew up among these

[1] Philip Henry Wicksteed, *Memoirs of Charles Wicksteed*, pp. 10–11.

Philip Wicksteed. Early Portraits

memories was the subject of this memoir, and the younger brother was his father, Charles. For two generations the name of the elder brother was given to the eldest son; Philip's eldest brother and his eldest son both bore the name of Joseph Hartley.

II

Charles Wicksteed, if less brilliantly gifted than either his elder brother or his son Philip, held a considerable place among the ministers of the Unitarian communion of the middle of the last century. Ten years at Shrewsbury under Butler and four at Glasgow University made him a well-grounded classical scholar, and in 1831 he was appointed minister at Toxteth Park, Liverpool. Liverpool was then, and for some decades remained, one of the most important and enlightened centres of Unitarianism in the country. Two fellow-ministers of lofty spiritual gifts, John Hamilton Thom and James Martineau, became his intimate friends. Four years later, at the close of 1835, he accepted an invitation to become minister of the Mill Hill congregation at Leeds. There he took an energetic part in public work and in the burning political questions of the day. The first Reformed Parliament had just begun to sweep away some of the grossest abuses of the past. Leeds, like the other great municipalities, acquired a relative self-government, and some of the disabilities of the Dissenters were now redressed. Nowhere were these changes welcomed with keener interest than in the municipalities of the West Riding, in all of which the party of Reform was strong, enlightened, and well-to-do. For the most part it was

Nonconformist in religion, and a large proportion of its most public-spirited and most educated members were Unitarian.

It was in the midst of this alert community, as the official guide of one of its principal religious congregations, that Charles Wicksteed in 1835 settled. It became for eighteen years his home. Young as he was, and brief as his experience of civic affairs had been, his union of engaging charm with clear and sharply-defined opinion soon brought him both a large circle of friends and social recognition and importance. In the stormy political agitations of those eighteen years he took a leading part. He was not a politician by temperament, but he was deeply conscious of the sufferings of the industrial north in those days of the "hungry forties," and they were aggravated by legislation which only political agitation could annul. He was one of the fiercest denouncers of the Corn Laws. But he flamed out with no less passion against the Fugitive Slave Act, which threatened no English material interest but made England co-operate with the American slave-owners against the American slave.

But it was not as the passionate denouncer of wrongs that Charles Wicksteed was most conspicuous to those who knew him. Even the official minister disappeared in the cordial friend. "Mr. Wicksteed did not call on us," said one later, "he came to see us." The Leeds Conversation Club, which he had some share in founding, was one of his most congenial relaxations. With three of the most distinguished Unitarian ministers of the day, J. H. Thom, James Martineau, his old colleagues in Liverpool, and J. J. Tayler of

Manchester, he edited the *Prospective Review*, the *Hibbert Journal* of those days.

Two years after settling in Leeds, Charles Wicksteed married the second daughter of a Leeds citizen, Arthur Lupton, whose family had been conspicuous through several generations for its sterling qualities and enlightened public spirit. Lupton himself had, in the dark years of Tory reaction after the fall of Napoleon, carried off his young family to the scarcely older republic beyond the ocean, returning disillusioned, after four years (1822). Some of his children shared his militant ardour. One daughter vowed to stamp on the shore of America when she left, and to kiss the soil of England when she landed. Another, some ten years old, fought with an American girl who had slighted England. This militant child, Charlotte (1812–88), became a remarkable woman, whom we shall meet again. It will suffice here to note that her indomitable will, her union of strong personality with indifference to wealth or fame, and perhaps her lifelong devotion to the prophets of Israel, reflect some Lupton qualities which came to the Wicksteeds, and not least eminently to her nephew Philip, with her sister Jane. In Philip's mother the Lupton character presented its most ingratiating aspect. Jane Lupton, in the words of her son, brought to her husband for almost fifty years a companionship "alike of the intellect and of the affections." She herself had the ordinary education of cultivated women in that day, but was in no sense, like her sister Charlotte, a learned woman. She made little attempt to follow even the more accessible portions of her son's many-sided culture. But we recognize in her beautiful and harmonious nature the source of the indomitable inner strength and security which his versatility only enriched and never disturbed; which made the many evolutions of his indefatigable quest for new truth, and his fearlessly enterprising thought, only like the facets of a polygon, distinct aspects of the same solid core of mind. She was one who, in her son's words, "looked straight into men and things with the guileless eye of unflinching and unsuspecting veracity, and had seized the good and rejected the evil with the quick instincts of truth."

It was in a home founded by these parents, and in the atmosphere quickened by these keen social, political, and intellectual interests, that their ten children were born. Philip Henry, the subject of this memoir, the second son, was born in October 1844. Only the first ten years of his life were to be spent in the Leeds home. During these years the children saw little of their father. He was an awful personage who dispensed decrees and imposed lessons in the otherwise inviolable "sanctuary" known as his study. But there was all the more freedom outside; and of Philip we have a glimpse, at seven or eight, as a curly-headed little lad, less prone to awe than to the *gaminerie* of the *enfant terrible*. A young minister, newly married, was visiting the Wicksteeds with his young bride. Philip danced on the sofa, chanting a stanza with the refrain:

> "What brats to rear,
> What stockings to be mended." [1]

But the scene was soon to be changed. Early in the fifties, Charles Wicksteed's health, never robust, began

[1] The visitor was Philip's later friend, Brooke Herford. Some fifteen years later, when he visited Philip, then himself just engaged, he reminded him of this, "not without a playful insinuation that he might by and by repeat it for his own edification."

Hafod-y-coed. Vale of Clwyd

to be gravely impaired. Mental lassitude was added to bodily suffering, and he was haunted by the fear that his ministerial work was futile. His keen enjoyment of social life made these symptoms invisible, even incredible, to outsiders. Many remedies were tried. The congregation, devoted to their minister, sent him on a three months' tour to Italy, and when the symptoms returned undiminished, proposed to give him three years' leave of absence on full salary. But Charles Wicksteed saw that he must give up the wearing struggle imposed by the nervous strain of the ministry, and in July 1854 he sent in his final resignation.

III

The course he now took, of settling in the heart of the country, was dictated not only by search for health, but by his passionate love of Nature. Devoted as he was to the eager and strenuous life of the town, and idolized by his people, he felt the close of his life at Mill Hill, the exchange of the city pavements for the country grass and roads, a spiritual as well as a physical emancipation; and he has described in a vivid sentence the rapture with which immediately after his departure he climbed the hill at Ilkley, a free man. He settled at Upper Eyarth, a beautiful spot in the upper Clwyd valley. It was a fine old timbered house, on rising ground, with a noble view of Moel Fammau, the "bosom" summit of the Clwydian range. Here an idyllic but active life began for them all, in which Philip, now a boy of nine, had his full part. The father, at first a wreck, scarcely able to walk a mile without rest, recovered his vigour and his joy. At

Leeds, rarely seen by his children, and then chiefly with awe, he now became the joyous and indispensable companion of their walks and talks. The scholar was now a farmer, and the walks had often a bucolic purpose in view, but the lively lads plied him on the way with a stream of questions on all things knowable and unknowable. Philip was already at work unravelling the riddles of nature and detecting the fallacious logic of men. "As we walked home last night," writes the father, "from investigations into the merits of some possible cow-purchases, by the light of the early stars, Philip tackled me with questions" as to how the sizes and distances of the heavenly bodies were measured, producing, he confesses, only a confused and unsatisfactory reply. And Philip was not easily satisfied. The passion for probing things to their roots, which later drew him to explore the sources of Dante in Aquinas and Aristotle, and the "common sense" of economics, often, at this stage, took the form of a provoking obtuseness to obvious matters of fact, winning for the baffled and brooding boy the reputation, we are told, of being rather stupid and "slow in the uptake."

Three miles from Upper Eyarth was the Grammar School of Ruthin. It was neither better nor worse than the mass of country grammar schools in those and much later days. The circle of the sciences and of humane letters were represented almost exclusively by "classics," mathematics, and "religion"; classics taught with a merely mechanical scholarship, in which criticism had no part and scientific archaeology and philology were as yet undreamed of. "Religion" meant (as with Fielding's Thwackum) the traditional theology of the Church of England, untouched by a breath of criticism, intolerant of "dissent" in all its forms, and particularly contemptuous of the Welsh Nonconformity of the surrounding countryside. Like most of the grammar schools in Wales it served as a stronghold of the English caste, and of the caste spirit founded on wealth and social prestige.

To this school, Philip and his elder brother, Hartley, were now sent as day-boys. Both for the father and for the school authorities the situation was novel; for us it is piquant and a little comic. Charles Wicksteed, though a large-hearted and genial man, and quite untouched by what Arnold later called "the dissidence of dissent," held his own religious faith with uncompromising security; he was not only a Unitarian, but he knew extremely well, as thousands learnt from his lips in after days, "why" he was one. And he was not minded to tolerate Anglican teaching for his sons. But the Anglicanism of the school was rigid and exclusive; exceptions to it were unknown among boys as among masters. No "dissenter" probably had ever sought admission before. This eccentric Unitarian had, however, one puzzling qualification: the old pupil of Butler and Sandford was a classic whose accomplishments inspired amazement and respect in head master and staff of the country grammar school.[1] A

[1] The boys' own prowess in classics was not at this stage remarkable. When examined by the head master in the elements of Latin grammar their replies were less satisfactory than those of the "poy" instructed by Sir Hugh Evans. "What is the genitive of 'ego'?" he asked. The two boys looked at each other, and, pooling the wisdom of their ten years, settled upon "tibi." Upon which the oracular sentence followed: "I see these young gentlemen's talents lie in some other direction." Before they left Ruthin, however, Philip had retrieved this disaster by at least one modest honour in the classical school.

compromise was grudgingly admitted, a sort of "conscience-clause" allowed, under which Hartley and Philip were excused the Catechism, while attending the Scripture lessons, the morning prayers, and the daily chapter of the Greek Testament.

This was the occasion of the beginning of Philip's religious education. It was strongly marked by his father's idiosyncracy, by the union in him of a religious passion which made public worship of some kind a necessity to him, with an extremely definite Unitarian creed. He was so far from reciprocating the Anglican aversion to his creed that he took his children regularly to the evening service at the neighbouring church of Llanfair. But when they came home he "took them carefully through the service, explaining which portions he could not accept or repeat," supplying a similar antidote to passages from the Bible which they had heard emphasized by the masters, or which their schoolfellows had flung in their teeth.[1] From his father's position Philip was to depart far. But that union of spiritual passion with intellectual definiteness and precision was resumed in far larger contexts in the son, who was equally himself in explaining the genius of Hebrew prophecy and in following the intricacies of Kuenen's criticism of the Pentateuch, the character of Dante's Beatrice, or the cosmography of his Hell.

But if his father bequeathed to Philip this happy union of gifts, he gave no help at all in the applications of them, which were to become so fruitful in Philip's intellectual life. His "antidotes" to Anglican teaching merely rebutted its claims to be founded upon

[1] *Memoir*, p. 67.

"Scripture." The authenticity of Scripture itself, the divergent history and significance of its several portions, he deliberately left wholly untouched. Hence Philip's school and home life in Wales left him a stout and single-minded Unitarian, indeed, but without a suspicion of the historical criticism which was undermining the traditional view of the Bible among the advanced minds of Unitarianism itself, and which he was himself to lead the way in making known to the "young people" of English-speaking lands. To those historical and critical studies his father, so far as he was acquainted with them, was not unfriendly, and to Philip's activities in this work, which he lived to witness, he brought the heartiest respect and sympathy. But an educational principle which, in after years, he gravely questioned, led him to "reverence his children" by keeping them, in these matters, ignorant. And such reticence harmonized with the idyllic or bucolic simplicity of the life these boys and girls lived in the beautiful Clwyd valley homestead; with the evenings when they listened to the father's reading from Scott and other classics. "For many and many a year," writes Philip, after the settlement in Wales, "Scott, read by my father as few can read him, was a part of the life of the household." The *Faery Queene*, picturesquely called by the father the scholar's Pilgrim's Progress, was in special request with one of the sons, who saw himself in imagination a knight-errant, and perhaps vaguely desired that he would be also a "scholar pilgrim" to many other shrines. But the Greek and Latin classics were called in as well; and Philip, in old age, reading the *Agamemnon* with a granddaughter, and finding it "jolly difficult," recalled how his father had translated it to the family circle, and felt impressed anew by the old man's scholarship.

The teaching at the school was, as already stated, apart from the "divinity," almost exclusively classics and mathematics, and classics taught more mechanically than in his father's day at Shrewsbury. The *Eton Latin Grammar,* the masterpiece of this mechanical method, excited the mature scholar's contempt, betrayed in half-suppressed exclamations, as he heard his boys recite its "ridiculous rules." But when Philip, catching at the word, asked "with a delusive gleam of hope," why if the rules were ridiculous they were compelled to learn them, he was met by the unsatisfying reply, "Because you would be ridiculous if you didn't." The question was natural enough; but the boy's repugnance to a mechanical task held the germ of the man's impatience of unreason in all its forms.

But if the scholastic discipline was not greatly based on reason, it was, in its rigid way, fairly comprehensive, and Philip became, like his father, a fluent reader of both classical languages.[1] A formidable amount of literature was read, and natural instinct for languages and keen mother-wit saved him, even then, from a merely sloppy scholarship.[2]

In mathematics Philip responded still more vigorously. The distinctions he won, at the head of the Upper

[1] The books read in the Upper School, during the latter half of 1859, when Philip received two distinctions, included books of Thucydides, Herodotus, the Attic tragedians, Pindar and Homer, and Cicero, Livy, Sallust, Juvenal, and Horace.

[2] One of his daughters, who had been entered at short notice for a scholarship in Latin, showed her father the examination-paper when she came home, and recalls the "it's all up" look on his face when she told him she had translated: "He was the first who said it"—"Primus erat qui hoc dixit."

School, in December 1859, in this field, show that he had already, at fifteen, given signs of the aptitude and zest for the lore of numbers and of measurement which runs like a red thread through all his far-flung intellectual adventures and researches, a symbol of their inner psychological nexus.[1] Whether in economics, in biblical criticism, in literature, or in philosophy, the mathematical fascination had a determining course upon the direction of his method or of his thought. It made him one of the first to adopt Jevons's brilliant application of the calculus to the problems of "the higgling of the market." Numerical discrepancies pointed out by Colenso in the Pentateuch text were to contribute to lead him to Kuenen and the *Bible for Young People*. The part which number plays in the structure of the universe of Dante was among the lesser attractions for him of the divine poem; and hearers might differ whether he was more completely himself when he was explaining the spiritual heights of a St. Francis, or when he was explaining the time-table of Dante's journey up the Terraces or through the Spheres. And if his last labour, the interpretation of Aristotle's *Physics*, was in one sense the goal of a path which led to Aristotle by way of his great medieval disciple Aquinas, in another it was a last proof of his inexhaustible interest in the phenomena which we measure and compute.

[1] An anecdote of Philip's boyhood illustrates his habit, always pronounced, of getting his teeth into any kind of loose inexactitude, numerical or other. When any well-meaning person quoted the rhymes "It is a sin to steal a pin, Much more so any greater thing." "Why should the sin be necessarily *much* greater," he would ask, "when the *thing* might be only a *little* greater?"

IV

The conditions of Philip's life became less easy and put a sterner tax upon his character when, in 1856, his father, encouraged by his two years' tenure, without disaster, of the small estate at Eyarth, embarked upon a more ambitious project, renting one hundred and eighty acres of farm land, some miles down the valley. One of the inducements was the prospect of providing easily the table of his large household. Here for twenty years he lived, never affluent, latterly with increasing embarrassment, which ended in disaster. But during the years of Philip's boyhood and early manhood Hafod was a Homeric home of growing boys and girls, mostly of robust health and pronounced character. The roomy homestead could house many guests, and here in time came his children's friends, and there were romantic meetings and partings at the neighbouring station of Trefnant. Philip has himself vividly described the twelve o'clock dinner, where eating and drinking were amply provided for, and properly enjoyed, but where no one, either, would have missed (or have been allowed to miss!) the seasoning table-talk of the head of the family; no monologue, however, but a game in which all were expected to share, and in which his two eldest sons, Hartley and Philip, never allowed the ball to drop. Philip himself, later on, was to know something of the satisfactions of the table-autocrat; but his father, he records, "was never at ease unless he could make his company talk as well as listen." The talk commonly began with the "news of the day," usually two or three days old; and every item started comment and

Hafod-y-coed

discussion. Whenever a question of fact arose, some boy or girl (called generically "Roger") would be despatched for the encyclopaedia. Book-learning had its part, and guests whose Latin was insecure avoided the risk of quoting it before a man who was known to hold that exile was the proper penalty for a man who perpetrated a false quantity. But the talk was not commonly bookish. Pedantry had to be equipped with the weapons of wit or fun, and culture itself to observe discretion, to have much chance with this audience. Life, at their doors, called to them on every side, and they had better and more joyous ways of getting home to it than through books or talk. Close by were the hills, the dome of Moel Flammau, and its companion heights, sweeps of heather and bracken, glorious for gallop and scamper. And in the stable, or more likely ranging freely in the fields, were four ponies, all Welsh, but all distinct in stature, powers, and characters. All the children above nursery age (one or two had come as infants to Hafod) were adepts in catching and bridling them, and the boys would spend any time in chasing them, rather than do their errands on foot. Philip, we are told, was never known to "go out for a walk," and mercilessly chaffed a studious college visitor, afterwards one of his closest friends, who habitually walked out with an umbrella. Their "walks" were a shouting gallop over the mountains, or a swim in the river. For the elders a quieter mode of locomotion was provided in two low four-wheeled carriages, one of which bore the traces of having at some antediluvian period come in two. In it the father and mother drove on market-day to the county town of Denbigh, four or five miles up the valley, to lay in stores for the week (piled up on the great hall table, after their return), enjoying on the way their only opportunity, during their busy daytime, of confidential talk.

But life was at the doors of a farming household in many other forms, too; and Philip, who "never took a walk," was a devoted lover of all living things. He would talk to the ponies as companions and brothers, and lie for hours by the pond watching the swarming myriads on the surface, and the inscrutable maze below. At an age when boys of his physique and temperament are often cruel, he not only hated cruelty as he did all his days, but felt "the mere living" of an animal, so "good," that he would not willingly let it be killed, even to shorten its misery. The household was sometimes disconcerted by his habit of bringing snakes home in his pocket. But he enjoyed a just triumph when a kitten, which had lost a fore-paw in a trap, was saved from execution at his urgency, and grew up to a long and happy maturity, under the name of "Tripod"—a feline parody of the Greek symbol for decrepit old age.

For games, there was cricket in an adjacent field, played by Philip with a fierce energy which made batting and fielding alike alarming to his young sisters, and also costly in balls, which often disappeared in the pond at the bottom. When, at intervals, the pond was cleaned out, numbers of them were recovered, and frugal young cricketers made valiant attempts to resuscitate them for the wicket. Sodden they were, however, and sodden they remained; yet with one compensation in the eyes of the gentler playmates, that Philip's terrifying vehemence was now effectually assuaged. As for other games, croquet, then in fashion, was too tame to be of much account. But we hear of an occasion when the strain of a succession of dull callers was relieved by Philip's proposal to have a croquet-match on stilts. Then there was dancing, jolly and informal, rural but not bucolic; gay evenings on the uncarpeted schoolroom floor. "How well those young men danced!" writes the sister of one of them, who became the wife of another: "Some of them parsons, too, and most of them embryo-parsons themselves. Though clad in simple country suits, each one of them had his white gloves in his pocket ready to don; for they would not have deemed it polite to present hot steamy hands in the dance." [1]

"Sport," in any other sense than games, was scarcely recognized at Hafod. Gun and fishing-tackle, if not precisely taboo, were very rarely seen. But most other country delights throve there, and the Hafod picnics were famous. In the sunset close of Philip's life at Childrey, where in so many ways Hafod was renewed, the memory of the Hafod picnics, "and the wind blowing thro' the grass," would come to him like a caress.

A less happy result of the removal to Hafod for Philip was that, owing to the distance of the school, he and his brother Hartley had now to board there, spending only the week-ends at home. The four years that followed (1856–60) were probably the unhappiest period of Philip's life, and, in spite of the lasting friendship of two of his schoolfellows, the memory of that experience was never effaced. That they were "always hungry" was a small matter, even for strong and healthy boys, and there was always the plentiful table

[1] *Inquirer*, 21 May, 1927.

at Hafod at the week-end. But the foulness of which adolescent boyhood is capable rioted there unchecked, and never ceased to embitter his recollection. All his life he retained an acute horror of every kind of sex stimulus in literature.

But these experiences added a halo to the Hafod home and quickened his love to passionate attachment. Among his brothers and sisters a specially close friendship bound him to his elder sister Clara. In the brother and sister was repeated much of the intimate understanding which had attached their father to his brother Joseph; and it did not lose intensity because the differences in years was much smaller, or because the elder was a girl. They read and wrote much together in Philip's little room, overlooking the Hafod farmyard. Clara at sixteen was, as commonly happens in such cases, the riper. But her feminine intuition divined that her brother's lesser accomplishment was only the slower groping of a powerful mind not yet master of its resources. One of their common occupations was to write sermons, in emulation of those they heard at the parish church, their frequent resort, with their father, on summer Sunday evenings. Clara's sermons, as both recognized, were better than Philip's. "But you," she told him, "will presently write better ones than I." And Philip was, in fact, occasionally called in by his father some years before he became a full-fledged minister, to give the "Sunday lessons," or even to conduct the home-service on Sunday mornings. Here, by the testimony of the few now living who heard him, the vehement boy promised to become a Boanerges of the pulpit; and it was one of these explosions of righteous passion which occasioned the beautiful maternal reminder, quoted at the outset, that Philip "had the blood of two martyrs in his veins." Their friendship only passed into a new phase when Clara became the wife of one of his closest and most honoured college friends, Richard Armstrong.

An intimacy, less close perhaps in the early years, but deepened with every year of his later life, bound Philip to both his parents. His memoir of his father is a record of social activities, some of which anticipated his own. Of his tender, exquisite relations with his mother, the letters from Italy in 1895, some years after the father's death, are a beautiful monument. Every evening, before retiring, he wrote the journal letter which he called his "Vespers service" at her "shrine"; playfully explaining to her, when he happened once to write in the afternoon, that the term "vespers," used in Catholic lands for an afternoon service, was thus actually more correct. Husband and wife had themselves travelled in Italy during his childhood, and he recalls to his mother the record in their diary of punctilious attendance at the Anglican services there. The economist, too, in Wicksteed owed something to his mother's principle of "making what you want out of what you have," and to her skill in applying what he pleasantly calls her "philosophy of cooking and entertaining." And we recognize another of the affiliations between the economist in Wicksteed and the social and spiritual thinker, in his association of that homely "domestic economy" with Ruskin's definition of "skill" in the arts. A like native "philosophy," touched with a more obvious inborn capacity for joy, had been instilled into her by her own mother, who always, Philip in a letter reminded her, "forbade her children to call any weather bad"; a trait which, in Philip, took the form of finding the "worst" weather particularly "good."

V

The most painful epoch in Philip's school life ended, but with it also the joyous week-ends in the Hafod home, on his transfer in 1860, to University College School, London. Here he found himself in an atmosphere which was in comparison austere. The home of Mr. Case, one of the tutors, at Hampstead, necessarily lacked the romantic joys and rural festivities of Hafod; but its refined simplicity was even farther remote from the things which had revolted him at Ruthin School. At the school Philip first made acquaintance with the disciplined severity of modern scholarship. At the Ruthin Grammar School he had learnt the fluent reading knowledge of Latin and Greek which he never lost. Under Hewitt Key, the professor of Latin and author of a Latin grammar of high repute in the 'sixties and 'seventies, he encountered a type of scholarship which spent an hour upon a few lines. Long afterwards, in his old age, Key stood out in his memory as one of the greatest of teachers.[1] But even deeper traces were left upon Philip, at school and college by the professor of mathematics, Augustus de Morgan. De Morgan, one of the most original English mathematicians of his day, bewildered many readers by his "paradoxes"; but his subtle applica-

[1] When Saunderson, the famous master of Oundle, died in 1922, Wicksteed classed Key with him as one whom he longed "to turn out in every tenth man to teach the children of the other nine." (To H. R. Beeton, 1 August, 1922.)

tions of calculation outside mathematics touched a kindred vein in Philip's eager mind. Twenty years later, the cognate work of Stanley Jevons was to initiate his economics.[1]

From the school Philip passed, in October 1861, into University College, living in rooms in the adjacent University Hall, exchanged later for lodgings in the then rural suburb of Camden Town. His neighbour at the Hall was a student somewhat senior to himself, Alexander Gordon, up to his recent death the doyen of the Unitarian ministry, a veteran scholar who had few living equals in mastery of the religious history of the Free Churches. He was then completing his last term as Hibbert Scholar at University Hall. Philip's predecessor in these neighbouring rooms had been a man, Joseph Dare, also a Hibbert Scholar, whose habits, questionably judicious for himself, had been highly satisfactory to his neighbour; for he habitually "lay abed all day, only rising in time to be late for dinner, and then passed the night in the enjoyment of coffee, tobacco, and philosophy, till breakfast; which despatched, he betook himself again to slumber."[2] Philip Wicksteed had not perhaps more self-control, but his self-indulgence, if any, was that of the robust and healthy boy of seventeen, not of the philosophic recluse. "He was very boyish," continues Gordon, "not to say bumptious, and a noisier neighbour I have never had. I kept to myself, and though we were always on good terms, I don't remember so much as a conversation between us."

[1] W. Stanley Jevons was probably a fellow-student of Wicksteed's at University College, where he entered in 1859, and took his M.A. degree in 1865. But he was nine years Philip's senior, and there is no record, and little likelihood, that they ever met.

[2] Alex. Gordon, in a private letter to the writer.

He did, however, overhear some of Philip's casual talk with his fellow-students; among the rest a declaration of faith by the future expounder of the Bible for Young People: "I don't know whether I am a Christian, I don't believe the miracles of the Old Testament." [1]

These student years at University Hall are described in letters full of affectionate confidence to his father, and slips in spelling, but not otherwise remarkable. He read much classics in his leisure ("Odd," he wrote, "that I shall invert the usual order, reading the Bible all the week, and the classics on Sunday"), and in "classics" as always he wandered far afield, and tasted with keen critical gusto much unwonted literary fare. Lactantius's *De Ira* he found "clear and flowing, both in thought and in Latinity, but not powerful or striking in either"; and a piece of Seneca's "about the most wonderful thing I ever read. I can't believe that he was insincere, however far his life may have been from embodying his principles."

It is credible enough that this "boisterous, not to say bumptious," young man, with his robust health and his good-humoured self-assertion, won from his riper associates a no less qualified approval than from Alexander Gordon. These were his "storm and stress" years, if any he had, but the ship was too well built to come near foundering, and its coming into port, whether "Christian" or other, was never in any question. But for two years its progress was slow. Then, in the third and final session a new spirit came into the young navigator, the spirit of Greek. To a good many young men and, in these days, perhaps to even more young women, the discovery of Greek has

[1] Alex. Gordon, in the private letter above referred to.

brought a thrill of rapture, usually disguised or concealed. A vivid phrase or two betrays the transport it wrought in the vehement temperament of Philip Wicksteed. A year after leaving college, when another and deeper passion had driven it into the background, he wrote to a brother-in-law from the home to which he had just brought his young wife: "You can't form any conception of it! Wedded bliss is what in my wildest classical mania I have imagined living *in Greek!*" One recalls the intoxicated fervours of Renascence Hellenism. And it is significant and prophetic that already Greek philosophy attracted him no less than Greek poetry, and of the philosophers, above all, Aristotle, Dante's "master of those who know," in interpreting whom he was, sixty years later, to lay down his pen.

But, in the meantime, Wicksteed was a university student, attending lectures, working for a degree. And if Philip was "Greek mad," there was, as always, method in his madness. He satisfied, at least, the officials whose business it is to apply those tests of repetition which madness, according to Hamlet, "would gambol from." And that, and something more, was needed to win even the *proxime accessit* for the gold medal for classics awarded to him, with the master's degree, in 1867.

It was not, indeed, given to Philip Wicksteed, then or later—unless in the very evening of his life—to "live in Greek." He was not to be of those who (if any modern may) pace delicately ever through the pellucid Attic air—ἀεί διὰ λαμπροτάτου βαίνοντες ἁβρῶς αἰθέρος—as the inmates of college cloisters and country rectories are sometimes fondly supposed to do.[1] He was destined to a busy life in the dustier and stormier air of lecture halls and committee rooms, chapels and schools; destined too to go on spiritual pilgrimages to shrines remote enough from Athens—Ibsen's Norway, Kuenen's Palestine, Dante's Florence. But—not to speak of a pocket Æschylus or Homer, an unfailing companion in the train—the Greek "madness" left its abiding traces. More even than the poetry of Greece, it was her philosophy and her citizenship, Aristotle's thought about Man in the universe and in the city—which struck home in his mind, entering there into rich fusion with the spirit of Dante, and communicating its organic and humanizing quality to the Hebraic vehemence of his temperament.

VI

We have passed lightly over the years of Wicksteed's studentship, first at University College (1861–4), then at Manchester New College (1864–7), to speak of its brilliant close. But the latter three years were memorable in his life if not for academic triumphs, for the fellow-students he met, and the lasting friendships and yet closer ties he formed. Looking back at the close of a life rich in experience of men, he regarded many of these young men, dedicated to the obscure calling of the Unitarian ministry, as amongst the elite of England; and he would often speak of them to his children. "It was lovely," wrote one of them after his death, "to hear father talk about them when they were all together at college; he used to do so often

[1] But Wicksteed in his most Attic moments could never have paced "delicately" (ἁβρῶς).

during the last years, and as he enumerated them, you felt what a splendid contribution to the world that circle of friends was, and how wonderfully they kept in touch with each other during their later lives, too. They have left a wonderful tradition behind them, and there are things they won for the intellectual and moral world so completely that they will not need to be fought for again by the younger men."

These college friendships were often, naturally, continued in the Long Vacations, and as hospitality ran in the family, his friends, almost as a matter of course, found themselves guests in the patriarchal home at Hafod. Among them were, in particular, five: Richard Armstrong, Francis Jones, Edwin Odgers, Francis Shepherd, and Joseph Estlin Carpenter. The first became the husband of the elder sister, Clara, Philip's closest confidante. The second married his younger sister Anne. Of the fifth, who occupies a unique position in his life, from this time to the end, a spiritual brother, who presents at the same time a fascinating contrast with him, something more must be said. And some of it may be said most fitly in this place. For we know from this friend's own memorable record, in a letter written long afterwards, to a former student of his own, that it was while a guest at Hafod in the Long Vacation, probably of 1865, that Estlin Carpenter, walking alone one afternoon along the country lanes, had the memorable spiritual experience from which he dated the profound religious faith which remained his to the last.[1]

The two men were to be in many outward circum-

[1] Cf. *Joseph Estlin Carpenter*, by C. H. Herford (Clarendon Press, 1928), p. 9 f.

stances of their lives, neighbours as they were in spirit. Fellow-graduates of London University, working at first as fellow-ministers or as scholars and teachers in adjacent districts—Taunton and Clifton, Dukinfield and Leeds, London, Childrey, and Oxford. Both lived with scarcely clouded vigour beyond fourscore; they died as they had been born, within a few months of each other, and their fraternal bond was accompanied as it rarely is by a deep intellectual agreement.

And the lives which touched or approached so constantly were alike, too, in the wonderful wholeness which each, with immense intellectual and spiritual resources at his command, achieved. Yet these resources were derived from different provinces of the intellectual world, and the kind of synthesis they won was different. Religion and the service of men were the deepest interest of both. But Carpenter was a theologian, who devoted his life to exploring in all their intricacy, as unfolded in the historic religions, especially of the Oriental world, men's ways of apprehending divine things; while the love of humanity which glowed an unfading flame in his heart, appeared chiefly in the boundless personal devotion to human service. Wicksteed was a humanist, whose most vital interest was concentrated on that type of human genius which Carlyle called the "hero as prophet"; men of large social purpose and intelligence, pre-eminently where this was united with the religious passion of those who proclaimed Jahweh, or the "Love which moves the sun and the other stars"; but also, when the religious aspect of that social purpose was wholly enigmatic as with Ibsen, or ambiguous, as with Comte. Both men came of Puritan ancestry; to both belonged some of the finer traits of Puritanism. "Plain living and high thinking" were ingrained habitudes of both; without creative gift for any form of art, both were deeply sensitive to certain modes of its appeal. Both began their careers as ministers of the Unitarian Church, and neither of them swerved a step from their fidelity to that body, in which, long before they died, they had become the most commanding figures. But neither of them left the Unitarian faith wholly as they found it; and both drew into the sphere of their thinking about human and divine things vast numbers to whom Unitarianism as such was obnoxious or unknown. Carpenter became deeply intimate with the mind of the East, and interpreted the ideas of universal religion to Indians in terms of their own. Wicksteed drew towards the Middle Ages of Dante and Aquinas, and to the Aristotelian foundation on which Aquinas, and through him Dante, had built; he claimed for Dante, that he made the religion of his own time and country vocal for ours and for all others, and he, if any man, became the interpreter through whom this claim was fulfilled, who, in the language of his most frequent utterance, disclosed the religion of eternity lurking, half disguised, in the lineaments of a religion of time. Both loved Nature with passion; both had hosts of friends in all stations of life. Carpenter, after his marriage in 1878, began that series of summers in his own boat on the fjords of Norway, and Wicksteed followed him. But Wicksteed's bond with both land and people went deeper, it was more in the blood. One of his children saw in him a veritable Viking, and he had the Viking's hardihood, his readiness to defy civilization, his fierce joy in pain. "The great test of health," he once said, "is to suffer violent pain, and not to mind." [1] Carpenter was never deterred by weather, however bad, but admitted the practical utility of an umbrella; Wicksteed refused to allow that any weather was "bad," loved rain with passion, and gloried in getting wet. Carpenter loved the mountains, and entered into Wordsworth's rapture in their presence. Wicksteed, too, found deep response in Wordsworth. But he shared also his father's passion for the earth as such, and the actual business of planting and hewing; and when, long before old age, he retired into the country, it was to a home much more akin to a Virgilian farm than to Wordsworth's Rydal Mount.

But joy in Nature was for neither man a barrier to the love of men. The mere delight in intercourse was a very real part of this, but the least part. Both spent much of their lives among people whose society offered little attraction in itself, and little basis for finer appeal. Both excelled in the gift of building intercourse and fellowship, upon these slender holds. But with Carpenter, this was sometimes a more difficult process. His rich humanity had to make itself felt through a manner somewhat austere and with little aid from humour; whereas, with Wicksteed, less inclined by nature to suffer fools gladly, brotherhood was instinctive and congenial, and many a boy could tell, like the one mentioned in a later chapter, whom he found reading Henry George, of the captivating man who had won his heart by talking to him about it "as if he were an equal."

[1] As an old man he had all his teeth extracted without anaesthetic.

CHAPTER II

TAUNTON—DUKINFIELD—LEIDEN

Taunton — Marriage — Comte — Dukinfield — O.T. Studies — Kuenen —Wicksteed and Kuenen—Bible for Young People—Visits to Holland

I

At the close of his college career, Wicksteed, like other young men, was faced with the problem of choice. It was not the choice of a career; the Unitarian ministry was his fixed goal; he saw in it only opportunity, not limitation, and dreamed of no other. But two alternative fields for these opportunities presented themselves at once; the congregations of Birmingham and of Taunton both required a minister. The first might well appear, in this as in other senses, the more eligible, and it was pressed upon him by three counsellors for whom he had the deepest regard—Martineau, Tayler, and his own father. But Wicksteed's own choice was set upon the little Somersetshire town, and he defended it in a letter to his father which may be quoted here, both as indicating his aims at the outset of his career, and as a quite admirable example of a firm and clear-headed, but not obstinate argument with authoritative elders for going one's own way. "I cannot in honesty," he writes (4 April, 1867, from University Hall), "say that I am convinced by [your letter] . . . but I am still open to conviction . . . I always wanted to begin without a colleague (unless I might choose him), in a small town, with a poor congregation, none of whom I knew. In all which, Birmingham opposes, and Taunton realizes, my ideas. I feel as if I should never be able to breathe again if I were to go to Birmingham now." In all which we recognize, at twenty-two, the man who at all times thought lightly of station and even of cultural opportunities, but demanded, like Milton, freedom to speak his mind. And to the impossibility (as he saw it) of working under an elderly colleague of conventional views, was added the call of need. Birmingham was wealthy and comfortable; Taunton was needy, divided, and might go to pieces if he failed them. Moreover, after hearing him preach, they forgot their divisions. "No one," wrote the secretary, after a congregational meeting, "would hear of any one else." Wicksteed chose Taunton. His mentors advised him at least to take a month's holiday first. He brushed that suggestion also peremptorily aside, impatient only to be at his life's work.

Wicksteed's ministry, at Taunton, placed him in a pulpit to which some notable, even classical, memories attach. That Somersetshire country had been, little more than half a century before, a haunt of great poets, and the cradle of momentous verse. Bristol, in the remoter precincts of which it lay, had then been a centre of letters, as well as of the slave trade, and the lucrative horrors of the middle passage like a fertilizing compost provided for her, as for her northern rival, Liverpool, many elegant amenities of civility and culture. No publisher of that day had a livelier flair for poets coming (but not yet come) than the Bristol bookseller Cottle, who published the *Lyrical Ballads* (1798) and composed an epic poem (on Abel) of his own; in Bristol the Utopian scheme of "Pantisocracy" was hatched, and Coleridge and Southey, two of the Pantisocrats, married the daughters of a Bristol linen-draper to prepare the Utopian tables and provide against the extinction of the Utopian breed. Coleridge, moreover, preached in Unitarian pulpits; it was in 1798 that he glorified the world for the young William Hazlitt, John Wicksteed's friend, by that sermon which "rose like an exhalation" (meteor) in the chapel at Shrewsbury, where Philip's father had worshipped as a boy.[1] And about the same time he had preached, probably wearing a blue coat and white waistcoat (as a sign that he "had not a rag of the Scarlet Woman about him"), in the chapel at Taunton, whose pulpit Philip himself was now to occupy.

To the neighbouring chapel at Clifton, too, nearly at the same time, came his fellow-student Estlin Carpenter, among whose many friends at Bristol Wicksteed was doubtless introduced. Two notable members of that family, of an older generation, he certainly knew. Mary Carpenter, Estlin's aunt, had her home in Bristol, in the intervals of working in India and entertaining and exhibiting distinguished Indians in London and elsewhere. Her brother, Russell Carpenter, was minister at Bridport in Dorset during all the later years of a long life, a man of wit and humour congenial to Philip's own.[2]

Of Philip's fortunes in the chapel where Coleridge

[1] Cf. Hazlitt's essay, *My First Acquaintance with Poets.*

[2] Wicksteed was fond of quoting his chaff of his sister's flair for lionizing illustrious and loquacious Hindus: "She 's a regular Circe, she turns heroes into lions, and then into bores," and his remark on a suave brother-minister who was commonly known as "the bishop of the west": "He has so much of the milk of human kindness in him that we must not wonder if it sometimes turns to butter."

had preached, little is directly known. But the Boanerges of the Hafod drawing-room was not the man to tame his fires because he was addressing a congregation as its official minister instead of his own parents and sisters. These ways were not, however, much in keeping with Unitarian tradition. Unitarianism had come to denote a distinct and determined body of believers in the eighteenth century, and it still bore very definitely the mark of eighteenth-century belief in "reason" and distrust of "enthusiasm." The Methodist movement initiated by the genius of Wesley in that century, grew up and flourished as a conscious reaction against that temper, and it stood in the opposite pole to Unitarianism. More formidable antagonistic forces emerged when, in the second quarter of the last century, Coleridge and Maurice, Newman and Keble opened up other avenues of religious experience and imagination, into the owl-haunted forests of German metaphysic, and the cloistral shrines of medieval Catholicism. To these reactions of the higher Romanticism upon the religious mind Unitarianism, strong as was its rationalist bias, could not remain inaccessible; least of all when they came to it enriched by a higher rationalism, in Schleiermacher, and the new Biblical science of the Hegelians Baur, Strauss, and Ewald. The Unitarians stood in the forefront of the English disciples of the new teaching; and the finest flower of modern Unitarian preaching was reached when this larger equipment of modern science, together with the high culture always traditional in it, was kindled or directed by the religious passion which, to the Priestleys and the Paleys alike, was suspect. If Paley within, and Priestley without, the Anglican pale, were of the same breed, an analogous kinship, on an immeasurably higher plane, as exponents of religion, was realized, half a century later, by Newman and Martineau. The tradition of the quiet, well-reasoned discourse was still powerful in the Unitarian pulpit. The spiritual fires of the prophet could not always be kept under, and there were souls, often ready and eager to be touched; but this fierce indignation rarely won complete success unless it came commended to the cultivated palate by polished periods and chosen phrase.

Wicksteed was at no time an orator precisely of this stamp. His eloquence—as when he was "letting himself go" at the beck of the greatest things in Dante—could be magnificent; but no one thought then of his periods or phrases, so perfectly fitted were they to their work. And at this time he was, in this sense, undoubtedly "raw"; neither inborn gentleness nor inbred courtesy disposed him to temper the wind of his fiery vehemence to the susceptibilities of his flock. There is some evidence that his preaching often "alienated many of his hearers"; and though no detailed information is available, it is likely that Philip, as a pulpit executioner, was rather of the school of Cassius than of Brutus; his way with the offender was rather to

> hew him as a carcase fit for hounds,

than to

> carve him as a dish fit for the gods.

But he could laugh at his own roughness. "You 'd be astonished if you heard me preach now!" he wrote to a brother-in-law. "Such queer stuff! It won't be a bit of good to me anywhere else if I ever leave here;

I don't mind what I say." In the same letter[1] he expresses qualified admiration for the "beautiful tender touch" in the sermons otherwise "threadless and pointless" of a fellow-student; faults from which he was himself perfectly secure, however hardly he might, as yet, achieve the compensating grace.

The young minister had begun by stipulating that he might be allowed to read another preacher's sermon once on the Sunday, instead of preaching twice himself. But the congregation soon found better relish in the native product, rough as it might be, and begged him to give them, for better or worse, only his own.

And we have evidence of the deep impression made by his preaching, whatever his private disparagement of it, upon an older minister, who, perhaps of all others, was qualified to see the spiritual force of a man, through whatever imperfections it had to struggle into expression. Brooke Herford, a friend of his father's, had already encountered Philip, fifteen years before, as a curly-headed lad of seven, as already mentioned. He now wrote to the father this report of a Sunday at Taunton, the first of Philip's ministry there: "I had not much fear for him, for the few days I had passed with him during the last week . . . had already made us close friends, . . . and taught me to have no doubt that he had the true stuff in him, and that one day he would come out. But at Birmingham I had heard he was thought youthful and stiff, so I had not liked to raise my immediate expectations very high. I tell you this because I could not otherwise convey to you any idea of the delight and pride I felt in the service to which I listened. The matter was

[1] To Frank Jones, 11 November, 1867.

Meadow Bank. Taunton. By Louisa Solly, 1868

thoroughly good . . . now and then roused even the Sunday School pews into eager listening—had in it the flashes of homely personal address and . . . illustration which I look to, more than almost anything else, as the sign of a preacher who is to *take hold* of his fellow-men. The tone and delivery were not youthful and stiff, but full of vigour, manliness and animation. . . . Nor was it with the preaching alone, or even mostly, that we were impressed. . . . I will only say how very deeply he carried us all with him in the devotional service. It seemed to me as if the having passed from preparation to his full work, and the consciousness of having entered on his ministry, of being the shepherd of that people gathered there, had roused and strengthened and developed his whole being."

Philip Wicksteed was still unformed; and there was apt to be in this initial stage of his sustained self-expression something too volcanic to be acceptable to the mellow culture of the older Unitarianism. "Birmingham's" criticism had some ground; his own sharper criticism was not quite without it. But, knowing his future as we do, it is perfectly clear that it was Brooke Herford's genial insight and larger-hearted faith that read aright the inner soul of the young minister. His crudity was the incipient form of a power which later made the conventional urbanities appear tame, as, on a higher plane, the provincialism of Burns and Wordsworth made the "glossy" elegance of the post-Augustans itself provincial.

And a new influence was about to enter Philip Wicksteed's life, adding to that "strong music of the soul," which Brooke Herford heard so distinctly, a rich clear undertone of gentler song, destined both to temper its harshness and to sustain its power. In April 1868, he married Emily Rebecca Solly.

II

A daughter of Henry Solly, minister of the Unitarian congregation at Lancaster, his wife was still in the first freshness of her twenty-three years; and she retained throughout their union of nearly fifty-six years, not in her husband's eyes alone, the radiant charm and the inner sunshine of her youth. From a very early date in their long journey together, Philip adopted Chaucer's "Emilye the bright" in the *Knight's Tale* as a romantic namesake for her, and he never wearied of recalling the delicious picture of the May morning in Theseus's garden at Athens in which Emily is seen by her future lover from his prison, gathering flowers in the early sunlight:

> Up roos the sun, and up roos Emilye.

A romantic namesake, perhaps; but the romance only suggested the richer and profounder romance of the reality. For both brought to their marriage a rare fullness of endowments for the ordinary as well as for the unwonted calls of married life; and hers, as little a mere counterpart to his as the gifts of a good woman can well be to the gifts of a good man, were yet wonderfully attuned to them, and contributed essentially to keep the impetuous genius of her husband from fruitless infringement of the terms on which the "philistines" of English society will consent to be enlightened, and the "barbarians" to be civilized. In fire and enterprise, in wit and imagination, in swift mastery of facts and solid power of thought, she had no claim to approach him, and would have been the first to dismiss such a claim herself. But neither did humility prompt her to efface herself. She had a clear judgment and a bright wit. No one ever thought her insignificant; she was never in danger of being "swamped" by his torrential energy. Not from self-will or even justified egoism, but from devotion to him and calmer appreciation of the needs of their common cause, she stood firm even when she had to bar his path. In the crisis of 1918, her insistence on a medical consultation probably saved his life. To his sensitive nervous exaltations she brought the medicine of what one of her daughters called "an inveterate sanity," the poise of a nature strong in its gentleness and gentle in its strength, the just sense of proportion even in nobler things. She shared his travels, and even his adventures. The temper of the crusader was no less inveterate in him than sanity in her; and there were occasions when the crusader's triumph was both securer and more complete because she had stood by his side; as there were others when his apparent failure was disarmed by her undaunted faith.[1] And when in the days of narrow means and a frugal larder, the crusader returned from his campaign, as large-hearted campaigners will, with a crowd of unexpected guests, it was sometimes well that the devoted comrade was also a most thrifty and resourceful housewife. But rich as their union was in the values, mundane and spiritual, which belong to unusual gifts of intelligence, thought and

[1] A faithful old nurse, in later days, put this in her idiom: Mrs. Wicksteed was "always 'opeful, always 'opeful."

will on both sides, these were all sublimated in that which made them, as he said when their long life together was over, "lovers from the first day to the last." And when, a few weeks after her death, an ensuing first of May brought the eightieth anniversary of her birth, he wrote to an absent daughter that May morning verse which had been so often on his lips:

Up roos the sun, and up roos Emilye.

They were married in April 1868. The symbolic springtide was about them as well as in their hearts. And he breaks into the ringing phrases of the *Pervigilium Veneris* in a letter to his father:

Ver novum, ver iam canorum, vere natus orbis est!

Then with an amused recollection of the far from lyrical pages of the founder of the Religion of Humanity: "I wonder whether Comte was proof against the spring!"

III

The seventh decade of the century which saw the most decisive chapter in Philip Wicksteed's passage from adolescence to intellectual manhood, was also, we know, notable in the history of the mind of England. The *Origin of Species* had set going currents of thought and controversy very various in sonority and significance. Far less regarded by the world at large, but acutely interesting to certain scattered but highly cultivated minds, was the prominence now acquired by the work and name of Auguste Comte, the most considerable French thinker of the century, who had died in 1857. In the following year a condensed paraphrase of

Comte's *Philosophie Positive*, by Harriet Martineau, had rendered the earlier of his two monumental books accessible to English readers. In 1865, Mill's important essay, *Comte and Positivism*, compelled the attention of thinking England to his ideas, notwithstanding Mill's pronounced repudiation of that final phase of his teaching, which Comte regarded as superseding the rest. In the same year Mill was answered by one of the weightiest of the English Positivists, John Henry Bridges. In France, shortly before, in 1863, Comte's chief French follower, Émile Littré, had published his classical monograph, *Comte et la Philosophie Positive*; while Herbert Spencer in *Auguste Comte* attacked fundamentally a system less modern but more far-reaching than his own.

The philosophy of Comte was thus a subject of keen debate in England and France in the very years of Wicksteed's studentship at Manchester College. No young man of his eager temperament was likely to pass through the 'sixties untouched by curiosity about the new philosophical system then under discussion.[1] The debate turned, moreover, precisely upon a feature in it most calculated to arrest the interest of such a young man, if he was a theological student preparing, somewhat restively, to enter the ministry of religion. For Comte's system rested upon a repudiation, peremptory and fundamental, of theology. In its first form (the *Philosophie Positive*) he had repudiated "religion" also; in its final phase (the *Politique Positive*) he had attempted to graft upon that non-theological philosophy a religion,

[1] A record of his reading in 1868–9, shows that on 24 October, 1868, he read Spencer's *A. Comte*, and on 3 November, articles in the *Theological Review*, Nos. VIII and IX on Mill's *A. Comte and Positivism*, and *General View of Positivism*, by Comte, translated by J. H. Bridges.

equally non-theological, but in which, as the "religion of humanity," the inspiring and upbuilding power of religion is, he thought, disengaged from the evils to which it had at all times been "able to persuade." Was Comte, in this rehabilitation of religion outside theology, betraying his "scientific" philosophy or completing it? Littré and Mill took the former view, Bridges and Beesly the latter. In the outside world, where the problem of Comte's consistency was not of interest, theologians and men of science in general dismissed with equal contumely, a religion that dispensed with theology, and one that professed to be scientific; while yet, in many minds where dogmatic beliefs were decaying, but the passion for the welfare and the service of men burnt with a steady glow, the conception of a "religion" of humanity established itself, sometimes as ancillary to traditional forms of faith, sometimes even as their vital core.

Among the personal forces in Wicksteed's *milieu* at University College Hall had been one which made some interest in Positivism not easy to escape; for Edward Spencer Beesly, one of its four English leaders, and Professor of History at University College, was Warden of the Hall. Beesly's commanding and incisive personality made him, with Frederic Harrison, the chief fighting force in the little Positivist band. His broad brow and other pronounced features were later recalled by those of Abraham Kuenen, his Leiden professor. But Beesly was no merely academic figure. A Radical reformer, a brilliant and fearless publicist, he freely put his formidable powers of learning and argument at the service of unpopular causes. In defending the right of the Sheffield Trade Unions to dispassionate inquiry (in 1867), he provoked the fury of all "respectable" England, and narrowly escaped blackballing at the Reform Club.

Such a man was likely to challenge the interest of the vehement student. It is certain that he had intimate talks with Beesly upon Positivism, and that in Beesly's presentation certain aspects of it acquired a deep attraction for him which for years remained powerful, and perhaps never entirely ceased; but it is certain, too, that he never gave it full intellectual assent. His approach, was, however, close enough both to persuade Beesly that his acceptance was complete, and to give his large-minded father some intelligible concern. His position at the close of his college years is fully and frankly stated in a letter to the latter (21 February, 1868):

"You seem half afraid that I am going to make Beesly my father-confessor and turn Positivist. I have no intention of doing so; but what between your guarded expression of apparent anxiety and Beesly's triumph or rather delight (for he seems to think I am a Positivist), I should scarcely know where I was if my little Emily (his fiancée) did not keep me steady! . . . As I know I inherit from you my horror of studying reviews and refutations in the place of going to the fountain-head, I send you Comte's *General View of Positivism*. You will find it well worth reading . . . Bridges (the translator) is one of the most earnest English disciples. I have at present *no* intellectual sympathy with Positivism, but I have far more practical and quite as much *moral* sympathy with the *real* Positivists (Congreve, Beesly, Bridges, Harrison, etc., *not* Mill and his lot) as with any people and men in theology. I think, as I said, that their influence is healthy and in the right direction though extreme, and put in a form which must be dreadfully painful to most Theists."

Even the distractions of the first months of marriage did not abate the keenness of an interest which his young wife, as we see, by no means shared. And her husband, as his letters to a brother-in-law testify, awaited with almost the same impatience, the arrival of a long-deferred volume of Littré and the advent of his first child. A few sentences from this epistle may be of interest to the psychologist engaged in measuring the hunger for intellectual satisfaction against the hunger of coming fatherhood: "For months past I have been in a state of nervous fever from the daily expectation and the hope, daily deferred, of Littré! At first the expectation was a pleasurable excitement. . . . New every morning was my hope! and it gave me an object to get up for! Soon it became like the expectation of my heir apparent—a source of eager anticipation not unmixed with anxiety. This went on for a long time—the baby came first!"[1]

A few days later he writes again, still in the same rollicking student vein. The book had come, and turned out rather bigger than he expected. "However, I can't say I regret my mistake, as it seems to be simply the stunningest thing ever written!" [2] This, on the face of it, tells us little but that the book cost him more and pleased him better than he expected; and no record of the immediate future remains to tell us of his adventures in the exploration of Littré's masterpiece, or how the claims of philosophy and paternity were

[1] To Frank Jones, 3 February, 1869.
[2] To the same, 7 February, 1869.

adjusted. But it is possible from what we know of Wicksteed's mind and of the lines of its later development to understand something of the impact which provoked this "Heureka!" cry. Littré, one of the first French minds of the century, a Member of the Academy as well as of the Academy of Inscriptions, had himself, after a vast training in medicine, philology, and literature, been enthralled by Comte's work, and his critical monograph on it, published some years after his master's death, was far better fitted to impress and fascinate an educated novice than anything that Comte himself had written. Rejecting that final phase, as fallacious, Littré had not only given a luminous account of Comte's organized cyclopaedia of the sciences, crowned by that "science of society" for which Comte himself had devised the name "sociologie"; but had explained Comte's "origins," and placed his philosophy in the evolution of philosophy at large. By that pregnant conception of a "science of society" Comte brought together a number of separate studies then being pursued to their hurt in isolation, among them that science of Political Economy of which it was to be one of Wicksteed's principal life-labours to elicit (in his own phrase) the "common sense."

But these two powerful preoccupations, his new wedded companionship and the imposing philosophy, did not distract the minister from his work. We may rather believe that they enriched and humanized it. The reputation of his preaching began to spread in the Unitarian world; and in the summer of 1869, he was invited by the congregation of the Old Chapel at Dukinfield, in Cheshire, to preach there with the tacit prospect of eventually occupying their vacant pulpit.

On 17 October, the congregation, by a unanimous vote, invited him to become their minister. With a promptness unusual in these cases he sent, two days later, a cordial acceptance. Impatient of all sham formalities, Wicksteed was not the man to affect the coy hesitation of one cautiously balancing the pros and cons of a resolve which both parties knew had, on his side, been already taken, when he went to preach on trial.

IV

This purely industrial township lies between two larger seats of mainly cotton industry, Stockport and Hyde, and within a few miles of the metropolis of the district, also then one of the capitals of northern Unitarianism, Manchester. For most men an obscure ministry in this outlying spot would have meant obscurity for life. But Philip Wicksteed, though he had many warm personal attachments at Taunton, welcomed his escape from "dear sleepy Somersetshire" into the keener atmosphere of the north.[1] And he soon became known, in the denomination and out of it, as a man of genial intelligence, for whom life was full of problems, but who was, above all, aboundingly alive, and radiant of vitality to all about him. An old friend, then a girl of sixteen, describes the impression he made when he first called on her mother: the bright boyish face, the cheery manner, and keen sense of humour . . . "You felt, here was a man as God would have him, and the vivifying effect of this thought was sometimes

[1] Letter to his mother, 11 September, 1869. He describes to her with amusement, in the same letter, the situation of the parsonage, on a hill-top, between the cemetery and the chapel yard. Some of his father's letters to him, of the same date, further describe this roomy parsonage.

almost too dazzling, as if you had suddenly met an angel, and had been smitten dumb.[1] And the young minister was quick to answer to the call of intellectual hunger, as he was, on occasion, to prick the bubble of conceit, which latter he had a happy way of doing with a jest that disarmed resentment, and cured, but left no sting. And if the men knew the young minister chiefly as the keen debater, the young people soon discovered the one-time leader in the gaieties of Hafod. He danced with an exuberant energy which satisfied even the Yorkshire standard of heartiness. "Bless 'is 'eart, ain't 'e enjoying 'imself!" an old lady of his congregation, looking on, was heard to remark. And this accomplishment (far from universal among his ministerial brethren) sometimes enabled him to provide an adroit solution for the small dilemmas of the ball-room. Seeing a young couple engaged in pleading with a tired chaperon for "one more dance," he promptly intervened by asking the chaperon if *he* might have the pleasure. . . . The young couple danced off without more concern for him or for the delighted chaperon; but Wicksteed would playfully describe this to his children as "one of the good deeds of his life."

Among the graver problems with which Wicksteed was daily confronted was one of a kind which never ceased to be urgent with him, and was to call out all the thinking power of his mature mind—the problem of the distribution of wealth. The little household budget, the question how to lay out a weekly wage with the best return, which figure so largely in his *Alphabet* and *Common Sense*, was itself the starting point of the ABC of his own economic science. What

[1] Miss H. Wainwright, in a private communication to the writer.

fascinated him in Jevons's theory was precisely that he provided a scientific account of these daily operations.

In the years, too, of Wicksteed's ministry at Dukinfield, the air of the industrial north still vibrated with the passion of recent controversy, and the pangs of recent hardship. The American Civil War, which had brought disaster upon the cotton industry and starvation upon thousands of operatives throughout the cotton area of which Manchester is the centre, was fresh in every memory. Nearly contemporary with the crisis in cotton caused by the failure of its raw material was the crisis in the cutlery trade, brought about in the other neighbouring city of Sheffield by the attempt of the Trade Unions to control the methods of production. The controversy stirred the interest, and the often uncritical indignation of the whole country; a Royal Commission, in 1867, brought about a very incomplete solution. Dukinfield, in its fold of the Pennines between Manchester and Sheffield, was subject to the industrial agitations of both. At Dukinfield, too, Wicksteed found, as he would have found all over the industrial north, working men who were keen students and hard thinkers; also, original types of social organization, run by the men themselves, for the benefit of their common studies. He was fond of telling of the little group of mill-hands there, field-naturalists, who each put by a weekly sum to enable one of their number, chosen not by rotation, but for his fitness, to devote a fortnight's holiday to the botanizing or entomologizing, and then communicate the results.[1] It was out of his reflection on such experience that Wicksteed, forty years later, built *The Common Sense of Political Economy*.

[1] *The Social Ideals and Economic Doctrines of Socialism* (1908), p. 4.

Associates of his own class, however, at Dukinfield were few—few, but choice. "I wonder whether you realize," he wrote to one of them when they were both approaching the close of rich and busy lives, "that with one, or perhaps two exceptions, you were the only man with whom I lived in continuous intellectual companionship during my years there." One of these was Henry Enfield Dowson, minister then and until his death at the neighbouring Unitarian chapel of Gee-Cross; a man whose saintly beauty of personality is still a fragrant memory in the wide circle of his friends. The little doctor, R——, was more doubtfully included. More intimate and important than with either was Wicksteed's intercourse with the third friend, to whom these words were addressed, John Reynolds, a schoolmaster at Dukinfield. The two men became close comrades, joined in publishing manuals and tracts for the enlightenment of teachers, and explored together the wild highlands of Derbyshire. Half a century later, after Mrs. Reynolds's death, Wicksteed wrote to his old friend recalling how her face, as she welcomed them on their return, was still vivid in his memory, and reminding him of sayings which had fallen from him, as they walked, and had struck root in the not very tractable soil of the younger man's mind. "Looking back upon that time," he adds in another letter, "I should see if I had never seen before, how much you count for in those years of early manhood. We had so much in common in fundamentals, and so much diversity of experience and approach to life." Some letters of that early time pleasantly illustrate those "diversities" which thus flavoured, without in the least disturbing, their comradeship. To the eager student of Comte, and of Kuenen, abstract dogma was already less alluring than the varying shapes it had taken in human minds; and though he offered Reynolds "any number of tracts" for his teachers, he stipulated that they would be historical, not moralist. And by way of tempering the seriousness of pedagogy, he sent him a copy of the once well-known burlesque "hymn" on King Saul which he had come across, worthy of an academic madcap.

But friends at a greater distance were not wanting. His fellow-student, Estlin Carpenter had settled, in 1869, at Leeds. And some three years earlier, the older fellow-minister who had divined his quality so wisely at Taunton, and whose influence now extended far beyond the limits of the Unitarian body, had passed from a pulpit in one of the two neighbouring great cities to a pulpit, still nearer, in the other. Of this henceforth intimate friend, a word may here be said. Son of a Manchester merchant, Brooke Herford (*b.* 1830) had spent nine eventful years (1855–64) at Sheffield, and then, at the height of his success there, returned to Manchester. At Sheffield he had shown himself, with little help from academic study, a master of Christian statesmanship; one who had both the courage and the power to face the gravest crises of modern civic and industrial life. Two such crises occurred at Sheffield during those nine years. The inundation which flooded the lower-lying parts of the city when the Loxley and the Don broke the embankment of their reservoir, found the minister in the forefront of the committee of citizens who coped as they could with the resultant misery. The crisis of the

Trade Union feuds called for rarer qualities, and, for its complete solution, knowledge and insight which at that time neither he nor perhaps any one else in England possessed. But by a union of fair-mindedness, high courage, readiness to do justice to both sides, and a burning and irresistible hatred of cruelty and meanness, Brooke Herford won a hearing from the workmen of Sheffield, for his lecture on "Trade Outrages and Who is responsible for them," in which he spared neither party.

Such a man was certain to attract the keen interest and attachment of the young minister of Dukinfield, fourteen years his junior, and Wicksteed's fine appreciation of his friend, after his death, in a Memoir prefixed to Brooke Herford's *Anchors of the Soul,* allows us a vivid glimpse of their relations. Brooke Herford was, as he incidentally declares, one of the two or three men to whom he had ever gone for counsel.

V

But Wicksteed's most absorbing interest at Dukinfield was one in which he neither sought help nor expected sympathy from this revered friend. Brooke Herford's extraordinary personal magnetism owed little to rare intellectual originality or penetration; it was the power of a grand but simple character, of a large brain and a larger heart, nourished by intuition, strong good sense, humour, and mother-wit, rather than by the stored-up wisdom of the past or the recondite lore of philosophy and science. A master of all the homely idiomatic wealth of his native tongue, he knew nothing, beyond a "little Latin and less Greek," or any other;

he accepted the disability on the whole with the cheerful complacency of those who, having the one thing needful in abundance, easily dispense with the rest. This did not prevent his tackling particular problems even of erudition, on occasion, with astonishing swiftness, efficiency and ease. But in theology and religion above all, he had little use for erudition; he knew the Bible through and through, and interpreted it by the light of his own passion for righteousness, his deep-welling faith in God; untroubled by the superstitions of ignorant bibliolatry, but also cheerfully sceptical of the conclusions of modern Biblical science. It was, however, precisely these which were about to enthral the alert and many-sided intelligence of Philip Wicksteed.

His interest in them was first awakened by a personal influence. One of the foremost of those who were attempting, in the second and third quarters of the last century, to make the Biblical scholarship of the Continent accessible, and understood in England, was a maternal aunt of his own, whom we have already encountered as a rather formidable girl of ten. Charlotte Lupton (1812–88) of Leeds, was one of the most cultured, clear-headed, and fearless women of her generation. She had studied German and theology in Berlin, and become deeply versed in the literature of historical criticism of which Germany was then the principal seat, and theological tradition, in all its branches, a principal domain. She corresponded with Blanco White, and his remarkable letters to her were published, after his death, in 1845.[1] A year before this

[1] White's *Remains*, ed. J. H. Thom, 1845, include his letters to Miss Lupton.

she had been invited, as a recognized authority in these things, to take part in a joint Reply to the scholar, D. F. Strauss, who had, in 1835, startled the dovecotes of even Unitarian orthodoxy by his *Leben Jesu*. But the editor, Dr. J. R. Beard, and her brother-in-law, Philip Wicksteed's father, applied to the wrong quarter, and Miss Lupton declined the proposal in a letter of admirable power and temper, not without touches of the ironical persiflage which the situation invited.[1] The work which engaged the energy and

[1] A portion of the letter deserves to be quoted, both for its own quality and as a lively illustration of the agitations and counter-agitations provoked in Liberal England by Strauss. " . . . I feel duly obliged by the honour of being selected as one of the contributors to . . . a defence of religious truth. But I cannot sympathize in the means which Dr. Beard seems inclined to use to accomplish this object. Supposing it is taken for granted (a supposition which in the first place will require a long proof) that Dr. Strauss entertains unphilosophical views, he has, at all events, brought them forward under the garb of . . . all the learning of the schools. It is due to the interests of truth to combat error in her own ground, and with her own weapons, and I certainly cannot regard as likely or even possible that a number of miscellaneous pamphlets could be made to embrace the subject under this point of view. It can be nothing more than a guerrilla warfare, unworthy of the noble position which the Unitarians used to occupy in the days of Priestley, when he could boast that he had defied to open combat the insidious underminers of Christianity, and that they refused the challenge. . . . The title is absurd, too, it seems to me—*The Voice of the Church in her own Defence*. It will prove to the public only that we are *dumb*, and have nothing to say, but being obliged to keep up a show of speaking, thus mimic the cry of other people. . . . But what is the Church? Not the stone walls, not the silver-toned preacher, not the quaverers in the organ-loft, but the men and women, whether singers or hearers, who truly feel that there is a divine reality in the Gospel of Christ. If such persons have a real faith and a real interest at stake, they will cry out, though it should be merely in the monotonous enunciation, "Great is Diana of the Ephesians." . . . But if the real Church knows nothing of their controversy . . . has, in fact, nothing to do with the matter at all, why should it be mixed up with it, and why cannot Dr. Beard write or print a civil answer to Dr. Strauss, clear his own conscience, and trust that the time will come either when the Church will care something about the matter, and follow his example, and give utterance to its opinion, or else trust that he himself, Dr. Beard, is equal to that other man, Dr. Strauss,

devotion of her later years was a translation of the great *History of Israel* by Heinrich Ewald (1843–59), which during the 'fifties and 'sixties held the field in Germany. When her nephew entered Manchester College she had for years been devoting time, labour, and money to the execution and supervision of this fascinating but formidable task, calling in to her aid his friends Russell Martineau and Estlin Carpenter.[1] She had also, as was natural, called his attention to the book, though his German was then too elementary to allow of his taking part.

It was this able and enterprising scholar-friend, then, who, soon after his settlement at Dukinfield, a few years later, brought to his notice a new voice in the Old Testament debate, the *Historisch-kritisch Onderzoek* of Abraham Kuenen, the first part of which, translated by John William Colenso, had recently appeared in English.

There was irony in the situation; for Kuenen was destined in a few years to make the Ewaldian view of Old Testament history obsolete. Whether Miss Lupton then divined this may be doubted, for she could not read Dutch and the most crucial parts of Kuenen were not yet translated. But her fire, undimmed on the threshold of old age, for the cause of Hebraism[2] led

who is, after all, only a doctor of that same country where Dr. Beard is himself so highly honoured, and thus try to settle matters by single combat himself, and hope that from henceforth Strauss being *bearded* in his stronghold will remain there safe and quiet, so long as life is granted to him? To get up a popular cry against a man is one of the greatest of follies, it can never serve the cause of truth."

[1] The translation was published in London, 1869–74, as the work of Russell Martineau and Estlin Carpenter, and had a wide success.

[2] Her hand was observed to tremble with nervous emotion, we are told, when she was chronicling the fight of David and Goliath. See the notice of her by Wicksteed after her death (1888) in the *Inquirer*, from which some other of the above details are derived.

her to welcome every new light. Certainly she was of the stuff which surrenders even Plato to truth. And as for her nephew, he was instantly won. He had seen Juliet; and if Ewald had been anything to him before, he henceforth, as a rival authority ceased, like Romeo's Rosalind, to exist.[1]

The Dutch author of the book,[2] which now, in Colenso's translation,[3] came into Wicksteed's hands, was to count greatly both for his intellectual and scholarly growth, and for his and his children's happiness; and it is necessary to dwell here awhile upon the career and personality of the man whose English friend became first an interpreter and disciple, and eventually the father of his son's wife.

VI

Abraham Kuenen, born at Haarlem in 1828, was even as a boy something of a phenomenon. We owe a vivid account of his childhood to a lady, then his governess, who later became the mother of a distinguished painter in Amsterdam; and quotation from it is the more apposite here, since it was Philip Wicksteed himself who after Kuenen's death, in 1891, took it down from the still vigorous old lady's lips. "Bram

[1] Not perhaps without a casual glance. According to Estlin Carpenter's private note-books (1870 and foll.), Wicksteed did at one time take some slight part in the Ewald translation. But this must have been towards the end, for Carpenter found his friend's German faulty, whereas "he is a master of Dutch."

[2] *Historisch-kritisch Onderzoek naar het ontstaan en de verzameling van de boeken des Ouden Verbonds, I, De historische boeken.* Leiden, 1861.

[3] *The Pentateuch and Book of Joshua critically examined by Professor A. Kuenen,* translated from the Dutch and edited, with notes, by the Right Rev. J. W. Colenso, 1865.

Kuenen?" she cried, when she learnt his errand, "Yes, I knew him from his third or fourth year, when he was only *so* high. It seems absurd to say of such a little tot that he was 'gifted' or 'talented,' but I can find no other word, he was so quick and so sure. Then, when he was nine, he sometimes came to stay with us, and what questions he asked! I was there, you know, as governess, and had to be fairly up in all manner of subjects; but when that child asked me anything I had not courage to give him an answer, or I had to look it up in my books to be quite sure it was right. . . . Nothing but the very truth was good enough for him. . . . Well, I was fifteen years older than he, but I tell you I was in awe of the child (*ik had respekt voor*); there is no other word for it. And a jolly little fellow! . . . And good to his mother and sisters. . . . And history; you can't believe what he read, and how quickly and clearly he grasped everything. And then so modest and so good-humoured. And that he remained his whole life long, always the same. . . . What was it that struck you when he stood before you? You could not call him handsome, no, he wasn't that. It was noble, that is what it was. . . . See, I am seventy-eight, and they say that feelings get dull at that age; but his death struck me like a dagger-stab. . . . You are going to write about him? You may say all the good you can, it won't be enough." [1]

This engaging picture of a great scholar's boyhood was wholly justified by the sequel. His first biographers had even to dissipate some heroic legends of

[1] From the Dutch *Levensbericht*, by W. van der Vlugt (Leiden, 1893), p. 10 f. This was translated from Wicksteed's English, itself, of course, his own rendering of his interlocutor's Dutch.

fabulous prowess in many fields. But there was true heroism in the young student who, on his father's death, quietly resigned his hopes of a scholar's career to serve in an apothecary's shop. Presently released by the generous intervention of an aunt, he returned to complete his course at the *gymnasium* and in 1846 entered the theological faculty of the University of Leiden. But theology, even in the large acceptation of the term current at that old and famous centre of learning, was too narrow a province for the already vast erudition, and large humanity, of Kuenen. A man of his brilliance, who at twenty was already proficient, not only in Hebrew but in Arabic, Syriac, Chaldee, and Sanscrit, was the marked prey of the Orientalists, and the two faculties "contended," in Wicksteed's lively phrase, "for the body of the living Patroclus." Under the influence of Scholten, his ablest predecessor in Old Testament criticism, theology eventually won the day, and in June 1853, after a Latin oration on the significant theme of the "importance of the study of Hebrew antiquity for the Christian theologian," Kuenen was appointed to an Extraordinary, and a year later to an Ordinary Professorship in that faculty. Eight years later appeared the first part of the *Onderzoek*, which immediately arrested the attention of Old Testament critics, and was eventually to play a chief part in the chief revolution effected, in that field, in his generation.

The ideas which it put forward were not startlingly novel: it might even be said, in the banal and equivocal phrase of a grudging German critic, to contain nothing new. But it presented, with commanding power and range of knowledge, ideas which had in Germany and

Holland long been fermenting, without finding any equally qualified exponent. A year after its publication Renan, then the recognized master of Biblical historic criticism, acclaimed it as the most adequate account of the Old Testament yet given.

The impression made by it spread to larger circles, both in Holland and abroad, when the *Onderzoek* was followed (1870) by the *History of the Religion of Israel.* "His departure from tradition," wrote Wicksteed later, trenchantly, "was so complete that we need not wonder if he was called sacrilegious, ruthless, and the like. But in reality, his most conspicuous qualities were an extremely anxious caution, simplicity, and self-restraint; and the structure was carried out with continuous patience and reflection from A to Z." But German scholarship long opposed a closed phalanx, and it was only in 1878 that Wellhausen's brilliant *History of Israel* announced her final surrender.

This is not the place, were it within the competence of the present writer, to offer an appreciation of Kuenen's work. But a word is permissible of the book which so deeply influenced Philip Wicksteed. It was the work not only of a great scholar but of a great teacher; and not only of a bold originator, but of a fearlessly honest man. To quote the testimony of his pupil, and successor, Dr. H. Oort: "It was a considered book; the writer had no desire to give up received opinions; it was an honest book; not only are divergent views faithfully reproduced, but the writer frankly points out the weak points in his own. It was, in a word, a strictly scientific book, sound through and through, penetrated by love of truth, and instinct for it."[1]

[1] Van der Vlugt: *A. Kuenen*, p. 21.

Kuenen was a single-minded scholar, little touched by the currents of philosophic tendency; he accepted the Grafian hypothesis under the impact of evidence, to him, as to the great majority of competent scholars since his date, irresistible, drawn from the Biblical texts. But even the tranquil tide of Kuenen's scholarship, "too full for sound or foam," might have been troubled, or diverted into other channels, had the Hegelian stream permeated the intellectual centres of Holland as it had done those of Germany. The Dutch intellect was shielded from this influence less by conservative caution than by the different temper of its own originality, a cooler, more objective daring in the recognition of facts, the spirit of the country which had sheltered Descartes and Locke, and been the home of Spinoza.[1]

And Kuenen was himself a moral as well as an intellectual force. It might mean little to the outsider that he was Professor of Ethics as well as of Hebrew Exegesis, or even that, in a rearrangement of subjects among the faculty, he insisted on retaining this great and arduous subject instead of being relieved of its exacting and, for many Biblical scholars of less eminence, distracting calls. But the teaching of ethics provided an opening for self-expression to Kuenen which the chair of Old Testament only indirectly offered; and his students often understood the soul of the man better than Leiden society, which knew only the austere and reticent scholar, or the world of Biblical scholars, who knew only the brilliant discoverer and fearless critic. "We went to him," writes one of them, now the eminent holder of a chair in Amsterdam,[2] "as a

[1] Cf. Herderschee, *De Moderne Godesdienstige Richting in Nederland*, p. 19 f.
[2] A. Y. Groenewegen.

Professor of Old Testament, who also taught ethics; we soon came to regard him as a great ethical teacher, who was also eminent in Hebrew." The other lecture-benches were rarely quite full; but at Kuenen's *Ethics* not a place was left; and the word which the audience of Dutch students commonly found to summarize their impressions was "*opgetogen*" (magnificent).

Such facts make clear the nature of the fire that moved and guided the brilliant intellectuality of Abraham Kuenen. His old governess found the right word for him: "noble." The revolution he wrought in Old Testament history was not the work of an iconoclast, but of a mighty rebuilder. And if his discoveries shook the religious faith of some weaker brethren, they never disturbed his own. His students and his friends noticed sometimes with wonder, that he remained the simple Christian of his boyhood. But the apparent paradox disappears when we recall that Kuenen was vindicating the primacy among the authentic voices of the religion of Israel, for the prophets to whom the world owes the sublimest utterances of the passion for righteousness. In proving the "priestly codex" to be, in fundamentals, of later date than Isaiah and Ezekiel, he was vindicating a more authentic and enduring type of religion itself. The path pursued with inflexible fidelity by the great Hebraist led to conclusions deeply acceptable both to the ethical thinker and the sincere Christian.

VII

That the work of a scholar of this type should arrest and fascinate Philip Wicksteed is not hard to understand. He was not, of course, strange to the view that the current tradition of Biblical history demanded radical revision. Neither his rigidly Anglican school, it is true, nor the more expansive yet on the whole traditional Unitarianism of his father, had prepared him for such inquiries. But the 'sixties had set currents of thought astir in England by which no young man of Wicksteed's powers could fail to be agitated. In 1859, Darwin's great book made evolution a ruling conception which was to transform the history of religion as fundamentally as that of nature. Lessing, long before, had foreshadowed that idea in Germany. And in 1862, an Anglican bishop, F. Temple, in his famous contribution to *Essays and Reviews*, building on Lessing's foundation, presented the history of religion as a gradual process. In the same year England was startled by the apparition of John William Colenso, a heroic and original figure, equally memorable in the annals of English scholarship and of colonial history. The career of this Cambridge mathematician was followed with deep and undisguised sympathy by English Liberals. Even those who were startled by his rejection of the Mosaic origin of the Pentateuch and of the doctrine of eternal punishment, honoured the great bishop who was championing the rights of the natives of South Africa, and who had begun by learning their language, and translating the Bible into it; and they deeply resented the bitter persecution to which he was subjected, on different grounds, by the white colonists. But Colenso's book, received in general with fierce hostility in England, was naturally read with keen interest by the author of the *Onderzoek*, published in the previous year, and, as he generously acknowledged, had some influence in the execution of the remaining parts.

It is doubtful, however, whether during Wicksteed's studentship even Colenso's researches had much affected the Biblical teaching in Manchester College. The liberal theology pursued there drew freely upon the copious springs of continental scholarship, and Henry Sidgwick's famous "trade secret," the "originality" attainable on easy terms by English lecturers who knew German, was there, even more than at Cambridge, a very "open" one.[1] But it had hardly yet occurred to any teacher in either quarter that "originality" was to be had, on securer if not on easier terms, by a knowledge of Dutch. And "daring Germany" herself, we know, refused for some years to accept, in this field, the yet more daring lead of Holland.

It was, then, substantially a new, yet an immensely alluring, world which was opened to Wicksteed when the first part of Kuenen's book, as translated by Colenso, came into his hands. And we can understand now why the book, alike in its temper and in its conclusions, was for him enthralling as well as new. In blunt terms, Kuenen had exalted the prophet and deposed the priest. Philip Wicksteed, whatever his nominal office, was never, either then or later, a very perfect priest, and he cared less than most of his colleagues in any ministry, of whatever theological shade, for the niceties of ritual, or the mint and cummin of prescribed form. Those who saw a mark of Norse blood in his high complexion

[1] Some readers may, I am advised, not follow this allusion. The anecdote refers to a Cambridge dinner at which Henry Sidgwick, probably the most eminent, certainly among the wisest and the wittiest of the Cambridge men of the later nineteenth century, made the speech in question. A bad stammer in no way hindered the influence of his wisdom, and even added to the savour of his wit. It was a trade secret among the university teachers, he declared, that a knowledge of German enabled a man to lecture with great *originality*.

and flaming hair sometimes clinched their argument by alluding to the newly-converted Viking who impatiently kicked over the baptismal tub. But whatever Philip Wicksteed's shortcomings as a priest, no Englishman of his day had more of the fire, the passion for righteousness, even perhaps in certain moods and aspects the inner loneliness, of the prophet.

VIII

But the gist of the book, from this point of view, was still hidden from English eyes in the untranslated second part. Philip Wicksteed, though never in the strict sense a linguistic scholar, had a singular zest for languages, and an unusual faculty of mastering their written expression. He threw himself upon Dutch, taking lessons from a Jewish tobacconist, of unattractive personal habits, in Manchester. He worked his way through the second and doubtless also the third part, and then through the great continuous *History* issued by Kuenen in 1870. He was soon in a position to undertake, single-handed, that translation of the popular exposition of Kuenen's results by his pupils, the pastors Oort and Hooykaas, by which Wicksteed's name first became widely known in England.[1]

Wicksteed's experiences as the translator of the *Bible for Young People* disclose the quite natural and intelligible resistance which Kuenen's "radical reform"

[1] *The Bible for Young People,* six volumes (London. Sunday School Association). Wicksteed's preoccupation with this work naturally influenced his preaching at Dukinfield. His hearers, it was said, spoke with especial interest of his sermons on Old Testament characters. (Rev. Alexander Gordon, formerly Wicksteed's fellow-student, in a private letter to the writer.)

encountered even in the left wing of English Liberal theologians. Wicksteed himself had not been at once converted; his brother-in-law and fellow-pilgrim to Leiden hung back longer; and even the Sunday-school authorities who had agreed to publish the translation betrayed some of the discomfort of Goethe's magician when they found what kind of spirits they had let loose. But the translator, after his first hesitation, became the doughtiest champion of his author, and fell upon the "stupid questions" of an intimate friend, who had delayed acceptance of the truth somewhat longer than himself, with fierce derision. "I did not expect to make it comprehensible to any but the cream; it was the *very* cream that asked me for it."

His letters to his father soon after he began the translation, illustrate the deep impression made upon him by the chief writer, Pastor Oort, at a time when he had not yet accepted fully Oort's theological position: "I am still delighted with my Dutchmen, and longing to see them 'face to face.' I have actually begun translating the *Bible for Young People*, to read specimens to my brother ministers. In richness of religious life it reminds us of Newman's *Soul* and of nothing else.[1] But Newman soliloquizes and the reader looks and listens, Oort pours out his love to his 'young readers' as well as to God, with a tenderness and strength which I do not think I could parallel from any other writer I know. I do not mean to compare Oort to Martineau in profundity of religious thought and mental analysis, but in richness of spiritual life he reminds me of him. In his historical and critical judgments he is what is called 'extreme' to a very extreme degree,

[1] Francis Newman's *The Soul, her Sorrows and her Aspirations.*

further sometimes than I can go with him even provisionally.''

It was in this connexion that he made his first approach to Kuenen personally. Wicksteed used to recount how, summoning his best Dutch, he addressed a letter to him putting some questions on the subject-matter. He received a very polite reply in the same language. To a second letter in Dutch, however, Kuenen replied, with equal politeness but in perfect English, remarking slyly that he knew English well enough to understand his correspondent's Dutch, so that it might be convenient if they continued to correspond in this language. Wicksteed was delighted both by the courtesy and by the humour, and used to tell the story to his children with much gusto.

When, accordingly, in 1872, the Hibbert Trustees invited Wicksteed to visit Holland on their behalf, for the purpose of reporting upon the position of the Liberal churches there, of which so much had recently been heard, Wicksteed eagerly welcomed the opportunity. Holland came to occupy too large a place in his affections and interests to be treated as merely accessory to his Biblical studies. But his sojourns there were holiday tours as well as pilgrimages; and as they are recorded in a number of his liveliest letters, we may allow ourselves and the reader a brief vacation in their company.

IX

Wicksteed paid three principal visits to Holland, one in 1872, during his Dukinfield ministry, one in 1874, after its close, and one in 1875, when settled in London. His principal letters were written to his wife, his father, and his brother-in-law, Frank Jones, or to a more general "public" of relatives and friends. Their intrinsic interest naturally grows as his growing mastery of the language and growing experience open more and more keys. The letters are remarkable chiefly for their freshness and perfect spontaneity. They begin with amusing recitals of the small adventures of a high-spirited young Englishman—still, in fact, rather young for his twenty-eight years—who is engaged in capturing a foreign language by force, and hugely enjoys both his disasters and his triumphs. He tells for instance, how he and his companion—a brother-in-law—sallied out the first morning, bent on getting tickets for the Dutch theatre; found that their tickets were for the German opera, which they did not want; how, the box-office refusing to return their money, Wicksteed appealed to a man in the street, who listened politely while he stated their case, but declined to state it himself to the box-office clerk: "What need, when Mynheer can argue it so well himself?" How at this juncture an energetic woman who had listened (for by this time a little crowd had collected) took him by the arm to the box-office and put his case so eloquently that the clerk sulkily refunded the money; how, finally, the Portia who had so successfully intervened intimated that her services deserved their meed, whereupon Wicksteed, a little taken aback, like Bassanio, pulled out five coins which he took to make the usual guerdon of twenty-five cents, and only discovered from the indignant looks of Portia and the spectators, that the five coins were *cents*—value together, one penny!

In October he is already established, hearing four or five lectures a day, taking three Dutch lessons a week, collecting a Dutch library, "polite literature, for there is a polite literature in Dutch,"—as well as theology, and dining out almost every evening. It is clear that the exuberant personality of the young Englishman, compelling a rudimentary vocabulary and a highly tentative pronunciation somehow to do its will, attracted his new acquaintances in the ancient university town, accustomed to more placid and equable modes of intellectual life, and to less enterprising English visitors. For even to educated Englishmen Holland was still too often a country of tulip-gardens and very clean cities, famous in history for realistic painters and for Motley's *Dutch Republic*. Oxford and Cambridge themselves were even more imperfectly aware of Leiden than of Leipzig and Jena; and Cobet, one of the most consummate classical scholars of the century, then professor there, was listened to by few pilgrims from those academic bowers. The ordinary English attitude was but too well typified by that of some well-to-do relatives, resident for years near Amsterdam, who received Wicksteed with cordial hospitality, but expressed unmeasured surprise that he found anything in Holland worth coming over for.[1]

In any case he found (as open-minded young men, from Saul downwards, will) far more than the immediate object of his coming. The *Report on the Dutch Churches* led him to the citizenship of a kingdom. He became intimate with the genius of Holland, with her art, her scholarship, her ethics of life. At the university he heard other than Biblical lectures, among other

[1] He brought back, at least, some piquant remarks. One of the guests at this house "lamented that the Unitarians were so intellectual and high-principled, it was such a bad example, and likely to lead others into their errors."

courses one by the great Cobet himself, his impressions of which are worth reading: Cobet was "a prime favourite with everyone," and "the university was very proud of him." He lectured in Latin, not pronounced in the English mode, and Wicksteed followed at first with difficulty. But he soon overcame this obstacle and enjoyed it keenly. "It was a spirited and humorous defence of the continued use of Latin in lectures and the maintenance of the classics as the most important element of education, of the necessity of learning Latin in order to understand anything else, and Greek to understand Latin; an attack upon 'handbooks' and 'extracts,' and an exhortation to the students to work hard, put away childish things, make themselves men, and keep up the reputation of the university." [1]

But his immediate business in Leiden, and also the focus of his interest, was to make closer acquaintance, and win, if he might, the confidence, perhaps the friendship, of the leaders of the Modernist movement in theology, and of those who under their inspiration and guidance were making its conclusions accessible to the larger educated public. These were, in the first place, Abraham Kuenen himself; with the pastors Oort and Hooykaas, who with Kuenen's help had prepared the *Bijbel voor jonge lieden*, on the translation of which Wicksteed was engaged. But also, the great founder of the Leiden School, still professor there, Johannes Henricus Scholten.

Wicksteed called on Kuenen on an early day of his first visit (20 September). He later told, in his *Memoirs of Abraham Kuenen* and elsewhere, the story of his

[1] To his wife, 20 September, 1872.

Philip Wicksteed, *c.* 1874

first personal approach to the revered author of the *Onderzoek*. He gave his first impressions of it in his letter of the same evening to his wife: "Imagine my feelings when we had rung the bell! We were ushered into a handsome house, and signs of children (Noah's ark etc.) were visible. Soon he came in. Such a man! Tall and distinguished looking. Very like Beesly. The same stoop and shoulders, the same broad brow, the same nose, the same cut of face, the same tonsure, much the same manner, but in some way *very* different also. He is a very striking and powerful looking man, and very prepossessing. He received us most graciously and spoke admirable English." Later in the day, Kuenen introduced Wicksteed to the privileges of the University Lesehalle and Library—he had a letter to the Librarian ("a little fussy man who talks very bad English with very great rapidity and infinite delight") from Henry Green, Unitarian minister at Knutsford, an antiquarian of note and author of a then classical book on "Emblems."

More intimate and important intercourse with Kuenen came two years later (September 1874), when Wicksteed, now tolerably proficient in conversational Dutch, revisited Leiden with his wife. She, too, was "completely taken captive," Wicksteed wrote to his father,[1] by Kuenen's easy and fascinating manners and his beautiful simplicity of life and character. "He is certainly the most faultless, and one of the most fascinating men I ever knew." "I have spent a good many hours with him," he goes on, "and have read him a considerable part of my Report. We have talked on many matters, for he is one of those who have

[1] 8 September, 1874.

the art of making you feel at home with them, and his enormous learning is worn so lightly that instead of cowing you it simply draws out and strengthens whatever one has in one. . . . I never feel ashamed of my ignorance in his presence, and he answers questions, and gives information to any extent." He even explained a cartoon in *Punch* which they had not understood, and told them particulars about Dr. Martineau's chapel which they did not know.

More dramatic was the first interview with Kuenen's elder colleague and master, the veteran Professor J. H. Scholten, who, thirty years before, had startled Holland by a vindication, then daring, of the fundamental humanity of Jesus, and was now the acknowledged founder and spiritual father of Liberal theology in that country. In the Christology of the New Testament, Scholten had intervened with as decisive effect as Kuenen was later to do in the theology of the Old. Refusing to build faith on dogma, he found a divine revelation in every form of religion. And these positions were advanced with the challenging emphasis of a man of granite character, a born leader, a stubborn defender; a prophetic nature, who demanded all or nothing; an architect for whom nothing fragmentary was of any use.[1]

The approach to this formidable person, whose impatience of "fragments" was understood to apply not least to fragmentary Dutch, meant, even for a tolerably self-confident Englishman, some searching of heart; and it was with a little trepidation that, one

[1] Based upon the sketch of Scholten given by Herderschee, *De Moderne Godsdienstige Richting in Nederland*, p. 92. He was, at the date of Wicksteed's visit, sixty-one.

evening between seven and eight, Scholten's hour for recreation, he sent in his card. He was shown into the salon, where the family was at tea. Scholten was "a tall, rather heavy, dark-haired, rather round-faced massive-looking man, with a harsh voice and manner, and something rather surly about him. He rose to meet me, and made a frightful sound which I imagined to be an attempt at my name and therefore assented. We sat down, but the scene that followed it is utterly impossible to describe! Hitherto I had been constantly surprising and surpassing myself in Dutch, but now every word of it was gone! People who have to talk in a foreign language they don't know are advised to have a small force of effective phrases for manœuvring. My effectives were all driven off the field! Scholten seemed deaf, and his harsh voice kept repeating inquiries that I had answered in a hopeless manner. Madame Scholten seemed much amused in a good-natured way, and I did my best in great discomfort. . . . At last he launched into a long disquisition on the history of English philosophy, explaining to me that we were always empirical and never speculative, with the single exception of Ockham. I had to recognize the names of the philosophers by the connection in which they came, as the sounds he made were about as intelligible as the cries of London! He kept smiling in the course of his harangue, and of course I grinned and giggled to any extent on these occasions, although it always seemed to me a most inappropriate time for any hilarity—(I afterwards discovered that his smile was a nervous twitch of the lips and not a smile at all!)—This did pretty well; but when he had brought the history down to the origin of the Broad Church

Movement he desired me to 'take up the wondrous tale,' and insisted on hearing all about Voysey, etc. I did my best, but I did not know the Dutch for 'Atonement.' When this was at last explained, it was 'But why, when every other European nation had quite a different word, should we have such a peculiar one?' At last Scholten said, as I thought in a tone of despair, 'Can you speak German?' 'If possible, still less than Dutch.' 'Oh,' he replied, 'your Dutch is good! very good! In a few weeks you will speak it perfectly.' This was a joyful surprise, and I discovered gradually that he was really pleased and interested, and that my interview with him too was a 'success.'"[1] The great man, in short, despite appearances, liked Wicksteed, as Dr. Johnson, when first encountered by Boswell in Davies's shop, "liked," according to Davies's encouraging assurance, the young aspirant, who "could not help" his Scottish birth.

And this friendship, like Boswell's, rapidly ripened, without diminishing Wicksteed's reverence. Two years later, in September 1874, he writes to his father: "I have not yet seen my idol—the mighty Scholten! . . . He is by no means faultless, like Kuenen, but he is one of the most powerful men I ever knew; he exercises a magic power over every one who comes in contact with him, and I am one of his most devoted worshippers." A year later still (September 1875), he is "enjoying Scholten's magnificent hospitality, something such as one does not experience many times in one's life. . . . Scholten talks by the hour, three or four hours on end if it happens, in the most intensely interesting and

[1] Letter to his wife, *u.s.*, J.

suggestive style. I feel as if I were drinking in wisdom by the gallon!"

The visit of 1874 was notable for the closer intimacy with Henricus Oort, one of the authors of the *Bible for Young People*. In the early summer Wicksteed had taken leave of his flock at Dukinfield, with deep regret on both sides, and had set out a little later for Holland, with his brother-in-law and old travelling companion Frank Jones, leaving Mrs. Wicksteed to superintend the removal and to follow later.

After landing and sleeping at Rotterdam, the two friends set out early, to the bewilderment of the hotel waiters, to walk to Leiden. The walk through the charming unexplored Dutch countryside, by Delft, was, he wrote home, "a magnificent success," with the "funny wooden carriages drawn high up out of the reach of floods," and the "handsome roadhuis" in every little village.

The husband and wife spent a fortnight with the Oorts at Amsterdam. Their enjoyment was marred by ill-health, and by the dank air, oppressive to both, but it was a memorable experience. "Oort is not such a man as Kuenen," he wrote in the same letter to his father, "but he, too, is a most delightful and fascinating companion, full of spirits, and as natural and simple in heart and life as any man could be." The straightforward simplicity of life in these cultured and well-to-do Dutch homes impressed them both. "It is a noble and exalted atmosphere to live in, and I feel it one of the highest privileges of my life to be able to call such men my friends."

He describes with keen gusto the routine of these Amsterdam days; "Our life was almost ideal . . . I got up in time to have a Dutch lesson before breakfast at half-past eight. Then Oort and I worked till about half-past twelve, when we had lunch. Then came picture and sight-seeing, walks, conversation, letter-writing, till dinner at five. Then work again, or conversation for an hour or two, during which I read *Hamlet* with Oort, then reading English aloud or reading Dutch poetry with Oort till supper and bed-time."

The friendship thus happily opened, ripened into an intimacy in which the two husbands shared equally. When Wicksteed visited them in the following year he exacted from Mina Oort a playful compact, signed with all formality, to return their visit at a given date.

Both men lived for half a century after these visits, and with unclouded friendship, and Oort in his last year paid a warm tribute to Wicksteed's services in the cause. "I have just been reading Oort's last essay," wrote Wicksteed, to one of his closest Dutch friends, in June 1926, "and admiring its 'construction.' How little I could have believed, in those old days, when under the spell of Kuenen's *Godesdienst* and Oort's [*Bible for Young People*], I felt that if I could be their mouthpiece in England I should say my *nunc dimittis*; that I should live to see Oort over ninety years old, and receive such a tribute from him as he has given me!"

The sequel, so far as it concerns Wicksteed, may be briefly told. In 1876, and later, Kuenen lectured in London and was Wicksteed's guest. Wicksteed's part in Kuenen's work scarcely went beyond that of the very capable translator and populariser of writings, composed in a little-known tongue. But the "Young People" whom he enabled to read the critically-interpreted Bible included the fresh-minded of all ages. In the meantime, after twenty years of intense discussion in several languages, a new edition of the *Onderzoek* had become necessary, and for Kuenen, a man as exempt from the scholar's vanity as from the sciolist's illusions, revision, under those circumstances, meant complete rewriting. The second edition of the three parts, separately as before, appeared at Leiden in 1885–9.[1] Immediately on the appearance of the first part Wicksteed set to work on the translation, published in London in the following year, 1886. He acknowledges the help of the author in verifying the references which pack every page.[2]

Kuenen was not yet sixty, but his career was approaching its close. He died in December 1891. Shortly afterwards Wicksteed wrote a brief sketch of his life, which has been noticed with warm praise by Dutch biographers, embodying in it the vivid descriptions of the boy Kuenen as taken down by him from his old governess's lips, which has already been quoted.[3] "Take it for all in all," was Wicksteed's final and sufficing summary of Kuenen's life, "it would be hard

[1] *Historisch-kritisch Onderzoek . . . Tweede, geheel omgewerkte uitgave.*

[2] *An historical-critical Inquiry into the origin and composition of the Hexateuch. . . .* Translated from the Dutch, with the assistance of the author, by Philip H. Wicksteed, London, 1886.

[3] Cf. especially Van der Vlugt's *Levensbericht,* already quoted. Wicksteed does, however, appear in his admiration, to have been at moments dazzled by the Kuenen "legend." Van der Vlugt, who is at pains to correct the heightened profiles, inquires with friendly sarcasm: "Who can have bamboozled Wicksteed into the belief that, at Leiden, the president of the student corps was 'commonly chosen on the ground of his high social position and ample means,' and that Kuenen's elevation to this honour was thus 'presumably an event unparalleled in the history of the university'?" But Van der Vlugt confesses his debt to Wicksteed for various particulars, especially for his account of Kuenen's father, as well, of course, as for the account of his boyhood. (*Levensbericht,* p. 16.)

to find one richer in the things for which wise men pray."

Only one event remains to be recorded in Wicksteed's relations with the Kuenen family; and this, though it followed by some years Kuenen's own death, was for him not so much the epilogue of the story as its climax and crown. In 1896, Kuenen's eldest son Johannes, a brilliant physicist, who was shortly to hold the chair of that subject at Leiden, became the husband of Wicksteed's third daughter, Dora. It was a source to him of peculiar delight, nay, rapture, when the man whom he had revered probably beyond any other, became the recipient in the person of his son, of one of the most precious gifts it was in his power to bestow. And looking back in old age upon his early study of Dutch, he told a correspondent how it had given him "a noble son-in-law and five glorious grandchildren." One of these, Emily Kuenen, became, in those last years, the skilled helper in the arduous labour which occupied him to the end.

CHAPTER III

1874: LONDON

Little Portland Street—The Home—The Lecturer—
University Hall—Books

I

In the autumn of 1874 Philip Wicksteed settled in London, as minister of Little Portland Street Chapel. Situated in a sombre and shabby street, near to the back doors of the ambassadors' houses in Portland Place, the chapel stood on the verge of the West End and outwardly suggested less of that proximity than in a topographical sense it possessed. Only a classic porch in stucco affirmed the decline among modern Unitarians of the austere Puritanism of which they continued to be proud. Within, neither the bare walls, the tall gaunt windows, nor the ungainly overhanging galleries, did much to distinguish the chapel from the dingy conventicle of tradition.

Yet this sombre and unattractive place was one of the focuses of spiritual religion in London. James Martineau held a place in the religious life of England much more important than either his church or the obscure college with its little band of ministerial students, over which he presided, might suggest. Shortly before this date he had become one of the original members of that "Metaphysical Society" in which Tennyson, Huxley, Cardinal Manning, Richard Hutton and others met for the unreserved discussion of ultimate questions. Debate among thinkers of such calibre and of schools so widely diverse was not likely to attenuate the differences it called into play; and Martineau's subtle, rather than catholic, genius was better calculated to explore and define the intervening chasms than to bridge them. But his noble and lofty personality, and the persuasive union of clarity and poetic charm in his speech, impressed his most pronounced opponents. Some of these stood nearer than he to the progressive forces of the age. Of the scientific movement led by Huxley and Tyndall he was deeply suspicious. Positivism he dismissed with impatience. To Socialism, now beginning to alarm the complacent prosperity of *bourgeois* England, he was hostile; and in the analysis of social phenomena, even when it did not lead to Socialism, he took little interest.

The congregation which worshipped in this outwardly unattractive place, under the guidance of this great spiritual teacher, had itself a very definite character. It was chiefly composed of families descended from the early days of Unitarianism, bound together by intermarriage, common intellectual and religious tradition, and by common experience of the tempered kind of persecution which, in people mostly of high culture and substantial incomes, under the conditions of modern England, tends to produce rather pride than discomfort. It has been computed that almost the whole Unitarian body of that day was descended from one or other of two ancestors, Philip Henry in the seventeenth, John Tayler in the eighteenth century. The members of Little Portland Street congregation were thus united by a bond in which a somewhat abstract theological agreement was touched with the familiar intimacy of kinship. The sect was also a a clan. Class differences, if they existed, were quite subordinate; "the poor" were cared for, befriended, and taught, but for the most part remained outside; the members were professional men, lawyers, university officials, with here and there a substantial shopkeeper from the neighbouring Oxford Street or Regent Street. Each family sat by itself in its own high straight-backed pew. Among the members were several notable in the future minister's history: his friend Estlin Carpenter; his friend's father, W. B. Carpenter, Registrar of the University of London; the distinguished barrister, Dr. Blake Odgers, and his Positivist friend and mentor, Edward Beesly, who, however, attended only in the person of his wife and their flock of fair-haired children.

The choice of Philip Wicksteed as minister to such a congregation, and successor to such a man may possibly have aroused some concern in those who asked only continuance of the even tenor of congregational life, or at least continuity in its evolution. Wicksteed's Old Testament innovations roused particular concern in some quarters. "Are we to change the faith of our fathers," asked one old member, "just because young Mr. Wicksteed has learnt Dutch?" Philip Wicksteed was, indeed, a scion of one of those ancestral stocks, as Martineau, child of an ancient Norwich home, was of the other; his father, too, had been Martineau's colleague, and was still his valued friend. But as Goethe said of the young Carlyle, there was "much future" in Philip; and its unfolding was not likely to be along normal lines.

He well knew that he could not offer the congregation

of Little Portland Street the literary brilliance and exquisite diction which clothed the spiritual intensity of his predecessor. He had accustomed himself, too, in addressing his Dukinfield working-folks, to a homely vernacular unsuitable to a "conventional" congregation. He was willing to prune his style, but he could not surrender the direct and simple address in which his strength lay; and he laid plans, while still at Dukinfield, for evening services (Little Portland Street had had none) to working-men "as a second string to my ministerial bow." [1]

He knew that the difference between himself and Martineau was not merely inferiority in experience or in power. In cast of intellect, in the fundamental assumptions and the habitual processes of their thinking, there was a cleavage which years were likely rather to deepen than to bridge. Martineau's soaring imagination and his impassioned religious genius Wicksteed sincerely revered. But the perils to coherent thought which accompany a union of those splendid and noble gifts could not escape the more positive and pragmatic intellect of the younger man. His considered judgment of Martineau, at the moment of entering his London ministry, is given in an important letter to his father, quoted below. [2]

[1] To his father, 4 April, 1874.

[2] Tyndall had just thrown England into a storm of angry discussion by his Belfast address at the British Association. Martineau was among its most indignant critics, and denounced it to Wicksteed as "blank and aggressive atheism." Wicksteed had not read it, and reserved his judgment. "I read it last night, however, and should rather describe it as scientific agnosticism than atheism. To-day," he goes on, "Martineau himself addressed a crowded audience in the [University] Hall. His address was very powerful and beautiful. . . . Some passages were masterly, both as oratory and as argument. And yet I never felt more keenly the weak side of his method of dealing with an opponent, and the

But whatever inner forces might later draw them apart, his first act on assuming Martineau's pulpit was a beautiful symbolic expression of the reverence which he never ceased to feel. On 4 October, 1874, his mother, who had come for the occasion, sent to her husband an account of his first service. "The most affecting part of the service was the reading of the Old Testament, where Joshua was exhorted to be of good courage, and the God who had led Moses would lead him; and where Solomon prays for wisdom to stand in the place of his father, for he is but as 'a little child.' Philip read these passages so that each was a sermon in itself, and no other allusion was made to his position. Many eyes were wet with tears of sympathy, and Dr. Martineau went up to him afterwards looking as kindly as a father; I do not think he could help feeling so." Nor did Wicksteed ever cease to revere him.

II

Wicksteed settled in a house near Regent's Park, two miles from the chapel. A keen-eyed little girl, playmate of his children and later an intimate friend, has recorded how she first saw him in the garden of their house near Regent's Park—"a leaping laughing figure on stilts, shouting as he bounded after the flying

absence of *lumen siccum* where it is the only satisfactory sort of *lumen*. He sometimes showered epigrams upon the materialists which had the appearance, but the appearance only, of arguments, and each of which, when analysed, depended for its point on an assumption of the matter under discussion. He was less successful, too, in his lighter vein, when he seemed to me, as in his essay on Comte, to attempt to make a thing look ridiculous, instead of respectfully and deliberately examining it." But Wicksteed allowed the less polemical part of Martineau's argument to be both profound and noble. (Letter to his father, 6 October, 1874.)

children who with shouts of delight scattered before him. . . . What a playfellow he was! . . . his full voice and personality dominating the house, flaming-haired, splendid—an Apollo touched with the joviality of Bacchus. For how jolly he was! yet with something of the awfulness of deity!"[1] A father who produced this conflict of impressions was naturally somewhat baffling to a child's mind. His presence flooded the home with genial delight, in which no one could feel dullness or doubt; yet in his gayest relaxation there was something of the giant at play, and his study was not so much a holy as a terrible place, to be summoned to which was the dread of the small evildoer. "I was horribly afraid of him," confesses one of his sons. Yet, once there, the chastisement was likely to be neither Christian reproof nor legal punishment, but some unexpected appeal which made the culprit feel that he was his father's comrade, a sharer in humanity and its rights. One of his sons relates how once, having been caught red-handed in the act of visiting a prohibited quarter of the garden, he received the summons of the unfailing Nemesis to the study. At the door he broke down. "Why are you crying?" asked his father. "Is it because you are going to be punished, or because you are sorry?" "Because I am sorry!" The boy was sincere, and his father accepted his word, "thereby," adds the son, "establishing confidence between us for life." Others of the children have confessed that, in those early years, they were thoroughly afraid of him. And the mere prodigality of his power, however genially it was exercised, might abash a defiant boy or a sensitive girl. But there was

[1] From private notes by Mrs. R. Garnett.

nothing deliberate or even conscious in this terrifying power. "I do not think my father knew," says the same son, "how terrible he was." In denouncing public wrongs, he could utter righteous anger with prophetic intensity. But in his home his power was felt as a perpetual radiation of life, energy, and joy, which did not so much put his children on their mettle, as impel them instinctively to be the best they knew. A faith, critical but boundless, in humanity, was a trait that lay deep in his nature; and with his own children it took the form of a beautiful certainty that if he planted and watered, "increase" would not fail. He never, devoted Wordsworthian as he was, credited them with having come into the world "trailing clouds of glory"; nor did he, on the other hand, indulge vast anticipations of what they might become; but he brought all into the presence of the best he knew. Even the baby, in its nurse's arms, attended with the whole household, his morning prayer; for education began in atmosphere, instinct, and feeling. And later on, if he won access to very unpromising orders of intelligence or stages of maturity, it was not by accommodating his matter to their supposed needs, but by awakening in them the aptitude to comprehend it. A commonplace rule of educational procedure, no doubt; but with him it was simply the outflow of his untamable spirit of human comradeship. It may be doubted whether Goethe's maxim (in *Wilhelm Meister*) that the child only achieves the best of which it is capable when it is treated as if capable of more was in his mind; this kind of paradox was not in his way; but it well expressed the magical operation which his sympathetic insight into childhood actually had.

That comradeship of a rich and abounding mind towards little beings much in awe of him, but also under the spell of his magnetism, was the spirit of Wicksteed's home-life. He was the soul of the household as well as the autocrat of the breakfast and all other tables. He overflowed with talk, but he was acutely sensitive to the quality of the hearers. If response was out of the question he would blaze away to a single intelligent listener. But he was hard to convince that the land was barren. In his home such an assumption was repudiated altogether, and the family table was saved by a host of ingenious devices from becoming a mere occasion for eating and drinking, the latter operation being, it may be said by the way, and remaining to the end, inflexibly and fervently teetotal. The table-games practised at Hafod in his boyhood under the guidance of his own father, reappeared, with added embellishments and excitements, in the London home. Stories were told by the children in turn on a subject previously given out. The asking of questions was turned into a game, of which the prize was to baffle the father; and the children would search their small experience and their daily talk for profitable treasure trove of this kind. In the "baffling" there were three stages of "triumph" for the victor; first, if he could not answer offhand; then, if he had to send for a book; third, if the book was not on his shelves at all. For so hearty a believer in individual initiative, Wicksteed had a keen relish for "institutionalism" in the home. The table "institutions" were not confined to these games. In table manners no nonconformity was allowed. There was a "clean-hands club," with a reward for the cleanest,

Little Portland Street Chapel

more needful in London than in wild Wales. Nor were the eating and drinking allowed to be "maimed rites"; the father, a perfect carver, presided as a most vigorous and watchful high priest. At the other end of the table, the mother sat, tempering the rigour of the game, and the urgency of the intellectual athlete, with her beautiful humanity, and diffusing her quieter enjoyment over the whole scene.

The children who grew up under this stimulating, but masterful regime were high-spirited young people, and they would not have been Wicksteeds if they had passively taken their father's mould. He himself, moreover, would have scouted the idea of being, according to a significant Dantesque image of which he was fond, "seal" to their "wax." There were wide diversities, too, of gifts and temperaments, as well as in years, among the eight children who survived infancy. A certain cleavage formed itself between those who were more and those who were less amenable to the more exacting saliences in their father's virile humanism, and the "opposition," as one of the latter group called it in later years, did not consist exclusively of the less docile sex. Its revolts against the "government" were indeed, in these years, innocent enough. The incipient Adullamites sometimes grew restive under the table discourse, and started a little backwater of talk in a lighter vein among themselves. But the father, a true democrat at heart, who wished nothing better than to set the tongues wagging in his hall, provided he set the brains working too, would probably, after a moment of natural disconcertment, join gaily in the rival talk, only to find it, too, all in his own hands. For Wicksteed was an autocrat *malgré lui*, a fundamentally humble man, who had authority thrust upon him by his own inveterate force of brain, and no less inveterate need to uplift and kindle the souls of other men.

With the beginning of the 'nineties changes gradually set in in the character of the home. The relation of the elder children, now growing to manhood and womanhood, to their father became freer, but also more intimate, less timidly constrained, but more critically receptive; and they learnt to parry his sarcasms with a disarming humour like his own. They also came to understand that there was no particle either of pride or of unkindness in his severity, and that he was his own sternest and most ruthless judge. "Your self-criticisms are the most devastating things I know," said his eldest son to him on one of those Norwegian cruises which seem to have most nearly released all concerned from whatever sheath of artifice they ordinarily wore, "they are just as nasty as the things you say about your children, but——" a remark cut short by a roar of Homeric laughter. The "opposition" ceased to be "agin the government" as it became better qualified to oppose. A daughter, married in a foreign city, confessed that she first learnt to understand what her father was when she left home. A son first grew intimate with his father on those same Norwegian tours, when he found, as a vigorous athlete of sixteen, that his father, of fifty, could beat him with the oar and the cycle.

A vivid reminiscence of a day on the fjord may serve to bring this home. "I shall never forget the look of his back as he swung back and forth, his cotton shirt rumpled in the spaces of his braces, his face and neck signal-red with sunburn, and shining with vaseline;

ten days' grizzle on his chin, and a rush deer-stalker on his head. Hour after hour would he plug away, tireless and serene, thoroughly enjoying himself in scorching sun, pouring rain, or shouting headwind. Sometimes an hour would pass with no sound but the chug of the oars. Sometimes a dissertation on the astronomical knowledge of the Greeks . . . and sometimes, it must be admitted, a pretty searching criticism of his companions."

"One day" (the same son relates), "he and I rowed the Kari (the boat), the six miles from Utne against a fresh wind. Father pulled hard for a spell (we had one oar each) then eased up, repeating the process perhaps a dozen times. In the pride of my youth I thought, he can pull harder than me, but can't keep it up so long. Presently he said, with some heat, 'You seem to be taking it pretty easy, young man, pulling with one hand.' 'It's very seldom I'm pulling with one hand,' I answered. 'That may be,' he said, 'but every time I look round you are doing it.' ('Dare I?' I thought, and risked it.) 'Then you shouldn't look round so often,' I said. He pulled in silence for a while, his whole outline gradually softening; then a chuckle broke to the surface: 'That 's rather good, S——,' and the row ended in harmony."

III

The twenty-three years of Wicksteed's London residence were the most strenuous period of a life in which every day was strenuous; the zenith of an energy which began, we are persuaded, in his cradle, and persisted literally to his last breath. The outer events were, indeed, without any unusual or sensational feature. They would rarely of themselves demand notice from the biographer. Perhaps the only incident in his life which would do to "tell over the wireless" was his encounter with a London burglar whom he found at night in his dining-room, and who ended the interview by stabbing him with a Norwegian knife which he had just brought home from a holiday there. The death, at ten months, of the little boy who derived from the same northern reminiscences his beautiful name, Sigurd, and of another infant child, were the only bereavements. In the 'nineties two of the daughters married: the eldest became the wife of Roger Lawrence, a rising barrister, later a judge of the Lancashire Palatine Court, who incidentally remarked of his father-in-law that he would have shone at the bar as well as in the pulpit; with his other son-in-law he had a yet closer tie, for Johannes Petrus Kuenen was, as has been said, a son of his old teacher at Leiden.

And the tours in Norway, if as has just been hinted, they sometimes occasioned events, were also, for Wicksteed and his family real events themselves. They began in the summer of 1878. A timely gift from the congregation eased the financial situation. He had invited his old Dukinfield friend, John Reynolds, to be his guest. "We would learn to *swear* in Danish, and have no end of larks. Emily (Mrs. Wicksteed) is very anxious that I should have someone with me who can *talk*, and is *not* a parson!" Eventually it was his wife herself (who satisfied both conditions), not his friend, who went. A little later he began the plan, at once economical and congenial to his hardy and simple tastes, perhaps, too, to some strain of the Norseman in his blood, of spending these summer weeks on some Norwegian fjord, in his own boat. These cruises, often with a child or friend as shipmate, were a peculiar joy to him, and the fjords were only the starting-point, not as with many English tourists, the limit, of his interest in Norway. He presently bought a boat from a Norwegian peasant, which during the winter was laid up there, to be launched again in summer. Many a summer night was spent in the boat; but he was no fanatic of solitude, and in the hospitable hamlet and country-houses he made hosts of friends, not a few for life; soon talking the pithy and forcible language, as he talked Dutch and Italian, with an effectual mastery not balked by his incurably inaccurate pronunciation.

But even more notable in the fruit it brought him, was the six weeks' journey to Florence, in 1895, to explore the sites of Dante. We know it intimately, for he described it in his letters, day by day, to his mother. It is of great interest in his life, and a more detailed account of it will be given below (Inter-Chapter I).

But the staple of Wicksteed's activities, outside his ministry, during the greater part of this period, was his work, now famous, as an "Extension Lecturer." The University Extension Scheme, initiated early in the 'seventies chiefly by James Stuart of Cambridge, had not long emerged from the contending fears and hopes of infancy, when Philip Wicksteed, perhaps the most remarkable figure in its history, in November 1887, began his long connexion with it.[1] The "scheme"

[1] Wicksteed was appointed, on 10 November, 1887, by the Universities Joint Board of the London Society for the Extension of University Teaching, to lecture for the society. His first course, on Dante, was given that autumn at Wimbledon. A list of all the courses given by him under the London Extension system is given in an appendix to this chapter.

had also in some degree the plasticity of infancy, and it became, in Wicksteed's hands, an organ not ill-suited to take the mould of his genius. For with him it was a "pulpit-," as well as a "university-" extension; he wore academic as little as clerical garb, but he held spellbound audiences which became in reality congregations, by a fusion of documented scholarship unusual in any pulpit with a prophetic fire rare in any university.

This twofold character appeared in the subject-matter of Wicksteed's lecturing courses no less than in their temper and tone. The University Extension Course, as originally designed, was literally to "extend" the teaching of the universities, to serve up some of the crumbs from the university tables, in a portable and nutritious form, for some of the multitude who had no chance of sitting there. A little history, economics, science, literature, was retailed, for the most part by young men fresh from the Triposes or the Schools. But the lectures being financed in part by payments from the districts concerned, supply was inevitably conditioned by demand, and local curiosity or interest in part determined the ingredients of the dishes offered. But from the first, there were lecturers of pronounced and captivating personality, who insensibly allured their audiences, especially the audiences of keen workingmen in the north, along ways then unknown at the English universities. Edward Carpenter, as a young Cambridge mathematician, was among the first, but the lectures of the future apostle of Socialism, even on astronomy, instilled, however unconsciously, suggestions of a spirit foreign alike to the courts of Cambridge and to the serene majesty of the stars. Elsewhere might be heard Richard Moulton, later famous in both hemispheres as an interpreter of Shakespeare, entrancing his audience by his eloquent discussion of the plays and dramatic impersonation of the characters; and English literature, in any form, was then only furtively beginning to cross the thresholds of the Cam and the Isis. When Philip Wicksteed, then, became engaged in this elastic system, it began to take the impress of his pronounced and masterful personality. Political Economy was already a subject at Cambridge, but on severely "orthodox" lines, and there can never have been much affinity between any academic economics in those days, and Wicksteed's "Getting and Spending", a first sketch of his later system, crowded with homely illustrations from practical life, and not concealing either his qualified admiration for Henry George or his ardent discipleship to Stanley Jevons, whose method of curves he, with its discoverer, believed to have riddled the base of the traditional schools. The title illustrates the constant interplay of poetic and scientific ideology in Wicksteed's mind. "The world is too much with us," lamented Wordsworth; "getting and spending we lay waste our powers." Wicksteed overcame what Wordsworth meant by "the world" at least as successfully as he; but by coming to grips with it, not by shutting it out; and he countered the poet's complaint by finding wise getting and spending one of the keys to economic progress. But Wicksteed was a devout, if inevitably a critical Wordsworthian; and in Wordsworth, beyond all other English poets, he found full scope for his peculiar power of studying a great personality in all the vivid circumstances of its historic setting in its own time, yet evoking whatever in it is expressive and vocal to ours. It is noteworthy, and may be thought to mark a limitation in Wicksteed, or in his methods, that the man who pre-eminently was both of his age and for all time was consistently rejected by Wicksteed as a theme for his lectures. He was an ardent Shakespearian, and one of the joys of his children and grandchildren in after years, were the evenings, and the Sundays, when he read entire plays aloud with the animation of a born actor. But Shakespeare's personality was impalpable and evasive; the authentic facts which the scholar in Wicksteed demanded were too meagre and fragmentary; the suggestions either of spiritual or of social vision which escape through the impenetrable mask are too elementary, to lend themselves to methods like his. "I have always declined to lecture on him," he wrote to Miss Knappert in 1921; "I have never felt any impulse towards any dealings with him except to enjoy him."

The other supreme poet of the medieval and modern world stood in acute antithesis to Shakespeare; and in Dante, Wicksteed found a theme which, beyond all others, touched all the chords of his genius, and of which he became, for more than twenty years, the most acceptable and accepted interpreter to the cultivated laity of England. In a secondary degree, and for a much briefer period, Wicksteed found, as will be told later, in Henrik Ibsen, at the moment when he was being most fiercely assailed in the authoritative literary circles of the country, a voice which his interpretative insight and eloquence could, and did, render vocal and moving for his countrymen, and the lectures delivered in Chelsea Town Hall in 1888, and immediately printed, were among the chief critical forces which contributed to dispel the cloud of obloquy.

Lecturing, as pursued by Wicksteed, was in a double sense "university extension" work. He brought teaching of university standard to men and women who, for the most part had not had access to universities; and he used it to initiate them in subjects which in the universities, for the most part, were not yet taught. For the lecturer, too, the system involved much less gratifying "extension" of normal academic wear and tear. The weekly journeys, sometimes to distant parts of the country, with the attendant hospitalities, not invariably congenial, curtailed the leisure, and tried the nerves, which masses of "exercises" to be marked and corrected would be waiting at home to engage. There was routine, and exacting routine, enough; but a routine full of human contacts, rich in the seed which Life everywhere scatters blindly for the seeing eye. Wicksteed was punctual; even, in questions of right and wrong, punctilious; but he was too exuberant to be, in any strict sense, orderly. The economist in him was mated with a generous giver, who was apt to spoil the symmetry of the "curves of his market." There was no grading of his output, no nice accommodation of supply to demand, no frugality in his response to the perpetual calls upon his time, his learning, or his inspiring and uplifting power. Single public utterances of his, like the speech at the Triennial Congress in 1891, and the Essex Hall Lecture of 1899, became events (real, if unregarded) in the spiritual history of the time. But even casual encounters with him were apt to be "events" in someone's history, and a note on the margin of a weekly exercise sometimes opened an avenue of eager interest to the imagination of some shy girl, or won the devotion of a lonely foreigner by an unexpected recognition of his national idols.[1]

He constantly took part, too, as an ardent Liberal, in the stormy politics of the day, and his powerful and impassioned denunciations of inhumanity and injustice, whether in Turkey (as in the crises of 1878 and 1897) or nearer home, became familiar on London platforms, and often (as Lord Morley, at the close of his life, said with modest consciousness of his own speaking) "made a difference" in the attitude of an audience.

Yet his perfect health of body and brain, still unabated at fifty, as they were to be at seventy—even, after a brief collapse and recovery, at eighty—bore him easily through the nervous and physical strain of these years; he seemed not to carry a burden, but to be a stripped athlete running a race. Men of more sluggish temper were kindled by a glow in which intellect and will had equal part. But he was of those very busy men who never plead want of leisure; he always had time for counsel, or for a pilgrimage to Westminster or the National Gallery, strange to so many Londoners. In pictures, without special knowledge, he had fine sensibility and very definite tastes; and it was his delight, in the earlier years of this period, to carry off a young daughter to be initiated in those treasures of our heritage in the National Gallery.

[1] Public occasions, of the kind just referred to, often in fact disturbed the routine.

IV

Some of the activities which grew out of his career as a lecturer call for fuller notice. Of the most remarkable and perhaps least known of them, the Economic Circle (of 1884–8), some account will be given in a subsequent chapter. Of his wardenship of University Hall something more must be said here. His mind had by this time worked off everything of youth but its freshness and spring, which were still to be his in old age. He was equipped to excel at the Bar or in Parliament as well as in the pulpit; but his rarest gift lay just in mediating between maturity and youth. It was as a lecturer in the "Extension" systems of London, Oxford, Cambridge, and Victoria Universities that he first became widely known. And when Mrs. Humphrey Ward, in 1889, after the phenomenal success of her *Robert Elsmere,* proposed to put in practice the "New Brotherhood" there projected, for the study and propaganda of Liberal Theology, it was in Philip Wicksteed that she finally found her most effectual support. Their enterprise, as originally conceived, failed, and few enough in that London of the "decadent" 'nineties, of symbolists and Yellow Books, heard of or regarded its passing or its birth. But the foundation, like many another brave but doomed venture in the chequered history of ideas, has an interest for the historian by no means commensurate with the trace it left in the moving tide of affairs. In the history of Philip Wicksteed, in particular, this episode has its dramatic and even heroic sides; he is here the strong man throwing all his power into the conduct of a vessel on which he embarked with misgivings too well justified by the issue. And a moment may be given to this story of a voyage which ended on the rocks, before we turn to Wicksteed's more prolonged and prosperous seafaring in the securer ships of a university institution.

Mrs. Ward's design to provide a social organ for what we now call Modernism attracted wide response, both among Unitarians, who were Modernists already, and among Liberal churchmen, who were often anxious not to have the movement confounded with Unitarianism. It roused the active interest, among others, of Canon Barnett, Warden of Toynbee Hall, Lord Carlisle, Dr. Blake Odgers, Miss F. P. Cobbe, and Stopford Brooke, with the professors of Manchester College, and Philip Wicksteed. In the autumn of 1889 Mrs. Ward visited Toynbee Hall, and her idea crystallized as a corresponding Hall, where the Brotherhood of the New Theology should reside, study, and teach.

The choice of a warden naturally exercised the committee. In their anxiety to avoid the label of a creed they even laid down, the Unitarian leaders warmly concurring, that the head of an institution devoted to propagating a virtually Unitarian faith should not be a Unitarian. The minister of Little Portland Street, the foremost English disciple of the Modernists of Holland, was thus excluded. But the attempt to find the required conditions anywhere else so eminently united, failed, and Mrs. Ward finally turned to Wicksteed.

But Wicksteed himself had grave doubts. He long resisted her overtures. But her conviction only deepened that he was the man she needed. She became urgent. "I want to wrestle with you," was her

Emslie's Portrait

greeting when, at her request, he visited her house in Russell Square. The talk closed with his acceptance. In a letter, a few days later, he explained his position. "I had never," he tells her, "been clear as to the exact thing contemplated in the Hall, I had never felt that it had any programme. Under these circumstances I felt that it would be false to myself, and in reality false to you, to allow myself to be overcome by your splendid faith and enthusiasm, and take it up without any true inspiration, in pity that so noble a 'quest' should find no knight-errant to try it. My talk with you has considerably cleared my vision, and has inspired me with growing *hopes* for the institution, but I cannot honestly say that it has given me any deep *faith* in its success." So far as Wicksteed's scepticism rested upon the supposed absence of an audience, in London, for Liberal-Christian lectures, the experience of the first few months seemed to disprove it. During 1891 and 1892, Wicksteed lectured on Sunday afternoons on the Old and New Testament, and the hall of Dr. Williams's Library was crowded to the doors.

Nevertheless, Wicksteed could not work whole-heartedly. "I did not believe the hall was doing the work that it set out to do." But Mrs. Ward's faith never flagged, and Wicksteed held loyally to the work he had undertaken.

One of the residents at the Hall during the later period of Wicksteed's tenure of the wardenship, Mr. R. M. Montgomery, has given some lively glimpses of the daily life there. Wicksteed himself continued to reside with his family in Camden Square, and was rarely present at breakfast. But he was almost always present at the seven o'clock dinner, and where he was present he, as always, presided in every sense of the word. Seated at the head of the table he carved, rapidly and skilfully, talking all the time. His talk was usually just the brimming-over of his full mind. Often he had just come in from an hour or afternoon in the British Museum hard by, and the carving-knife would do its rapid execution to the accompaniment of an equally rapid exposition of a logical imbroglio from the schoolmen, followed by a challenge to his men to offer their solutions; finally, when the beef had disappeared, submitting his own. The diners at University Hall were thus sometimes the first to receive the announcement of the warden's happy finds, and they happened to this indomitable verifier of references quite as often as to the merely curious browser. Thus he came in, one day in 1892, full of a gay old French poem which he had just read in the manuscript-room—that charming *Our Lady's Tumbler* which, a few weeks later, translated by the discoverer, was given to the press. A little later he was facilitating the study of Blake—still the cult of a coterie—by assembling a collection of his drawings on the walls. And any one who strayed into the Hall in the evening at nine or ten, would be likely to find the warden exercising his rare gifts as an educator, helping late learners to Latin by the new method, or initiating them unconsciously into the ideas of the calculus by his uncanny lucidity with chalk and blackboard.

The residents of the Hall were also, sometimes, the first to hear their warden expound one of those original ventures in sociology which, just then and later, stirred his interest more deeply than the chronology of the Old Testament. In October 1891, a younger friend,

John Trevor, recently assistant at Little Portland Street, then minister of Upper Brook Street Church in Manchester, had founded there the first "Labour Church." Of Trevor and his attempt to organize the "religious aspect of the Labour Movement" an account will be given in a later chapter. In Trevor, Wicksteed, with the moving humility which was always his, recognized a man who, otherwise frail and ineffectual, possessed something of poetic and prophetic power, in the presence of which he felt himself "commonplace and timidly compromising." But Wicksteed had given as well as received. At the Triennial Conference of Unitarian Churches in London, April 1891, in a debate on "The Church and Social Problems," Wicksteed had made a speech which Trevor described as "magnificent," and as almost reaching the idea of that "Labour Church" with which Trevor's mind was big, and which came to birth on 4 October of that year. Wicksteed responded instantly, enthralled one of the first meetings of the new church by an address, and in February 1892 described the meaning and purpose of the movement to his residents.

But with all its apparent vitality, the "Toynbee Hall of Liberal Theology" eventually collapsed. It rested on an unstable combination. A rift appeared between the organizers and the majority of the residents; between those who had planned it as a centre of enlightened religious teaching for a comparatively educated public, and those who wished to make it literally a second Toynbee Hall, a Bloomsbury counterpart of the Whitechapel prototype. For the large humanity of Wicksteed himself there was naturally no incompatibility between scholarship and slumming.

But he understood, perhaps with a touch of humorous sympathy, the unwillingness of young men eager for social work to be regarded as an academic "New Brotherhood" devoted to propagating the doctrines of a popular novelist. Finally, the rift became a cleavage; the residents founded another Hall near by, for boys' clubs and kindred activities. The Biblical studies on the other hand, flagged. By 1893, University Hall had become too large for its dwindled functions, while Marchmont Hall was not nearly large enough. Wicksteed resigned the wardenship. But it was without any of the bitterness of failure. He had worked, as Mrs. Ward's daughter and biographer has testified, with splendid energy and resource for an ideal never entirely his own, in homage to a faith which he very imperfectly shared. And when a few months later (May 1894) the generosity of Passmore Edwards enabled Mrs. Ward to start the new foundation called by his name, Wicksteed summed up the history of the movement in these words, as remarkable for insight as for generosity: "It will be seen readily enough that it was on the side of the school rather than on that of the residents that Mrs. Ward's ideals seemed to have the best chance of fulfilling themselves. Yet in truth it was in the residents that the germ of future development lay." [1]

[1] Pamphlet issued by the Passmore Edwards Settlement. The account of this episode is based upon Mrs. Trevelyan's *Life of Mrs. Ward*, supplemented by some of his letters.

V

Wicksteed during these busy London years wrote several books. But like some others whose writings have left a mark rather deep than wide, he carried no trace of the "man of letters." There was nothing of affectation in this, or of the voluminous George Borrow's scorn for authors. "I don't think I am of the nature of an 'author,'" he wrote simply, towards the end of his life, to a brother; "for they often speak of the 'impulse to create,' and the need of self-expression, to both which things I am a stranger. I have always wanted to express something that had come to me, not *myself*; and I suppose that is why I can always believe that something I have expressed has really been of vital significance to people, but always feel kind of bashful at being mentioned in that connexion; it seems irrelevant."[1] Of the books produced during these London years, one—*Our Lady's Tumbler*, already mentioned—was a gay casual fling. The others, though often of lasting moment in the history of their subject, were not, with one exception, final. They were the overflow of a full and rich but still growing mind, from which a more sustained and complete elaboration of the theme might be expected later on. In the case of two of these that expectation was fulfilled. The *Six Sermons on Dante* (1879) preluded the translations and commentaries on his work, *Dante and Aquinas* (1911–13). *The Alphabet of Economic Science* (1888) preluded *The Common Sense of Political Economy* (1910). If the *Four Lectures on Ibsen* (1888) remained isolated,

[1] To T. Wicksteed, 11 August, 1921.

it was confessedly even less final, for Ibsen himself had still nearly twenty years to live, and some five further plays of European significance to produce. But Wicksteed, regrettably, never, save in a brief necrologue, delivered his mind on Ibsen's complete work.

Of all these books notice will be taken in the later chapters of the present volume. One other, the exception above noted, was in its nature final. The *Memoirs of Rev. Charles Wicksteed,* 1885, edited by his son, had been undertaken soon after the father's death in the preceding year. Three-fourths of the volume consist, in effect, of matter thus "edited"; a selection of the sermons, widely famous in their day, and of his correspondence, including the delightful account of an Italian tour enjoyed by the young minister in 1834, sixty years before his son's. But the book is of interest here chiefly for the memoir prefixed, a succinct but beautiful piece of biography. Wicksteed portrays with delicate insight a personality which at many points touched his own—a first sketch of it, one might suppose, in gentler hues, and with less robust saliences of contour. A deep affection between them rested in part upon inner congeniality of nature. The stuff of enterprise was in both men, and while Philip followed, with sympathetic concern, his father's exploits in agriculture, his father admired, without emulating, his son's more fortunate adventures among the radical theologians of Holland. The inscription placed, at the father's own request, upon his tomb, *Obiit felix pietate natorum,* had a hidden significance. For Philip had himself used these words, wishing that his father might be thus blest, at the close of a letter, eleven years before, in which he tenderly explained a difference between them.[1]

But Wicksteed's most important writings during these London years pointed, as has been said, to the future, not to the past. They were creative, not commemorative, and it was principally with the view of devoting himself with fewer distractions to the work of completing both by teaching and writing, the expression of what he had to say to his generation, that Wicksteed, in the spring of 1897, resigned the pulpit of Little Portland Street Chapel, and removed into the country from his London home. But other causes concurred. The congregation had for some years steadily declined. Residential London was moving westward and northward; and the rift between minister and congregation, always latent, grew more pronounced. It became unmistakable when Martineau himself transferred his membership to Bedford Chapel. But Philip Wicksteed felt also the call of the country. It was in his blood as well as in his brain. The Wordsworthian in him concurred with that which he inherited from his father, the minister of Mill Hill, who had likewise, as we have seen, in the middle years of life thrown up his ministerial charge to settle on a Welsh farm. Philip did not propose to become either a farmer or a recluse, but he wished to do his work in a home out of earshot of the great world, but with ready access to it, and amid scenery genial and peaceful, but not austere or sublime,

[1] A saying of the father's, with the son's comment upon it, may help to detach their kindred profiles: Charles Wicksteed used to declare that if people were neither clever nor rich nor beautiful, he had no use for them. He was sorry to say that it was not enough for him if they were only good. On which Philip remarked that he could do very well with the people who were only "good," provided they did not *talk*.

where the still music of humanity came to the sensitive ear neither from the silence of the wilderness, nor from the roar of cities, but from the sound of the reaper's scythe or the woodman's axe. After two sojourns in the nearer home counties,[1] a daughter adventuring farther afield found the roomy old manor-house of a Berkshire village, Childrey, near Wantage, and here after some misgivings, Wicksteed decided to settle. In 1901 it became his home for the remainder of his life.

[1] The first of these, the beautifully situated farm of Bix Bottom, near Henley, had immediately won their hearts, and when (in March 1898) an unexpected decision of the owner forced them to quit it, they felt its loss as acutely as a bereavement; "We loved it," his daughter writes, "with the romantic affection of a first love"; and her father wrote her a letter of that grave consolation in which so many wounded hearts found their best support; yet touched with humour, as of one who shared the grief but knew that in such a case, though you might be very, very sorry, it would be unreasonable to be deeply grieved. "We are full of wonderful schemes," he ends, "and pretend we are happier than we are, but *are* quite happy—shame on us if we were not." The second abode, at the village of Sydenham, in Surrey, proved less attractive, and less healthy, but remained their home for nearly three years (1898–1901).

INTER-CHAPTER I

JOURNEY TO ITALY: TRAVEL LETTERS (1895)

Wicksteed's six-weeks' tour with his wife and their friends John and Alice Cruikshank, in Italy (April-May, 1895) nearly coincided with the close of his London residence. It is represented for us by his vivid daily letters to his mother, and a brief account of it may here be interposed, before entering upon the period of his country residence. The tour had as its immediate aim the enrichment of his Dante studies and lectures with a deeper and first-hand knowledge of his *milieu*. About one-third of the time was thus given to Florence and the neighbourhood, and the remainder almost wholly to cities closely associated with Dante's history or writings—Verona, Ravenna, Assisi, Siena. But Dante did not overshadow other great memories. Florence is hardly less the city of Fra Angelico than the home of Dante, and Ravenna is even more the city of Theodoric and of the infancy of "Gothic" art than the city where Dante died.[1] Wicksteed had the true versatility which can apprehend facts of different orders with eagerness and accuracy at once; and his Dante scholarship, exact, minute, and enterprising as it was, left a host of other interests free play.

There was, however, one aspect of old Florence, of

[1] Nearly thirty years later, the news that his friend Miss Knappert was about to visit it stirred him to a transport of reminiscent enthusiasm. Ravenna, he wrote to her (19 April, 1923), he thought "absolutely the one most revealing place that I had ever seen in my life."

deep interest to most of his contemporaries, which aroused only antagonism in Wicksteed. Its Renascence art and literature repelled or left him cold. Whatever in it sprang from the attempt to recover the antique world fell under the ban of his healthy abhorrence of the derivative and secondhand. But his repulsion extended much farther, to the magnificent creative work of Michelangelo, work not less creative because he had learnt from Roman sculpture (Greek was still unknown) all it had to teach, before immeasurably transcending it. Yet Wicksteed confessed, with his usual perfect frankness, that even the Night and Morning in the Medici chapel left him cold. "I did not care for them in the least."

And Raphael, as might be expected, excited an even less qualified distaste. Raphael's portraits in the Pitti he finds "superb," not an epithet which connotes very deep admiration with him, but he misses "revelation" in the eyes of his madonnas, though "the Madonna della Seggiola is exquisite in its way." The originals tell him no more than the familiar photographs had done. The Pitti collection altogether, seen after a morning with the Fra Angelico's in San Marco, he recalls with a sense not of disdain but of wounded harmony. "I went there conscious of a kind of discord and fall in the act. After seeing frescoes that belong to, and are part of, the place in which they have grown, a 'picture' that can be carried about seems like a cut flower."

But there was a further cause for Wicksteed's antipathy to the Renascence, for the facility with which his modern temper surmounted that "barrier"—moral abhorrence. Italy only confirmed this energetic condemnation. "I had all my life," he writes, when about to leave Florence, "that is, ever since I knew anything about it, wondered how it was possible for anything so splendid as the Renascence art of Florence to spring out of such rottenness as the rule of the Medici and such pedantry as the 'revival of learning,' but I had always taken it for granted, and came to Florence with the full expectation of being taken into a new and glorious world of art. Well, the result so far has been a most astonishing one to me, viz. that the effect of the Renascence on art was bad, and bad only, just what one might have expected from its moral rottenness and intellectual feebleness. It made the scholars desert their own and Dante's language to play at making themselves immortal in Latin, and it made the artists aim at classical beauty and pagan freshness and variety with somewhat similar results. I now know why I never did, and I suppose never shall, admire Botticelli adequately. It is because he has the fifteenth - century trail upon him. All this is not deliberate judgment, but a record of a most astonishing and even unrealizable first impression. Fra Angelico is in the fifteenth century, but not of it. Filippino Lippi has some of the old spirit still, but the rest do not seem to have anything but cleverness and elegance. Raphael's portraits are superb, and his children a prophecy and glory; but I have scarcely seen anything else except single heads of his that seems really to possess a soul. My mind turns with renewed wonder to Shakespeare. He, almost alone, embraced the vast region thrown open by the Renascence, and with an enlarged horizon kept his balance and lived in his own age, uncorrupted, but in sight of all the ages. It is true of him, with his little Latin and less Greek, as a fourteenth-century man said of Dante, 'He had nothing, yet he saw everything, and gave it all to us.'"

Wicksteed felt too keenly to be easily cosmopolitan in his taste, or easily patient with the ordinary tourist, English, American, German, whom he saw "doing" the Fra Angelico's. But here his humanity, his large and sympathetic understanding for the common mind, one of the secrets of his power as a lecturer, intervenes to check the natural (and probably deserved!) scorn. "I daresay there were many of them just as conscious as we were that nothing short of living in these cells for a month or two would be in the least adequate. I should like to sit in them one after another and read the *Paradiso* in them. Then in the course of a year one might know them. But they are so gentle, so simple, so pure, that even our hasty visit has left, I trust, an indelible impression."

And then he tells another similar experience, where men not more finely strung than he, might have found refuge in abuse at a vulgar intrusion. "I remember looking at a great bosom of snow from an Alpine peak, and being surprised by a band of noisy tourists, who uncorked champagne bottles and threw them away when empty. But the snow seemed not only to be silent, but to pour out silence that swallowed all the noise, as the snow itself would have swallowed a falling stone! So from those angelic pictures there seemed to emanate a peace and gentleness that made one not only independent of disturbing surroundings but able to embrace even one's fellow-tourists in the love and peace that they bred!"

With Fra Angelico came Giotto, both, though Fra

Angelico spoke out of a later generation, exquisitely attuned, for Wicksteed, to the spirit of Dante. The arena at Padua had been, with Ravenna, the supreme experience of the outward journey. Ruskin, the interpreter for many English minds of Giotto's Florence, as of Venice, he consulted of course, but with a criticism very alert and somewhat cool. At no time very sensitive to style, as such, Wicksteed felt the slight disdain of a fundamentally masculine intellect for the emotional and florid elements of Ruskin's eloquence, and willingly allowing his stimulating power, and his insight in artistry, perceived the limitations of his knowledge, and believed that his judgments, even of the great artists, whom he had interpreted to the world, and whom he and Wicksteed worshipped in common, were impaired by his ignorance of the medieval civilization outside art.

He was not less deeply stirred by the fourteenth century reliefs at Orvieto. "O mother, mother, have you ever been in Orvieto?" so opens the daily letter on 6 May; "if not, you must come with us next time and see it. There are many beautiful and wonderful things there, but *the* thing is a series of reliefs in marble on the façade of the cathedral. . . . They are by unknown masters. So they ought to be. The men that made them did not think of fame. They are a prayer and a song. . . . All the 'comparative superlatives' that one is tempted to have recourse to . . . seem foolish and inexpressive. I can only say that I never saw painting or sculpture before that did, as a matter of fact, remind me of Dante's descriptions in the *Purgatorio*, in the Circle of the Proud, except by contrast, and these did so constantly. Two things seemed marvellous from the technical point of view: the marble angels *float,* and the eyes of all the better preserved groups *speak,* and this not by any *tour de force* or trick, . . . but by sheer purity of emotion and exquisiteness of sympathy . . ."

But this tour did more for him than deepen his intimacy with Dante's kindred among painters and sculptors. That intimacy with men who had devoted transcendent genius to the expression of religion through painting, as Dante in verse, facilitated his access to the secrets of the medieval mind itself, and of medieval religion. "The attempt to get near to the central thoughts of the architects and painters of the fourteenth century is a perpetual Service. I am in a state of permanent contemplation and reflection on the difference between the religion of those people and our own religion; but I hardly dare to formulate ideas about it. When one is receiving impressions at this rate it would be premature to do anything with them."

Such words do much to define the impression made by these letters as a whole, that this tour meant much more for him than a gathering of fresh material for his Dante lectures, or a revision of the material he had, or even a making of discoveries about him, though in all these ways it bore abundant fruit. It enlarged and deepened his conception of the religion of the Middle Ages, and even of religion as a whole. In the same letter, just before, he had referred to the journal of a similar tour by his father and mother. "I often think of the punctual Sunday entries in your journal of attendance at the Protestant churches, and how dear father always found attendance at public worship a necessity of spiritual existence." "I feel," he continues, "as little inclined to attend English or Protestant service as can well be imagined; but I do not feel that there is any great departure from father's spirit in it." No, but it was yet a spirit with which English Protestantism, Nonconformity, and the Unitarianism of Wicksteed's youth was only distantly related; a spirit for which religion could be poured forth, not only in specific acts and times and places.

The study of Dante and his age centred, as I have said, in Florence. But it was just in Florence that this keen-eyed and devoted lover of Dante failed to find him. At Fiesole he writes: "I cannot explain, but whenever I am out of Florence, everything converges upon Dante; when in it, he vanishes." "Yes! Dante was banished from Florence!" Florence was the city of the Renascence, not of Dante, and he now approves of the people who thought only of Browning and of *Romola* there. That chance remark finds response, no doubt, in the visit of every Dante-lover to the oppressively "modern" Florence of to-day. No doubt this very modernity ministered to Wicksteed's keen appetite for problems; the historical geologist was only put on his mettle by the number and elusiveness of the overlying strata through which he had to penetrate to the traces of that precious fourteenth-century vein of gold. And how contagious is his zest—no brief dilettante enthusiasm, but the driving-passion of a man let loose at last upon the object of years of longing—as he pursues these mining operations! Watch him for a typical day! "This morning (13 April) I woke earlyish again, and was out of the house just at seven, with our friend—a Dante pupil and an ardent student. We did some old-Florence hunting, that is to say, tried to identify an old church, and we thought we succeeded. It is mentioned by Villani, the old Florentine historian contemporary with Dante, and is of some interest in connection with Florentine topography. We thought we succeeded in finding it—now a store-house for funeral appliances. We also made some investigations apropos of a fortress that apparently commanded the Arno in ancient times, to include which the walls of the city made a 'horn' as Villani calls it. All seemed to fit in perfectly with Villani's description and it was certainly interesting. Then we came back to breakfast." And be it noted that Wicksteed, no scholar of the spare ascetic type, but a humanist living his life in every pore, neither omitted his meals nor omitted to record them, though he never describes them. After breakfast a walk with Mrs. Wicksteed to San Miniato, where they read a passage in Dante describing it. Then down to the Piazza del Duomo, where all Florence and the neighbouring countryside were gathered for the Easter Saturday ceremonies. They looked down from the campanile on the Piazza and neighbouring streets crowded to the last square foot with the throng; he pleasantly touches the festive details—the fireworks, the "dove" moved from the High Altar along a cord to set them alight, to the great disturbance of "the real doves"; and the four solemn white oxen, decorated with gaudy green, scarlet and gold, who drew the car away through the shouting multitudes, giving dignity to the whole, for "nothing can make an ox ridiculous." After lunch, further Dante explorations, or work in the libraries, then dinner and an evening with friends.

Among the more exacting objects of examination were the frescoes in the Spanish chapel in Santa Maria Novella with their Latin inscriptions. Their first visit was devoted to the inscriptions—deciphered in a dim light through an opera-glass as they lay on their backs. "It is almost the hardest work I ever did it seems to me!" Wicksteed wrote. "Mr. Cruikshank knows no Latin, but has a marvellous faculty for spelling out inscriptions, letter by letter; and between us we managed to get through a small fraction of the material." Then, in the evening, "I have been working hard at St. Paul's epistles in the Vulgate, to find some of the texts that had puzzled us." Exacting, yet of peculiar fascination. For here were the same fundamental ideas which dominate the *Divine Comedy*, conveyed, imperfectly and obscurely, yet with profound sincerity, through the medium of an art potentially of boundless capability, but as yet far less adequate than Dante's verse. "It is curious," writes Wicksteed, "to see how the old painters deliberately set out to tell a story or to expound a doctrine, and how great the difficulties, how largely dependent upon conventions the method, and how obscure the result very often; and yet how massive and dignified the total resultant impression; how architectural and structural, not merely decorative or ornamental they are. I am sure I shall feel this more than I realize at present, when the whole cumulative effect settles down." And what confirmed the hold of these frescoes (as of the Orvieto reliefs) upon Wicksteed was, more even than their spiritual content and their Dantesque significance, what he calls their "structural" quality. They were an integral part of the art-creation, not like pictures detachable and "hung"; they participated in the complete impression which the "Chapel" as a whole was designed to produce, participated as the sounds in a spoken sentence participate in its meaning, whereas the pictures in a gallery, however cunningly arranged, rather resemble movable types which the printer assorts for one piece of writing, and redistributes for another.

The same feeling gave Wicksteed a new joy, certainly not native to the Protestant, in the elaborate musical performances of the Catholic Church. "There was some Schubert, and must have been some Mozart I am sure. A great deal was rather conventional and shallow perhaps, but the performance was beautiful and congruous. The absence of the vulgar associations and surroundings of the concert hall or theatre made it extremely impressive. . . . It certainly makes me long for conditions of life in which beautiful art, including music, can be made a part of life in some way. To hear beautifully performed music in a great public church as part of a service, and to see beautiful pictures as part of a church seems to give them roots and make them belong to life."

On 23 April they broke up their Florentine sojourn, devoting a last hour, after an afternoon of packing, to Orcagna's frescoes in Santa Maria Novella, "perhaps the strongest painting," Wicksteed thought, "in the world." Yet he found the faces too expressive of the temper of the Church Militant, wanting in the "beatific insight" of the saint.

Siena had her own saint, St. Catherine, and she lost none of her due. But Wicksteed's first feeling was relief from the encrusting modernity of Florence.

"Ah, my mother, we are really in Italy again now!" It rained most of the first days, but "every moment has been full of life." And if the "life" still converged upon Dante, it was from a wide circumference, in which the politician and the soldier had as secure a place as the visionary and the poet. On the very first afternoon he walked for five and a half hours through rain to the scene of the battle of Monteaperti (1260), repeatedly alluded to by Dante, which for six years put Florence in the hands of the Ghibellines. But Wicksteed was not one of the pilgrims who have eyes for nothing but their goal. History, and even Dante himself, here counted hardly more in the joy of the pilgrimage than the road, than the rain! For the road, eagerly followed with map and compass, was irregular and hilly. "I was out of one little valley and into another all the way, my course being from west to east, and all the streams flowing from north to south, for we are over the watershed of the Arno basin. If it had been clear I fancy I should have seen Siena from every ridge." And then the rain! Italian rain filling the fragrant air—that might be enough to explain the delight of many another healthy and vigorous Englishman. But with Wicksteed it touched the springs of a yet more intimate joy. "When I think of the very real passion for literature, for water (from the Skjaeggedal Foss or the wine-faced deep to a London gutter in a thunderstorm, or the patter of rain on a window-pane, an umbrella, or my own bared head), and for every kind of weather, I wonder whether music and art have really more than a casual meaning for me. I love them, sometimes I think passionately, but I *know* that I love Literature and Water, and

Weather, with a keen edge of unfailing delight that must surely last as long as I live, and that I could not do without and yet feel that I was living!"[1]

And here is a vignette of Dante memorial hunting, near Siena. Wicksteed and Mr. Cruikshank, after breakfasting at seven, took train for Castellina, which they reached by nine, and walked thence to Montereggione. "It is a huge ruined castle, in appearance," he writes, "with shattered turrets all round it, some nearly level with the wall, and some still rising to a considerable height above it. From some points of view it has a long shape, from others it looks circular. When Dante was making his way towards the centre of Hell he thought he saw through the murk a ring of towers rising 'as they do round Montereggione,' and asked what they were, but Virgil took him gently by the hand to still his fears, and then told him that they were not towers, but giants, rising from the middle upwards above the sides of the central pit of Hell. Then, as Dante drew near and saw that it was so, his error vanished and his terror grew. The whole scene as we approached was quite solitary, and we passed under the old gateway. What was our surprise to find a village inside—houses and well-tilled gardens and wells. There are three hundred inhabitants, we were told, and there is a post office. So we bought postcards and wrote to friends at home. Then we walked round the walls outside, accompanied by a decent percentage of the population, and when we reached the best point of view I found myself, rather

[1] Wicksteed's joy in rain recalls Meredith's; but his elemental passion scarcely ascribed to it the spiritual and ethical powers which it exercises in *Richard Feverel* and the *Earth and a Wedded Woman.*

to my own and my companion's amusement afterwards—delivering a little lecture, illustrated by a diagram traced in the dust with my stick, on that central pit of Hell and its connection with Monteriggione. . . . It was wonderful to see how eagerly they listened, and how they felt the spell, and kept crying 'Santo!'"

CHAPTER IV

CHILDREY

Childrey—Nostalgia and the Country Life—The Home—Holidays—Friends—The Lecturer—The Reformer—In the Study

I

NOSTALGIA for the country life in which his boyhood had been passed was, as we saw,[1] a chief determining motive in Wicksteed's choice of his new home. After two experiments in the nearer home counties, he settled at the little Berkshire village of Childrey, three miles south-west of Wantage; and its "old manor house" became, for the almost thirty remaining years, his home and the point of repair for his children—now for the most part settled at a distance—for their children, and for countless friends. Cut off from the highways of traffic, the village straggles with a wayward charm along the gentle northern slope of the north Berkshire downs. From the churchyard, the eye wanders northward over the rich alluvial valley towards the invisible towers of Oxford, some fifteen miles away.

And apart from its fortunate situation, Childrey had a certain unspoilt naturalness which fitted it to receive, as before many years it very distinctly came to do, the impress, the accent, of the Wicksteed mind. Not prosperous enough to be an Arcadia, nor beautiful enough to be a resort of tourists, it was sheltered from the more self-conscious modes of felicity. Its very

[1] See close of Chap. III.

The Old Manor, Childrey. Front View

The Old Manor, Childrey. Back View

insignificance exempted it from some of the insidious perils of modern village life, and the more ordinary conventions which disturb the idealist and the reformer, though they existed, were not aggressive. No great proprietor had aspired to make it a model for the country of what a rustic village might become—a show place where every house was an example of picturesqueness and propriety, and the passing of the squire's carriage the signal for demonstrative or diplomatic obeisance.

Nothing could be less like this than Wicksteed's Childrey. His house, in spite of its name, had none of the outer features of a manorial "hall." You approached it, neither by avenue nor drive, nor even through a modest garden, but by a little flight of two worn, moss-grown steps, directly from the village street. Any suspicion of such pretension was promptly dispelled when the owner of the "old manor house," on the day of arrival, carried a pail of water through the village. As little did he think of playing, in however figurative a sense, the "parson." A Unitarian minister, though no longer in harness, did not need the highly unclerical habiliments which were his habit, not his costume, at Childrey, to make that clear. But not many years passed before this unconventional and unorthodox settler had become without seeking, almost without consciousness, a sort of king and bishop of the place—invisibly "crowned and mitred" like his own Dante, in an "Earthly Paradise" of his own choice. It was a purely personal authority, as little courted as imposed; the authority instinctively accorded by good-hearted village folks, as to a natural chief. It was supported by his magnificent physique; the grand, leonine head, the powerful limbs, which at eighty could outwalk and outride much younger men, and made hewing or chopping wood his habitual relaxation. Such things impressed the roughest village boy. But for older folks he was the oracle to whom every kind of puzzle was brought for solution, all the more because they knew the oracle to be just a neighbourly friend, who knew a thing or two more than the rest. Even the officially appointed spiritual guide, the rector of the parish, brought his "difficulties" and "doubts" to the study of this unapostolic dissenter, whether they were household accidents, legal disputes, or questions of scholarship or science, even in the interpretation of that "Holy Writ," about which Wicksteed was understood to hold, and even to have promulgated, opinions still tabooed by the Church.

Like other old villages, too, Childrey had its other characteristic and indispensable personages, but they were all good friends, on terms of human fellowship with the Wicksteed family. There was a village blacksmith, whose forge drew the children according to immemorial usage, as they trooped home from school in the gloaming, but whose cunning was also available on occasion to repair a bicycle or a lock; the village carpenter and woodman, who gave Wicksteed his first lessons in the hewing of trees; and the village baker, whose marriage with a Norwegian maid of the Wicksteed household recalled to the next generation the Norse predilections of its head. As for the "village idiot," it has been surmised that this rudimentary "appendix" of village life disappeared after the advent of the Wicksteeds, finding the atmosphere of Childrey uncongenial to his habits of mind.

II

And for Wicksteed himself the change meant far more than a release from the incubus of the streets. In June 1897, shortly after resigning his charge at Little Portland Street, he addressed election meetings at Hampshire villages on behalf of the Greek and Armenian victims of Turkish power, whose sufferings were treated with cynical indifference by a large part of the London press. "That day and a half," he wrote to one of his daughters, "has made a new heaven and a new earth for me. The Hampshire peasantry care, and care tenfold more, about the Greeks and Armenians, than about their own rates and taxes and compensations for injuries. It has been a grand experience. The dry rot has not reached the heart of our sons of the soil. I believe in Wordsworth and democracy more than ever."[1] In the face of such words it is but pardonable hyperbole to say that Childrey appeared to be the Promised Land to which Wordsworth and democracy, pillars of fire which neither on that, nor on any later day, turned to "smoke" or nebula, had (after a wrong turn or two) guided his steps. His keen eye for the generous impulses of the English country folk, which his own eloquence had perhaps done more than he admitted to elicit, was probably quickened by his admiration for the fine peasantry of Norway, among whom he had moved so intimately and made so many friends.[2]

[1] To R. W., 9 June, 1897.

[2] The Norwegian girl mentioned above, a trophy or *trouvaille* of the summers there, who became a maidservant in Wicksteed's house, ultimately, as we just said, providing the village school with numerous examples of the Anglo-Norwegian child.

But it was not the outcome of an enthusiastic moment only. In the striking essay, *Education and the Village School,* he enforced, a few years later, a more considered view of the kind of training which ought to be provided for the village child. The explorer of unread folios of the schoolmen, the devoted lover of Catullus and Aristophanes, has little place for books in the regimen he prescribes for the sons and prospective fathers of ploughmen. With much apposite and felicitous illustration from Norwegian ways and educational methods, but also from the tact and shrewdness of the English countryside, he urged that country-school education must be brought into vital relation with country occupations. And in Wicksteed's hands this did not remain the pedagogic commonplace it sounds. The peasant brought up to understand and enjoy the country instead of hankering after the town, was brought nearer to the heritage of Wordsworth, to the contemplative fruition of divine things which is the consummation of the *Prelude* as of the *Paradiso,* where out of their alien and remote ages, in the synthetic minds of men like Wicksteed, the two great poets join hands.

It is easy then to understand the passionate indignation with which, a few months after the date of that pæan over the Hampshire peasants, Wicksteed saw the might of England let loose upon the "embattled farmers" of the Transvaal. The Boer War, as he said towards the close of his life, began the disintegration of his whole "scheme of things" which the Great War and its sequel were, in effect, to complete. But the problems with which that vast cataclysm confronted Wicksteed belong to a later section.

III

The Wicksteed home, half old-world manor house, half farmstead, was straggling but roomy, as became the varied age and habits of its inmates. In one wing, Mrs. Wicksteed's father, the Rev. Henry Solly, passed his remaining years. Behind lay a kind of orchard pleasance, full of plum and other fruit trees, where native luxuriance was allowed to have its way without too curious a regard for trimness. The focus of the home was naturally the library—a single spacious low room, lined from floor to ceiling with plain book-shelves all round; a large writing-desk stood in the middle, and a bust of Dante over the fire-place. On the shelves there were not many beautiful or very costly books. Ibsen, Kuenen, Dante, Jevons were a matter of course. But there, too, as in few other English private libraries, were the massive folios of Aquinas, and a still rarer treasure, a sumptuous edition of St. Thomas's master, Albertus Magnus. Gifts, too, from fellow-writers, of their books, among which search might discover (for it was not likely to be displayed) Mr. Shaw's *Commonsense of Municipal Trading*, inscribed by the author to Wicksteed, "my master in economics."

But Wicksteed was now less than ever a slave of his desk. The vacations and week-ends at Childrey opened the way to new applications both of muscle and brain denied to the townsman. Not least notable of these were the readings aloud. It was a family "institution," begun early in Wicksteed's home life, and even during the busy London years rarely allowed entirely to lapse. Now, at Childrey, it began to fill the spacious leisure of Sundays and holidays. Childrey, in fact, restored the rich opportunities of his boyhood at Hafod, and the man of sixty proved as fit in nerve and muscle as the boy to make use of them. Felling trees was the congenial sport even of his extreme old age, as of Gladstone's, but he would turn his hand with just as hearty good-will to the humbler business of chopping wood. "I have cut down a small tree," he writes to a son in September 1926, on the eve of his eighty-second year, "and stubbed up the stump" —pushing home to the root, as usual—"and I find," he adds, in apology for this slackness, "I can't do much of a day's work with axe, spade, and pick, though I have become rather cunning." The felling of an old ash near the house marked a red-letter day in his education as a woodman, if not in the annals of Childrey, and he described it with many vivid touches in a letter to an absent daughter. He had called in the village wood-cutter, R——, to direct the critical operation. "I wish you had been here to admire R——. He marked where I was to cut down the roots, so as to make the bole of the tree free to roll when we had it down, and told me how to do it. I did it, as I thought, in the spirit of his remarks, but he said I was doing it wrong, and explained why I must obey the letter, which thenceforward I did. . . . Presently I made the discovery that I put too much work of my own in it, and so wore myself out too fast. What I had to do was to make the axe do the work by its own weight, and confine myself to telling it where to bite. . . . I was nearly tired out when he set me to cut off a big attachment from behind the tree, . . . a passer-by offered to help, as Wordsworth offered to help old Simon Lee, but

I declined his "proffered aid," saying that I had so nearly done it all myself that I should like to finish it, and that R—— could have polished the job off half an hour ago if he had not known that. R—— was evidently much pleased at the assurance that his mind had been read and appreciated. . . . After two or three strokes the tree fell, almost without warning, exactly where it was meant to fall." Wood-cutting, like cycling, Wicksteed carried on until he had long passed the threshold of old age. Even when his right arm was disabled, so that he had to use the left to lift it with the axe in it, he refused to desist, and his daughters held their breath in suspense till they had seen the axe, dropped heavily, like a guillotine, safely hit on the wood.

At Christmas, too, the large hearth of the old manor house demanded a Yule-log. The modest bounds of the homestead did not always yield one, but it was a country of rich woods, and they usually managed to secure one for payment after marking it for their own on their autumn walks. Later, a practical-minded daughter substituted a modern grate.

But wood-cutting was not Wicksteed's only "sport." The sports of most brain-workers do not call for extensive notice by their biographers. But Wicksteed put something of himself into whatever he did. He cycled, as he cut wood, with a "fine excess." He astonished waiters and landlords by cycling in Switzerland at eighty; and during many earlier holidays at Childrey, drew his wife or an invalid sister through French plains or over Norwegian passes in a "trailer." [1]

[1] A few allusions to these pleasant jaunts may be quoted from his letters. In May 1909, when the *Common Sense of Political Economy* was almost complete, "the last knot untied," he felt too fagged to undertake the "lopping and trimming" that alone remained. "I am quite pumped out,"

And nearer home there would be more idyllic excursions; days of boating, for instance, on the beautiful reaches of the river at Abingdon, to Nuneham or Sutton Courtney; Wicksteed himself handling the sculls, sometimes with a "lady-cox" less inured to the water than himself, whose embarrassment he would chaffingly enjoy when they encountered another boat. After one such occasion, when the suffrage movement was on the eve of triumph, he gleefully reported to an absent daughter, the dialogue "not wholly imaginary" which then ensued: "Which side must I take?" "Whichever side they want you to take; it is their choice." "But they are all women!" "Then whichever side they will let you!" The "cox" was her mother.

Thus it came about that the old rich life of the London home expanded without growing less rich, in this country retreat. The filaments of attachment to the centres of cultural activity grew more manifold and complex, as children and grandchildren, and friends of three generations, came and went. For Wicksteed himself the four or five days weekly spent away from home brought frequent intercourse with friends and with his married children and sisters, whose homes were in the lecture-towns.[1] At the week-ends there would

he wrote to his brother Tom, "and am off to France, for a two or three weeks' 'trail' with Emily." Two years later they took a Norwegian tour, when he pushed his sister Clara (Mrs. Armstrong) in a wheeled-chair. "We were a most harmonious party," he wrote with rollicking gaiety to the same brother. "I was at Clara's service all the time, but she was very considerate, and Emily and I had any amount of Sundays out, and area-railings kind of larks. My principal feat was in pushing Clara (with a little assistance) up a pass 3,400 Norwegian feet high. It took two days up."

[1] He was thus often the guest of his sister, Clara Armstrong, in Liverpool; of his sister Anne, whose husband, Rev. Frank Jones, was now Librarian of Dr. Williams's Library, in London; and of his daughter Mabel (Lawrence) at Liverpool, and Birkenhead.

be a vast correspondence to dispatch, and at the end of term he would sometimes take a day's "delicious holiday, reading Greek," as he wrote to a daughter. But for him as well as for the younger members of the large household, the week-ends and vacations were seasons of exhilaration, sometimes touched with awe. The pulse of life beat faster in that rural quietude, and few who entered its orbit failed to catch something of the excitement. There were endless stories to be told, reminiscences of old days, of the kindred home at Hafod, of Taunton and Dukinfield, anecdotes of his most recent adventures amongst the minds of Extension students. If the disorderly methods, or methodical disorder, of the London home suffered no abatement in this less closely knitted household, the autocrat was the more securely enthroned in its affections and admiration. Wicksteed understood, at least as effectually as Victor Hugo, if without his sentimentality, the "art of being a grandfather." He was in his element rowing a crew of children all day long on Derwentwater. The great classics, if less systematically read, flowed as freely as ever into his talk. "Whenever any one says anything," remarked a grandchild wonderingly to its mother, "grandfather always says a piece of poetry."

IV

Wicksteed was richly endowed with the gifts which win enthusiastic friendship, and they flowered to the full at Childrey. In part because his mind and temperament were fundamentally masculine, he was even more signally the friend of women than of men. Women responded readily to his magnetism; but this magnetism was itself only the living expression of his spiritual ardour, of the passion for great ideals which was the stuff of his mind, and neither such attraction, nor the hobnobbing of fellow-students and fellow-specialists easily ripened into friendship where the lure of some kind of spiritual humanism did not lead the way. Hence the causes for which he had laboured, the countries which had been the scenes of his pilgrimages, or the home of his "prophet-poets," were each the nucleus of many friendships. Ibsen's Norway, Kuenen's Holland, Dante's Italy, each was the home of some of his friends; and common interests attached him also to hosts of English men and women. Most of these friendships have now vanished without trace save as a far-off glow in a few ageing memories; but we shall not see Philip Wicksteed aright if we do not imagine his face, as Dante saw those of his saints in Paradise, on a living background of other faces, now indistinguishable.

A few only can be singled out here. In addition to those who have passed away, a few friends of old date, still living, have been briefly referred to. Of the men who had welcomed him to their lecture-rooms and to their homes on his first visits to Holland, one only survived his settlement at Childrey. But his daughter's marriage at Leiden sealed other intimacies than those with her husband's family, and some of these were continued in the younger generation on both sides. Dr. H. Oort, the professor referred to, whom Wicksteed had visited at Amsterdam in 1874, as already told, was eight years his senior, but lived to send him, at ninety, a letter of grave farewell which reached Wicksteed a few days before his death. He and his wife followed Wicksteed's later career with affectionate interest, and an insight, difficult to attain in the atmosphere of a continental university, into the perplexing mentality of this unaccountable Englishman, this unprofessional professor, this layman among divines, this enthusiastic exponent of Thomas Aquinas, Henrik Ibsen, and Stanley Jevons, who had something fresh to say to the specialists in all these fields, this adventurer in many lands who was at home in them all. The Oorts and the Kuenens were among those who impressed upon their circle the difference between the "Jack of all trades," or even the clever eclectic, and the man who hews stone in many quarries to build into the same fabric. "He was doing one thing all his life," wrote Wilhelmina Kuenen, after his death, to his eldest son.[1]

Close, again, to Wicksteed and his children stood another, Miss Emilie Knappert, whose friendship began in those years, to whom allusion only can here be made. Some of his letters to her will be quoted below. There are few of his interests to which she did not bring the stimulus of her shrewd and eager intelligence.

"Economics," too, initiated many friendships. But here, likewise, fellowship in study scarcely grew into friendship unless it was enriched by the larger humanism of social ideals. It will suffice to mention here the host, in his London house, of the "Economic Circle," Mr. H. R. Beeton of the London Stock Exchange, for Wicksteed, like Shelley, found an intimate and understanding friend in this profession.[2] It was to Mr.

[1] V. *supra*, p. xi.—J. H. W.

[2] Wit and sense
Virtue and human knowledge, . . .
Are all combined in Horace Smith. *Letter to Maria Gisborne*, 247.

Beeton and his wife that Wicksteed dedicated his *Alphabet of Economic Science,* the first-fruit of those discussions. And it may be permitted to mention here the relations of cordial and mutual esteem which subsisted to the end between Wicksteed and his chief antagonist in the "Circle," Mr. Bernard Shaw. The dissonance in economic theory remained; but Mr. Shaw (like a Proteus who discovers that his disguises no longer deceive) appreciated the perspicuity of a critic who, in the years when he was, not inexcusably, held to be a brilliant buffoon, never ceased to insist that the buffoonery was the mark, and the brilliance the weapon, of a determined, if freakish reformer, and a serious (if not very profound) philosopher. And he often recurred to those moments in *Major Barbara* or *Back to Methuselah* in which Mr. Shaw appears of the kindred of the prophets, and forgets his freaks.

But closer likeness of mind bound Wicksteed to Dr. Graham Wallas. The second title of his *Common Sense*—"a study of the Human Basis of Economic Law"—marks clearly enough the analogy of his method and point of view with the author of *Human Nature in Politics*. Graham Wallas had been a member of the Economic Circle, and the intercourse between two minds, alike so rich and so expansive, so ideal in their aims, so concrete and positive in their assumptions, was not likely to wane when Dr. Wallas entered upon his professoriate in that London School of Economics which is now the chief English stronghold of their common studies.

Among those whose relation to Wicksteed was in the most intimate sense a friendship in Dante, was and is Edmund Gardner, lecturer in Italian at Univer-

"I will not cease from Mental Fight."—*Blake*

sity College, now professor of that subject in the University of London. Dr. Gardner approached Dante as one who shared his Catholic faith. That way of approach, seemingly so "broad and easy," is notoriously not free from perplexities or embarrassments for the implicit believer.[1] To Gardner, needless to say, these were of as little account as were the repugnances of the Protestant or the superiorities of the modernist, for Wicksteed. Their acquaintance began in the early days of Wicksteed's Dante lecturing. They collaborated in the well-known edition of Dante's friend, Del Virgilio. Gardner's *Dante Primer* guided the steps of the novice when he closed the *Six Sermons*; and his classical *Dante's Ten Heavens* was the companion of those who listened to Wicksteed's not less, but otherwise, inspired lectures on the *Paradiso*. In 1922, Wicksteed, who viewed very humbly his own services to Dante scholarship, was genuinely gratified by Gardner's dedication to him of his re-written *Primer* "with deep affection and high esteem." The words which Gardner wrote after Wicksteed's death: "it was impossible to be intimate with him without becoming his disciple," remain a moving tribute to the power of a common religion to transcend divergences of theology, and yet more striking differences of temperament.[2]

The Dante lecturer sowed the seeds of many

[1] The anecdote is often told of the traveller in France who asked the *vicaire* of a country-church whether he had read the *Inferno*. "Non, monsieur; M. le curé nous le défend, parce que c'est très-inexacte."

[2] Professor Gardner will pardon our recalling an occasion at Childrey when he took part in one of the family charades, *The Rivals*, but was cast for a ludicrously inappropriate part. Wicksteed at the close laughingly congratulated the biographer of St. Catherine on having been "the very worst 'Jack Absolute' he had ever seen."

friendships, with men less known to the world, some of which became intimate. Among these friends in Dante were John and Alice Cruikshank. They were Scottish Quakers, settled, when Wicksteed first knew them, at Haslemere. John Cruikshank was interested in the scientific breeding of cattle, and had made an ample competence in this pursuit. But their deepest interest, suggested neither by this calling nor by their Quaker upbringing, was a passion for art and its historic monuments. They travelled widely, and ultimately made their home at Florence. We have already met the husband as the companion of Wicksteed's explorations there in 1895. It was at their instance, too, that he first visited Chartres and other French cathedrals. From their house at Haslemere the Cruikshanks came in to Wicksteed's Dante courses, duly writing the regular class-essays for him; and no one will ascribe to Wicksteed's warm friendship for them the distinction which these essays invariably received, of being marked in the highest class. The friendship was, however, indeed intimate, and inclusive; the Wicksteeds and their children were frequent guests at Haslemere, entertained with inexhaustible lantern-slides and comments. Nowhere but in Cruikshank's study, Wicksteed would say, could he work so well as at home; and Cruikshank's long study table, where there was room for two or three separate workers at once, was the model for that at Childrey. Cruikshank was deeply concerned, too, to make the objects of his own artistic delight more widely accessible and understood, and edited several popular handbooks with this aim. Charles Lamb's abominable libel about the Quaker rule, "which doth the human feeling cool," is belied

Philip and Emily Wicksteed, *c.* 1905

every day, but seldom more signally than in John and Alice Cruikshank.

Dante was one of the ties, too, which bound Wicksteed to another husband and wife in the earlier Childrey time, Herbert and Alice Rix, in their headland cottage, near Limpsfield, Surrey. Rix was a former minister and assistant secretary of the Royal Society. Wicksteed valued, beside his sterling qualities as a man and an administrator, his "most delightful gifts of conversation." Alice Rix had even rarer gifts. She was a "Martha and Mary in one," who felt, with even more unfailing instinct than her husband, the oneness of material and spiritual things. There was something better than plain living and high thinking in their home, for the phrase suggests an austerity which the wealth and generosity of Alice Rix's nature forbade. Alice Rix "seemed never to forget and never to neglect anything. New claims and new possibilities of kindness seemed to enter her life without displacing anything that was already there; she had the genius of order that makes the full life of its fortunate possessor more leisurely and reposeful than the empty life of another." The Rix's may be said to have discovered Limpsfield. One friend after another settled there, and Headland Cottage became a centre of philosophic thought and a fountain of spiritual influence. His study became, says Wicksteed, a laboratory of the truly "higher" thought. Alice Rix's part in these discussions was that of a "permeating" rather than a commanding personality. When her face was in repose she might have sat for Mary or Rachel whom the medieval imagination symbolized as the contemplative life. The Rix's had arranged for him to talk to the village folk of Limpsfield, one summer morning, on the *Comedy*. Perhaps that comparison came into his mind as he watched her listening face.

If the Dante lectures won for Wicksteed hosts of potential friendships and not a few real and lasting ones, his devotion to the laborious discipline of Dante's master, Aquinas, did more perhaps to repel than to conciliate. A Unitarian Thomist was bewildering or suspect to the orthodox of either order, a religious mongrel with whom the true-bred did not mate. But there was one contemporary who had undergone phases of experience outwardly analogous to his, only in the inverse order. Charles Hargrove had been a Dominican monk; then at thirty left the Roman Church, and after drifting for a while embraced Unitarianism, and entered upon a career of rare mark and significance as the minister for thirty-five years at Mill-hill Chapel, Leeds. "You and Philip Wicksteed are the only Aquinas scholars among us," wrote Estlin Carpenter, his predecessor in that pulpit, in later days from Oxford. But the relation of the two men to Aquinas was only outwardly similar. To Wicksteed, Aquinas was the master of Dante, a revered theologian, from whose distinctive theology he stood wholly aloof. To Hargrove, the Dominican, his theology had been the object of a sincere, if uneasy, belief. But in both men religious vision was coupled with a critical modern intellect. Hargrove, as a young man still feeling his way to truth, had long hesitated between the divergent signposts of Strauss and Newman, and his final "apostasy" from Rome was only a return to a recognition, on a higher plane, of a faith in which critical reason and spiritual vision alike found scope. It was no accidental, but an inner necessity which caused Hargrove to "find" himself in the Unitarianism of Martineau, Beard, Carpenter, and Wicksteed. To people who asked why Hargrove, on ceasing to be a Catholic, had become (of all alternatives) a Unitarian, Wicksteed gave the simple, if half jocular, explanation that a Thomist who rejected the Christian "Revelation" became, *ipso facto* a Unitarian; the pea, as it were, relieved of its pod. More seriously and profoundly he said of Hargrove, in the beautiful dedication of *Dante and Aquinas*, "Dominicanae quondam, Dominicae nunquam non gregis," a tribute to the inner spiritual oneness of his friend's perplexed course which it was doubtless easier for Wicksteed to accord than for his former Catholic associates to echo.[1] Hargrove, who could be the gayest of companions, with grave humour deprecated the praise, and suggested a substitute to the effect (in Latin): "To the lazy servant, who, having received five talents, buried three of them in the earth and negligently used the other two, his industrious fellow-servant offers this compassionate testimonial." (C. Hargrove to P. H. Wicksteed, 17 April, 1911.)

An intimacy with a friend better known to the world had its origin in the same lonely explorations of a modernist in the scholastic mind. Robert Bridges, the late Poet Laureate, was fascinated by the *Reactions*, which Wicksteed had sent him on its publication in 1920, and gave it a place in the little shelf of choice reading that hung at his bedside. But the book opened

[1] Hargrove's career and personality have been presented in a book of great power and beauty, his Life, by Principal L. P. Jacks.

up other fountains of community in both men, and the symposia of the two veterans at Childrey or Boar's Hill are reported to have resounded with a gaiety not always derived from the rare jests of Aristotle. Wicksteed was privileged in his last months to read the unfinished MS. of the *Testament of Beauty*.[1]

An older friendship and perhaps a deeper sympathy bound him to another distinguished Oxford neighbour, then even better known to the world, Professor Gilbert Murray. Greek and internationalism, Athens and Geneva, were lodestars of both men, and for both, religion had disengaged itself from the traditional theology.

And there were other friendships where a common interest became the instrument which Wicksteed's riper mastery touched to more immediate and personal issues of uplifting or consolation. Among the many whose debt to Wicksteed was of this kind, Alice Rix's sisters, both blind, whom he visited weekly to read to, have allowed the use of his letters to them. Another has permitted us to record an experience. Her home in London had been visited by a tragic bereavement. "It was," she writes, "as if he had nothing more pressing to do than to browse in his favourite classics. I sat and listened, and for the first time there dawned on me the living beauty of those old words, which had before only stood for toil with

[1] A letter of Bridges' to him (22 December, 1926) throws a valuable light on the composition of the *Testament*. "I hope," he writes, "that your work has gone on well, and that you will have leisure to look at mine some time in January. I have made a struggle to get through the first section of my poem before Christmas, and I think I have accomplished it. It is about eight hundred lines, and I shall get it set up in type as soon as I can."

dictionaries. It was generally Virgil, but I remember vividly a first morning with Catullus—our shared delight in the charm of *Lesbia's Sparrow*, the poignant grief of Catullus at his brother's grave. We had both of us lost a brother at an early age in foreign parts." Comradeship was thus the very spirit of Wicksteed's friendship. To all his friends, whether men or women, young or old, he brought that fine blend of human attachment and common loyalty to an ideal which comradeship implies.

Of the most intimate of all Wicksteed's friendships something has already been said in speaking of the student years when it began. But this summary account of his Childrey life would want a vivid note if his later intercourse with Estlin Carpenter, now Professor, and then Principal, of Manchester College, Oxford, received only passing mention. The fires of scholarship and of social service burnt with equal intensity and continuity in the breasts of both men, and this singleness of purpose in their often alien pursuits was still the soul of their intimacy. It mattered nothing that the instrument of Wicksteed's exact and meticulous scholarship was Dante, of Carpenter's, the Buddhist scriptures; or that Carpenter sought a more definitely religious faith, disengaged from the limitations of East and West, but enriched by their kindred sanctities, while Wicksteed, using, with magnificent freedom, the most highly elaborated instrument of medieval theology, sought to disengage from it, for his own time and for all times, the inner core of all religion. During the whole of the Childrey period the intercourse was frequent; and the "earnestness" of the evening discussions in Banbury Road was sometimes interrupted by an unacademic but ever-welcome apparition, glowing from his fifteen-miles' ride, and very likely without a tie, who might startle the argument with a paradox, or waylay it with a jest, but was quite certain, in any case, not to leave it where he found it. And there were corresponding and equally delightful apparitions at Childrey, when the tall and stately figure of the Oxford friend was seen dismounting from his horse at the gate, and the "Master of a College" discoursed familiarly of things that "were not knowledge" to the children and grandchildren gathered round the long hospitable tea-table.

Both men were athletes in build, and even, for scholars, when they rowed or cycled, in prowess; and both wrought side by side at their cognate tasks in the spirit of that "holy athleticism" which Dante ascribed to the sternest of his saints. And when the veterans reached four-score, the outer aspect, too, of each came to acquire a grandeur that mirrored the soul within; more majestic and venerable in the one, more leonine and formidable in the other; to one who watched them as they sat together for the last time in the study at Childrey, a few months before their death, a Hebrew prophet in his serener hour might have seemed to have found fellowship with an aged but still indomitable Stoic. The beautiful dedication which Wicksteed prefixed to the *Reactions* is the fittest commemoration of their friendship:

Josepho Estlin Carpenter
Amice constantissime dilectissime
Tu mihi primitias ingenii tui
Dedicasti iuvenis
Tibi post octo lustra

Membra haec libri disiecta
Senex retuli
Majora viribus meis
Tu semper de me sperabas
Minora heu quanto spe tua
Benigne tamen accipias.

To Joseph Estlin Carpenter. Most constant and beloved of friends, you, as a young man, offered me the first-fruits of your mind: I, as an old man, have brought to you after forty years these fragments of a book. You ever expected from me things beyond my power: receive indulgently these offerings, far, alas! below your hope.

V

Thus richly furnished was the scene of Philip Wicksteed's later labours; the home of a peopled hermitage secluded from traffic, but attached by countless affiliating ties to the centres of civic activity, and to the invisible background of distant friends. Of those labours themselves something must now be said, reserving for a later chapter their more detailed appreciation. Measured by the range and depth of the impressions they left, the most important of these activities was perhaps the humblest in scholarly status—the business of Extension lecturing. Begun as we saw in the later years of his London ministry, this became at Childrey, during the whole period preceding the collapse of 1918, the staple of his external activities. But the courses now grew, both in comprehensiveness and in individuality. One such course which bears the stamp of Wicksteed's synthetic mind, provided a conspectus of the spiritual history of Europe, as reflected in great literature, from the Hebrew psalmists and prophets, through Homer, Æschylus, and Virgil, to Dante.[1] Portions of this vast field were handled in separate courses. In particular, his lectures on the Greek tragedians, hardly less than his Dante lectures, were the vehicle of his enthralling power of interpreting masterpieces. The Dante courses themselves, without losing any of their power of appeal, became less elementary, richer in examples of Wicksteed's singular power of lucidly expounding the abstruser matter of Dantesque philosophy and technique, and thus more instructive to the Dante specialist. The Dante lectures became widely celebrated, and attracted hearers for whom from different, perhaps opposite points of view, "Extension Courses" were in no way designed. Distinguished critics were allured by curiosity, maidservants invited by their mistresses, and both "remained."

It is not easy to convey to those who never listened to Wicksteed's Dante lectures any vivid notion of their quality. To say that the preacher "out of harness" *found* himself when he interpreted Dante at the lecturer's desk more completely than when he conducted a devotional service from a pulpit, though probably true, would only mislead. The pulpit could not shackle nor the lecturer's desk set free a man who, like Wicksteed when he interpreted Dante's vision, transcended, as Dante himself had so supremely done, whatever is conventional and vulgar in the distinction of secular and sacred. He had no pulpit accent or idiom to

[1] It may be mentioned that when in 1918 Wicksteed was compelled by illness to give up his lectures, his successor in this and other courses was the "boy" whom he had found, some thirty years before, reading Henry George, Rev. J. H. Weatherall, now Principal-elect of Manchester College, Oxford.

transport to the lecturer's dais, none to discard there. He remained the layman he had always fundamentally been. But a layman who breathed as his native air the atmosphere of the "sacred poem," so that the Dantesque sanctity, which is so much more intimate and personal than the sanctities of institutions, rites and priesthoods, became through the instrumentality of his mind and life a transfiguring as well as an uplifting power.

An experience not unjustly described in terms like these was the privilege of countless audiences during twenty years before the war. Various currents of tendency favourable to the acceptance of Dante were percolating the soil of cultivated England during these years. Mysticism, Anglo-Catholicism, St. Francis, Thomas à Kempis, were loosening the stiff texture of Protestant prejudice, and undermining the exclusiveness of insular religiosity. Of none of these causes was Wicksteed in any sense an "apostle"; but they undoubtedly rendered the soil more responsive to the Dantesque seed he sowed.

The following personal impressions illustrate the ready access he found to several different types of hearer:

"I had heard much of him as a lecturer," writes a young lawyer, "but he far surpassed my expectations. I knew Dante dealt with elemental emotions, and so might appeal to the crowd; but I had no notion that in a short hour any one could so imbue an audience like ours, which consisted largely of ex-Sunday scholars and the like, with a whole system of politics, philosophy, and religion, and imbue them in such a manner that they were electrified. Neither had I any idea how extraordinarily applicable to everyday affairs in England to-day these systems were. I regard the lecture from every point of view as an extraordinary achievement. The greatest critic present was much impressed, and, on the other hand—a maidservant said she wouldn't have missed it for anything, and that she could have gone on listening for hours."

Would Dante himself have wished for a better interpreter of the poem by which he meant to communicate to the wisest of men the means of salvation, conveyed in terms which every "muliercula" could understand?

The following describes the experience of an old fellow-minister. The lecture (on the *Purgatorio*) was heard a quarter of a century ago, but the impression it left, only recently put on paper, was of unfading freshness. Its scene was a Surrey village, the time a summer morning, the audience mainly villagers.

"I had listened to this lecture before, when delivered to a crowded assembly at a large hall in Liverpool. But the full significance of that toilsome pilgrimage from circle to circle—to the heights of the Earthly Paradise, I had but faintly apprehended or realized prior to this so favoured hour, which was to make the time and the place for ever sacred to me. I have often wondered since, if ever speaker was more possessed by his theme, or hearer more subdued and receptive. As he led us from the lowest margin of the Mount . . . upwards, round by round to the summit's clear light and air, it was as if we who followed were no longer dwellers in this modern world of England; we were companions of those two pilgrims on their toilsome ascent. . . . Yet Wicksteed seemed to make that ascent . . . just a dramatic representation of life as we know it here . . . and the spiritual and moral import of it all seemed to disentangle itself from it, and the innermost truth of the poetic vision to emerge. . . . Thus, to at least one listener . . . it was as if the whole of his moral life, its inward struggles and aspirings, its sins and its sorrows, its defects and partial triumphs . . . were mirrored before him. . . . He knew himself living through all again, as in the atmosphere of a higher, holier world which the poet-seer and his prophet-interpreter disclosed, the light whereof shone into the deepest recesses of mind and heart. Tears of strangely mingled joy and penitence and grief were flowing down the listener's face when the speaker ended, and silence, the silence of released attention, fell on that little company; and though he was sitting with beloved friends, of whose sympathy he was assured, his one desire was to escape and be alone, lest any impulse of that hallowed hour should pass before it had become an abiding reality of experience, never to be taken away from memory or from love." [1]

These reports testify to the magnetism which Wicksteed exercised upon minds very variously constituted. And the spirit which enabled him to make Dante live for modern audiences was not first wakened by Dante; it found its way through many other channels than the lecture or the lecture-room. Such a channel he found, in particular, in the gatherings at Swanwick, a country house among the hills of Derbyshire.

The Swanwick Summer School had been founded in 1912 chiefly on the initiative and under the inspiration

[1] Privately communicated by W. J. J.

of Philip Wicksteed himself. It was designed to provide a meeting-place in which members of all denominations or of none might discuss in common, the subjects of deepest interest to them all. It was a piece of constructive organization (if that much abused adjective may be used), analogous to the equally inter-denominational Summer School of Theology which his friend, Estlin Carpenter, was carrying on with no less signal success during the same years at Oxford.[1]

At these informal gatherings of keen minds unembarrassed by the frontiers of creed, race, or class, the lectures often mattered less than the ensuing debates, and the appointed lecturers than the impromptu speakers attracted by curiosity or interest. Power, personality, knowledge, alone determined dominance. Many who attended them in the earlier years will recall occasions when such dominance was spontaneously accorded to two men who were alike incapable of seeking it. One was the late Friedrich von Hügel, whose catholicity reconciled more powerfully than his catholicism, and his spirituality more than his arguments. The other was Philip Wicksteed himself, a humanist whose catholicity had fewer reserves, and effected its reconciling purpose by a less disguised handling of the rapier of logic. Nowhere was Wicksteed more in his element than in this greenwood Academe, secluded, like that of the Shakespearean

[1] The Swanwick School was in some sense the prototype of the later Copec conferences in Birmingham and Stockholm, and of the Christian Social Council. Some share in the success of these organizations must be ascribed to Wicksteed's fertilizing thought. He had earlier taken an important part in similar attempts to overcome local and other insularities, such as, in particular, the Leicester Union of Sunday Schools, in 1906, as I learnt from the late Miss K. Gittins of Leicester.

Navarre, from officialdom and red-tape, from towns and courts (but certainly not "from women's eyes"), where he could apply at will his kindly but keen Socratic dialectic, disarming pretension, but meeting the humblest student on his own terms.

VI

But the Socratic business of clarifying thought and (in the fine older sense) ascertaining conviction, by no means exhausted the calls that throughout these busy pre-war years interrupted the routine, and riveted the energies of the study and lecture-room. What Wicksteed most profoundly cared for was to put his countrymen more fully in possession of their spiritual heritage. This was, for him, the very core of that "reform in the interest of the unprivileged," which he declared to be the true aim of social action, for to participate in that heritage was the supreme privilege, as to be debarred from it was the supreme disability. Wicksteed was no leveller. The democrat in him never made the student of genius less keenly aware of the hierarchy of human wit, nor the student of history less aware of the hierarchy of social divisions. If he held that there is in every man a spark of the divine, the devoted interpreter of Dante was not likely to ignore the difference between a spark and a flame.[1] If Henry George had for a time captured his acceptance of an equalizing law, Comte had impressed him with the sense of the social origin of wealth, and the conviction that the condition

[1] It is said that Wicksteed, once being asked: "Do you deny the divinity of Jesus?" replied, "No, nor the divinity of any other man."

of progress is order. He rejected the methods, as he embraced the ideals, of socialism. In the address on land-nationalization, to be noticed below, in 1900, he showed how little the idyll of Childrey had blinded him to the abuses of landlordism in the country, as well as in the town. But he deprecated any hasty anticipation of general opinion. In a later paper on Socialist ideals he had even won the applause of the *Morning Post* by his emphatic acceptance of capitalism as an economic institution. Deeply as he desired a more equal distribution of wealth, he understood too well the complexity of the causes which affect distribution, and was too fundamentally just, even to the large landlord and the "idle rich," to be prepared for a radical and summary revision. There was, too, in Wicksteed, a vein of frugality, of good husbandry, a touch of Franklin, even,[1] which impelled him to make the best of what you have instead of reaching out for endowments or unearned increment. This homely wisdom had been his mother's familiar maxim; and it is hardly hyperbole to say that the art of intelligently using what you possess, thus early instilled into the boy was the substance of the man's economics.

Wicksteed was not, then, conspicuously, what is commonly understood by a reformer. His immense intellectual and moral energy was devoted less to bettering existing conditions than to equipping men with the spiritual viaticum which lightens the toil of the journey and makes its goal clear. The social work which most perfectly expressed his aims was probably

[1] A Franklin, indeed, who like Emerson, "hitched his wagon to a star," or rather, since the "hitched wagon" could only, at best, be a clumsy flier and probably spill "the wagoner," a wagon convertible at will into an aeroplane, impelled upward from within.

the "Labour Church" of the 'nineties, described in a later chapter. There are signs that he did not accept its failure as final. The phenomenal success of the Salvation Army in carrying "religion" into the slums led him seriously to consider whether similar transformations might not be achieved with a less crude theology. In an extant letter of 1899 to Sir J. Brunner he expresses complete confidence in the power of the pure and rational teaching of Unitarianism to emulate the "Army." But nothing came of this, and when his friend and "disciple," Mr. Shaw, a few years later (1906) playfully introduced a Greek scholar beating the Salvation drum in the streets, it was another distinguished friend of Wicksteed's who had to serve as his model.

It thus becomes intelligible that Wicksteed, democrat as he was, did not take a conspicuous part in a reform movement which was forcing itself upon the averted ear of England during these Childrey years, and at the outbreak of the war had become strident and menacing. The claim to the suffrage affected primarily only the machinery of government. Wicksteed held the claim to be just. But, like many other Liberals, he was repelled by the violent methods of the "suffragettes," and deplored the injury they did to the cause. And while he felt and denounced the "horror" of forcible feeding, his logic was humorously alive to the paradox of protesting against a punishment you deliberately incur because it is severer than you expected. "Those who choose martyrdom," he would grimly, but not cynically, remark, "must not bargain just how hot the fire is to be."

The women, moreover, were not helpless, they were

also vocal, and they used their voices with singular ability. It was otherwise with the Armenian and Greek victims of the ruthless Ottoman, whose cause Wicksteed, as we saw, went to plead in the Hampshire villages. Otherwise, again, with the Chinese victims of the indefensible, but stubbornly defended, traffic in opium. It was otherwise, too, with a class of beings, neither vocal nor capable of self-help, who were the victims of an exercise of human power less passionate but even more cruel. From the early years of his London pastorate Wicksteed opposed vivisection. He became closely associated in this crusade with Miss Frances Power Cobbe, its secretary, one of the most resonant names among the women reformers of those days. It became one of the leading preoccupations of his Childrey years, and his active support gave notable encouragement to the little band of "agitators" in the north. Miss Cobbe's successor in the secretaryship, Miss Alice Lucas of Darlington, became a close friend. Their cause had recently been called into public notice by the trial of their leader, Dr. Hadwen, for refusing to use a drug derived from the practice of vivisection. The prosecution, supported by the whole authority of the medical profession, placed Dr. Hadwen in the category of a heretic vindicating his unpopular faith against established orthodoxy—a *prima facie* recommendation to men of Philip Wicksteed's mind. But neither this nor his rejection of the claim that vivisection was "necessary for science," indispensable for the discovery and use of the medical safeguards of human health, was the determining factor in Wicksteed's position. He believed, after investigation, that that claim was not justified. But even if it were, he insisted, vivisection would, none the less, be a sin against the "moral health" of man himself. To seek his own health at the cost of animal torture his generous nature regarded as so mean an abuse of superior power that abolition must follow its clear recognition. "As soon as scientific men take a wide view of their function," he wrote in one of his eloquent and stirring addresses to the society, "our cause will be won; for in truth it is *not* for animals only that we are pleading, but for humanity also; and when science has taken a point of view at once more lofty and more practical, the evil and folly of the practices which we denounce and oppose will be seen in all their nakedness." In 1920, when slowly recovering from his illness, Wicksteed reluctantly accepted the office of president of the society, warning Miss Lucas, however, that his days of lecturing were definitely over. His friendship with Miss Lucas, initiated by their work for this public cause, was drawn closer as the years went on, by other bonds; fellowship in suffering, in illness and bereavement, and in the courage which, as he wrote to her "continues to face life bravely and to go on fighting for the cause of living and loving beings that cannot fight for themselves."

VII

But if Wicksteed was widely recognized as one whose words made a difference, no one was better aware of the evanescence of the most impressive talk, as no one was more completely indifferent to oratorical triumphs. His Dante lecturing, above all, ran the risk, as all lecturing upon a difficult foreign poet must, of being water poured upon sand, so long as the original text was not easily and cheaply accessible, with all legitimate aids, including the contemporary history, and a literal prose version, to its intelligent interpretation. To provide for this vital need had long been a cherished plan, and was one of the first preoccupations of his retirement.

The earliest of these was the translation of relevant passages from the Florentine chronicler, Villani, by Wicksteed and Miss R. Selfe (Constable, 1896). A little later (1898) he testified to his lasting sense of the significance of Karl Witte's Dante work by co-operating with his eldest daughter in a translation of the famous *Essays*.[1]

The English edition of Dante in six volumes (as it ultimately became), in the Temple Classics, was a joint enterprise, two specialists in Italian, Dr. Oelsner and Mr. Okey (afterwards professor of Italian at Cambridge), being also concerned, especially in editing the text. Publication was undertaken by the then young firm of Dent. Mr. J. M. Dent, its founder and head, was doubtless encouraged by the immense vogue of the beautiful and scholarly Temple Shakespeare, and the dainty and compact format of the Dante pocket-volumes, doubtless owed something to the careful study bestowed upon the externals of the earlier series. The Dante volumes were also a decided, if less phenomenal, publisher's success, and the value of their wide diffusion in view of the relative inaccessibility of Dante in any other form, was, for the mass of serious English readers, let us say boldly for the higher mind

[1] Wicksteed and Lawrence, *Essays on Dante, by K. Witte,* 1898.

of the English people, very much greater.[1] In these little volumes, too, every kind of insidious cunning was used to allure the possessor, step by step, along the path which divides the sight of a dapper book in a window (to be had at the price of a moderate cigar), to competent Dante scholarship. Here was neither text alone nor translation alone, but according to the plan now familiar in the Loeb classics, then perhaps adopted for the first time on a large scale, text and translation printed face to face. More than this, the English version was designed and treated, not as a substitute, but as a "crib"; the attempt, usually made by the accomplished Loeb translators, to produce, by a dexterous use of the stylistic resources of English idiom and diction, as perfect an equivalent as is attainable in the English tongue, being deliberately forgone in order to provide the novice with a ready clue to the meaning. With this policy, it may be frankly said, Philip Wicksteed, whose power as a writer lay rather in the force and clarity of his thought than in "curious felicity" of phrase, and whose zeal in the cause of Dante entirely dominated any literary ambition of his own, found it easy to comply. The translations, on the whole, and Wicksteed's more particularly, have the quality of tempting the reader to try the original; not because it is not clear, but because the matter seems to betoken a nobler vesture of expression than it wears. It is otherwise with the

[1] His experience as an Extension Lecturer had made Wicksteed acutely aware of the reluctance of even the well-to-do to lay out money in a book if it could by any device be otherwise secured. A group of such hearers came to him one day after the lecture, to inquire where they might borrow a copy of a book he had referred to, "I 'll tell you what," he rejoined, "just club together all of you and *buy* one!"

"Argument" prefixed to each canto. Here the problem was not to render the words in a form controlled at every step by the course of the original, which it had to reproduce but not to simulate. The matter is cast into a new medium, a prose paragraph which the writer can, within limits, order and mould at will. Here Wicksteed's power of lucid presentment found full scope. And lucid presentment of Dante meant much more, be it remembered, than the not uncommon cleverness of a good précis-writer. It meant seeing with Dante's eyes, sharing in some sort his spiritual vision, not merely summarizing the gist of his thought. And this, it is not too much to say, is the impression that the finest of Wicksteed's "Arguments" leaves upon his readers. Only a word need be added upon the notes, not always the work of Wicksteed, or the "appendices" and excursuses. Here the immensely various essential matter of Dantesque scholarship was succinctly but effectually set forth; here the mathematician who was twinned with the medievalist found his opportunity in tabulating the symmetries and harmonies of a poet for whom, as for Plato, Number was itself mystic and divine; the time-table of Dante's Journey, of the classifications of sins in Hell and Purgatory, the cosmology of his three Realms, and the genealogies of his historic or mythic families.

It was no accident that the *Paradiso* was the first portion of the *Comedy* to be thus made widely accessible.[1] Wicksteed never ceased to expose the superficiality of the popular and even of the educated judgment, fortified by the crude sensationalism of illustrators like Doré, which regarded Dante as primarily

[1] *The Paradiso of Dante Alighieri*, J. M. Dent, 1899.

the poet of the *Inferno*, and ignored the *Paradiso* as a tissue of scholastic sermons. Those who listened to Wicksteed's lectures could not easily retain that belief. The graduated ascent in sanctity of the spheres through which Dante leads us certainly has not a counterpart in any corresponding ascent in poetic power. The power shown in the *Inferno* and the *Purgatorio* is unsurpassed in its kind. But the kind is less rare, less beyond comparison than that of the great scenes of the *Paradiso*. It was not merely the fact that it was the spiritual climax of the Vision, that held his hearers as Wicksteed retold that final canto which some have placed at the head of the poetry of the world. This opening volume of the Temple Dante was further commended to less initiated palates by a frontispiece from the illustrations of Botticelli, a noble quotation from Bonaventura, and a title-page of choice beauty.

It is needless to dwell upon the other volumes. The *Inferno* followed in the autumn of 1900,[1] then in rapid succession the *Purgatorio*,[2] his translations of the *Convivio* (1903), his translations of the *De Eloquentia*, the *De Monarchia*, and the Latin *Eclogues* (1904), and the translation of the *Canzoniere*, with the *Vita Nuova*, translated by Okey (1906).

All these books, of almost incalculable value as they were for the diffusion of a more familiar acquaintance with Dante, were addressed to the cultured or culture-seeking public, not primarily to scholars, much as these might incidentally glean from them. The volume on Dante and Del Virgilio, on the other hand, produced

[1] The edition of the *Inferno* included valuable "Notes" by Wicksteed on the arrangement and chronology of Dante's Hell.

[2] The translation was by Okey, the Arguments and a "note" on the Chronology by Wicksteed.

in collaboration with that distinguished younger colleague who was soon to become one of his closest friends, was addressed chiefly to the narrower circle of Dante specialists.[1] The brief but very attractive relations of Dante, in grey old age, with the young and ambitious poet of Bologna were in effect an episode of the early Renascence, and there is a touch of irony in the fact that Wicksteed's most definite contribution to Dante scholarship should have been concerned with that "Revival of Learning" for which he entertained a rooted and outspoken abhorrence.[2] For Del Virgilio (whose very name indicated his great exemplar) was a leading figure among the Latinists who were attempting to oust the vernacular from the language of poetry, as written by and for, educated men. But Dante, the

[1] Wicksteed and Gardner, *Dante and Giovanni Del Virgilio* (London, 1902).

[2] This antipathy, founded partly on moral repugnance, partly on the scholar's contempt for "derivative" literature, was freely expressed in the letters from Italy (1895) already noticed. It found even more energetic expression, ten years later, in letters to his collaborator in the present volume. Mr. Gardner had passed on from Dante studies to steep himself in, precisely, the age of Humanism. Wicksteed was not easily disconcerted, but his letters acknowledge the receipt of Mr. Gardner's *Dukes and Poets in Ferrara* (1904) and *Ariosto* (1906) betray something that may not inaptly be so described. "The student of the thirteenth and of the fifteenth centuries," he writes (to E. G. Gardner, 25 September, 1906) "may be two men in one without any very definite and direct relations; but the student of the thirteenth and of the sixteenth centuries will have to settle accounts with each other one way or another; they cannot do with a mere nodding acquaintance and an occasional reference to show that they have not forgotten each other!" Wicksteed's antipathy to the Renascence extended, in a milder degree, to the whole sixteenth century; even Shakespeare, we have seen, he delighted to read but consistently refused to lecture upon. It rested in part upon deep-seated temperamental instincts, but involved, as the book just noticed shows, an undue limitation of the "period" of the Renascence. An eminent medievalist of our acquaintance, the late T. F. Tout, declared himself unable to decide whether we ought to say that "there never was a Renascence" or that "it was there all the time."

stubborn medievalist, persisted in conveying his really new and weighty matter in the vulgar tongue. The *Inferno* and the *Purgatorio* were before the world; the *Paradiso* was known to be approaching completion; and Del Virgilio's expostulation in an "eclogue" so full of classical allusions that it required a commentary even for its contemporaries, gives us a lively notion of the forces Dante had to overcome when he decided to give his great matter to the multitude, and not to the pale scholar. Dante's reply, in his first eclogue, is well known; it is a model of good temper, touched, as the editors say, with his rare humour; Milton, exhorted towards the close of *Paradise Lost*, to write it in Latin, would have answered with grimmer sarcasm. To make this faded background of Dante's Latin eclogues alive for English students was, then, a task entirely worthy of Dante scholars; and the editors discharged it with the ungrudging labour and care bestowed upon a classic; while the "Prolegomena" presents a living portrait of the most illustrious Latin poet of that circle, exiled like Dante from his native city, Albertino Mussato.

But the first decade of Wicksteed's Childrey retirement bore fruit of more significance and originality than any of these volumes. The desire for more concentrated study had been one of the chief motives of his withdrawal from the active ministry and from London; it possibly gave the initial impulse to this step. Two classes of subject matter stood foremost in the urgency of their claims upon his less restricted leisure: the working of the economic organism of society, and the history of the thought of Dante. Thirty years before, the *Alphabet of Economic Science* and the *Six Sermons* had foreshadowed, in the form of a popular presentment, Wicksteed's fundamental ideas. In the former field he was conscious of things definitely fresh to say, and there were times when he regarded it as his chief work in life to say them. "I believe (rightly or wrongly)," he had written to a correspondent before his retirement, "that I have the power of throwing essential light upon (economic and social science), that the best account I can give of my life will be given if I can say I have made the fullest contribution I can to this study." [1]

Ten years later, when the book was approaching completion, Wicksteed wrote to a younger colleague who had become an intimate friend, in closely similar terms: "I am nearing the time when I shall commit the work of ten or twelve years to the public. It is my life effort to do something real for thought and life; and I can honestly say that I look forward with perfect serenity to the possibilities of being entirely ignored, of being violently attacked, or of being convinced that I was mistaken and presumptuous in thinking that I had any serious contribution to make to the subject." [2]

The result of these aspirations and this protracted toil, the *Common Sense of Political Economy*, appeared in 1910. The effort left him for the time exhausted. Shortly after the publication he excused himself for not replying at once to his brother Tom's warm praise: "It is because I feel nothing at present, having, it seems, *given* myself to this book."

[1] From a private letter, written in 1897, to a lady who had consulted him on the question how far intellectual culture was justified under present circumstances of social need.

[2] To E. G. Gardner, 11 November, 1907.

Of Dante's doctrinal and philosophic sources he had, for a different audience, not less important things to say. The principal source, the theological system of St. Thomas Aquinas, had no doubt been expounded with immense learning by illustrious scholars. But they belonged almost exclusively to St. Thomas's own church. A survey of the philosophy of Aquinas and of Dante's qualified discipleship to him, by a scholar who brought to both a critical reverence wholly unbiased by doctrinal agreement was something new and important. And it satisfied instincts in Wicksteed himself which the closest analysis of the technique of getting and spending left inert. Hence it was with openly confessed relief that, on completing the *Common Sense,* he turned to the preparation of the lectures, delivered in the following year, 1911, on "Dante and Aquinas." They were published as a volume two years later. And this, perhaps the most perfect though not the greatest of Wicksteed's books, was itself only a step to the more elaborate handling of cognate problems in the *Reactions between Dogma and Philosophy,* illustrated from the works of St. Thomas Aquinas, which he delivered as the second course of Hibbert lectures in the autumn of 1916; they were ultimately issued, after long delay through illness, with a vast apparatus of notes, in the volume so entitled, in 1920. And that study led in turn to the concentrated occupation with "the philosopher" himself, which was to engross the last years, weeks, even the last hours, of his life. Of the whole of this body of work, the ripe fruit of Wicksteed's synthetic genius, some account will be offered in the closing chapters of this book.

CHAPTER V

CHILDREY: LAST YEARS

The War—The Golden Wedding—Last Journeys—Last Work—The End

I

A YEAR after the appearance of his *Dante and Aquinas,* Philip Wicksteed had occasion to invoke the "medieval" wisdom of his great poet in the presence of the most appalling calamity of the modern world. In the autumn of 1914 he contributed to the *Nation* a paper on "Dante's Vision of Peace." "Dante," he wrote, "and especially the *Paradiso,* reveal their meaning to us in proportion as they transfigure our conception of peace, transmuting it from the negative suggestion of 'relief from conquest' into the positive sense of fullness of realization and fruition." Dante's "peace," then, did not exclude the use of war to maintain or secure it. "To no great poet," as Croce has said, "is militarism so completely abhorrent as to Dante." Yet Dante had passionately called the German emperor of his day to crush with arms the disorders of Florence; and with no less conviction he had gloried in the Roman conquest of the world which prepared the way for the rule of Christ and of the Roman law. Wicksteed was a pacifist in this sense and in no other. For him, as for the immense majority of Englishmen at that date, the contemporary "German emperor" had wantonly shattered the peace of Europe, and he held that England had no choice but to take the course she did. His faith in his country was, therefore, not exposed to a blow comparable with that inflicted by the war of purely imperialistic oppression, as he thought it, with the Boers. But the partial justification of his country's action could not lighten for him the horror of the world-war itself. He saw in it a sudden and complete failure of the forces which had appeared to be steadily making for an organic unity of the civilized world. The greatest calamity brought by the war was not, then, the possibility of defeat. On 15 May, 1915, soon after the sinking of the *Lusitania,* he wrote to his brother Tom: "I am not a peace-at-any-price man, I never was; but I am not a war-by-any-means man either, and the danger that A—— spoke of at the beginning of the war, that 'we should overcome the German armies and be overcome by the Prussian spirit,' seems to me nearer than it was. Every day makes the idea of Prussian world-supremacy more hideous, but some days make the prospect of an Allied victory less inspiring." Most sensitive onlookers sought seasons of relief from the tragic tension of those tremendous years. Wicksteed had moods when he would sit in his study "reading Aristophanes hour by hour, as old-fashioned people read their Bibles," and when he turned, as he often did, from the derider of Athenian militarism to Æschylus, it was, we suspect, with the sublime poet of Prometheus, not with the singer of the glory of Salamis, that he took refuge. To a friend who invited him to preach in his pulpit he replied that, if he did, his subject would be Shelley's *Prometheus Unbound*—Humanity nailed to the rock by Force and Violence, and liberated by the might of Love. Force was now having his unimpeded way; and whatever the issue, the real triumph would be his. That triumph only a renunciation of the war-spirit could annul. For Wicksteed, as for many others, the peace which actually followed only deepened the gloom by making more precarious the prospect of that peaceful evolution which the war had shattered. It postponed indefinitely the liberation of Prometheus. More than this, it made more insecure than ever his belief that this was a world in which Prometheus had any prospect of being liberated at all.

Some sentences from Wicksteed's private letters disclose how deep was the reaction of these events upon his faith in a moral order of the world. "The Boer war," he wrote later (September 1922) to Miss Knappert, "and the war of 1914, and still more its aftermath, these destroyed my world, and told me that the things I thought could not happen, could; and the things I thought must happen, need not. These things tended to make hope pale and faith totter, and challenged the question whether I was *saying* to myself that I retained faith and hope because I would not face the fact that I had lost them, or whether I still 'believed in the Holy Ghost.'" Symptoms of the same temper before the Great War are disclosed by a letter of 1911 to a ministerial colleague who had reviewed his "Dante and Aquinas" lectures: "Honestly, my position is becoming more 'agnostic' in what I take to be the proper meaning of the word, viz. having no system of positive beliefs which I dare to affirm I believe." [1] Wicksteed does not add, what the sentence implies, that agnosticism in the *im*proper sense, of a dogmatic denial of the possibility of all grounded positive beliefs, was not the goal he was approaching.

Thirteen years later he wrote, to the same friend, of

[1] To Mr. Lloyd Thomas, September 1911.

his "ever more tenuous beliefs," [1] a description rather illustrated than qualified by the affirmation, elsewhere, of "something akin to us in the universe." Such a faith, he adds in the same context, justifies neither exultation nor extreme despondency. And if Wicksteed's habitual temper inclined far more to the former emotion it was because there glowed within him a faith, never attenuated at all, in the spiritual values to which human life as he saw and interpreted it is so richly charged. Within a few weeks of the letter to Miss Knappert above quoted, he had replied to a group of students and friends who had addressed him: "All that I have offered and felt as 'vital nutriment' during long and strenuous years of teaching is to me vital and nutritious still, and the life it feeds is good."

II

Yet the war years also brought occasions which interposed a little ease in the harrowing tension, even for those who felt it most acutely. In April 1918, Philip and Emily Wicksteed completed the fiftieth year of their flawless union. The thought of festivity in this hour of national crisis was abhorrent to him. But one of his daughters struck out the idea of a "golden honeymoon," and this was accepted. A cottage was hired, high up on the adjacent wolds; they called it "the Sæter," with a fond reminiscence of the upland chalets of Norway. Here, as he wrote

[1] This phrase occurs in reference to a contemporary notice by Mr. Thomas of Otto's *Das Heilige*. "The 'optimism without frivolity, and pessimism without despair' coupled with 'ever more tenuous beliefs' comes as near hitting my own case as possible—I think better expressed than I could have done it myself" (April 1924).

to a young friend, they could literally rise "*audessus de la guerre*," and court peace and the return, for a space, of the *Saturnia regna*"; here, in the intervals of planting edible herbs and other rural activities, he took up again the appropriate *Georgics* (in the vellum Heyne of his college days). There was now a more poignant meaning in the great apostrophes to the peasants, happier than they knew, who lived exempt from the vices of imperial rule; and even the directions for planting and ploughing acquired an added relish for one who had just been engaged in these operations himself.

He sent a jocose account of the wedding-breakfast which preceded the "golden honeymoon" to an absent daughter; the "golden bridegroom," as usual, prepared the coffee, but something went wrong, and spills and stains had to be made good before the meal was ready. Then the "golden bride" sailed into the room (amid quiet but full-toned acclamations) attended by two bridesmaids, her own grandchildren, led by one of her original bridesmaids.

Then there were the hosts of greetings from the vast circle of those who loved and revered them. "There is nothing in the world," he wrote to the same young friend, who had been brought near to him by a common reading of the *Alcestis* at a time of bereavement, "there is nothing in the world that is more life-giving . . . to old people than this affection (as differing from the kind attention, which is very beautiful and touching, but another thing) of young people. We seem to be rich in this blessing, and as we go on we still make new friends among the generations coming along after us, and increasing our vital 'holding' in the future as well as in the dear past.

People talk about the 'compensations' of old age. We have been singularly blessed, and though 'we daily lose things that we fain would keep,' yet on the balance we . . . feel more inclined to think of the broadening stream of life and the wider collecting ground of acquisition and suggestion that comes with age than of the fading vividness of local impressions for which some seek 'compensation.'"

But this happy festival, in which all the idyllic potencies of secluded but busy Childrey might seem to have conspired to create a moment of real idyll for the husband and wife, was soon to be followed by events of graver tenor, of more than one kind, which exacted to the full his powers of heroic endurance. Early in October, shortly before the opening of his Extension lecture course, a tension of the heart of which he had for some time been aware, became a severe and dangerous strain. Nothing would induce Wicksteed to cancel or postpone his opening lecture, or to see a specialist till—afterwards. But here Mrs. Wicksteed's "inveterate sanity" at length overcame his stoical vehemence, and he consented, reluctantly, to see the specialist *before*. Only a day then remained before the lecture was to be given. "Why is he so anxious to give the lecture to-morrow?" asked the doctor. He then said: "If he does it, he does it at the risk of his life. He could probably do it, I have very little doubt that he would get through it; but I have very grave doubts whether he would leave the lecture-hall alive." He then explained to Mrs. Wicksteed and to her daughter Jane, a trained masseuse, who was present, the risk of complete fatal collapse, in such a condition, after such an effort. "Now how much of this," he asked, "am I to tell to him?" "Oh, tell him all that, doctor," the wife replied; "nothing but the truth will stop him!" Wicksteed yielded. It was only just in time. When he reached Hampstead (in a taxi, to his great disgust, instead of by tube), he was scarcely able to mount the steps, and slept for some nights on the ground floor.[1] The period of exhaustion that followed was so complete that he could scarcely move hand or foot, and though he could talk and recite poetry, was unable to read, or to occupy himself in any other way. Rheumatism stiffened almost all his joints, greatly retarding the recovery, which, largely through the massage applied for several weeks by his daughter, eventually came about.[2]

How completely the fears, naturally excited by this event, were belied in the *anni mirabiles* of Wicksteed's last decade remains to be told. But the abandonment of his lectures changed his entire way of life, and financial anxiety was not out of the question. He suffered little pain and no grave discomfort; immunities of less importance to his stoical temper than the enforced inactivity.[3]

The calamity naturally moved the deep sympathy of his many hundreds of hearers, and especially of those whose lives had been uplifted by his interpretation of Dante. A large number of these scattered and mutually unknown friends joined in a letter of sympathy, accompanying a gift. His reply to them is full of

[1] The house was that of his friend Rudolf Gunther, who became, six years later, his son-in-law.

[2] This account is based upon details supplied by Miss Jane H. Wicksteed.

[3] Wicksteed, we know, was not "stoical" in the conventional sense only. He did not merely bear pain with fortitude when it had to be borne; like the stoic "wise man" or the Norse chief, he valued the bearing of pain for its own sake, and liked to try how much he could bear. How, in his old age, he had all his teeth extracted without anodynes has already been told.

Philip and Emily Wicksteed
The Golden Wedding Day, 1918

indomitable cheer. He well knows, he writes, what rare privileges he has enjoyed; but far from tempting him to presumption, they have sometimes given him the deep humility with which Dante, himself exempt, walked among the sufferers in Purgatory. Meanwhile, even if he can do no more active work, all his faculties are still keen; the masters of literature who have been his constant companions are still accessible to his unimpaired eye and ear; his memory is richly stored with home and foreign travel; and his fifty years' companion is still by his side.

But Wicksteed's powers of stoic resignation were not yet to be so severely called upon as he thought. His immense physical vigour triumphed, and in the course of 1919 he became convalescent, and then enjoyed for some seven years a wonderful Indian summer of almost perfect health. In 1921 he gave a highly successful course on the Latin poets at the Oxford "Summer School." He made repeated journeys to distant parts of England, and three to the Continent. The occasions were sometimes mournful. The death, in October, 1922, of his son-in-law, Johannes Kuenen, of Leiden, summoned him to his daughter's side. Wicksteed had loved the son as he revered the father, and grieved deeply at the passing of his "great and noble personality." [1] But there were more cheerful occasions also. Wicksteed was not indifferent to university honours, though he would have been the last to court them. But had he deliberately sought to evade them he could not have planned his intellectual achievements on lines

[1] "I have not only lost a very dear son, but I have lost my oracle," Wicksteed would say. "Whenever I want to know anything, I ask Jo" (Johannes).

better calculated to secure the dismissal of his claims by those who recommend such awards. To be distinguished at once in economics and in the lore of Dante, was in these days of specialism, to discredit one's title to distinction in either; in neither field, moreover, did Wicksteed's work fall easily within recognized categories. When, in 1915, the University of Leeds conferred on him its Doctorate of Letters, Wicksteed with beautiful modesty accepted it as an honour done to his father, minister there sixty years before. In November 1919, a similar honour, for which there was no such pretext, was conferred on him by the University of Manchester. His convalescence was still far from complete, and Wicksteed's friends, at the university and elsewhere, looked forward with some apprehension to the possible effects of the strain. In September he wrote from Bournemouth to his old friend, Reynolds, gaily picturing himself "hobbling with a stick to the presence of the vice-chancellor before the eyes of the world." But the ceremony was only the occasion of a happy reunion with old friends.[1] The Dean of the Arts Faculty, Professor W. B. Anderson, a distinguished Latin and Italian scholar, presented him to the vice-chancellor in a felicitous speech which perhaps surprised the modesty of the recipient by the familiarity it appeared to display with his varied achievements as a scholar.

But more moving to Philip Wicksteed than the stately honours thus accorded to him by two great universities was a second tribute of grateful affection offered to him three years later by some hundreds of

[1] Mr. and Mrs. G. W. Brown, of Leeds; he was an old fellow student in London.

his old students—the "Gentiles" of the outer courts of academic study, for whom he had opened the gate into the inner shrine of Dante. The address, accompanied by a travelling clock and a cheque, was presented to him at Childrey by his devoted friend, colleague, and "disciple," Edmund Gardner. The donors asked him to propose an inscription to be engraved on the clock. "So how," he declared in reply, "when I heard its beautiful note in striking, could I help thinking of the heavenly horologue in *Paradiso* X, and how can the sweet chiming of its earthly representative ever fail to find my spirit 'well-ordered' to the affection that speaks through it?

> Tin tin sonando con si dolce nota
> ch' il ben disposto spirto d' amor turge.

Old age has dealt kindly with me, and though forced to give up public work in 1918, still has left some enterprise and some ambition to measure my strength against a task that seems to be worth doing. . . . Your assurance that it has meant, and directly or indirectly still means something to you, crowns my work and lays a benediction on my rest."

But this beautiful serenity was now at length to be more gravely tried. The companionship which had made his compulsory cessation from active work easy to bear was now to be withdrawn. In February 1924, a little before the completion of the fifty-sixth year of their union, Mrs. Wicksteed died. Her physical strength had for some time been waning and a severe attack of congestion of the lungs in the spring of 1922 marked a definite stage in its decline. Increasing deafness, too, had its part in her gradual withdrawal from the active life of the household; she was eventually almost entirely confined to her own two rooms. Here she still "held her court"; and absent children and grandchildren coming home on visits spent many happy hours in her sunny sitting-room hearing new tales about old times and receiving her ever ready sympathy in their own affairs. These quiet times were varied by sudden inroads from the master bringing his letters to read aloud to her. But eventually her deafness made her unable to hear him, a loss which both of them felt acutely.

In her last illness she had many willing nurses, but it was always he who took the night-nursing, she always "felt so safe" when he was with her; and during these quiet hours when he had her entirely to himself he learned to face the future.

She was laid in the village churchyard, with its far outlook over the tranquil valley, where the bell-ringers rang their muffled peal in the twilight of the evening.

III

The autumn which followed that sorrow-fraught spring and this summer of happily renewed activity was a time of steady work, cheered by the affectionate care of many devoted friends. In July hisy oungest daughter, "Molly," married his old and intimate artist friend, Rudolf Gunther.[1] His eightieth birthday (25 October) brought a shoal of affectionate letters—lines of deeply felt brotherly greeting from the friend of sixty-three years, Estlin Carpenter, two months his senior, and young devotion from Dutch and English grand-

[1] "I always felt as if I were their son," he said, "now I really am."

children. His granddaughter Emily Kuenen came for a visit. It was a great joy to him, too, and to the scholar and critic not less than to the father, to receive, early in October, his eldest son's book on Blake. "'*Exegi monumentum,*' you can say," he wrote to him (2 October, 1924), "beyond any that I have ever experienced, or am likely to do." He recognized in his son's book his own ideal of scholarship. "I think you know how your Blake work stands as a solid piece of work to me, responsible and craftsmanlike, in which vision is not allowed to grant dispensations for neglect of spade work. It has been and will be a sure refuge and support to me when inclined (as I have been and shall be!) to criticize or challenge you in other branches of intellectual activity."

For Blake's own work Wicksteed felt rather wonder than whole-hearted admiration. His essay "On Art and Artists" he read "with immense amusement," and desired to hear his son's exposition, and Rudolf's comments. (To Joseph Wicksteed, August 1925.) But for Blake's Dante illustrations his admiration was unbounded.

With another son, too, whose name has since become widely known, Wicksteed had cheering intercourse this autumn. Mr. Alexander Wicksteed, after some years of stress, was established as English teacher in the University of Moscow. His letters home freely recorded his impressions of, and experiences under, Soviet government, and like those subsequently collected in his book, *Life under the Soviet,* by no means tallied with the views current in England that "Red Letter" autumn. "All that you write greatly interests us," wrote his father, "but we are in doubt where you are.

You date from Moscow, but we know all about that, and it is quite evident that that is not the place or country you are living in."

Time and strength remained, too, after the three hours' morning work at Aristotle was finished, for other relaxations of the strenuous kind he loved—long cycle rides among the old-world villages of Berkshire with Emily Kuenen, or the reading aloud of classics old and new. And very apropos, this same October, came Mr. Shaw's *Saint Joan*, a presentation copy from his quondam pupil in economics, still a loyal friend. It was promptly read to the assembled party.

The Wordsworthian in Wicksteed was never far off, and a call to the mountains, in the form of a pressing invitation from his cousins, Mr. and Mrs. Arnold Lupton, to go with them, that summer, to Switzerland, received a prompt assent. All three were over seventy, but it was to be a cycling tour, and Wicksteed was not to be denied the company of his bicycle, though it had lain by for six years. But he satisfied himself by repeated trials that he could still handle it. The Alpine rides of a man of eighty who had a few years before lain prostrate, became something of a legend in the wide circle of his acquaintance. But Wicksteed knew what he could do; the strength which had brought him to fourscore years, though he had undergone sorrow and labour, remained almost unabated, and like a good economist he meant to use it to the full while it was his. He could even write to a friend (Miss Hargrove): "Physically I have been, to my own great puzzlement, growing younger these last six years. I never *expect* to go anywhere again, but sometimes I *do* go all the same." Of bravado he was entirely incapable, but he no doubt enjoyed the amazement of Swiss landlords, when they discovered the age of the guest who had descended from his cycle at their door; and the discomfiture of one of them who pointed out to monsieur the obvious error in the entry of the date of his birth. The letters he wrote almost daily to his daughter at home are full of vivacity. And the following summer (1925) saw the cycle-tour of 1924 repeated, with a year added to the fourscore, but no apparent decline in the strength. And what hardened scorcher could better the casual nonchalance with which this youth of eighty-one jots down his proposed route to a son-in-law: "I leave home to-morrow morning and London on Sunday morning to bicycle to Dover, cross to France and then go I don't know where. . . ." It proved to be South Germany. A month later, at the end of July, he and his friends returned without accident. He wrote to his correspondent from Rothenburg (after comparing its museum, severely, with those of Nuremburg and Naples, "the greatest that I know"): "I don't know when I shall be able to write to you again; but my adventures on the wheel, such as they have been, are now closed. I wonder whether I shall ever have any more. I have not lost the power of appreciating them, but I think I have lost the impulse to seek them." [1] Nearly two years remained, and one more summer of intact health, before the end. But that autumn his son-in-law, a very dear and cherished friend, himself passed away.

[1] To his son-in-law, Vice-Chancellor Roger Lawrence, 27 July, 1925. Mr. Lawrence was confined to bed by the disease from which he never recovered. The letters were written daily during the tour for his amusement.

IV

But other adventures than those of travel were to fill this wonderful "Indian summer," and we must retrace our steps a few years to follow their course continuously. He was not the man to be cheated by illusive hopes. He was like the shrewd annuitant who, having outlived his "expectation of life," instead of playing fast and loose with his added income because it was unforeseen, lays it out with the severer economy because he cannot tell how long it will continue to accrue. He knew that he must prepare to say his last word on the matters of deepest concern to him, and he gathered his powers to say it while they were still his. Some older tasks had, in the first place, to be completed. In 1920 the Hibbert Lectures of 1916, on the "Reactions between Dogma and Philosophy," at length appeared, enriched with justifying citations, of almost equal length, from the text of Aquinas and Aristotle. In the same year he contributed to the appendix of Vol. II of the new edition of the *Dictionary of Political Economy* his final statement of "the pure theory of Economics."

But two tasks, of yet more powerful appeal than these, were to engage the years of his recovered strength. The catastrophic riot of human unreason in the war added to the motives which drew him to the two lodestars of his faith in the Spirit of Man, Dante and Aristotle. In January 1921 he was busy with a final essay on Dante; it was published in the following year by the Manchester University Press. The *From Vita Nuova to Paradiso* is no mere summary of what he had said before. He was trying, in this essay, he wrote to a fellow-Dantist, "to bring all Dante's work into relation with the 'Visio Dei' at the end of the *Paradiso*."[1] And this meant a presentation, in many respects new, of the works, especially the *Convivio* and the *Monarchia*, which, as ordinarily understood, were very indirectly thus related. This attempt to reorganize the evolution of Dante's work Wicksteed regarded as his principal contribution to Dante scholarship.[2]

This book was Wicksteed's last published word on Dante. His edition of the *Physics* of Aristotle, on the other hand, was to occupy all his remaining years, and to offer the final challenge to his failing powers and his indomitable will. But the work had a more immediate motive. He was impelled by a conviction of the vital importance of the *Physics* for contemporary thought. "I believe it will be the bit of work most likely to affect thought that I have ever done," he wrote in November 1924, to Miss Knappert, still hoping to complete it "if I live a year or two longer." It was an inspiring and a sustaining purpose, for one living in the presence of the eternities of thought. Like the imperishable creations of music and poetry Aristotle afforded a refuge and a stronghold from which the vicissitudes of politics and other transient events could be seen in their just proportion. "Is not it a comfort to reflect," he wrote after the Liberal *débâcle* of the "Red Letter" election, "that the late election will not affect the symphonies? To know that the Ninth Symphony is *there* in the nature of things means immeasurably more to me than the hope of hearing it." So he went out little and gave himself up to Aristotle.

[1] To J. Lloyd Thomas, January 1921.
[2] To E. G. Gardner, 7 October, 1923.

He was still hoping, then, at the date of this letter (November 1924) to complete the translation and commentary in "a year or two." He lived, in fact, more than two years longer. And he was cheered and fortified in the following year by the acceptance of his edition for the Loeb series of translations. And until the summer of 1926 he held on his way with vigour and spirits apparently little abated, and able to work some three hours a day at the book. In June of that summer a young visitor, brother of one of his most devoted friends, sent his sister this vivid account of a day at Childrey, which he then saw for the first time: "I hardly know what to say of the visit. The atmosphere that pervades the place is indescribable. One stays in it quietly given up to veneration, mostly mute, while Dr. Wicksteed talks, and one comes away pervaded by it, humbly grateful and rather awed as from the experience of something that transcends the life of every day and is for all time. Last night he read to us, beginning with some selections from forgotten eighteenth-century dramatists—very good fun; and then the whole of Gilbert Murray's translation of *Alcestis*. In the afternoon he walked out with me about four miles in the rain—it rained all day—talking hard and going just about as fast, if not faster, than I should go when off to catch a train. We then came in and I sat down to a reading of Plautus, joining in with a Wantage Grammar School boy who attends for tuition that afternoon. Dr. Wicksteed works at Aristotle in the morning, and one gets a good deal of Aristotle at meal-times, which last a goodish while, particularly breakfast, but at breakfast politics came up with the arrival of the post and the *Manchester Guardian*. . . .

In the evening we all went in to Wantage to a League of Nations meeting. Dr. Wicksteed moved a vote of thanks, saying to perfection and patently to every one all that the lecturer had tried to say in a long and complicated paper."

A month later (2 July), Wicksteed could write to his third son [1]): "I go on pegging at my Aristotle, and am in fuller spirits about it than I have ever been before . . . I think I may now fairly say that I mean to put it through, which will be very wonderful indeed."

V

But the beginning of the end was at hand. A few months later a rapid failure of physical power made the handling of heavy folios impossible. No ordinary secretarial help would have availed to deal, in addition, with the technicalities of Greek texts and Latin commentaries. But the situation was saved by the intervention of the granddaughter already mentioned, who suspended her own studies to help his; devotion the more prized because her other grandfather was his friend and master of fifty years before, Abraham Kuenen. With her help Wicksteed continued to work till within ten days of the end. Miss Wicksteed described to a friend this co-operation (recalling Romola and her father) [2] of the young scholar with the old. "Father is lying on the sofa in the window, in the sun, with a big volume of Aristotle on the reading-desk before him, and Emily by his side reading

[1] Mr. Samuel Wicksteed, of Edinburgh.

[2] Notwithstanding that Wicksteed himself strongly disliked George Eliot's Florentine novel and its heroine.

the original and then his translation aloud to him. It is a beautiful sight, and more beautiful still to see the way she helps him and smooths out the difficulties." It was only the muscles and nerves that were crippled, the mind remained as clear, the will as fiercely vehement, as ever, and in the hours when he could not work at the translation or commentary he found unfailing delight in his familiar classical poets.

In February, his son "Sam," who had not seen him for some weeks, came from Edinburgh. He tells how he entered his father's room fearing that he should find a wreck. He found "the body indeed twisted, but by no means disabled, and his mind perfectly clear. He would fall asleep, indeed, in the midst of a talk, but wake, a minute later, and resume the conversation where it left off, sometimes with the remark that he had 'heard the other man snoring.'"

A week before the end graver symptoms set in. An obstruction in his throat impeded breathing and prevented his taking solid food, and he believed that his life would end by choking. His eldest son arrived from London, and Mr. Francis Cornford, who had relieved Wicksteed's anxiety by undertaking, together with an older friend, Mr. Saunders of Hull, the editorial charge of his book, from Cambridge. "He greeted me on my arrival," writes the former, "with radiant delight at having completed an exceptionally good day's work, that had taken him to within a few pages of the end of that part . . . which he still hoped to complete." Mr. Cornford, who arrived the same evening, stayed in the house till the eve of his death. "He wished to welcome me," he writes, "and I was taken up to his room. He was propped up in bed. The shawl was turned back from his paralysed arms in order that I might take his hand, which he could still move. The white hair was combed back from his forehead. His face had the transparent whiteness of a dying man. He welcomed me in the most generous words. But neither the face, though it grew daily more beautiful, nor the words, had any suggestion of mildness. The clear-cut profile, with the fine straight nose and keen eyes, often reminded me rather of a hawk ready to pounce on the least mouse of false sentiment, or flattery, or humouring, such as most people show to the sick and dying.'' It was the face of a man entirely fearless in conflict with Death himself, and holding the phantom at arm's length until he was assured that his work was done: holding it, too, with full mastery, as if his mind were independent of the body, and could do with it what he would. In his presence I felt none of the embarrassment or distress one associates with a visit to a dying man.''

Each day he dictated to Mr. Cornford for an hour or two, speaking at first as fast as the pencil could travel, then with growing difficulty, often syllable by syllable, but always with a mind entirely clear. Sometimes he would forget Aristotle, deliver dicta on Catullus or idioms of medieval Latinity, beg his hearer to re-read the *Politicus* of Plato, or to study the principle of a new device in fire-tongs. His manner was often abrupt, even fierce, as if the fountains of his native kindliness had to be sternly suppressed, as not now in season. He would sometimes call for ''that man Cornford.'' ''Are you happy?'' he asked a young maid who had come into his room, and then, when she lingered, dismissing her with a rough, kindly ''get along with you." When he was to be helped to a new position he gave directions for every motion with imperious particularity, not because he feared discomfort, but because everything had to be exactly right.

And the scholar's passion could still not merely master but, as it seemed, efface the body of the paralysed veteran. The day but one before his death (16 March), in the afternoon, he said to his daughter, "Rebecca, help me to stand up. There's going to be a surprise for you: I'm going downstairs." And he walked and climbed down, still sustained, it seemed, rather by his own will than by the arms thrown round him. "He seemed to enjoy," said his eldest son, "seeing what his body could still do." As his weakness grew he seemed to be the more possessed by an exultation which glorified all about him. There was "just one more bit of the Aristotle" that he wanted to do with Emily. "If I cannot do it, it will not impair the brightness of this day; if I can, it will add lustre. Praise God! Praise God!" he cried again and again.

That evening the exultation began to efface for him the hard limits of actuality. The book was finished, and that imaginary fulfilment blended itself with another, yet more sacred and more dear. "At nine-thirty he sent for me. He was lying in bed, hardly able to speak. He said, 'I have finished my book, and this day on which it is done purports to be our diamond wedding-day. *Gloria Deo, nunc dimittis,* according to Thy word, amen.' But the indomitable vitality surged up against this. 'It does not follow,' he immediately added, 'that I shall die. I may have many jolly larks with Cornford yet. But I am set free, and I shall go when I want to.' Then he sank into sleep."

The following morning, about daybreak, Mr. Cornford heard him, from his own room below, crying out "Hur-rah, hur-rah," again and again; he seemed to be greeting the sunrise.

In the evening of the following day (Friday, 18 March), he died, only a long breath followed by silence marked the moment of his death.

It was a farewell to life in which the Stoic as well as the Christian would have found himself. That long labour, crippled and in pain, with Aristotle, brings Browning's Old Grammarian inevitably to our lips:

> So, with the throttling hands of Death at strife,
> Ground he at grammar.

—lifted above the torment of the moment by a like clear vision of the things that endure, and driven on by a like "sacred thirst." The passion for spiritual realities which had informed all his work still burnt within him when the end was at hand. All thought or concern for what might follow death, as he wrote to his old friend Gilbert Murray, he dismissed. Yet, to some who saw him in those last weeks, he seemed to be invested with the sanctity which is not the appanage of Christian faith alone. "I saw him for the last time a fortnight before his death," wrote an intimate friend of thirty years whose religious faith was not his but who held that "to know him intimately was inevitably to become his disciple." "He was dying as he had lived . . . and I came away with the conviction that I had been in communion with a saint." [1] Yes, a saint; who did indeed die as he had lived; not, it may be, "greeting the Unseen with a cheer," but hailing with an old man's quavering

[1] Edmund Gardner, in *University College Magazine*, 1927.

"Hurrah! Hurrah!" as his last dawn broke, the Eternities that are revealed in Time.

The funeral service was in the little Wesleyan chapel at Childrey, which the whole village, and the rector, attended. The rector conducted the service at the graveside, and later in the day held a special memorial service in the church, assisted by two of his colleagues who had been friends of Wicksteed. In addition, two memorial services were held elsewhere. One of these, in London, was a Catholic service held at the instance of his friend, Edmund Gardner. At the other, Dr. L. P. Jacks spoke noble words of heartening and consolation in Manchester College chapel. Estlin Carpenter, himself frail and bowed with illness, and in two months more to follow his friend, listened to the service. It was to be his last.

Philip Wicksteed was laid beside his wife, in the village churchyard. The coffin was carried shoulder high by relays of his village friends from the house to the chapel, and thence to the churchyard gate, where it was taken up by his sons and grandsons who carried it through the church to the grave, while the rector read the Fifteenth Psalm: "Lord, who shall dwell in thy tabernacle; or who shall rest upon thy holy hill? . . ."

Both graves were entirely covered with flowers: the cross given by the villagers was laid on the grave of the wife, "because," someone explained, "we thought he 'd like it." At nightfall, the muffled peal "rang him out over the fields and downs" as it had done his wife three years before. "He was always our friend," wrote one of the bell-ringers to his daughter, asking to be allowed to keep a book he had lent.

Philip Wicksteed, *c.* 1917

INTER-CHAPTER II

INNER SYNTHESIS

BEFORE entering, in the ensuing chapters, upon a closer examination of Wicksteed's work, it is necessary to face a question which at once presents itself to any one who reads a catalogue of his books. How were the widely severed provinces of study which engaged him, and in at least two of which he was eminent, related in his mind? How exactly did it happen that the interpreter of Dante was also a notable economist, the explorer of Aristotle and Aquinas an exponent of Ibsen and of the prophets of Israel? No one will now suggest that Wicksteed was an eclectic sciolist, dabbling in a number of studies at the beck of a versatile and curious taste. Still less, that he was a dexterous educational caterer, supplying his tasty pabulum according to the demand of the Extension public. He justly resented a reviewer's patronizing compliment to one "favourably known as a popularizer of Dante." Nor did Mr. Bernard Shaw take his old friend and antagonist's measure quite accurately when he described economics as his hobby and Dante as his job. None of these labours was taken up as a "relief" while he rested for another. An inner nexus held, for him, all those studies together. Each, in its proper context, became a channel of his deepest convictions. But was there not, at least, some incoherence, some inner struggle, some conflict of mind and outlook? Did he really drive his many-horsed chariot with the serene security of Plato's *Nous*, and have merely the waywardness of one or other of his steeds to overcome? More apt, surely, in his case, is the less dignified image of the circus-rider, who drives his three horses with the the same successful control as one.

Wicksteed was fond of saying that in any group of men, however unlike—St. Francis, an English farmer, an African negro, Michelangelo, Richard III—there is always one thing which you can predicate of them all at any given time—within a few hours, each has had a meal. Even the soul of St. Francis, in other words, had an economic basis. Wicksteed was saved by his own abounding endowment both in physique and in spirit, from the perversions to which such a dictum might point. A hearty eater, a mighty athlete, no one was ever less inclined to solve life's enigmas by Feuerbach's trivial epigram: *Der Mensch ist, was er iszt.* On the contrary, he was only the more acutely aware of the inner diversity of the different worlds to which humanity has access, because he was himself a privileged citizen of both. He would not have drawn the contrast between the city of man and the city of God with St. Augustine's scorn. The "religion of eternity," for him, spoke more and not less home to the human spirit because it transcended the religion of Time. And one, perhaps the chief, source of his deep and enduring attraction to Aristotle was the union in him of the exaltation of metaphysic and the particularity of natural science.

Wicksteed, then, never confounded these remote realms. He was, on the contrary, acutely alive to their sometimes piquant contrasts, and often used these to point an illustration. In the *Alphabet of Economics*,

St. Francis is introduced to drive home his distinction between economic and real value. St. Francis might indeed be said to have thrown down a challenge to the unborn science of political economy when he took the "Lady Poverty" for his mystic bride, and Wicksteed's doctrine of "Value" only gained added richness because he had entered with spiritual insight into the meaning of saintliness.[1]

But far as Wicksteed was from confusing the appeals of these two regions of life and experience, or even because he was so far from that confusion, it was natural that he should be powerfully drawn to any system of thought which offered a legitimate bridge between them; a synthesis in which religion and science, St. Francis and sociology, both had their legitimate scope and their defined place.

That it appeared to offer such a synthesis was, to many perplexed minds of that day, one of the most impressive features of the philosophy of Auguste Comte. The "Positive" philosophy, expounded by

[1] This sentence will be sufficiently illustrated and justified by the following published reference to one of Wicksteed's "Extension" lectures on St. Francis. The writer had been overwhelmed with grief by the death of his son: "It was in the intimate days in this time of sorrow that I heard Wicksteed give his extraordinary lecture on St. Francis of Assisi. Nothing else in the world was a bit like it. . . . It caught the spirit of the saint and transmitted it without loosing the rare loveliness and perfume of the life. I saw into two souls at once, the soul of Francis and the soul of his lover who was interpreting him. It was an epoch. I found then and there the man who has ever since been one of the major guides of my life in the sphere of love. I should have been a different person if I had not found in Francis the revelation of 'the second mile' and at the same time a transmitter of the love of God. But now I know that nothing has ever carried me back, or up or down into the life of God or done more to open out the infinite meaning of love, than has my visible separation from dear Lowell, for the mystic union has never broken and it can know no end."

RUFUS M. JONES, *The Trail of Life in College.*

a group of very able disciples, had been before the English world, as we have seen, for some twenty years, and Wicksteed himself, as a budding minister, had studied it with feverish curiosity. The five years that had passed since those days at Taunton had enriched his experience both of society and of religion; but his keenest thought and labour had been given to problems of remote Hebraic history, of little relevance to modern issues. His settlement in London brought him at once into the focus of modern issues of every kind, and among them into close personal touch with some of the leaders of Positivism. With Edward Beesly, in particular, his old professor and mentor, he renewed intimacy on more equal terms, and Beesly became one of his closest friends. Positivism still, it is clear, continued to appeal powerfully to the riper mind of the man of thirty, and we have fortunately the means of measuring the nature, the extent, and the limits, of the attraction.

Shortly after his settlement in London occurred an event of importance in the history of Positivism in England, the appearance of the English translation of Comte's *Politique Positive*, that monumental afterthought of the founder of the Positive Philosophy, which had repelled the whole-hearted allegiance of Stuart Mill, and the application of which was to divide his most eminent English disciples into two camps. In the early 'seventies, however, they were still in substantial accord, and the founder of English Positivism, Richard Congreve, with his three chief disciples and associates, John Henry Bridges, Edward Beesly, and Frederic Harrison, had combined in the arduous labour of translation. The first volume, including the *General*

View of Positivism, by Bridges, the most synthetic intellect of the four, was published in the first instance alone. The translator, a busy professional man, had spent ungrudgingly his time and labour, and provided the utmost help to the reader in marginal headings and detailed analytic summaries. Yet the mastery of this massive volume demanded unusual qualities. Comte's writing, abstract and diffuse, disdained all the stylistic attractions common in French prose, and the philosophic reader was put off by the slight and distant recognition of the philosophic past. Few reviewers made any serious attempt to cope with the book, and of these, many misunderstood or mis-stated it, in grave points; in most quarters it was dismissed with cursory and impatient notice.

Philip Wicksteed was one of the few, and his review in the *Inquirer* (22 May, 1875) must be counted one of the most remarkable documents illustrating the nature of the impact of Positivism upon able and candid English minds of Wicksteed's generation.

The opening paragraphs give a lively picture of the impact not of Comte, but of what Comte was popularly supposed to stand for, upon hosts of English minds to which neither of those adjectives would apply. The conflicts he had excited in high quarters had left a wake of excited discussion among the lesser organs of public opinion. Positivism was a "topic of the day," a mysterious subject which educated people wanted to hear about, and the half-educated to affect to understand; a subject dangerous and alluring, inviting cheap refutation, yet always requiring to be refuted again; a philosophy which the philosophers ignored; a body of abstruse science which the scientists scoffed at; an atheistical heresy which had no God, yet claimed to be a new religion. These phenomena of the 'seventies Wicksteed sketches with merited sarcasm. Even the more important figures on either side he criticizes with the frankness of one who had earned by close study the right to criticize. Thus Huxley, then the most authoritative name in English science, whose neat algebraic formula for Positivism ("Catholicism *minus* Christianity") probably harmed it more than many weightier attacks, is convicted of doing injustice to Comte's immense range of secular and scientific learning. And Harriet Martineau, carried into repute as a popularizer of Positivism by Comte's own recommendation of her paraphrase, is convicted of the gross blunders which Wicksteed could least of all pardon in derivative work.

Then, after explaining the scope and purport of the earlier of Comte's two works, the *Philosophie Positive* which both Littré and Mill had accepted, he states his own attitude to it. "In spite of its faults—and I am far from thinking that either friends or foes have pointed out all its defects—this work must ever be regarded as a colossal monument of the human intellect."

But what of the second great work, the *Politique Positive*, the first instalment of which, in English, was before him? Mill and Littré had scornfully rejected it; but Comte himself had no less definitely declared that it was to supersede the *Philosophie*. Wicksteed, with remarkable penetration, insists on the continuity of purpose which underlies their disparity. He saw that Comte's aim had always been not doctrine merely, but practice. "It is clear that Comte never swerved from his conviction that the goal of his philosophy must ever be a Polity,'' and the future work is definitely intimated in the closing volumes of the *Philosophie* itself. What was new was, not the Polity, but the presentment of the organizing power of the "polity" as a "religion." And Wicksteed dwells with admiration on the "treasures of thought and feeling and practical wisdom" scattered through the chapters of the *General View*.

But Wicksteed makes perfectly clear his fundamental divergence from Comte. He did not, like many ministers of religion, repudiate it because it denied Christianity. He found in the "Positive" method itself what he called the fundamental fallacy—the πρῶτον ψεῦδος—of Comte's system, his rejection of the validity of "inner observation," and with it, of all psychology. Comte, attempting to found all conviction upon the "positive" knowledge of science, and to dismiss as illusory the "theological" and "metaphysical" beliefs which had hitherto overlaid it, had wrongly identified this distinction between science and illusion with that between "outer" and "inner" observation. That mistake was the necessary preliminary to his "colossal negations." But this was cutting away the ground, not merely of theology and metaphysics, but of any religion and any ethics; not merely of the faith in God, or in abstract entities, but the faith in love and duty. This fallacy had been present implicitly from the first, but had only gradually become apparent as Comte passed from the "objective" sciences, from mathematics and physics, to sociology and morals. It was thus that both his critics and he himself could mistake for a change of method what was really only the gradual bringing into prominence of a factor which had all along been active but which only became apparent in the elaboration of the "sociology."

At the outset of his career in London, then, Wicksteed regarded Comte's *Positive Polity*, as represented by the *General View*, with a reasoned and unconcealed, if critically qualified, admiration, which everywhere stopped far short of complete acceptance. He saw in it a synthesis, capable of both disciplining and fertilizing the thought of the citizen of our loosely aggregated polities. "A study of the *Polity* would regenerate many of our social and political ideas," and such study would have "enormous value" for us. But the actual scheme of social organization presented by the *Polity* he held to be purely provisional, and much of it he cordially disliked. In any case, immense work in detail would be necessary before the application of sociology to polity could be effected.

The review excited much attention. Bridges, the translator, wrote to him in warm acknowledgment. "It has been so rare, so almost unexampled, to meet with anything but the reverse of common candour and honesty, that your sympathy, even when it takes the form of conscientious opposition, diffuses an influence at once soothing and breezy" (1 June, 1875). To similar effect wrote Edward Beesly. And outside the ranks of professed Positivists, the distinguished lawyer, Sheldon Amos, invited him to a reception at the Temple, in order to "talk over the subject of the review" with him.

Wicksteed himself did not explicitly modify the position assumed in the review. And his own thought and interest moved from the beginning of the 'eighties into regions which the Comtian synthesis might embrace, for which it might provide a frame, but on which it could exert little vitalizing power. The sociology of Comte continued, nevertheless, to be a source from which he sought to enlighten and enrich the pure and noble but somewhat elementary social thinking of his generation, and to relieve the excessive emphasis of its theological creed.[1]

There is no reason to suppose that Wicksteed ever came near to acceptance, as a whole, of the Positivist faith; it encountered some irreconcilable antagonisms in the very stuff of his mind. But certain aspects of it supported and encouraged mental appetencies in him which were imperfectly satisfied either by the Unitarianism that it was his office to expound, or by the Unitarian community which sat, somewhat restively, at his feet.

For Positivism was a way of life; a religion at least in moulding and guiding power; not merely linked with, but founded on, and nourished by, a deep, comprehensive, and instructed, social sense. No English denomination then offered any real parallel, and those which were most securely and justly conscious of intellectual enlightenment often fell further short of it than the adherents of more emotional and intuitive faiths. But even the incomparable services of the Evangelicals and the Friends to humanity rested upon very rudimentary types of social philosophy; while the

[1] After one of his Sunday evening addresses, in the 'eighties, an acquaintance—member of a well-known Unitarian family, remarked to him that the sermon seemed to show much interest in Positivism. Wicksteed warmly admitted it. "And what more wholesome influence would you wish?" The visitor agreed, having become, he said, a Positivist himself. Wicksteed appeared a little to regret the heartiness of his agreement.

early Puritans had with unconscious *naïveté* hitched their unworldly religion to the star of a solid and successful promotion of capitalism;[1] while Unitarianism had never completely disengaged itself from that preoccupation with a highly abstract theological dogma which its infelicitous name suggests. Social service enlisted workers in the Unitarian churches as nobly devoted as in any Christian church whatever; and no form of religious ministry offered more signal examples of it than theirs. Nevertheless, Unitarianism not only had not, as such, a social philosophy, but philosophic thinking about society in any form was a study not easily accommodated to its individualistic habits of mind. The large social intelligence of Wicksteed's friend, Estlin Carpenter, insensibly widened these horizons wherever he worked and taught; and the organized social passion which he found in the religious minds of India both attracted and enriched his own. In Wicksteed, the organized social thinking of Positivism played an analogous part. For his vehement nature, the call of social thinking to the religious mind was not an appeal only, but a challenge, and he took up the challenge with characteristic vigour. In response to his proposal, a course of lectures on sociology was delivered by him in Manchester College in the session 1888–9. The opening lecture, on "The Place of Sociology in Theological Studies,"[2] is a powerful plea for the recognition of these studies as an integral factor in the training of the student, in particular of the Unitarian student, of theology. The use of the

[1] The close nexus of Puritanism with the growth of capitalism has been traced by Ernst Troeltsch, and Mr. Tawney's fine essay only qualified his contention.

[2] Printed in Carpenter and Wicksteed *Studies in Theology*, 1903.

term "sociology" would itself point to the prominence of Positivism among the sources of his social thinking. But Comte also contributed to quicken his receptive sensibility to allied sources—to the sociality of Hebrew and of Greek, of Amos and of Aristotle. Yet he owed in a greater degree to Comte that sense of the intimate dependence of the highest developments of the human spirit upon the complex social basis. "The higher development of our humanity rests upon an industrial society. . . . It is only in society that man is human; and it is where society is most concentrated and developed that humanity culminates." Wicksteed well knew, indeed, that the problem of the individual and society is not so simple as that; that society, like religion, may be the organ of the direst cruelty and oppression; and in a splendid image, rare with him, and of which Comte would have been incapable, he compares "society" to the Cross, in the Old English Vision, which "shimmers and changes before our eyes, at once the rood-tree of crucifixion and the throne, on which humanity is martyred and glorified." But if sociology is needful for the student of theology, so no less is religion to the sociologist; and it was precisely here that he expressly invokes the support and authority of Comte, who had, in the ordinary sense of the term, repudiated religion altogether. "Auguste Comte saw far and deep, when he denounced, as materialistic and immoral, the study of industry apart from the general structure and purposes of society, and the isolation of the selfish and gain-seeking impulses of man, and their erection into a self-contained system." [1] This side of Comte's thinking

[1] *u.s.*, p. 297.

was profoundly congenial to Wicksteed, and found much and varied expression in his work. In particular, it led to his powerful advocacy, some three years later, as will be described below, of John Trevor's "Labour Church."

Yet it is clear, as has been said, that if Wicksteed vindicated, with Comte, the need of sociological study, his own sociological conceptions and methods were radically different. The individualism of the English Protestant for whom the Athenian city-state counted more than the empire of Rome, asserted itself against the collectivist mentality of the Latin Catholic. Comte subordinates the individual; his conception of social order is based upon this subordination in "love for others," in reverence for the past, in continuous submission to the purposes of a larger whole. Wicksteed did not undervalue these dispositions as factors in social order. But he was too vividly aware of the urgency of personality, in others as in himself, to accept this as a complete analysis either of actuality or of an ideal; "order" for him was reached through the play of personalities, the give and take of will, even "the higgling of the market," and the self-surrender of Love was not for him, any more than for St. Paul, an abnegation of thought, but a liberation of the higher self from the seductions and inertia of the lower.[1]

The affinities and repulsions thus sketched may perhaps shed some contributory light upon the complex

[1] Wicksteed used characteristically and justly, to insist that St. Paul's great chapter on Love (1 Cor. xiii) ought never to be separated from the preceding account of the various "gifts of the spirit," the talents and accomplishments of men which "Love completes and harmonizes but does not supersede."

of spiritual activities which set in, for Philip Wicksteed, with the early years of his London residence. He was not a system-maker, and the methodic execution of his projects rarely escaped signs of the vehemence of his impulses. Men of smaller powers have offered a parallel such as he never even attempted, to the cosmic thinking of a Spencer, or of Comte. But a book came his way, and its impact, touching the hidden springs, let loose a stream of power unsuspected often by himself before. The young minister had "seen Juliet" when he discovered Kuenen; and his eagerness for the promised volume of Littré had contended with his impatience for the arrival of his first-born. And the effect upon the London preacher, in his thirties and forties, of Dante and Henry George, Stanley Jevons and Ibsen, was even more transforming and even more eventful and sustained. Wicksteed who was to bicycle in Switzerland at eighty, retained, in spiritual things, too, the expansive enterprise and energy of youth.

But we may regard that attraction to the Positive synthesis, and also his definite reserves in relation to it, as foreshadowing the nature of the intellectual currents which thus emerged, the particular course which they now took, and the inner nexus which (to most eyes invisibly) sustained and nourished them all. Comte's magnificent conception of humanity as a Polity, in which science and religion, industry, the State, all had their ordered place and part, remained. But the individualist temper, so richly fed, both by lineage and culture, moulded and created freely the erections which he raised upon this vague ground-plan. He took up the economic aspect of society at the very point—the orthodox English school—which Comte had slighted, and handled it with his sturdy concrete particularity, his zest for the daily business of the home. And his Germanic individualism asserted itself no less in the more imaginative plane of his work. Dante, Ibsen, and Wordsworth became for him and his entranced audiences, not only great poets, but the centres and sources of a veritable religion of humanity; they were neither priests in a hierarchy nor calendar'd saints, but lonely prophet-poets; and whether their loneliness was that of the homeless exile, of the Enemy of the People, or of the inspired Recluse, they uttered their words of catholic and universal significance with lips that had also flamed with the challenge of the seer in the wilderness.

CHAPTER VI

PART I

ECONOMICS AND SOCIOLOGY

Wicksteed's Economic Preparation—Review of Marx—Economic Circle—Nationalization of Land—Labour Church

I

PHILIP WICKSTEED entered the field of economics comparatively late in life, and with the advantages and the disabilities, the privileges and the handicaps, of the highly gifted but (in this field) self-taught man. His education had included no tincture of economic theory, very rarely as yet an item in any college curriculum; his experience no training in business; and his profession had brought him into personal contact only with that discreet and decorous "market" in which the salaries of Unitarian ministers are offered or declined. From the academic and the commercial bias alike Wicksteed was, like Adam Smith, remarkably free.[1] And he had, like his great predecessor, several valuable qualities, rarely found together—a delight in abstract theory, close touch with concrete things, strong common sense, and an overmastering moral sympathy; "and where these meet in a single mind," said a distinguished reviewer of his *Alphabet*, "the man is a born economist." [2] And Wicksteed's moral sympathy was, moreover, of the

[1] Smith was, of course, a professor, but in his time there was no "academic" bias in economics.

[2] Professor H. S. Foxwell, in the *Inquirer*, 11 May, 1889.

kind which enlarges horizons without blurring outlines. It gave him a lively insight into the minds of housewives setting out to shop (he had seen his own mother at it before the weekly expedition from the Hafod farm to Denbigh); but it saved him from the unreal abstraction of the Benthamite "economic man." It gave him a profound feeling for the "unprivileged producer," whose interest he came to hold should be the guiding principle of all social reform; but it did not prevent his looking coldly on all vague schemes of benevolence which helped people otherwise than by helping them to help themselves; or regarding with acute satisfaction original methods of self-help, such as that little club of Dukinfield mill-hands, described above.

Wicksteed entered the field of economic science at a moment when its very foundations were in dispute. The whole "orthodox" theory of political economy was being challenged from many different quarters. Socialists impugned the validity of a "bourgeois" science; historians avenged upon it Bentham's, Ricardo's, and even Mill's open neglect of history; Jevons claimed to have riddled it by his differential curves; Comte condemned it as a pseudo-science, illegitimately isolated from what he was the first to call sociology. Mill himself had largely revised and deepened the earlier Benthamite teaching; and Arnold Toynbee, in the 'seventies, could brand Ricardo's theory as "a declared imposture." Abroad, the more philosophical and instructed Socialists of Germany were beginning to force their alien ideas upon the notice of her imperialist aristocracy; to Bismarck they were now a foe to be crushed, now a useful pawn in the game. The great book of Marx, with its Hegelian heritage of historic vision and specious fallacy, was slowly becoming known; in 1878 Bismarck himself spoke with deep respect of the brilliant Lassalle; and the tradition of philosophy and erudition impressed upon German socialism by these two men of genius remained.

Meantime, a not less radical attack upon the prevailing social order was made, in England, from a very different quarter, under the impulse of very different ideas, by a very different type of man. In 1879, a plain, straight-thinking American, Henry George, published his recipe for curing the economic ills of civilization, *Progress and Poverty*. It was Henry George's book which first arrested Philip Wicksteed's attention, and drew his eager and enterprising intelligence to the economic problem, and the economic solutions of many problems not primarily economic, which were to be a chief occupation of his mature mind.

That a book so crude, with all its trenchant power, as *Progress and Poverty*, should have had this effect is not difficult to understand. Wicksteed's deepest interest in economic facts sprang from their relation, not as with Adam Smith, to the "wealth," or even to the "welfare" of nations, but to the welfare of the individual citizen. The Benthamite economics had, like the Benthamite jurisprudence, been extraordinarily successful; and England, measured by the standards of that school, had become, in the 'fifties and 'sixties, the most prosperous nation in Europe. The glaring inequalities in the distribution of that prosperity were for the Benthamite (or "classical") economist its inevitable accompaniments; accompaniments scarcely regrettable, since poverty stimulated thrift and industry, and thus led automatically to the creation of wealth. Labour was a commodity which the capitalist bought and the worker sold, at the market price, and if either was dissatisfied with the price to which they agreed, they had as little ground as the buyer or seller of any other commodity to complain. That the agreement was often not a free contract was indeed frankly admitted, but rather as an incidental defect in the working of the mechanism than as an integral feature of the system. It was this which incited Marx to that analysis of the relation of Capital and Labour which became for better or worse the basis of his doctrine.[1] Marxism was thus a blend of profound truth and paradox; for while he insisted that labour is not a commodity, all responsibility for the production of which ceases when it is paid for, and when he, on the other hand, ascribed to labour, exclusively, the creation of value, Marx insisted that the glaring inequalities in the distribution of wealth were an ineradicable consequence of the capitalist system. But while Wicksteed then, as always, rejected with trenchant emphasis, in common with English economists in general, the specific doctrines of Marx (in particular the notorious "surplus value" doctrine), the inequality in the distribution of wealth was the fundamental spring of Wicksteed's thinking.

He later expressed his sympathy with the socialist ideal of a society organized in the interest of the unprivileged, while wholly repudiating their economic methods of attempting to bring it about. This at once distinguishes him from all propounders of short cuts to "equality," while it explains the interest

[1] Cf. the Master of Balliol's essay *Karl Marx's Labour and Capital* (1925).

excited in him by the ideas of George, whatever he thought of his methods. It also explains the attraction exercised upon him during the last months of Arnold Toynbee's short life, by one who, if any in that day, deserved the name of the apostle of the unprivileged.

Of his friendship with Toynbee, prematurely closed by Toynbee's death early in 1883, the chief memorial is Wicksteed's articles on Toynbee's lectures, and his tribute after Toynbee's death in the *Inquirer*. Wicksteed and Toynbee were spiritually akin, in so far as both took poverty seriously; for both, this was the central problem of economics. Their attitude towards it was, no doubt, radically different; Toynbee was aristocratic, fastidious; Wicksteed robustly human and passionately sanguine. In Toynbee, then, as a trained economist, Wicksteed sought an ally. At his instance Toynbee delivered the two lectures upon George, which were shortly followed by his lamented death. But both stood apart alike in temper and in method from the dominant economists, whether of the academic or of the business world. To both these classes George and his book were, in general, anathema, and both mercilessly exposed the blunders of his untrained intelligence. Toynbee and Wicksteed were no less acutely alive to his limitations, but they agreed in doing honour to the bold, constructive essay of an honest and generous mind.

But the direction in which Wicksteed finally turned in his search for a method of handling the inequality problem was determined by an influence with which neither Toynbee nor George had anything to do. In 1871 William Stanley Jevons, professor in the Owens

College (the nucleus of the present University of Manchester), published his *Theory of Political Economy,* a fuller statement of a discovery announced without attracting notice to the British Association some years before. His analysis of the phenomena of exchange, which by aid of the conception of "final," "limiting," or, as they are now called "marginal" values, eliminates the old antithesis between "Value in Exchange" and "Value in Use," has long since been absorbed into the structure of accepted economic theory. Wicksteed seized upon it with the eagerness of one in whom the joys of the mathematician were as innate as the ideals of the sociologist, and who had found a scientific nexus between them.[1] Jevons was, for Wicksteed, the Epicurus of Economics, and he celebrates him with an exaltation which recalls the rapture of the Lucretian *Primum Graius homo*. The doctrine of "marginal utility" became in Wicksteed's hands, in fact, much more than an explanation of the economic phenomena of exchange. He found in it the key, not only to a healthy economic order, but to a healthy mentality and a healthy way of life. It enabled him to reject, on reasoned grounds, both many Utopian expectations and many pessimistic fears; to resist revolutionary schemes of social reconstruction, yet to reject equally the cruel determinism in dealing with Labour which had consorted so ill, in the Benthamite school, with its canon of Free Trade. Social reform was thus scientifically justified. There was, for Wicksteed, no hiatus between the daily operations of the housekeeper, and

[1] He supplemented his own mathematical training for the purpose by taking lessons in differential analysis from the mathematical tutor at University College, John Bridge.

the economic policy of the State. National welfare was resolvable into a right use of the resources which the nation, the *polis*, commands.

II

Philip Wicksteed appears to have been actually the first to apply the Jevonian calculus to the burning controversy between the advocates and the enemies of Socialism which agitated England in the early 'eighties.[1] In the industrial world access to Jevons was barred in general by his mathematics. Mill's classical book on Liberty was the bible of the individualists. To meet this influence the abler socialists were beginning to call in a new and formidable ally, the German economist, Karl Marx. Not every worker could grapple with the complex periods and abstruse arguments of *Das Kapital*; but a few, like Mr. G. B. Shaw, then becoming active in London Socialist circles, were deeply impressed by the "literary power and overwhelming documentation" of a book far removed in its Hegelian range of thought from all English economic tradition. *Das Kapital* was not yet the "bible" of Socialism; but it was rapidly becoming its final court of appeal.

It was not, however, as a partisan but to expose a fundamental fallacy in it that Wicksteed, in the autumn of 1884, published a powerful criticism of it in the columns of the Socialist journal *To-day*. "I have long wished to lay before the disciples of Karl Marx certain theoretical objections to the more abstract portions of *Das Kapital* which suggested themselves to me on my

[1] Pease, *History of the Fabian Society*, Appendix by G. B. Shaw.

first reading of that great work, and which a patient and repeated perusal of it have failed to remove." [1] How imperfectly even the most capable English Socialists of that day had mastered the teaching and ideas of Marx was apparent in the defence put up, in reply to Wicksteed's challenge, by the Fabian "intellectuals."

Wicksteed sets forth at the outset Marx's now well-known theory of "surplus value." Marx had taken over from the English economists the Ricardian doctrine that "value" is constituted by labour, and then turned it against them by arguing that the capitalist who sells his commodities at a price determined by this value, has obtained the labour which produced it at the cost of maintaining it; and derives his "unearned" profit by pocketing the difference. Wicksteed does not attack all the propositions which constitute this theory. "Against the doctrine that . . . normally wares are bought and sold at their values I have nothing to urge." He concentrates his attack upon the point, that the (exchange) value of all commodities, including "labour-force" is constituted by the amount of labour required to produce them. He points out that Marx's admission that "labour" is not to count, for the purpose of this doctrine, unless it be "useful," surrenders his case. That the Marxian doctrine was popularly current among the Socialists of 1884 may be gathered from the argument of a supposed objector introduced by Wicksteed at this point. Instead of directly meeting it, he calls in at once the theory which had, for himself, definitely and finally decided the matter. "It is the complete and definitive solution of the problem thus presented which will immortalize the name of Stanley

[1] *To-day*, October 1884, p. 388. (See Appendix.)

Jevons"; and all that he here attempts, he adds, is to apply to it "the potent instrument of investigation which he has placed in our hands." He proceeds to explain in detail the application of the laws of "indifference" (commonly known as diminishing returns) and "marginal utility"; to demonstrate that exchange value is not a function of the labour expended on producing the article sold. This suffices for his purpose. But at the close of his review Wicksteed recognizes, as few of its bourgeois critics then did, that *Das Kapital* does not stand or fall with the theory of surplus value. "In the latter part of the published volume Marx appears to me to have made contributions of extreme importance to the solution of the great problem, though I cannot see that they stand in any logical connexion with the abstract reasoning of the early chapters."

Wicksteed's criticism demanded a reply; but qualified vindicators of Marx were not easy to find. Mr. Shaw, appealed to as an enthusiastic Marxian, sent a brief reply, which he has himself described as "not bad for a fake." It is a mixture of plausible argument, brilliant fencing, and ingenuous admissions. He regrets that he can put forward only a "counterblast" to Wicksteed, not a thorough analytic discussion: and while canvassing, acutely and amusingly enough, Wicksteed's illustrations of the working of the economic phenomena in question, he disclaims any adequate competence either in economics or in mathematics for dealing with the Jevonian calculus on which Wicksteed rested his refutation of Marx. Of mathematical methods he even affects complete distrust, and his future biographer may like to be referred to his story of a plausible schoolfellow who had proved "by strict mathematical method" that 2 equals 1, as the original source of this scepticism.[1]

Wicksteed's rejoinder was brief but, under courteous forms, unsparing, and as Mr. Shaw later acknowledged, final. He refers at the close to the confirmation afforded, since his criticism of Marx, by Carruthers's book, *The Industrial Mechanism of a Socialist Society*, where he shows that in such a society prices may be apportioned to labour cost, but only in so far as these prices correspond with the "final utility" of the commodities in question.

III

The controversy thus carried on in the columns of *To-day* excited interest by no means confined to the economists and the business world. The antagonists were unequally equipped for it; Wicksteed carried more powerful weapons and commanded larger resources of thought and knowledge, for which Shaw's agility of intellect did not make him an equal match. But his concern for the bettering of economic conditions was genuine and deep-seated, as was also his relish for discussion and debate. He was a Fabian Socialist; no debate on problems of the "dismal" science was ever "dismal" when he was there. And he presently found occasion for the exercise of these qualities in a society, at once study-circle and intellectual arena, where the dominant figure was his antagonist in the columns of *To-day*, soon to become an honoured friend.

The initial impetus to the formation of this society was derived, not from the still recondite doctrines of

[1] See Appendix.

Karl Marx, but from the more elementary revolutionary proposals of Henry George, in the early 'eighties the most powerful solvent of comfortable bourgeois complacency which the popular mind of English-speaking countries underwent.

English nonconformity opposed on the whole a more stubborn resistance to socialism in any form, than the Anglican church. And even the Unitarians, who were leading the way in accepting the revolutionary discoveries of Colenso and Kuenen in biblical history, looked no less askance than their theologically more orthodox brethren at ideas which threatened the capitalistic structure of society; for capitalism was deeply engrained in the Puritan tradition, and this part of their common heritage proved more enduring than either its theology or its asceticism. Yet here, too, many of the bolder spirits and of the younger men were deeply stirred, and sharp discords arose between ministers and their congregations. At Little Portland Street, in particular, Philip Wicksteed found his congregation very imperfectly responsive to the sociological convictions which now began to colour his preaching. Among those who declined to follow him was his most illustrious hearer, his own former teacher, the *coryphæus* of contemporary Unitarianism. For James Martineau, who saw the hope of human salvation in the spiritual uplifting of the individual, distrusted the claims of even the most ideal social reformers. He eventually resigned his membership. But the enemy was busy sowing tares in that quarter of London in those days; for Stopford Brooke, at Bedford Chapel, to whose ministrations he had turned for refuge, presently himself showed symptoms of the same heresies. And among the young men studying under him at Manchester College some keen minds were also discussing the ideas of Henry George. This was of importance, for it is, in fact, to their initiative that we owe the formation of the "Economic Circle" now to be described. They included several men who afterwards became notable as ministers in the Unitarian body, and sometimes in wider fields. Among these was Mr. E. I. Fripp, later minister at Mansfield, and elsewhere, and now widely known to Elizabethan scholars by his researches in the history of Shakespeare and his Stratford *milieu*. Alone, it would seem, among the frequenters of the circle, Mr. Fripp took careful notes, and it has been possible, through his kindness, to give some account of gatherings not without importance in the history of English economics. For the time was astir; and the circle, which eventually included several men then or later distinguished in English economics and public life, became a court where the claims of the orthodox political economy and its modern critics were informally discussed.

The meetings, originally a study-group formed among themselves by the Manchester College men, were from the first conducted by Wicksteed, who had willingly responded to their appeal, requiring them, however, to equip themselves for the purpose with the instrument of mathematical analysis provided by Jevons. The meetings began early in 1884, and were held at the house of Mr. Hodgson Pratt, near Regent's Park. In March, several members attended a lecture given at the Hampstead Liberal Club by Mr. E. K. Blyth. The lecturer was incisively attacked by the ardent Georgians present. Among the hearers was one destined to play a notable part in the circle. This was Mr. Henry R. Beeton, a member of the London Stock Exchange. Mr. Beeton spoke, after the lecture, with emphatic approval of Henry George, and his advocacy was immediately endorsed, no less emphatically, by Philip Wicksteed. After the meeting the two men who had thus discovered each other "fell into each other's arms" (as the family legend describes it); the occasion was, in any case, the beginning of a lifelong friendship. Mr. Beeton began to attend the meetings of the group, and its place of meeting was, in October 1884, transferred to his house in Belsize Square. In this congenial and stimulating atmosphere the circle developed a new vitality and importance. Wicksteed led the discussions, not as a lecturer promulgating ideas, but as an ardent investigator who had now found a unique opportunity of pressing the economic problem home to the core. The circle began to be known. Two London professors of economics, Mr. H. S. Foxwell, of University College, and Mr. F. Y. Edgeworth, of King's, with Mr. Sidney Webb (as he then was), frequently attended and took part, reducing to insignificance, in Mr. Fripp's modest phrase, the students to whose zeal the circle was ultimately due. But Wicksteed's leadership was unchallenged, and this meant the strict application of the Jevonian curves and equations; a preliminary inexorably insisted upon, but which Wicksteed, prodigal as always of his time and strength, generously assisted the less agile to surmount, by a special class for their benefit.

The transfer of the meetings to Mr. Beeton's house nearly coincided in time with the appearance of Wicksteed's notable review of Marx, already noticed.

This arrested the attention, as we know, and challenged the criticism, of the Fabian Socialists, and his antagonist in that controversy, Mr. Bernard Shaw, presented himself, one evening, at the debate, and set upon it, as it was his way to do, the indelible stamp of his impish wit. He was led there, he has told the present writer, by a desire to understand the drift of Wicksteed's "last word in their debate." [1] The scene deserved a record which, thanks to Mr. Fripp, it may here receive. The problem under discussion that evening was the element of choice in value, exchange, and purchase, and was carried on, as usual, with the help of the chalk and the blackboard. "I remember Mr. Shaw's advent somewhat vividly," writes Mr. Fripp. "He stood up with red hair and beard, in a grey suit (most of the company being in evening dress), and chaffed both Wicksteed and the rest of us with an audacious wit, sometimes too pointed to be entirely relished. 'You fellows,' he declared, 'have been talking a great deal about "choice." You would know better what choice is, if, like me, you had every night to "choose" between a bit of fire and a bit of supper before you went to bed.' And as to 'curves,' the 'curves of supply and demand' had much less to do with a man's control of the market, than the curves of his profile. He himself had earned only £100 in the previous twelve months, whereas, with our host's resolute curve of the chin, he would be making £10,000 a year. And he proceeded to illustrate his point, amid the embarrassed laughter of the

[1] In a private letter, January 1930. He tells us that he himself also, as a consequence of the debate in *To-day*, "put myself in Wicksteed's hands, and became a convinced Jevonian."

company, by drawing their own profiles in lively caricature on the blackboard."

These, however, were only preliminary flourishes of the cap and bells; and they did not prevent Wicksteed, then or later, from doing justice to the serious thinking and purpose which Mr. Shaw's coruscations have often served rather to conceal than to illuminate. At these meetings, in any case, where economists so distinguished as Foxwell, Graham Wallas, and others were present, the two *coryphæi* of the discussion were Wicksteed and Shaw; and Mr. Fripp declares that their encounters were the most brilliant he has ever heard. Common ground with both was the policy of redressing the gross inequality in the distribution of wealth by some form of land-nationalization, and both seem to have favoured the project, then widely current, of "buy or tax," as a practicable method of realizing it. This plan could be accepted without inconsistency by men who wholly diverged in their conception of the ideal State. And this line of cleavage continued, as might be expected, to divide the fundamentally individualist Wicksteed from the socialist Shaw. Shaw, in accordance with the Fabian policy, advocated, in Mr. Fripp's words, "a capitalistic state, slowly acquiring and holding all essential industries for the benefit of the whole population, including among the industries a national bank which should employ the national credit in loans at low interest; while Wicksteed looked to the extension of private enterprise, which, without private ownership of land and natural resources, could never create monopolies in goods or exchange, and might be trusted to stimulate energy and invention, without risk to the community, and to its ultimate benefit." In these discussions the theory of "interest" seems to have played incidentally much part. The epigram, supposed to embody the doctrine of usury, that "if you ate your cake slowly enough it would last for ever," "thrown about like a ball at the heads of opponents," may perhaps be ascribed to Mr. Shaw. But as it ignores essential factors in the economic situation, it is not likely to have greatly troubled the serious defenders of interest. A considered account of interest, as the Fabians viewed it, was no doubt given in a paper, by Sidney Webb, of which no record but the title is preserved.

The circle continued to meet until 1888, at least. But the close of Mr. Fripp's studentship, followed by his absence for a year (1886–7) in Germany, and then by his settlement at Mansfield, prevented his attending more than an occasional meeting. During the winter of 1887–8 the artist, A. E. Emslie, a member of the circle, painted his fine portrait of Wicksteed, now in possession of Mrs. Estlin Carpenter. He also made an interesting etching of one of the meetings, which was sent out with the invitations to view the portrait. It represents Wicksteed, standing at his blackboard, erect, dominant, methodical, chalk in his hand, pointing to the converging curves on the board; while twelve of the more habitual members sat in groups before him. The scene is Mr. and Mrs. Beeton's hospitable drawing-room, then in Maresfield Gardens. The host and hostess sit at Wicksteed's right, Edgeworth is making a remark to Shaw, Mr. Fripp and some of his fellow-students are listening. Stopford Brooke, who saw the etching, but was unable to attend the meeting, pronounced the rendering of Wicksteed capital, that of Shaw less successful.

It was at one of the later meetings, in 1888, that Wicksteed read to the circle the last sheets of the book which was to be the first fruit of their meetings, and was shortly afterwards published under the title of *The Alphabet of Economic Science*. It was appropriately dedicated to their warmly sympathetic hosts. And when, thirty years later, his friends were about to remove from Maresfield Gardens, Wicksteed, then slowly recovering from illness, in 1919, wrote to them, gratefully recalling the welcome which "came out to meet us before we had touched the bell," and "the world exquisitely cushioned spiritually and materially which awaited us within." [1]

IV

All Wicksteed's economic writings convey a reminder, however indirect, that he had once been fired by Henry George, that he never ceased to be a disciple of Stanley Jevons, and that before he met with either he had been deeply impressed by the social philosophy of Auguste Comte. Of all the economists of his time he was the most completely free from the Benthamite abstraction, denounced by Comte before Carlyle and Ruskin, of an "economic man." He was more in danger of finding the "common sense" of political economy in considerations which do not obviously belong to political economy at all. But he justly insisted that man in his economic relations could only be understood in the light of the entire context of his social relations. This social

[1] To H. R. Beeton, 3 April, 1919.

context, however, he interpreted with a passionate humanity, which rendered him acutely alive to the inequalities in the distribution of privilege, and indefatigable in the pursuit of means to mitigate them. Finally, in all his systematic handling of economic problems he consistently applied, with brilliant developments of his own, the Jevonian calculus.

These systematic applications, which contain the core of Wicksteed's economic labours, will be handled in the second part of the present chapter. But, as has just been implied, the range of Wicksteed's economic outlook would be imperfectly exhibited if we ignored activities which touched economics only on one side, and politics or religion on the other. Of this kind, with the distinguishing difference indicated, were his deliverance on land-nationalization, and his association with the Labour Church.

Whatever his other assets or handicaps as an economist, Philip Wicksteed brought to the study open eyes and ears, and a mind not curiously seeking problems, but quick to perceive them in all the circumstances of his environment. In the industrial north he had watched the factory clubs at work; in London he had elaborated a theory of value derived from the transactions of the market. But there, too, he had already, as we have seen, in 1884, begun to agitate for land-nationalization. And when, in 1897, he settled for good in the country, the scene of his boyhood, his attention was constantly engaged by the problems of the village, of the country landlord and the farmer, nowhere in England more urgent than in those beautiful home counties, his new abode.

His address on the nationalization of land (1900)

bears the clear mark of this change of environment. He is acutely alive to the abuses of landlordism in town and country alike, but those in the country have been freshly and sharply brought home to him; they lie at his door, they affect the buying and selling, the getting and spending, of his neighbours; and they offered, he thought, more hope of early reform. He can still do honour to the "fervid genius" of Henry George, and he is far too deeply impressed with the social origin of every kind of property to attach any ultimate importance to the argument from possession. But he well knew that every kind of property, including those which the possessor of land, capital, or labour may apply to the creation of wealth, derives much or most of its value from the action of other members of the community; that "the land" which would be communalized or nationalized is the result of long and complex working up by human effort of those original gifts of nature. He was, moreover, preserved from some fallacies of the land-nationalizers by his repudiation of the doctrine of special laws applying to rent. He was far less hopeful of the effect of any change of land-tenure in easing the problem of overcrowding in the towns than in relieving the incubus of landlordism in the country. But even in the towns communal ownership would bring many advantages to the community. And Wicksteed held that communal ownership of land was, as a final condition, both legitimate and practicable. But it was to be brought about gradually, not by any sudden revolution, nor yet in defiance of, or in advance of, the general sense of justice. And the Hebraic passion for righteousness that lay deeper in Wicksteed than his economic theories, if it did not rather lie at their root, flashes out when he presses this point home: Woe to the community whose responsible representatives outrage [its sense of justice]. But his conception of righteousness itself, if Hebraic in intensity and authoritativeness, was in its character psychological and relative; the popular sense of justice must not be outraged, but it could be enlarged and enriched by new elements, until it was ready to condemn what it had once approved. "We may set ourselves to devising measures which will bring about the desired result along the lines of least resistance and will, at the same time, be progressively educating the public mind and enabling it to move with increasing swiftness until our goal is reached."

Wicksteed's handling of land-nationalization, then, reflected the characteristic union in him of fervent social idealism with an acute sense of economic facts. A pamphlet published some years later, *The Social Ideals and the Economic Doctrines of Socialism* (1908), clearly marks the temper of his reforming aims. His attitude on labour and capital was as far as possible from being the balanced *via media* of a "Mr. Facing-Both-Ways," but it might at moments persuade each side that he was its advocate. He accepted capitalism, and even won the approval of the *Morning Post* by a defence of competition as "an immense driving force which we must not waste."

But the man who defended capitalism because it makes for vigorous production was only the more alive to the defects of a system which guarantees secure possession to hosts of individuals irrespective of their value to society. That system he would not forcibly disturb. But this conservatism did not diminish the fervour with which he hailed an attempt to give labour a share in other kinds of value accessible without party conflict or legislation. An original and remarkable example of such attempts has now to be described.

V

There was one form of such privilege to which it might be thought the outcast from all other privileges had direct and easy access, and to which the chosen life-work of Wicksteed himself might appear to point the direct way. Religion had been brought by Jesus precisely to the unprivileged, the poor and needy, the slave, as their supreme consolation and compensation. The Founder of Christianity had not attempted to reorganize society in the interest of the unprivileged, producers or not, but to endow them with a supreme privilege which made every other superfluous or hurtful. The servant was told that spiritual blessings beyond price were within his reach, but he was to "obey his master."

And the Christian churches had accepted this teaching. But they accepted also, and with increasing emphasis, the secular class-inequalities which the Christian religion was to assuage. If they founded religious orders devoted to the cult of Poverty and based upon mendicancy, they claimed divine sanction for a society based, implicitly, upon the cult of privilege. Any sect, which, like the Anabaptists, attempted to enforce the democratic aspects of Christianity, was savagely suppressed. The other-worldliness of

Puritanism had been a chief incentive to strenuous industry in this world, and thus become a principal source of the growth of capitalism and of the glaring inequalities of privilege which that has involved.

Of one of the Christian churches Wicksteed was himself a minister. But he faced the situation squarely. The "primal lie," he declared, that the truly human life can only be secured to the few at the expense of some form of slavery to the many, and that spiritual things can only be enjoyed by those who are secured from the pressure of need, was repudiated by Christianity, as by every religion worthy of the name. But a conception ultimately cognate, of the place of the working-classes in modern society, was deeply engrained in the minds of those who composed the existing churches. "What workman," he asked, "could walk into a middle-class congregation with the consciousness that the underlying assumptions, both in the pew and in the pulpit, as to the proper organization of active industrial life . . . are his own? And if he cannot do that, then in asking him to join in the worship you are not asking him to express and nourish the religious aspects of his own higher life, but to suppress or suspend that life in order that he may join in the devotions of others who cheerfully accept and would in many cases defend the things against which it is his mission to fight." And the immense majority of workmen would have emphatically endorsed this statement. Of no type of Christian congregation, moreover, was it more peculiarly true than of that in which Wicksteed himself was a minister. The middle-class and intellectualist left wing of English Christianity was perhaps least of all inviting to the Socialist worker from the streets. By irony of circumstances, the man who saw this dilemma most clearly and felt it most deeply was placed precisely at one of the points where it was most acute.

Wicksteed, like many of his colleagues, had laboured hard to mitigate its acuteness. His church was the centre of a host of social activities of every kind. And it was the need of help in this extraneous work that brought him into intimate relations with a man who was to discover, what he believed, and what Wicksteed also believed, to be the solution of that dilemma. In 1887 John Trevor entered Manchester College as a student. Trevor had already, at thirty-two, traversed several phases of that "quest for God" which he narrated twenty years later in the remarkable volume so entitled.[1] His mind, hampered by many limitations and disadvantages, was lifted to significance by a spiritual thirst for the divine. There was something in him of the poet, something of the prophet. But that thirst for the divine found in life, and in the world and Nature, only transient moments of satisfaction. Like Browning's Sordello, he seemed to be for ever attempting, in vain, to "fit to the finite his infinity," and he betrayed part of the secret of his failure in the casual remark that "man can only express the infinity of his nature by being everything by turns."[2] But another part of the secret was his absorption in his own thoughts and emotions. For him, it seemed, the world was a place in which God was hidden, and life a period of time to be occupied in looking for him.

It was a notable moment in his "quest" when

[1] *My Quest for God*, London, 1907. [2] Ib., p. 225.

Trevor, by the counsel of the then secretary of the London Ethical Society,[1] applied for admission to Manchester College. Wicksteed was immediately drawn to Trevor, and Trevor to him. Wicksteed saw the touch of the poet and the prophet in him, and entered with the sympathy of experience into the temper of his rebellious discontent. But Trevor, too, saw in Wicksteed's immensely rich and fruitful contact with men and with affairs a corrective to his own self-centred dreams. "My eyes were opened," he said, "to the necessary relation between politics and religion."[2] It is not surprising, then, that Wicksteed presently sought Trevor's help in the work of his church. In 1888 he was appointed assistant-minister, his special province being to "draw more closely together those social activities which had grown up around it." But the effect upon Trevor himself of this more intimate contact with London's mean streets was only to convince him of the "frightful gulf between the churches and the world," and of "the helplessness of the churches in facing the world's problems." It was in this mood that he received, in 1890, a call to the pulpit of the Free Church of Upper Brook Street, Manchester. Here Trevor at first felt, with some reason, that he had the opportunity of his life. For his predecessor, Silas Farrington, a great-souled and pregnant-minded New Englander, who owed more to Wordsworth and Emerson than to the Unitarian tradition, had in effect, though not in form, detached the church from that tradition, and made it the resort both of persons inured to other forms of

[1] Mr. John H. Muirhead, later professor of philosophy at Birmingham.
[2] *My Quest for God*, p. 219.

religious belief, and of men ready to welcome any new religious force, whatever its complexion.

But the freedom of the Brook Street Church did not, after all, help it to bridge that "frightful gulf"; and Trevor was tormented by a sense of his futility as its minister. Many of his congregation admired him the more for the intensity which sent them home (as one of them said), "uncomfortable to their Sunday dinners"; but Trevor, walking to his church through the squalor of the city, asked himself whether they or he ought to eat a Sunday dinner at all. He had said in his first sermon in the church: "We must get outside these four walls." He soon began to feel those four walls "the walls of a grave, and the roof the earth above—with no daisies or lesser-celandines springing in it."

From this *impasse* Trevor was lifted by Philip Wicksteed. In the spring of 1891 he attended the Triennial Conference of Unitarian and other Free Churches in London. He expected little from such a source; but heard, to his surprise, a debate in which his own problem was handled by a great preacher and by a great champion of Labour. Ben Tillett "burst on the conference like a Titan"; Wicksteed was "magnificent," and "both men almost prophesied the Labour Church."[1] He returned home, "frightfully stimulated," though still "blind and miserable." The germinal impulse was given, and a talk with a working-man, who enjoyed Trevor's sermons but could not stand his congregation, sufficed to strike out the idea of a Labour Church. Wicksteed instantly accepted an idea which was, in effect, the keystone of the arch he was himself rearing, and gave it from the

[1] Trevor, *u.s.*, p. 239.

outset the support of his incomparably richer experience, larger culture, and weightier thought. "The Labour Church rested on Wicksteed's broad shoulders as long as I was connected with it," wrote Trevor long afterwards, at the close of his life.[1]

Trevor's "idea" was simply this: Labour, debarred from the churches frequented by the privileged "possessors," and serving as organs of the existing order, should have a church of its own, in which the fundamental aim of the Labour movement, to reorganize society in the interest of the unprivileged producer, if not actively promoted, should be taken for granted; while, at the same time, in the words of one of his oldest supporters, the individual worker would be "led to a truer individualism . . . in the effort to develop the highest capacity of his own soul, and to become a channel for the divine spirit which exists in every man."[2]

The proposal seemed to many people laughable, even a contradiction in terms. Outside the Labour party they said: If Labour wants religion, let it go to church; inside, they said: What has Labour to do with religion? Our business is revolution and propaganda. Don't "accept gifts from the Greeks." But it was not as a solvent for material wants of any kind that Trevor and Wicksteed saw the opportunity and justification of a Labour Church. It was not to be a sort of Christian mission carried on "for working-men, by working-men" in working-class neighbourhoods. It was to create wants rather than to relieve them, to discipline as well as to console. It was to build a

[1] In a letter to the present writer (2 August, 1929). He died a few months later.

[2] H. V. Herford, *A Democratic Religion*, *c.* 1902 (out of print).

spiritual culture upon an organization devised to satisfy material wants, and to animate the builders with the conviction that while the superstructure would be impossible without the basis, the basis would be useless without the superstructure. "What is the Labour Church?" he asked, in a phrase which aptly symbolizes the union of the religious thinker and the economist in his philosophy, of the seer and the athlete in his temperament; "what is the Labour Church, but a recognition that whereas we cannot be either saints or lovers or poets unless we have quite recently had something to eat, yet it is no use having anything to eat unless we are so far at least saints and lovers as to be true men living a human life."

The few paragraphs which Wicksteed (in *What the Labour Church stands for* and elsewhere) devoted to describing the religion of the Labour Church as he conceived it are instinct with the large and energetic spirituality of his own religion. The Labour Church was not an organ attached to, or auxiliary to, the Labour movement; it was the Labour movement itself "in its religious aspect." Man's heritage was not material comfort only, but the uplifted spirit which can hold communion with Nature, Man, and God—the communion which the sublime prophetic lines of the *Recluse* declare shall one day be "a simple produce of the common day." To that heritage, Wicksteed declared, "only a Labour *Church* can lead man; if it is not a Church, the fruits of the Labour movement will turn to ashes in the mouths of its followers."

Wicksteed well understood the hostile suspicions which the new organization was bound to encounter, and the special virulence to which he himself, the minister of a middle-class church, was exposed as their advocate. He had to face the opposite criticisms of his fellow-bourgeois who saw him making religion an organ of revolutionary Labour instead of an instrument for making it piously contented with its lot; and of revolutionary Labour, in whose eyes he was "drawing a red-herring across their path," to divert dangerous social upheaval into innocuous devotion. He knew that it was vital for the Labour Church movement to be, and to be recognized as being, a working-class creation, and himself carefully avoided the position of leader, while holding out generously the helping hand. But *nolo episcopari* is often vainly pleaded, however sincere. Wicksteed had not founded, and would not lead, the Labour Church. But the theory of it inevitably took the stamp of his mind; of his large culture, of his Dante and his Wordsworth; of the synthesis of material and spiritual ideals so organically knit in his thinking.

Manchester, the scene of Trevor's ministry, was thus the birthplace of the Labour Church. Its first meetings were held there, in October 1891. There Trevor founded its organ, the *Labour Prophet*, a periodical now of capital importance for the history of the Labour movement in those days. Wicksteed, then Warden of University Hall, London,[1] gathered a group of his men together, soon after, for discussion. And on 3 February, 1892, he addressed a large Sunday meeting of the "Church" in a Manchester hall. The meeting began with a devotional service, and Wicksteed's address was in effect a sermon—such a sermon as

[1] Of this episode in his career some account is given in Chapter III, iv, above.

he might have delivered at his own church, yet such as only he could have delivered there. The Labour Church was still in the first glow of its inception, and Wicksteed's account of this meeting in the *Manchester Guardian,* a few days later, is the most authentic evidence now available of what the Labour Church in practice meant; and in particular, our chief concern here, of what it meant for Wicksteed. A few sentences must be quoted.

Wicksteed begins by dispelling the easy misconceptions already noticed. "The Labour Church is frankly, even passionately democratic. It contemplates the organization of society in the highest interests of labour as the work of the age. Any one who should look on Mr. Trevor's movement as a means of clipping the lion's claws would be woefully out of his reckoning. But in its very being it is devout and not mutinous. My own doubts on this point, if I had any, were removed last Sunday, when I had the rare privilege of conducting a service for the Labour Church. I was struck at once with the purposeful air with which the six or seven hundred members of my congregation gathered. They were of all classes, but the great bulk I took to be workmen. We had, I think, the most genuine and spontaneous religious service in which I ever engaged. As a matter of fact, the hymns, prayers, solo songs, pieces of music, lesson, and address had all been arranged beforehand, but one felt at the time as if each one came just where and when it did in response to the present want of the eager souls that were drinking in every word and sound. There were none of the traditions, customs, or habits of worship in the dingy, draughty, and not over reputable hall, in the boxes, gallery and pit of which, my congregation was gathered; but *the reality of worship was there*. The hymns were sung with the utmost heartiness, the solo singers and musicians were felt as part of the congregation, not as performers. . . . My lesson was the first canto of Dante's *Divine Comedy*, recited, or rather paraphrased, with interpretative comments. . . . I showed them Dante struggling to gain the Sunlit Hill of good government and *well-regulated life on earth*, thwarted by lust, pride, and greed, and urged by his guide and master, while never relinquishing his hopes of reform, also to seek another way to peace. In the address I led them, with Dante, to seek the permanent conditions of all fruitful reform in a knowledge of the roots of moral good and evil; and when we brought our pilgrim back from the very presence of God, where the life of 'knowing' and 'loving' is focused, back into the miseries of exile and poverty, and the never ceasing struggle against wrong . . . the strained attention of my hearers released itself in prolonged and repeated applause that showed how every word had gone home. The impression was produced by the congregation not by the preacher, and I shall not soon forget it. It will be strange if Manchester is blind to the significance of such a movement. Hitherto it has been shaped by a single man, and he a man with little physical strength, with no pretension to eloquence, with no means, and with no influence, save such as springs from absolute devotion and singleness of purpose and the passion inspired by a great idea." [1]

For some years the Labour Church idea attracted much interest in two classes of English minds. It

[1] From the *Labour Prophet*, No. 2, February 1892.

appealed to men who, like Stanton Coit, were themselves seeking to organize religion outside the recognized churches. And it appealed, as its founder was confident it would, to the religious strain which lay deep in the nature of hosts of English working men, who found access to the churches of the middle class difficult or uncongenial.

But the Labour Church did not strike lasting root. Its founders perhaps assumed too easily that elements which fused in the glowing genius of a Mazzini can enter into other than precarious union in the rank and file of any class. Theistic and democratic faith have a different root and a different history; they may cohere but they seldom integrate. The Theism of the Labour Church made a frank appeal to undemocratic enthusiasm. Its God was a king who would lead it to the reorganized society of which it dreamed. When Wicksteed, the apostle of the movement, four years after its inception, addressed his searching "Letter"—"What does the Labour Church stand for"[1]—to the "Gentiles" of the factory and the mine, the Labour Church was already verging on decay. The process was hastened by its founder's engrained distrust of established things, even when they were his own work; by the rooted individualism, for a time overcome by the large social conscience of Wicksteed, which led him to feel all organization, even one of his own creation, as an obstacle to spiritual advance, not as its instrument; by the failure of resources, notwithstanding generous contributions by no means only from "Labour" men, and, finally, by his own frail physique and feeble health.

[1] The *Labour Prophet,* 1895.

But Philip Wicksteed never lost faith in Trevor, or in the Labour Church idea. "I have a sincere and inextinguishable affection for Trevor," he wrote long after (April 1924) to a fellow-minister, "and recognize the strain of genius (heroic and prophetic) in his character, which always makes me feel commonplace and timidly compromising in presence of his inspiration." But this fragile man of genius needed the "commonplace" giant's support. We have already quoted the letter in which Trevor described the Labour Church as having been "borne on Philip Wicksteed's broad shoulders." Wicksteed used his wide and powerful influence both to support Trevor, who had, rightly, no doubt, but in spite of warm appeals from many of the congregation, severed his connexion with Upper Brook Street Church, and to finance the organ of the Labour Church, the *Labour Prophet*.[1] For a few years the *Labour Prophet* was, in effect, the organ of all that was idealist in the Labour movement; it was

[1] An example of these efforts may be quoted in a note. In October 1897 he wrote to a cousin, "The *Labour Prophet* perhaps you see, and I hope you think it worth supporting. I believe it to be a really valuable thing, and to have great possibilities before it in keeping alive the somewhat feeble spark of spirituality in the Labour character. Well, Trevor ran it at his own risk and incurred a heavy deficit. He was forced to drop it and to rely upon its old supporters to clear off his debt (to say nothing of his subsistence which is most precarious). But several friends determined to carry on the *Prophet* on a cheaper scale, and want £50 a year to do it on. If they get this from Trevor's old subscribers, they will practically (so far) be taking over his supporters to their venture and *leaving him with his deficit*. . . . Under these circumstances I am trying to raise the £50 on new ground. Game is scarce on these moors! I would pick up half-crowns sooner than nothing. But what I want is £10 notes. I have got one and I want more. If I can raise this £50 Trevor will be in possession of his own, viz. his supporters and his deficit. If I cannot, no one will, and Trevor will be left in possession of his deficit and without his supporters; who do not, and will not, understand the position, and to whom Trevor can hardly explain it."

perhaps too brilliant to live. In 1897 a heavy deficit compelled its cessation. For some years of the present century "Labour Churches" were carried on in several factory towns of northern England, at Leek in Staffordshire, Selly Oak near Birmingham, and perhaps elsewhere, though these efforts probably in no case survived the war. But Wicksteed, as has been said, never lost faith in the idea. And it may be that nowhere was the vital core of that idea more completely embodied than in this strenuous worker with head and hand, whose life-labour, whether as economist, teacher, or scholar, was inspired by the desire to diminish the unequal distribution of privilege, and chiefly of the supreme privilege, the access, through man, nature, and religion, to spiritual things.[1]

[1] The fortunes of the Labour Church, and the after life of John Trevor, are relevant only as they concern Philip Wicksteed. But a brief note, as appendix, may be permitted. Trevor lived on, poor and unknown, till his death in 1929, in a tenement house in Hampstead. He was supported, latterly, almost entirely by the contributions, and cheered by the visits, of his old friends. A recent letter (5 April, 1930) from one of them, Mr. H. A. Atkinson, now in New Zealand, to another, Mr. H. V. Herford of Manchester, formerly treasurer of the Labour Church, throws a valuable light on its significance for the Labour movement. "I think the 1893 conference in London, which floated the Independent Labour Party into a national movement, adopted the Manchester and Salford Constitution as they certainly did the most distinctive part of it. Although Blatchford [did] the writing, much of the inspiration came from John Trevor. He it was who had the idea that the different elements in the movement towards Socialism in Manchester at that time should be got to work together. So we had two leading spirits from the Social Democratic Federation, Evans and Purvis, two from the Fabian Society, Settle and Dugdale, he and I, his assistant, from the Labour Church, and the great man of the day, Blatchford, of the *Clarion*. I have not seen any evidence yet which weakens my belief that the starting of the Manchester and Salford I.L.P. under such auspices and in such manner, was the true inauguration of the Third Party movement and the beginning of the British I.L.P."

PART II
The Economic Works[1]

BY LIONEL ROBBINS
(Professor of Economics in the University of London)

I

To the general public, it is probable that Wicksteed is known chiefly for his work as a classical and medieval scholar. For various reasons, some of which it will be our business to analyse later on, his work as an economist, although often expressly addressed to the generality of educated readers, has not received such extensive recognition. In this he has been unfortunate. Among professional economists his reputation has always been high: and as years go on it is likely to increase rather than to diminish. Nor is this reputation confined to this country. From the outset of his career as an economist, he received international recognition; and it would be difficult to find a really important work on pure economics written during the last twenty years which does not contain some reference to his work or some trace of his influence. His various books, never issued in large editions, have become extremely rare, and are greatly sought after, not only by the regular collectors of the literature of Economic Theory, but by the workaday economist, endeavouring to provide himself with the indispensable instruments of his craft. An English economist, anxious to ingratiate himself with some American or continental colleague, could find no more certain claim to instant

[1] This section has been published separately in *Economica*, November 1930.

friendship than the gift of one of these much-prized volumes.

The beginnings of Wicksteed's interest in economics and his connection with the early Fabians have been described in an earlier section. The object of this section is to give some account of his main works in this field and to attempt a brief estimate of the significance of his various contributions.

II

Wicksteed's first extensive contribution to the literature of modern economics was his *Alphabet of Economic Science*, a slim pocket manual which was published in 1888. The formative influence on his thoughts as an economist was Jevons. A copy of the second edition of the *Theory of Political Economy* which was purchased by Wicksteed in 1882 is in the possession of the present writer: and the marginal annotations on almost every page show how profoundly and how extensively he had meditated on its doctrines. In an earlier essay on the labour theory of value,[1] he had used the Jevonian theory to demonstrate the inadequacy of the classical and Marxian theories of value. The *Alphabet* was an attempt to restate and to elaborate positively its central guiding principles. The book is avowedly an introduction. Forty pages of careful mathematical illustration of the notion of limiting rates preface the attempt to apply this notion to the explanation of exchange values, and copious and minute illustrations accompany every step of the subsequent argument. In the history

[1] *To-day*, April, 1885, pp. 177 *seq.*

of theory, the book is perhaps chiefly notable for its introduction of the term "marginal utility"—a rendering of the Austrian "*Grenz-Nutzen*"—as a substitute for the Jevonian "final utility," which, for obvious reasons, had tended to lead to confusions. But the book is not merely of historical interest. It still preserves considerable pedagogic value. Much as has been written on the subject it deals with since that date—not least by Wicksteed himself—it still remains one of the best available introductions to the so-called utility theory of value. Other introductions may be easier to read and perhaps more entertaining to the student. But none is more calculated to give him real grasp and comprehension of the subject. In broad outline, of course, nothing can be simpler than the general notion of diminishing marginal utility. But in closer application to the problems of commodity prices, the notion is apt to prove elusive, at least to the non-mathematician. And more than one economist of standing has been betrayed into grotesque misconstructions. It is the great merit of Wicksteed's book that, starting from a point at which no knowledge of the calculus is assumed in his readers, he succeeds in expounding the theory with such minuteness and precision, that misconstructions of this sort should be impossible for any one who has read it with a normal degree of attention.

The book was an immediate success among economists. With one stride Wicksteed had secured a place in that esoteric circle whose pronouncements on pure theory command international attention. It was referred to approvingly by Edgeworth, and the great Pareto, most ferocious of critics, most uncompromising guardian of the sanctities of pure theory, gave it a prominent place in the bibliography of works on "*Economie pure*" which appeared in Part I of his *Cours*. With the general public, however, it was not such a success. When the general public picks up an introduction to economic science, it expects to discover a handy guide to the solution of all the most controversial problems of the day—a few neat paragraphs about trade unions and wages, a chapter on trusts and big business, perhaps a diagram or two to lay bare the intricacies of the monetary system, all rounded off with a few sound generalizations about the future. But here was a book pretending to be an introduction, which started off with a series of graphs and algebraic formulae exhibiting the behaviour of falling bodies and the cooling of iron bars plunged into baths of cold water, and continued with exhaustive diagrammatic discussions of trivial household calculations, such as buying a coat or a loaf of bread, never saying anything which was short and snappy and simple. Small wonder that the hungry sheep, as usual, refused to feed, and continued to bleat to all the world that no nourishment was forthcoming in these pastures.

The preface to the *Alphabet* had promised that, if it proved to meet a want amongst students of economics, it should be followed by similar introductions to other branches of the science. This plan seems to have been abandoned. For the next work was one which by no stretch of imagination could be described as introductory or simple. This was the celebrated *Essay on the Co-ordination of the Laws of Distribution*, which was given to the world in 1894.

By the beginning of the 'nineties the centre of gravity

in theoretical economics had shifted from the narrow problem of commodity value to the wider problem of distribution, or, as it is sometimes called, the pricing of the factors of production. Jevons and the Austrians had suggested a theory which as a first approximation might be held to elucidate the prices which could be secured for "ultimate commodities." The problem now was to decide in what proportions the prices were "distributed" between the different factors co-operating in the production of these commodities. It was this problem which the *Essay* was designed to solve. The solution offered was a form of what is sometimes known as the marginal productivity theory of distribution. If the product to be distributed is P, then to use Wicksteed's own statement, "the rates of participation in the product on which any factor K can insist . . . will be $\frac{dP}{dK}$ per unit and its total share will be $\frac{dP}{dK}K$." [1]

How far this result had been reached independently of the work of others it is difficult to say. Just as, at the beginning of the 'seventies, the utility theory of value had occurred simultaneously to Jevons, Walras, and Menger, so at the beginning of the 'nineties, the productivity theory of distribution was "in the air" and different variants had been put forward by Marshall, Clark and others. It is certain that Wicksteed was acquainted with Marshall's work in this field, for there are footnote references to it in the *Essay*. But it is probable that his solution was reached as a result of his studies of Jevons, which were carried out before Marshall's *Principles* were published.[2] This is

[1] *Essay*, p. 9.

[2] *Quarterly Journal of Economics*, 1889, pp. 293 *seq.*

what seems to follow from Wicksteed's own account of his discovery,[1] and we may be sure that a man so scrupulously honest and so modest about his own achievements would have acknowledged the debt had it existed.

By the time the *Essay* was published, the idea that the notion of marginal productivity might play a part in the explanation of the price of the factors of production was becoming widely accepted among the more advanced economists. The same cannot be said, however, of the main proposition of the *Essay*, namely, that if each factor is rewarded according to its marginal productivity the sum of the remuneration of each separate factor will exactly exhaust the product—in other words, that the marginal productivity analysis is a *sufficient* explanation of "distribution."[2] This bold generalization has always been associated with the argument of the *Essay*, and it is true to say that, even at the present day, it remains the subject of lively controversy. Wicksteed himself, as a result of criticism by Mr. Flux and Pareto became dissatisfied with it, declared it to have been a premature synthesis[3] and in *The Common Sense of Political Economy* announced the proposition to be finally withdrawn. The grounds of his dissatisfaction, however, were technical and mathematical; it would be wrong to suppose, as has sometimes been done, that he renounced the productivity

[1] *Essay*, p. 43.

[2] See e.g. Knight, F. H., "A Note on Professor Clark's illustration of Marginal Productivity," *Journal of Political Economy*, xxxiii, pp. 550–4. Also Schultz, *Journal of Political Economy*, xxxvii, pp. 505–551, "Marginal Productivity and the Pricing Process."

[3] *Economic Journal*, 1906, pp. 553–7, and *The Common Sense of Political Economy*, p. 373.

analysis in general.[1] Certainly the solution offered in its place in *The Common Sense of Political Economy* does not differ so noticeably from that of the *Essay* as to suggest that the earlier version was to be regarded as wholly misleading. And, so far as I understand them, the criticisms which have been made by Pareto and others relate to the nature of the assumptions made rather than to the internal logic of the argument. That is to say, if I am not mistaken, Wicksteed's proposition is not untrue; the only criticism to which it is exposed is that, in certain circumstances, its assumptions render it inapplicable. It is not so exhaustive as its author at first supposed. This is not a very grave defect in a new theory. We are none of us so near the goal as we tend to believe ourselves to be.

For sixteen years after the appearance of the *Essay,* Wicksteed published little on economic questions. A couple of reviews in the *Economic Journal,* on Jevons' *Principles* [2] in 1905 and Pareto's *Manual* [3] in 1906, constitute the sum of published utterances. But all this time his mind was revolving the terms of a synthesis wider than anything he had hitherto attempted, and in 1910 he published his *magnum opus* in this field, *The Common Sense of Political Economy*.

It is not easy in a short space to give an adequate idea of this work. The title conveys less than nothing. Indeed, never was a work of this kind more unfortunately named. It is not "common sense" in the ordinary sense of the term, and it is not *political* economy. It is, on the contrary, the most exhaustive

[1] It is worthy of note that Knut Wicksell expresses great surprise at Wicksteed's apparent recantation. See *Vorlesungen*, Bd. I, p. 156.

[2] Op. cit., p. 432.

[3] Ibid., p. 553.

non-mathematical exposition of the technical and philosophical complications of the so-called "marginal" theory of pure economics, which has appeared in any language. The only work with which it can be compared in this respect is Wieser's *Theorie der Gesellschaftlichen Wirtschaft*, but even Wieser, like Marshall and other authors of "systems," really covers a much wider field, and does not enter into nearly the same degree of detail.

The aim of the book was twofold. On the one hand it attempted a systematic exposition of the Jevonian and Austrian theories, such that any reader commencing from no previous acquaintance of Economic Analysis would be in a position to achieve "an intimate comprehension of the commercial and industrial world." On the other, it involved an attempt "to convince professed students of Political Economy that any special or unusual features in the system thus constructed are not to be regarded as daring innovations or as heresies, but are already strictly involved and often explicitly recognized in the best economic thought and teaching of recent years."[1] As usual, Wicksteed made no claims to originality. Indeed, he refrained from making claims which might very well have been made. But he did definitely hope that his work would compel recognition of the degree to which economics had been changed by the discussions of the last forty years. "I believe," he said, "that the reconstruction contemplated by Jevons has been carried to a far more advanced point than is generally realized even by those who are themselves accomplishing it. Adhesion to the traditional terminology, methods of arrangement, and

[1] *Common Sense*, p. 2.

classification, has disguised the revolution that has taken place. The new temple, so to speak, has been built up behind the old walls, and the old shell has been so piously preserved and respected that the very builders have often supposed themselves to be merely repairing and strengthening the ancient works, and are hardly aware of the extent to which they have raised an independent edifice. I shall try to show in this book that the time has come for a frank recognition of these facts." [1]

The book is divided into three parts. In the first comes a systematic working out of the marginal analysis. This is introduced by an extensive analysis of the economics of household administration, in which the principles of what the Germans call *Naturwirtschaft* are exhaustively examined. This is followed by a minute exposition of the notion of margins and limiting rates of expenditure, unparalleled in the whole literature of modern economic theory for clarity and precision. "Nowhere," said the late Professor Allyn Young, reviewing the book for the *American Economic Review*, "is there so clear a (non-mathematical) explanation of the meaning of marginal significance, or so effective a refutation of those writers who have thought that the existence of indivisible goods puts insurmountable obstacles in the way of the marginal analysis." [2] The analysis then opens out to include the phenomena of money and exchange. The implications of the Economic Nexus in the *Verkehrswirtschaft* are expounded. Markets, earnings, interest are systematically examined, and finally, at a great height, the interrelations of distribution and cost of production are made the basis

[1] *Common Sense*, p. 2. [2] *American Economic Review*, 1911, pp. 78–80.

for an exhibition of the whole notion of economic equilibrium.

The second part of the book, which is described as "Excursive and Critical," consists of a series of special studies of technical problems of analysis. The notions of the diagrammatic representation of margins and total utility are investigated with a precision and minuteness which provides a significant contrast with the cursory treatment usually afforded these matters even in respectable textbooks. There follow special studies of the supply curve and markets, and an examination of the concepts of increasing and diminishing returns and their relation to the theory of rent, in which some of the subsidiary propositions of the *Essay on the Co-ordination of the Laws of Distribution* are expounded and developed. Finally, in Part III, the general system of analysis elaborated in the earlier chapters is applied to the elucidation of certain practical problems, housing, unemployment, redistribution of wealth, taxation, land nationalization, socialism, and so on. The treatment here is less detailed, more discursive than before, the Lucretian passage which prefaces this part of the book suggesting perfectly its intention. "But this faint spoor suffices for an alert mind: so that thou thyself mayst come at all the rest. For just as hounds, when once they have found the true track, full often search out with their nostrils the lair of the mountain-roaming quarry, hidden though it be with foliage; even so mayst thou, in such things as these, see for thyself one thing after another, work thyself into the secret hiding-places and thence drag out the truth."

The book was the culmination of Wicksteed's life-work in this branch of knowledge. Into it he poured all the subtlety and persuasiveness, all the literary charm of which he was capable. It is a masterpiece of systematic exposition. It is the most complete statement of the implicit philosophy of economic analysis which has been published in our day. But with all these great merits, it did not succeed in attracting the notice of the general educated public, and even among professional economists it has not exerted the influence which might have been expected.

Why is this?

Three reasons, I think, are to be discovered. In the first place there was the misfortune of the name, which I have already discussed. It did not succeed in attracting the general public. And many economists, I imagine, having learnt from bitter experience what is usually to be expected from works which profess to treat economic problems in a "common-sense" manner, have been positively deterred from investigating its contents. I well remember as a student, unaware as yet of Wicksteed's high repute among the inner circle of the craft, feeling definitely that a work which devoted seven hundred pages to a "common-sense" exposition of theorems which I already knew to be highly intricate and technical, was "extra-marginal" so far as *my* reading time was concerned.

Partly, I think, on account of its length. It is a weighty book, and although the exposition is most exquisitely organized, the nuances of argument most delicately fluted, yet it cannot be denied that it is possible that at times it may drag a little, may become a trifle *langweilig*. I do not find this myself, but it must be set on record that this was the impression it produced on so sensitive and so learned a critic as the late Professor Allyn Young.

But mainly, I think, what failure there is must be attributed to the nature of the task which Wicksteed set himself. Wicksteed lived at a time when it was still thought necessary for economists to write mainly with the general public in view. Economics was still a subject which was read and discussed in the clubs. The result was that at every point the economists' wings were clipped. Whenever the use of a technical term or a reference to the periodical literature of the science would have simplified and sharpened the argument, the exposition had to be loaded with recapitulation and periphrases which only tended to hinder its progress. It is notorious that Marshall's great work on *Principles* suffers from this deficiency. But Marshall's *Principles* is high technicality itself compared with Wicksteed's *Common Sense*. Marshall, at least, permits himself the luxury of footnote discussions, a mathematical appendix, and copious reference to the classics. Wicksteed goes serenely on, even in the most controversial sections, almost as though no other economist had ever written. Moreover, Marshall was professor in one of the great centres of economic study, where every shade of technical implication would be daily sifted out from his smooth flattened prose by tutors learned in the more esoteric oral tradition of the School. Wicksteed was an isolated classical scholar and Extension lecturer, respected indeed by fellow economists, but with no regular pupils or assistants to make explicit the intimate affiliations of his thought. In such circumstances the only sure path to recognition was to keep to the tradition of the

Essay, reserve his best thoughts for the expert public of the journals, and leave to professors, secure in the comfortable eminence of academic chairs, the thankless task of enlightening the general reader. But the preacher in Wicksteed died hard and he chose the more arduous endeavour.

III

Wicksteed's place in the history of Economic Thought is beside the place occupied by Jevons and the Austrians. The main stream of economic speculation in this country in the last forty years has come via Marshall from the classics. By this I do not mean that it shows no advance on the classics. That, of course, would be absurd: it has made the most superb advances. The judgment relates merely to tendencies. Marshall's position was essentially revisionist. He came, not to destroy, but to fulfil the work of the classics. Wicksteed, on the other hand, was of those who, with Jevons and Menger, thought that "able but wrong-headed man David Ricardo" had "shunted the car of Economic Science on to a wrong line, a line on which it was further urged towards confusion by his equally able and wrong-headed admirer John Stuart Mill"[1]; and that complete reconstruction was necessary. He was not a revisionist but a revolutionary. I have cited already the passage from the preface to the *Common Sense* in which he says that the time has come to recognize that modern economics is not a reconstruction of the old, but a new and independent edifice.

[1] *Theory of Political Economy*, third edition, p. 1.

The same point of view is very strongly presented in his review of Sir Sydney Chapman's *Political Economy*.[1]

The difference is perhaps very largely one of emphasis and *conception* of theory, rather than in the *substance* of theory itself. But none the less it modifies materially the presentation of theory by representatives of the Schools concerned. In spite of a very real agreement on the broad outlines of analysis, there is a world of difference between the "*look*" of Marshall's *Principles* and Wicksteed's *Common Sense of Political Economy*, Wieser's *Theorie der Gesellschaftlichen Wirtschaft*, or Schumpeter's *Wesen und Hauptinhalt der Theoretischen Nationalökonomie*. Nor must the degree of fundamental agreement be exaggerated. There are differences in the central core of theory. This is specially noticeable in the theory of costs—Marshall, and (up to a recent date) most of his followers, insisting that costs in the last analysis were something "real" and absolute, Wicksteed and the Austrians denying that they were anything but foregone alternatives. No doubt, in part, this difference of theory was due to a difference in ultimate assumption concerning the nature of the conditions of economic equilibrium.[2] But in part it was due to an ultimate difference of opinion concerning what psychological comparisons were *relevant* in the determination of *any* equilibrium. So far as this was the case, time, I think, has decided in favour of the revolutionaries. The conception of real costs as displaced alternatives, which Wicksteed so eloquently

[1] *Economic Journal*, 1913, pp. 72–5.

[2] I have tried to exhibit this difference of assumption as between Marshall and the Austrians elsewhere. See my article, "On a Certain Ambiguity in the Conception of Stationary Equilibrium," *Economic Journal*, 1930, pp. 194–214.

expounded, is now accepted by the majority of theoretical economists, though even now its implications are not always fully grasped.[1]

But it would be a great mistake to regard Wicksteed as merely a disciple of Jevons and the Austrians. He was much more than that. He was an independent and original thinker. Even where he expounded the main elements of the utility theory it is safe to say that he touched nothing which he did not make his own. Nor was his own position one of stationary equilibrium. He was continually reformulating and improving. I have mentioned already his willingness to jettison his original theory of distribution. An equally interesting example of this tendency is to be found in the comparison of the utility theory expounded in the *Alphabet* and the utility theory of the *Common Sense*. Superficially the two theories are the same, and no doubt they do belong to the same family. But a closer inspection will reveal important points of difference. The *Alphabet* starts from the idea of the rate at which total utility is increasing; the *Common Sense* from the positions on the relative scale of preferences which marginal units of different commodities occupy. In the *Alphabet* the utility relevant to the determination of value is treated as if it were something absolute and measurable. In the *Common Sense* the sole relevance of *relative* utility is emphasized and the idea of *measurability* has given place to the idea of *order*. In the *Alphabet* the analysis is definitely "one-thing-at-a-time." In the *Common Sense* the emphasis of the simultaneity of

[1] For a superb application of the Austrian theory of costs to the examination of certain theories of fluctuation, see Hayek, *Geldtheorie und Konjunkturtheorie*, chapter ii *passim*.

the determination of all values is continuous. And so one could go on. There is no feature of the presentation which does not bear evidence of reformulation and improvement.

Apart, however, from his services as exponent of the general theory of equilibrium, there are certain particular contributions for which Wicksteed will always be remembered. I have discussed already his studies in the theory of distribution. Whatever the ultimate decision as to the truth or falsehood of the particular theorem he advanced with regard to the adequacy of the productivity analysis, there can be no doubt that economists owe him a high debt of gratitude for having focused attention on this aspect of the problem. It is not always those who are finally right who make the greatest contributions to progress.

A second contribution which must always be associated with his name is his famous demonstration of the reversibility of the market supply curve.[1] The general proposition that the reservation prices of sellers are in the ultimate analysis demands, was one which he continually reiterated with varying shades of emphasis. "What about the supply curve that usually figures as a determinant of price, co-ordinate with the demand curve?" he asked in his address as President of Section E of the British Association in 1913—an address which epitomizes many of his most characteristic doctrines.[2] "I say it boldly and baldly: there is no such thing. When we are speaking of a marketable commodity, what is usually called the supply curve is in reality the demand curve of those who possess

[1] See *Common Sense*, pp. 493–526, and *Economic Journal*, 1914, pp. 13–16.
[2] *Economic Journal*, 1914, pp. 1–23.

the commodity, for it shows the exact place which every successive unit of the commodity holds in their relative scale of estimation. The so-called supply curve, therefore, is simply a part of the total demand curve. . . . The separating out of this portion of the demand curve and reversing it in the diagram is a process which has its meaning and its legitimate function . . . but is wholly irrelevant to the determination of the price.'' [1] It is safe to say that no one who has followed through his beautiful diagrammatic analysis of this proposition, and realized its wider implication that *all* psychological variables can be exhibited as phenomena of demand acting on fixed stocks of products or factors or time, will deny that the whole of the analysis of economic equilibrium has received thereby a transforming elucidation.[2]

Finally, in the realm of technical contributions, we must notice his analysis of the relation between the marginal productivity theory of distribution and the Ricardian theory of rent. The discovery that the rent analysis of the classics is the productivity analysis with, as Edgeworth put it, the relationship between dose and patient reversed, was, of course, not peculiar to Wicksteed. By one of those singular coincidences which seem to characterize the progress of our science, the idea seems to have occurred almost simultaneously

[1] For a very elegant demonstration of this last possibility in relation to the problem of hours of labour, see Wicksell, *Vorlesungen*, Bd. I, p. 159.

[2] It should be noted that the same general point of view was enunciated independently by Professor Davenport in his *Value and Distribution*, and further elaborated in his *Economics of Enterprise*. Nothing that has been said in praise of Wicksteed's work in this connexion should be understood as derogating from the merits or the helpfulness of Professor Davenport's exposition, for which, indeed, when he came to know it, Wicksteed had himself a very profound admiration. See *Economic Journal*, 1914, pp. 421–5.

to at least three writers in the early 'nineties, Wicksteed himself, J. B. Clark, and the much-neglected H. M. Thompson, author of *The Theory of Wages*.[1] But of the demonstrations of this proposition, Wicksteed's was incomparably the most precise and convincing; and, at the present day, a teacher who wishes to convince some recalcitrant student of the truth of this doctrine cannot do better than refer him to the classic reformulation which is to be found in part ii, chapters v and vi of *The Common Sense of Political Economy*.

IV

But apart from these technical contributions and far transcending them in general importance come Wicksteed's elucidations of the implications for social philosophy of the results of the theory of economic equilibrium—particularly those discussions of the nature of the economic relationship which are to be found in the chapter of the *Common Sense* entitled "Business and the Economic Nexus."[2] This, if I read him correctly, was the feature of his work to which he himself attached greatest importance, and it is for this above all that he deserves to be remembered. Yet, curiously enough, no aspect of his teaching has been more completely neglected. The reason is not far to seek. In England, at any rate, the average economist, secure in the tradition of an empirical approach to his subject-

[1] See *Co-ordination of the Laws of Distribution*, pp. 18-20. J. B. Clark, "Distribution as determined by a Law of Rent," *Quarterly Journal of Economics*, 1891, pp. 289 *seq.* Thompson, *The Theory of Wages*, chapter iv *passim*.

[2] The curious should consult a tract entitled *Getting and Spending*, reprinted for private circulation from the *Inquirer*, 1888, for an earlier and much inferior statement of Wicksteed's position in this respect.

matter, is apt to be impatient of inquiries which linger on implications and modes of conception. The man in the street, egged on by the inexpert practitioners of other branches of the social sciences, may reproach him for an ingrained materialism and an assumption of a simplicity of motive unwarranted by the complexity of the situation to be analysed. But such reproaches leave him indifferent. He knows in his bones that they are unjust. He knows that, unlike his traducers, he is in possession of analytical instruments which do genuinely elucidate the understanding of complicated social relationships, and he is apt to regard with impatience those semi-metaphysical inquiries which harp on ultimate assumptions. The instinct, no doubt, is a healthy one, and has saved us from the torrents of empty methodology which at times have threatened entirely to submerge economic analysis elsewhere. None the less not all inquiries of this sort are empty, and it may be successfully contended, I think, that by their researches in this field a small group of economists —Wicksteed and Knight in English-speaking countries, Schumpeter and Mises in Central Europe [1]—have raised the whole discussion of equilibrium analysis on to an entirely new plane—a plane on which economics is seen to be a discussion not of the nature of certain *kinds* of behaviour arbitrarily separated off from all others, but of a certain *aspect* of behaviour viewed as a whole. It is perhaps too early to evaluate the individual contributions to this stream of thought, for the movement is by no means exhausted, but when the final

[1] See in particular Knight's essay on "The Limitations of Scientific Method in Economics" in *The Trend of Economics*, ed. Tugwell; Schumpeter, *Das Wesen und der Haupt-Inhalt der theoretischen Nationalökonomie*; and Mises, *Die Gemeinwirtschaft*, II Teil, 1 Abschnitt, "Das Wesen der Wirtschaft."

history comes to be written, I think it will be found that Wicksteed's exhaustive examination of the "economic relationship," and his insistence that this, and not the pseudo-concept of the "economic motive," is the chief sociological preoccupation of economic analysis, will be seen to be by no means the least important contribution.

V

Such in broad outline was the main achievement as an economist of this noble and penetrating intellect. It is an achievement of rare distinction. Economics in England can boast a long succession of devoted and dispassionate practitioners. There have been none more devoted or dispassionate than Philip Wicksteed. It has been said that his work was detached and remote from reality. In a sense this is true. He was the purest of pure economists—always occupied with the general, always searching for the one in the many. He tried to erect a structure of principles which should be valid for all time and all conditions. His work is indeed destitute of statistical tables and discussions of contemporary business structure, but it is informed throughout by continuous regard for the intimate texture of conduct. There are many economists who have had wider contacts with the life of their times, there are many who have had a greater range of immediate practical usefulness: there are few who have done more to bring economics as a science into relation with life as a whole.

CHAPTER VII

THE PROPHET-POETS

Wordsworth — Ibsen — Wicksteed's return to Dante — The *Six Sermons*—Aspects of Dante; Language—Dante the Lover—Dante the Philosopher—Dante the Statesman—The *Comedy*—Religion of Time and Religion of Eternity

WHAT Philip Wicksteed wrote about Wordsworth, Ibsen and Dante, differed widely in scale and in literary importance. Wordsworth, so often on his lips, so near to the inmost springs of his thought, was expounded by him only in a single course of lectures, which remained unpublished and generally unknown. The *Four Lectures on Ibsen*, a brilliant and revealing essay, remained, save for an obituary notice, isolated. The *Six Sermons on Dante* were only the prelude, though a most stirring and effective one, to the long series of Dante labours which closed with the *From Vita Nuova to Paradiso* more than forty years later.

I

Wordsworth was, for Wicksteed, the poet of reconciliation and the poet of permanence. A course of Extension Lectures, delivered repeatedly in the later 'nineties, on "Poems of Revolt and Reconciliation," originated, as he tells us, in a desire to interpret the obvious contrast between the philosophy of *The Excursion* and that of *Prometheus Unbound* and *Cain*. The contrast, as may be supposed, in the hands of a man in whom both tempers were so engrained, proves to be complementary, not exclusive. Revolt "declares war on conditions of life," but in the interest of a truer harmony; "Reconciliation" confronts the combatants with an olive-branch, but for a Peace whose virtue is to create opportunities, not to restore repose. Wordsworth appealed from "our meddling intellect" to instinct and intuition, from passion to the natural affections. But these were precious to him as the sources not of virtue only, but of heroism and vision; as these in their turn were precious, not merely as manifestations of character or genius, but as means by which humanity may break down the barriers, and pierce the integuments, which divide it from a life in and with the things that endure.

Hence Wordsworth, the poet of reconciliation, was also the poet of permanence, and Dr. A. N. Whitehead in our time has singled this out as his supreme contribution to poetic philosophy. And Wicksteed, too, the worker and thinker of tireless energy, shares the solemn joy with which Wordsworth speaks of the permanences of geometry as types of permanence in the universe. It was only under a different vesture of thought that he contrasted progress, and the religion of Time with the timeless religion of Eternity. These passages will be noticed in the sections on the *Reactions*, and on Aristotle's *Physics*, of the following chapter.

II

Wicksteed's congenial intimacy with Norway and the Norwegians has already been glanced at. Norway was, from 1878, the most frequent goal and haunt of his summer travel. There, in his own boat, with one or two intimate companions, he could live face to face with the simplicity, grandeur, and loneliness of the fjords, while remaining attached, by a tenuous but not wholly imaginary filament, to the amenities of civilization, including those of an infrequent but regular post. Thus he cruised through the long summer days on the Sogne or the Hardangr, pitching a night's camp on whatever wild spot commended itself. For the dwellers in the little fjord-side homesteads his friend and frequent associate Carpenter was "the English gentleman who had rowed up the Sogne." But Wicksteed, with his flaming hair and blue eyes, his elemental boisterousness, his less fastidious urbanity, and very soon his fluent and idiomatic if not very accurate Norse, became the northerner from England, whose unmistakable affinities mental and physical, made him as much at home in Norwegian farmsteads as in Norwegian solitudes; he had hosts of warm friends there.[1] He delighted in the sterling character of these peasants of the "land of the thousand homes," who had learnt to know both the seen and the unseen world in battling with nature for a livelihood, but who were also cultivated and well read. He keenly relished the frugal resourcefulness that pitched a homestead on every patch of fertile land among the rocky braes, which made these peasants living exemplars of his own economics; and he relished these virtues none the less because in these houses he could discuss Ibsen and Shakespeare with his host. The daughters of these homes were often eager to go to England, and having no other

[1] A son, as has already been told, bearing the heroic Norse name of Sigurd, died in his first year.

means, engaged in domestic service there for a year or more. Many were thus introduced by Wicksteed in his own circle; several passed through the Wicksteed household; one at least, as already mentioned, settled permanently at Childrey.

His children, in after years, mischievously chaffed him with the reminiscence of a day when one of them had landed with him at some wild nook on the Sogne. One of the girls declared that she did not know a man with whom she would spend her life in such a spot. "Oh," cried her father, "I know a dozen men, and *hundreds* of women!" And a son records, from these Norwegian tours, another vivid utterance of his zest of life. He never wanted, he said, to "say to the present moment 'Stay!'—he was too busy enjoying it." It was a matter-of-fact version of his grave doctrine of "eternity!"

All this helps to explain the power and swiftness with which Wicksteed in the early 'eighties penetrated into the genius of Henrik Ibsen, then obscured by clouds of obloquy and insular prejudice from all but a few eyes in England.

The *Four Lectures on Ibsen* were delivered in 1888. Henrik Ibsen had, then, for at least ten years enjoyed a secure fame on the Continent. In England his claims were still hotly disputed. By the mass of the periodical Press he was covered with abuse, against which a few voices of enthusiastic devotees strove to make themselves heard; and neither denunciation nor cult made for critical interpretation. That he had introduced a new and powerful stage-technique was grudgingly admitted, and the first performance of *A Doll's House* (Nora) was a tonic in the London dramatic world, sated with the conventions of the French "well-made play." But the angry protests in the name of "desecrated family life" overpowered that measured critical approval; and when, two years after the original production of *A Doll's House,* Ibsen turned upon his *bourgeois* assailants in Norway with the terrible and unanswerable retort of *Ghosts* (1881), and the cries of protest became frenzied shrieks, and reputable journals allowed themselves excesses of language and allusion, for which Ibsen's drama, severely reticent, as Ibsen always is, within the limits imposed by the subject, gave no kind of excuse. The frenzy reached its climax in England with the performance of the play in London in 1891.[1]

But in this confused agitation two aspects of Ibsen had received little notice. That he had invented a new stage-technique, and found an effective motive in social iconoclasm was beyond denial. But few understood that he was a great original poet, and that behind the social iconoclast stood a powerful if untrained thinker. There was much excuse for both forms of neglect. For the dramas in which his philosophic thought and his brilliant poetic imagination were embodied were as yet only in part, and very inadequately, translated in English, his lyrics not at all.[2] But it was precisely in these two aspects that Ibsen had

[1] It is not surprising that the authorities of Little Portland Street, in particular, Dr. Martineau and Mrs. Humphry Ward, refused to countenance the delivery of either sermons or lectures on Ibsen in the Chapel, and that even the University refused to admit Extension lectures on him. They were given as public lectures at the Chelsea Town Hall, and immediately published.

[2] Several verse translations of *Brand* (1866) existed in Germany, where the poem had been enthusiastically hailed as a kind of Norwegian *Faust*; but none of them were of high quality.

powerfully stirred Philip Wicksteed; and it was the lasting service of the *Four Lectures* to make it impossible any longer to ignore them. They were not intended to offer a detailed account of Ibsen, still in mid-career, nor to satisfy curious appetites about the "scandalous" social plays. His aim he defined at the close as twofold. "I have tried in the first place, to show some of the ground upon which I claim for Ibsen the name of poet, and in the next place to point out the clues to the meaning of his later work which are to be found in his earlier lyrics and dramas."

What Wicksteed undertook, then, in the *Four Lectures* was something of fundamental importance for a right understanding of Ibsen in England. The poems and poetic dramas were not to be dismissed or ignored as the stammering speech of the immature artist whose mature art found itself in the prose plays. It was no apprentice, in any case, but a man in his later thirties—the age of Shakespeare at the date of *Hamlet*—who had produced the two great poetic dramas and the finest of the lyrics.[1] For this task Wicksteed indeed, as he frankly confessed to the reader, wanted one qualification—he was not himself in any sense a poet. The faculty of verse and the impulse to write it were quite absent, so far as we know, in the Wicksteed tradition; nor did they emerge, as in Shelley, unheralded by ancestry, in the otherwise rich endowment of Philip. Nor was appreciation of the poetic art, of poetic imagination and poetic speech, apart from its human and ethical contact, very much in his way.

[1] How little Ibsen himself regarded verse drama as an apprentice stage which he had outgrown, may be judged from a remark he made to the present writer at Oslo, in 1895. "I mean to write my last drama in verse. Only" (he added) "one never knows which will be the last."

But it was happily, just the human and ethical content which was, for Ibsen's poetry, of the first importance. That is not to say that it could be disengaged from the imagination or the metrical expression as the kernel from the shell. The terrific force of his *Miner* needs the hammer-like clangour of rhyme and rhythm; the magic of *With a Water-Lily* depends upon a subtle interweaving of imagery and allusion impossible in prose. But verse was always with Ibsen an instrument or a weapon, never an altar at which he worshipped, or a toy with which he played. On the other hand, Wicksteed brought to the interpretation of the human and ethical element of Ibsen's poetry qualifications in which no one else in England, of the few who had touched this side of Ibsen, approached him. The delicate literary organ of Edmund Gosse, whose vivid account of *Peer Gynt* in 1872 was perhaps the first notice of Ibsen in England, owed little of its fascination to philosophic depth or ethical intensity; and William Archer, the best Norwegian scholar of his generation, and later, Ibsen's principal English translator, was, above all, the champion of the epoch-making innovator in stagecraft. To disclose, however imperfectly, the poet and the brooding and pregnant thinker in Ibsen, was to add some very essential traits to the crude image of him entertained by the English public. The author of *A Doll's House* was imagined to be an anarchist bent upon undermining the sanctities of the home, and blind to every kind of marriage but that which is built upon a lie. And that prose of his, deliberately denuded of literary phrase and figure, how could such a writer be capable of the lyric cry? The lyrics quoted in Wicksteed's first lecture disclosed unmistakably, not an anti-social doctrinaire deliberately working out a programme, but a poet, torn by the struggle between passions of terrific intensity, an egoism capable of the utmost extremes of anti-social cynicism, and a deep, often violated and trampled on, but ineradicable faith in love. The terrific picture in *På Vidderne* (*On the Moors*) of the struggle between the Faust and the Mephistopheles in Ibsen himself, threw a revealing light upon the whole of Ibsen's later work. Through *The Eider Duck* sounded the passion for his northern homeland which underlay his scorn for the Norwegian character; in his exquisite *Thanks,* the deeply felt gratitude of this anarchic wrecker of the modern home to the woman who had made his own.

Brand and *Peer Gynt* needed still more urgently the kind of interpretation which Wicksteed brought to bear upon them. Brand, as Ibsen saw him throughout the first half of the poem, was a Hebrew prophet, a young Isaiah denouncing, in a speech sometimes not unworthy of his exemplar, the invertebrate feebleness of his countrymen, the policy of compromise, which masks its dearth of heroic will. And Brand, like the old prophets, is stoned. Ibsen's letters, published only since his death, show that this fierce denunciation was the original motive of the poem—conceived as he watched the Danish cannon drawn in triumph through the streets of Berlin.[1] But other and deeper forces in his nature asserted themselves in the poem as he went on, and Wicksteed sees them more clearly than Ibsen himself. The prophet in him was mated, as we know, with the citizen;

[1] For a fuller account of the origins of *Brand,* as well as of the rather earlier *Love's Comedy,* the reader may be referred to the writer's Introductions to these plays, prefixed to his Translations of them in the original metres in the Collected Edition of the dramas (Heinemann).

the vision for things of the spirit with a shrewd recognition of physical conditions and material needs. Love, which Ibsen, an old "romantic," imperfectly repentant, now invests with a halo of sentiment, now cynically derides, is for Wicksteed the Christian Love, greatest of all things, which yet does not dazzle but clears the apprehension of all the rest. And he points out what excusably escapes Ibsen's readers, how Brand's failure in love, which blinds him when he tramples on his own love for wife and child, blinds him also to the real merits of the honest State official who stands in his way. Ibsen, as his letters to Brand make clear, was no less fanatical than Brand in his scorn for "the State," and Brand is here simply the mouthpiece of his scorn. But Wicksteed's English political sense found attractive traits even in Ibsen's portrait; this official who does his duty "only in his own district," does it faithfully and even wisely there, and when his office is on fire, risks his life to save the archives. The man stood on a spiritual plane immeasurably below Brand's, he "could not, of course, understand Brand in the least; but Brand might have understood him, respected him, worked with him, and ultimately even taught him something." But there is no indication that Ibsen thought his Brand thus at fault. The seer in him was too little touched with everyday humanity to stoop easily to the homely virtues; whereas the heroic and prophetic strain in Philip Wicksteed was inseparable, as we know, from a humanity which found itself in helping the simplest and homeliest to rise.

Wicksteed was thus in some respects better equipped than Ibsen for apprehending in all its aspects the problem of the life of the individual in society which he finds at the heart of all Ibsen's work. He knew Aristotle, and he knew Comte, he was a minister of religion and an English citizen. The Greek ideal of citizenship, in which the individual citizen finds his own complete life, Comte's ideal of living for others, and the Christian "die to live," were made as real to him by the practice of a full and public-spirited life, as the direct demands of his personal will.

And in his closing pages Wicksteed faced the ethical dilemma which Ibsen continually provokes in the high-minded English citizen, but which he himself nowhere clearly states, far less solves (unless it be in the mystic vision of the Third Kingdom). "How shall the self-abnegation demanded by society be combined with the self-realization that is the legitimate demand of the individual, and the salt of society itself?" . . . And he replies, "When the ideals of a community are dead, and their place has been taken by conventions and lies, then the common life will seek to choke and do to death the life of him who dares to live." But "when the ideals of a community are living, the common life will magnify the life of the individual, and room for self-realization will be found in self-surrender." And it is just this second type of situation, this second half of the dilemma, which in Ibsen never clearly emerges. His merciless penetration presented with incomparable force both the diseases of society and the tragedies of idealism; he could brilliantly mock at its masquerade in *Peer Gynt*, and scathingly expose its deadly futility in Gregers Werle; he discovered for the modern drama the tragedy, which broods over the Æschylean drama of an ineluctable inherited past. But his insight into the working together of the forces that make for a healthy society is far more elementary. His "ghosts" of the past are all deadly and doom-bearing; they ruin Osvald, they plunge Rebekka and Rosmer, albeit through the purifying fire, into the mill-stream.

But imperfectly as Ibsen understood the healthy social organism, and remorselessly as he exposed the sores and scabs and scars of the community on a stage accustomed to have them decently ignored, it was a singularly obtuse criticism which represented him as one who had an eye only for ugly and obscene things. It fell properly to Wicksteed, a man of abounding and untainted health in mind and body, to vindicate for this resolute "miner" among the dark places of life, a rare but sure vision also for the loveliness of souls naturally sweet and pure, growing often in the interstices of a poisonous vegetation and perhaps destroyed by their malign environment, but untainted by it. "If Ibsen," he declares, "were the mere cynic, with no eye to beauty and no belief in nobility of character, he would have little enough significance for us. But we are speaking of the creator of Lona Hessel and Martha Bernick . . . of Dr. Stockmann and his wife and daughter and seafaring friend, of Hedwig Ekdal and Juliane Tesman." In some of these the spiritual beauty emerges, like that of Hero or Cordelia, through their reticence; it should not have been difficult to see that this scornful repudiation of Romance had brought into the European drama a kind of beauty in womanhood as free as Shakespeare's from sentimentality and emphasis. To Wicksteed's audience this was made abundantly clear.

Wicksteed's interpretation of Ibsen inevitably

suffered, like that put forward three years later by Mr. Shaw, from the fact that Ibsen was still in the full tide of his creative activity. He was to live eighteen years longer, to produce five [1] more plays, each of them a European event, and whether they marked the climax of his powers (as Mr. Shaw thought of the last four) or their still splendid decline, they showed the veteran poet embarked upon strange seas of thought and art, and had to be reckoned with in any adequate account of him. Nor did Wicksteed ever, like Mr. Shaw, supplement his necessarily imperfect earlier book after Ibsen's death. He wrote indeed a necrologue immediately after that event, published in the *Inquirer* (6 June, 1906). This is, as might be expected, an eloquent and powerful piece of writing. But it scarcely does more than repeat, with new emphasis and the air of finality with which, on the morrow of death, we sum up a closed career, the substance of the *Four Lectures*. None of the plays produced after 1888 is mentioned, and there is no hint that Wicksteed recognized in them, as criticism even then commonly did, a new and highly original phase of Ibsen's art. *Brand* and *Peer Gynt* still occupy the place of honour, and the many-faceted richness of *Peer Gynt*, he could even declare (as we do of Shakespeare), "would furnish any man who knows it well with an epigrammatic comment on all the experiences, all the scenes, and all the characters with which life can present him." The picture of the "Poet of Doubt" exposing the inner rottenness of institutions, movements, passions or characters, and dragging our secret weaknesses relentlessly

[1] *Hedda Gabler*, 1890; *The Master-Builder*, 1892; *Little Eyolf*, 1894; *John Gabriel Borkman*, 1896; *When We Dead Awaken*, 1900.

before our eyes, is repeated without any hint of the new temper and attitude which make these formulas not untrue but insufficient when applied to *The Master-Builder* or *When We Dead Awaken*. But the main currents of his thought and energy were now focused in two regions apparently remote, but as we have seen, for Wicksteed entirely congruous, Economics and Dante. Both these absorbing interests tended in spite of Wicksteed's Norse proclivities, to thrust the terrible "Poet of Doubt" somewhat into the background of his mind. It is neither paradoxical nor hypercritical to believe that Wicksteed's exuberant healthiness, the eternal youth which fourscore years could not subdue, impaired his living interest in the great pathologist, whose art, more prevailingly than Goethe's, had been devoted to exposing the sores of an ailing generation.[1] And in those last four plays which had not been written when Wicksteed wrote, Ibsen, as Mr. Shaw says, "passes into the actual shadow of death," albeit for his art it is rather "the splendour of his sunset glory." "They are tragedies of the dead, deserted and mocked by the young who are full of life." And for youth, too, they are tragic, and they are built upon the unnerving belief that the normal relation between the coming generation and its predecessor is merely a clashing discord.

[1] Ibsen had not, like the greater "physician of the iron age," merely laid his finger on the place, and said, "Thou ailest here and here"; he had probed and cauterized the sore; but no poetic surgery would, as such, have repelled Wicksteed.

III

When Wicksteed, in 1888, delivered the four lectures on Ibsen, he was himself already well known, if not to entirely the same audience, as an interpreter of Dante. Beyond the necrologue just mentioned he wrote no more on Ibsen: Dante became a chief preoccupation for more than forty years. In both cases Wicksteed used the form and the function of a popular lecturer for purposes of much larger significance and scope. In both, he is vindicating as well as expounding. In Ibsen, denounced or applauded as a social iconoclast, he is vindicating the poet and the ethical thinker. Dante stood in no danger from the noisy passions which colour and distort contemporary fame. He was a literary classic, securely sheltered by his six hundred years of fame from the grosser buffetings of criticism. But those six hundred years also debarred him from certain kinds of glory which contemporaries lightly win. For between him and us stood two formidable barriers, popularly known as the Renascence and the Reformation. To the modern educated and Protestant Englishman the great Catholic poet of the thirteenth century was, in general, a subject for respectful, but in every sense distant, homage, not of living concern. It was precisely from that sheltered remoteness, that empty prestige, and across those barriers of "enlightenment" and Protestantism, that Wicksteed, more signally than any other Englishman, drew Dante forth; to vindicate his enduring value as a living force in shaping and building up the soul of the modern man.

For this task Wicksteed had some unusual qualifications. Among them was the fact that he was a genuinely "modern" man himself, a man of his own time and place, with open eye and heart, as we know, for the ideals and problems of the England in which he lived and worked, and sharing to the full the changes in characteristic mentality which distinguish the English, and the European, nineteenth century from its predecessors. First of these for our present purpose was beyond question the growth in imaginative sensibility which has enabled the scientific humanist to enter into the soul of religions which he does not share. And at the root of that enlargement of imaginative sensibility to divergent forms of religion lies, it is no less certain, a consciousness of the intimate kinship of all forms of religion. The welter of alien and incompatible religions become "varieties of religious experience." Hence, for men like Wicksteed, medieval Catholicism was accessible to his intimate apprehension without being a whit nearer to his faith.

More than this. Wicksteed was among the earliest Englishmen of his Puritan Nonconformist breed to enter, not merely with interested curiosity, but with passionate devotion, into the religious mind of the thirteenth century. Of neo-Catholic, as of Pre-Raphaelite sentiment, he was wholly devoid. Rossetti, save in his renderings of Dante, repelled him; Keats, the idol of the Pre-Raphaelites, he could not read.[1] To the specific enthusiasms of the altar and of the studio alike he was normally strange. He regarded the Reformation with little more favour than the

[1] This I learn from his son, Mr. Joseph Wicksteed.

Renascence. Luther, after his first phase, left him cold.[1] Of that neo-Catholic nostalgia which sought to cancel the Reformation in order to recover, if it could, the Middle Ages he had not a trace; but he shared profoundly in that new Renascence of the nineteenth century, which did not so much cancel as enlarge and supplement the old, so that its frontiers took in the medieval no less than the ancient world. Hence he, no less than the neo-Catholic, could look across the sixteenth to the thirteenth century, to Chartres and to Assisi, to Giotto and St. Louis, to St. Francis and St. Catherine and St. Thomas, with the clear-eyed attachment of one who approached them at once with masculine philosophic intelligence, and with the Christian tenderness for the child.[2] And it was as the supreme figure in that company, the singer of Francis, the friend of Giotto, the disciple of Aquinas, that Wicksteed saw Dante. Yes, but also as one who stood among these associates fundamentally alone; the lonely prophet who like Isaiah had thundered at unrighteous rulers, and interpreted the will of God to a stubborn and recalcitrant world.

IV

Wicksteed's first public utterance on Dante was the series of six sermons delivered on successive Sundays in 1879 from his Little Portland Street pulpit. To a

[1] To E. G. Gardner, 25 September, 1906.

[2] Shortly before the appearance of his friend E. G. Gardner's beautiful monograph on Saint Catherine of Siena, he wrote to the author with keen expectation, recommending disdain for the reviewers, of whose verdict upon a book so eloquent of the devotion inspired by the Catholic saints its author had professed himself apprehensive.

casual observer who read the announcement outside, or who strolled in out of curiosity, the contrast between the setting and the subject was extreme. In this London back-street, to this congregation of the rationalist and enlightened left wing of English Nonconformity, the magnificent paradoxes of the medieval Catholic poet were to be expounded, by a modern preacher, not chiefly as interesting literary matter, but in the service of moral and spiritual life, of religion. Yet those who looked back afterwards understood that across the gulfs of apparently irreconcilable disparity, the preacher had magically thrown a bridge. The great medieval Catholic was medieval and Catholic still; he had abated not a tittle of his paradoxes, nor a day of his six hundred years; and yet he was in their midst, their own.

But if Dante's value for Wicksteed might be said to be, in the last resort, his value for the preacher, his potency in the ethical and religious building-up of life, this, though true, would be misleading. The eclecticism which singles out in a great mind what will serve our turn he left to dilettantes and sciolists. His stringent maxim that you had no right to quote a book which you had not read from cover to cover, had a corresponding corollary, that you had no right to speak about a man whom you had not studied through and through. Wicksteed had become noted among English Dantists not less for the range of his Dante scholarship than for his enthralling power as an interpreter of Dante's soul; he was as much himself when he was tramping over hill and dale to visit the site of a battle in which Dante might have fought, or deciphering Dante manuscripts in the Florentine libraries, as when he was carrying eager men and women with him in spirit through the circles of the *Paradiso*, and making them see, as he told how Dante saw, the point of intense light in the centre of the empyrean from which all heaven hung, and whose splendour penetrated the universe, irradiating one part more and another less.

But fundamentally one as Wicksteed's Dante work was, there were variations in the manner as in the scale of the presentment. The *Six Sermons* (1879) he never ceased to regard, and, as his way was, frankly to recommend, as, on the whole, in spite of its immaturity and what he sometimes spoke of disparagingly as "the trail of the preacher," the best introduction for English readers; not a substitute for the admirable *Dante Primer* later provided by his friend, Edmund Gardner, but a general survey of the course, which that book would help them exactly to pursue.[1]

The book already gives us Wicksteed's Dante; a portrait boldly, swiftly drawn, not stippled or subtly articulated, but in his very habit as he lived, swiftly and boldly flung upon the canvas. "Philosopher, prophet, poet, supreme in each, unique as a combination of them all." [2] And in this first portrait it is the prophet whose traits emerge with most salient sharpness from the rest. It did not require the student of

[1] How deeply they impressed their first hearers is evident from the appeal made to him by a representative body of members of his congregation to allow them to arrange for their publication. The terms of the letter imply that the sermons had attracted much attention outside its confines, and were thought likely to attract still more.

[2] "It is most desirable," wrote a fellow-minister who had once been a Roman Catholic, and never ceased to be a Catholic, in acknowledging the *Six Sermons*, "that our people should know something of other prophets than Isaiah and other apostles than Paul."

Hebraism to discern them, but they derive an added poignancy from the remembrance, never far away, of the prophets whom Israel stoned, and whose passion for righteousness first uttered the burning sense of sin. Such memories cannot have escaped those who listened to Wicksteed as he recited the great canzone *Tre Donne,* the exiled poet's picture of Righteousness and her daughters, driven, ragged and in beggary, through the world. But Love, the vindicator, exhorts them: "Let those grieve whom it concerns: what is grief to us, who are of the eternal rock?" And the lonely poet, in the presence of those sublime sufferers, thought his banishment his glory. Still less remote are such suggestions when Wicksteed is laying bare the inner meaning of the torments which horrify and repel the sensitive imagination in the *Inferno*. Not questioning for a moment Dante's belief in the orthodox Hell, Wicksteed insisted that the *Inferno* is not a document of nor a representation of that Hell. It is not a picture of the terrors of Hell displayed to frighten sinners into good conduct; it is, in Dante's familiar words, a picture of Man, choosing, in the exercise of his freewill, to sin, when he might have chosen goodness, and thereby incurring the divinely imposed penalty. The burning purpose that fills Dante's soul is not to deter by exhibiting consequences, but to reveal the horror of sin itself. "Oh, the pity of this sin, the unutterable, indelible pity of it! Its wail can never be stilled in our hearts while thought and memory remain. The misery of some forms of sin, the foul shame of others, the vileness, the hatefulness, the hideous deformity of others yet—this, and not horror at the punishment of sin, is what Dante stamps and brands upon our hearts as we descend with him." [1]

Only, perhaps, one who himself entirely rejected the dogma of eternal punishment could have thus sharply disengaged the ethical core of Dante's poem from its pictorial investiture. Yet Wicksteed is no less free from the opposite illusion of the "emancipated" interpreters, who would release Dante from the superstitions of his age, and make him, medieval only in date, a morning star of the Renascence, a forerunner of the Reformation and the modern world. Dante, he insists, was a medieval Catholic through and through. The shafts of scorn and indignation which he discharges at the Church of his day, though often eagerly borrowed by the early Reformers, were aimed with a different animus. As little could the Church brand him as a heretic by putting his treatise on Monarchy on the Index. Even Virgil's sublime farewell to Dante, when he leaves him, at the threshold of the Earthly Paradise, the "mitred and crowned" lord of himself, is not that first trumpet-note of modern spiritual autonomy which liberal interpreters have willingly heard in it. It applies only to the brief interlude between the departure of Virgil and the coming of Beatrice; and Wicksteed allows it a correspondingly limited significance.

It is not through "anticipations" of modernity that

[1] The distinction so incisively seized in his interpretation of the *Comedy*, between the dread of punishment and the dread of sin, was always acute in Wicksteed. It is illustrated by the story, already told, of one of his sons, convicted of a childish delinquency. "'Are you really sorry, or is it just because you know you are going to be punished?' 'I 'm really sorry,' I said. He took my word for it, and thereby gained a confidence that he never betrayed."

Dante counts for the modern world. Nor is it even only through his consummate and imperishable poetry. Wicksteed's analysis went deeper, when he insisted, and it is the very core of his Dante teaching to insist, that Dante, by and through the Catholic and medieval vesture of his thought, penetrated to the universal elements of all religion, and thus spoke, in his own great idiom, to universal man.

V

The *Six Sermons*, then, were already something more than a prelude to the years of brilliant exposition, interpretation, and research that followed. Between them and the "epilogue"—*From Vita Nuova to Paradiso*—of 1922, more than forty years intervened, during which he won a place of lasting repute among English Dante scholars. In the first book he had scarcely entered, in the last he had for some years withdrawn from, the arena of specialist debate upon Dante. But all his Dante work from first to last was informed and impelled by the same fundamental purpose and the same fundamental belief: the missionary aim to make the soul of Dante accessible to and operative in the growing minds of the English people; and the conviction that Dante's life and work were an organic whole, to which all merely fragmentary approach was futile. Three years before his death he wrote to a correspondent (2 January, 1924) who had expressed high appreciation of that last book: "I am sometimes tempted to think that few readers of Dante care much to form a synthetic view of his work either as psychologically and biographically connected, or in its relation to the age to which it belongs but from which it stands off, and transcends. I have long lost touch with the minute discussions that sometimes seem to distract students' sense of the whole organism, and it is a true happiness at the close of my life to find here and there one who considers my aim in my farewell work worth attention."

This, however, is not to say that all the component parts, in the vast complex of Dante's experience and achievements, attracted or detained Wicksteed's attention in the same degree. Of least interest to him, without question, were those researches into the technique of poetic form, and of literary speech, which are nevertheless so astonishing by their reach of prosodic and linguistic insight at that date. The treatise *On the Vernacular Speech* (*De Vulgari Eloquentia*), was, in its linguistic portion (Book I), although surprising in philological grasp, of direct concern only for Italians, and the Italians of Dante's time, and Dante himself was to play the chief part in making it obsolete, by deciding once for all in what kind of Italian the poets of Italy were henceforth to write. The diversity of dialects set forth in his brilliant survey symbolized only too faithfully the clashing discords among the states—cities, republics, dukedoms, kingdoms—which then, and for five hundred years more, frustrated his dream of a united Italy. But in literature his triumph was already won.

With Dante's linguistic inquiries, then, Wicksteed was only in this general sense concerned. Nor did he dwell with very eager scrutiny upon the subtleties of Dante's rhythmical sense, the structure of the canzone, and the other complex lyric forms, or on the niceties of the noble *terza rima* itself. Even in his translations of Dante's verse he never affected any of the fastidious delicacy of diction, idiom, and vocabulary, which a writer who cared more for language as an art would have called more assiduously into play. On exactness of speech he insisted; but the curious felicity of the virtuoso in phrase was not his affair, and the unsubdued and unsubduable Puritan in him made him always readier to laugh at this æsthetic virtuosity than to emulate it. It was only in the *Comedy* that Dante professedly wrote for the "muliercula"; but Wicksteed in all his translations of Dante disclaimed, and not only or chiefly from modesty, any purpose but to provide access for plain folks to the soul of Dante. Yet grave injustice, as has already been noted,[1] would be done to Wicksteed's mastery of language if we looked to his translations only. "Translation" as such had in it something repugnant to him; its secondary and derivative quality balked and thwarted the current of his elemental and *primesautier* mind. It was only when he was thrown back upon his native fund of expression, when he had to put Dante's thought in his own way, that the richness and resource of his speech have full scope. Hence it is that the incomparable "Arguments" of the successive cantos serve, even better than his longer expositions, to replace his lectures, for those who have not heard them.

[1] Cf. Chapter IV, section vii.

VI

Far nearer to Wicksteed's interest, and even at one point touching the core of his intensest sympathy, lay Dante the *lover*. The topics of the loftiest poetry, as enumerated by Dante in the treatise just referred to, are three only: virtue, war, and love; love being the discovery of the modern poets, especially of the troubadours of Provence. Love, as cultivated at the Courts of Provence, was a brilliant but unwholesome flower. In the troubadours' songs and ballads human nature inspired poetry at the cost of human society; the loyalty of lovers presupposed (since the lady was always married) disloyalty between husband and wife. But the seed of Provençal poetry fell upon the richer soil of Italy. In the schools of Bologna where Dante is supposed to have studied, there grew up a love-poetry as noble as any in the world, even if its nobility was won at the cost of an attenuation of the nature of love itself. For Guido Guinicelli honoured love as a purely spiritual potency, so alien to the body that it not merely controlled or, as in ideal marriage, transfigured bodily appetite, but destroyed and annihilated it. Love was declared, in Guinicelli's famous verse, to be the very negation of evil:

Amor e gentil cor son una cosa.

It is the secret of that "new sweet style" which he originated. But Dante, who had previously learnt from the troubadours all that they could teach, surpassed his master, and the greatest monument of the "new sweet style" was that *Vita Nuova* which enshrines his spiritual love for Beatrice.

Of the historicity of Beatrice, Wicksteed from first to last admitted no doubt. But after the death of Beatrice Portinari, in 1290, Dante underwent experiences of love materially other than those reflected (if reflected they were) in the *Vita Nuova*. At some time not long after her death he married, as she had married. His wife bore him four children before his exile in 1302; she survived him, and nothing is known in her disfavour; unless it be a ground of dispraise to have inspired no poetry in a great poet, and to be never certainly alluded to in his work. What little is known, or can reasonably be inferred about her, is entirely to Gemma's credit, and Wicksteed always repudiated the slighting judgment of her put forward, on quite inadequate grounds, by some Dante critics. And probably during the same years that followed the death of Beatrice, Dante knew a fiercer passion; a love terrible and tormenting, lawless, sensual and fruitless. This love found utterance, not in brief bursts of liquid song, like the love of Burns, but in complex and magnificent canzoni, whose intricately woven rhythms never impede for a moment the vehement onrush of passion and thought. It may be that we must find, with Mr. Abercrombie, the climax of Dante's sheer poetic splendour in the last of these enigmatic Pietra odes.

It is clear that Dante the lover, in all these phases offers a problem to the Dante interpreter, and a touchstone of Dante interpretation; he has, moreover, complicated the whole matter by resorting to the elusive medieval instrument of allegory. For we have now to recognize a fourth kind of love, his intellectual passion for a "lady" who, if she did not replace Beatrice in his affections, consoled him for her loss. Allegorically, she was the "Philosophy," whose spell engrossed his intellect after her death.[1] His prose treatise, the *Convivio*, or *Banquet*, is an imposing feast of medieval learning in the form of a commentary on three of his canzoni. Two of these, ostensibly songs of love, are deliberately interpreted, as inspired neither by Beatrice nor by any other woman of flesh and blood, but by the Lady Philosophy.

Now here Dante put into the hands of the after-world an instrument dangerously seductive. Allegorizing is an easy game, and if Dante himself could declare one of his odes to Beatrice to be allegory, why should not she herself and her whole story in the *Vita Nuova* be allegory no less? But if so, in the great central scene of the *Comedy*, where Dante is examined by Beatrice, confesses his aberrations, and is rebuked, what kind of aberrations is he confessing?

It was upon these subtle and elusive controversies that Wicksteed brought to bear his insight into the heights and depths of human nature, and his own experience of the kindred exaltations of thought and passion, of philosophic enthusiasm and ideal love, his masculine humanity and his clear good sense.

The crucial passage, then, is the examination and confession (in *Purgatorio*, xxxi). "What," asks Beatrice, "were those fosses, and what those chains, that thou foundest across thy path, barring thee from hope of further progress?" Dante hangs his head in deep and bitter shame; then confesses that "the lure of false pleasures had turned his steps astray."

It is in interpreting this confession that authoritative

[1] It is needless to touch here upon the further complication introduced by Dante in the "Screen-Lady."

exponents have diverged. For the school of Witte this scene marked the central moment not only of the *Comedy*, but of Dante's whole career. For it represented Dante's final return from the aberrations of Philosophy to the Catholic Theology of his early faith, a process symbolized by his reconciliation with Beatrice, who after his ascent through Purgatory becomes his escort to Paradise, as she had once inspired his youthful vision of "The New Life." [1] Wicksteed never ceased to acknowledge his debt to the epoch-making essays of Witte, which cleared away the "political pamphleteer" view of Dante, vindicated his profound religious faith, and presented his life as a sublime and organic whole,—an epic trilogy of which the hero was Dante himself, and the theme his spiritual progress through error and recovery to Truth. But the trilogy scheme bore too obviously the stamp of that Hegelian dialectic of which, at the date of its inception (1824), few of the most alert and eager German minds escaped the spell. Wicksteed was not alone in holding that that imposingly symmetrical arrangement of Dante's life was purchased at too heavy a cost. Witte was an ardent Catholic, and in no part of his work was he more completely justified than when he repudiated with scorn the view then widely current, that Dante was a modernist born before his time, a morning star of the Renascence or of the Reformation. In this repudiation, Wicksteed, as we know, heartily concurred: it was the very core of his Dante exposition. But he held no less decisively that Witte in vindicating Dante's medievalism had not been medieval enough. In his eagerness to emphasize the

[1] Karl Witte: *Ueber das Misverständnis Dantes* (1824); *Dantes Trilogie.*

gravity of those philosophical aberrations from which Dante had returned to Beatrice and to Catholicism, he ignored that Dante's "philosophy" was that of the great Catholic doctor St. Thomas, and that its "paganism" was merely that of the Aristotelian ideas incorporated by Aquinas into his great fabric of Christian doctrine. Aquinas's system is based upon the doctrine that human reason, though it cannot attain to the truths of Revelation, is trustworthy within its own sphere, that "philosophy," the domain of reason, is therefore not a digression from "theology," but an incomplete step towards it. That Dante put forward in the *Convivio* some opinions which he subsequently abandoned for others, which he puts into the mouth of Beatrice in the *Paradiso,* does not affect the fact that in the *Comedy* he treats the transition from philosophy to theology not as a recantation of error, but as an advance from imperfect to complete truth; an advance symbolized by the relation of Virgil to Beatrice, for Virgil, the representative of the wisdom attainable by reason alone, has been dispatched at the instance of Beatrice herself to guide Dante's steps to the Earthly Paradise which marked the limit of his sphere. It was not then his pursuit of Philosophy that brought upon Dante the reproaches of Beatrice. His wooing of that purely allegorical lady involved no infidelity to her.

But what, then, was the offence for which she so sharply reprimanded him, and which he, with so much contrition, confesses? That Dante's love for Beatrice had been deflected by any attachment which could not be expressed in doctrinal terms would have impaired the symmetrical coherence of the trilogy. The fierce eroticism of the Pietra odes was either explained as merely bold imagery for a philosophic passion; or huddled into a wholly hypothetical corner of Dante's adolescence before he had fallen under the spell of that virginal adoration for the girl on whom, as a boy of nine, he had gazed with awe. The "philosophy" was thus conveniently clothed in the hues of a diabolic temptation proper to whatever distracted the lover of Beatrice from fidelity to the faith of the Church.

To this view, as to the Manichæan conception of "philosophy" which occasioned it, Wicksteed opposed an explanation which consorts better with the interpretation both of medieval thinking and of Dante's mind. The Pietra odes reflect a real passion for a real girl; an experience, he urged in his last book, "not rare in natures of exceptional energy, and high devotion to intellectual pursuits." [1] This enthralment was the chain which had barred his progress, and which he confesses with shame to Beatrice to have caused his infidelity to her. It was thus a passion of his mature manhood, subsequent to her death. That Dante meant to allegorize it in the *Convivio,* as he allegorized the real and beautiful love song in the canzoni of the second and third treatise, is probable; the shame it caused him may even have been among the motives which prompted the whole scheme of allegory in the *Convivio*. But fortunately, as Wicksteed says, he never reached that point. Had he done so,

[1] This interpretation inevitably impairs our conception of the virginal Dante, derived from the *Vita Nuova,* just as the "Annette" episode impairs our conception of the virginal Wordsworth. Wicksteed accepted it with deep and natural reluctance, and expressed it with a reticence which may well have disguised from his readers the real nature of the Pietra odes. But he makes clear that this was his solution.

one asks, could even he have turned into persuasive allegory his superb but terrific picture of Love's vengeful coming to the "stony" maid? How could the most ardent love of philosophy symbolize itself in this lover who would "seize those locks that have become my scourge and lash, lay hold of them ere tierce and pass with them vespers and evening bells, and have neither pity nor courtesy in my sport"? For this nice distinction to which Dante compels us, between allegorical and literal interpretations, Wicksteed laid down in his last book a canon as important as it is characteristic of himself. "If what seem like mere elegances or conceits when literally interpreted begin to glow when referred to the experiences of the baffled but indomitable student, then Philosophy is the lady of the poet's love. If the passion becomes pale, the images less vivid, and the expression strained when Philosophy is substituted for a human personality, then it would be wronging Dante's genius to take the poems on any other footing than as love poems in the primary sense. And this wrong we must not do him even though it should be at his own bidding.[1] From this canon, Wicksteed drew the conclusion which we hold just, that the Lady Philosophy was simply—Philosophy, and the object of the Pietra canzoni simply—a woman.

This view alone adequately explains both the deep contrition of Dante, and the anger (such anger as celestials feel) of Beatrice. Dante did during these years fall into intellectual error; he adopted a mistaken explanation, for instance, of the spots in the moon. But when Beatrice, in the *Paradiso* sets him right (in

[1] *From Vita Nuova to Paradiso*, p. 74.

a way that shows, as Wicksteed remarks, that she herself might, with even more profit, have been "examined" by modern science), it is not with the grieved resentment of one chastising, but with just such intellectual sarcasm as a modern astronomer might have applied to herself. To make the emotional tension of that confession scene in the Earthly Paradise plausible we have to conceive Philosophy as severed from Beatrice, and Dante from Theology, by a yawning chasm, such as divided the eighteenth-century *philosophes* from the Church, not by such trivial "errors" as these.

To sum up. The virginal loveliness of the passion enshrined in the culminating passages of the *Vita Nuova* did not need a Wicksteed to praise it, nor can his words be compared for kindred beauty with the prose rendering of Rossetti. Some fine scholars have refused to accept the reality of the story it tells. We need not speak slightly of them; the allegorical theory can be made on internal grounds very plausible. But Wicksteed was never among them. Least of all would he have admitted in its support the argument that the spiritual adoration described there is a psychological *Unding*, real only as the lovely dream of a poet. He knew the lover's adoration too well. But neither would he consent to dissolve in allegory the utterances of fierce and torturing erotic passion. He refused to attenuate any of the elements which contended in Dante's complex nature. As the young man's bodiless, ecstatic love of Beatrice was real, so was the mature man's encounter in the trackless forest with the wild beasts of passion. In Dante Wicksteed saw one of those in whom the senses throw out a challenge to the soul, who impress us by the fullness, as well as by the transcendence, of the experiences they communicate. And powerful as was the vein of inherited Puritan asceticism in himself, he watched and interpreted those "conflicts of sense and soul" in the spirit of Browning and Meredith, not of Tennyson. And if Dante, who touches us at so many points, remains strange to the modern conception of wedded love, he knew something of wifely devotion in other men's experience, and Wicksteed delights to dwell on the brief glimpses of devoted wives which refresh us at moments in that tremendous journey.

VII

If Wicksteed, then, refused to see in the "Lady Philosophy" a woman for whom Dante was unfaithful to Beatrice, or a woman at all—what was this "Philosophy"? The answer must be sought of course, in that philosophical treatise, the *Convivio*, to which Wicksteed devoted some of his most powerful critical discussion. The title hints, and the glowing first chapter discloses, one aspect of what "philosophy" meant for Dante. It meant wisdom gathered from a rich table to be scattered broadcast before a hungry world. Like Aquinas, whose treatise, *Against the Gentiles,* Dante here emulated, he wrote, not only with speculative, but with missionary ardour. At that banquet the bread of angels is eaten; but few, as he said later in the *Paradiso,* are they who eat it. Dante himself, proudest and humblest of men, is not one of the guests, but has left the common herd of careless livers to gather up the crumbs that fall from it, and scatter them among the hungry flock. It was in this temper that Aquinas, like St. Paul, approached the "Gentiles"; and it is easy to understand Wicksteed's inexhaustible interest in a book that opened with this parable, in which Plato and Christ mingled, and the answer of the Samaritan woman to Jesus was carried to a yet further height of spiritual beauty. To Dante distributing his crumbs of the bread of angels among the hungry multitude the lecturer and teacher could bring the devotion of the disciple as well as the homage of the scholar.

But it was also in the *Convivio* that Wicksteed found the principal record of the formative period of Dante's intellectual nature. There are signs in it of immaturity, and it is distinguished from the *Comedy* by clear differences, both of tone and atmosphere, and in the details of opinion. But it is, on the whole, a homogeneous and impressive body of erudition and thought, which the *Comedy* superbly enriches and supplements, but does not repudiate. This would be impossible if Dante's "Lady Philosophy" had been an antagonist of Theology, or of Beatrice in its impersonation. As has been already remarked, we must not apply to the fourteenth century reasoning proper to the conditions of the eighteenth, when Christian theology was confronted by a definitely irreligious "philosophy" in the person of a Hume or a Diderot. The "philosophy" of the *Convivio* was not even exactly symbolized by Virgil in the *Comedy*, who leads Dante to the point where Beatrice is to meet him. It did not prepare for theology, it included it.

To find such philosophy in or before Dante's time, and known to him, we have to go outside Christendom altogether to the ancients, or the Mohammedans of

East and West. All these, from Aristotle to Averroes and Avicenna, Dante placed, as his theology required, and without a murmur of question, in hell; but it was in that pleasant forecourt of the *Inferno* which to our eyes rather resembles the Elysium of the ancients; and even the Arabs, who were not heathen, but in the Christian view infidels, who had even "blasphemed Christ," shared this favoured treatment, to the indignation of some of the early commentators. Clearly the poet who, at the outset of his sublime Christian allegory, thus manifested his large charity not only to philosophers who had never known Christianity, but to those who had known and actively assailed it, was not confessing to Beatrice in the same poem his bitter repentance for having devoted himself to philosophy at all, even had it been one expressly heretical.

And it is certain that the philosophy which won Dante's devotion during the years between the death of Beatrice and the supposed date of the vision was in no sense heretical at all. It was not even distinguished from theology, as secular from "divine" wisdom. It comprehended all forms of wisdom, secular and divine alike, under one name. The philosophy of which Dante is enamoured included all branches of human knowledge from theology to arithmetic. Between theology or revealed knowledge and secular knowledge there was thus for Dante a clear division, but there was not a cleft. And this was equally true, as we have seen of his later mind: in the *Comedy*, too, the division between theology and philosophy is not a cleft, but a step.

The *Convivio*, where Dante describes his devotion to the Lady Philosophy, and sets forth its first fruits, is the key then to this problem, and Wicksteed's admirable exposition of it is the key to his interpretation of Dante. Two points are here made clear. First, that Dante's interest in philosophy was at this stage predominantly in its secular elements. The substance of the teaching which his missionary passion seeks to make the common possession of his Italian fellow-citizens, is drawn mainly from Aristotle and Boëthius. He can speak of heaven as the "Celestial Athens," and he draws examples of the contemplative life, not from any Christian mystics, but from Plato, Aristotle, and Seneca.

But further, theology, as represented by Aquinas, though it still holds a second place in Dante's interest, has never been for a moment displaced in his faith. St. Thomas is his master as well as Boëthius, and Aquinas, clearly as he marked off sacred from secular wisdom, had been the most powerful instrument of reconciliation between them; for his herculean task had been, precisely, to weld the philosophy of Aristotle into the edifice of Christian dogma, so that the study of knowledge became not a desertion of the study of sacred knowledge, but a necessary approach to it—the approach which Virgil was to symbolize in the *Comedy* when he led Dante up to the threshold of the Earthly Paradise.

The Dante reflected in the *Convivio* is one who, however, symbolically unfaithful to Beatrice, was in reality preparing himself by many-sided intellectual study for the culminating spiritual vision which in the *Comedy* under her guidance he achieves.

VIII

All ways in Dante lead to the *Comedy,* and so they do in Wicksteed's interpretation of him. But they were not all equally congenial to the interpreter's tread. Dante's *statecraft,* in particular, makes large demands upon the modern student of politics, not least upon the English Liberal. We pay all honour to the able and energetic citizen of Florence, whom his fellow-citizens chose as its envoy on a difficult and dangerous mission to the Pope. But what are we to make of the political solution which Dante found and ardently embraced until it was frustrated by events? What are we to make of that passionate appeal to the German Emperor Henry VII to impose peace and unity upon Italy by arms? It is enough to reply that for Dante—and no one has ever made it clearer than Wicksteed—the decisive ground (precarious or fallacious as we may think it) was not a military triumph, but the assurance of peace. Henry stood for the Roman Empire, and the Roman Empire was the empire of the Roman law, the empire first won, indeed, by arms, but only (he held) as the preparatory instrument of that peaceful rule, and therefore symbolized in the poem by Justinian, not by Cæsar. Nor did he ever put his magnificent symbolism to more significant use. For the early Christian centuries Pagan Rome was, as in Orosius's invectives, the power which by rude violence shattered the elementary (the pacifist or Tolstoyan) "peace" of Jesus. From Virgil, the poet of the Roman empire who had heralded the birth of Christ, Dante learnt the larger pacifism of a law-abiding society, just as he had learnt from Aquinas the larger Christianity which included instead of repudiating philosophy. No other great poet, as Croce has justly said, is so completely free from the taint of militarism.

Dante's political ideal, then, was the application of the Roman law to the distracted society of his country; and an ideal set forth with superb eloquence in the treatise on Monarchy, written shortly before the death of the emperor, which turned what had always, during Dante's life, been a visionary but credible Utopia, into a shattered dream. With "monarchy" in the ordinary sense the book has little to do, for there is as little of the royalist in him as of the militarist; courts and camps were equally places where, whatever hospitable favours they might afford him, he only thought how bitter were the alien stairs he mounted, and the alien bread he ate. None the less, his readers in a century for which "monarchy" has come to signify an office mainly, or often, otiose, will discover the grandeur of which the conception is capable, when used, as Dante uses it, to denote the counterpart on earth of the divine government of the universe. Nothing less august than this was the prerogative, in theory, of the emperor who inherited the imperial titles and attributes of Rome; and when Dante, with passionate vehemence, called on the German Henry VII to cross the Alps and restore order in Italy, he was not betraying Italian patriotism, but summoning Cæsar to assert and enforce his rightful sway, that authority of law which the Roman Empire had created and the Italian chaos of rival parties, states, and cities destroyed. It is only on the surface that Dante's policy appears to offend against either true patriotism or wise citizenship. It was fundamentally inspired by both alike. And as such, Wicksteed, his exponent, was clearly at one with it.

But with another aspect of Dante's argument in the *Monarchia* Wicksteed was in yet deeper accord. This was the repudiation of the claim of the Church to infringe upon the secular power. For Dante, here, God speaks to man directly through his secular vicegerent, not only through ecclesiastical mediation. His position here is analogous to that of Hooker, nearly three centuries later, with us; he is vindicating the divine authority and authenticity of the State against the medieval Church as the great Anglican vindicated it against the left-wing Protestants; the politics of immanent Reason, Greek in essence if not in form. He was opposing a politics based upon Canon Law, as Hooker a politics based upon biblical texts.[1] The polemics of the *Monarchia* were not wholly obsolete in Wicksteed's time and country. Encroachments of the ecclesiastical upon the civil power, if chiefly through the medium of civil legislation, were not unknown; and Wicksteed, since the beginning of his ministry, had witnessed at least three capital vindications of civil justice—the disestablishment of the Irish Church (1869), the abolition of University Tests (1871), and the Elementary Education Act (1872). These events Wicksteed had followed with deep moral and

[1] Incidentally, Dante dismisses some of the stock biblical arguments of the papal casuists for committing temporal as well as spiritual power to the Pope, with a quite modern freedom. Peter's offer of two swords was interpreted to signify the right of Peter's successors to the two kinds of authority. "This is to be entirely denied," Dante says; "first, because the answer was not according to Christ's wish, secondly because Peter, as usual, was answering in haste and superficially." *Mon.* III, 9.

intellectual satisfaction, analogous to that with which he had followed Kuenen's deposition of the priests of Israel from their traditional priority to her prophets; and they gave an acuter relevance, for him and for his hearers, to the arraignment of the Roman priesthood by the sublime prophet of medieval Italy.

Yet this point of view, though very real in Wicksteed, as of course in Dante, does not fully explain his deeper mind, just as it marks, for Dante, only a step itself incomplete, to the sublime synthesis he finally attained. The *Monarchia* is not entirely homogeneous. Dante is borne by the very course of his argument to conceptions which modify its purport. In this very treatise, designed to vindicate the authority of the secular power, we nevertheless encounter the quite new conception, "a twofold government of the world corresponding to his twofold destiny for earthly and for heavenly bliss." [1] It is natural to surmise that, as Wicksteed puts it, the Christian and Platonic elements of Dante's thought, were undermining the Aristotelian. Spirit and Matter, the "things pertaining to Cæsar" and the "things pertaining to God," two divinely recognized and distinguished realms—did not these demand distinct provinces in the government of the world? And if so, could the things of God, and of the soul, be assigned to the lower? In other words, the Empire and the Church acquire in Dante's hands, without any conscious inconsistency, a quite altered significance. The Church appears in the closing chapters of the *Monarchia*, no longer as the arrogant power from whose usurpation he has to vindicate the claims of its rival, but as the power whose function, recognized as higher, her temporal

[1] *From Vita Nuova to Paradiso*, p. 128.

rival ought to revere "as the eldest son the father." [1] But Dante never confounds reverence with prostration. He never swerves from the assertion of the rights of the "things of Cæsar," of the body, however subordinate in function to the things of God, and of the soul. The greatest of the singers of another world is the farthest from other-worldliness. The graduated ascent of the *Comedy*, where Eden, the Earthly Paradise, is the subordinate, but indispensable, first step to the heavenly Beatitudes, is already present in germ. And, if we abstract the magnificent apparatus of medieval dogma and symbolism, Wicksteed, Dante's exponent, is here his disciple, too. For no man of his time had the things of the soul a deeper and more glorious import than for this man of rich senses and abounding health: to none was the "religion of eternity" more clearly visible than to this adept in the varieties political, social, economic, and "natural," of the religion of Time.

IX

But whatever its enduring significance, the immediate purpose of the *Monarchia* was frustrated, as is well known, within a few months of its completion, by the death of the emperor. His fatal sickness had been preceded by long and unnecessary delays, which provoked his own advocate to outbursts of expostulation, as Hebraic in phrase and vehemence as those addressed to the common enemy. But with his death, not only did the *Monarchia* become, as a practical argument, obsolete, but the entire edifice of Dante's

[1] *Mon.*, III, 16. *From Vita Nuova to Paradiso*, p. 130.

politics fell to the ground. It was a blow from which few men would have recovered. And Dante was nearly fifty, solitary, poor, and worn by twelve years of exile. If, as Wicksteed had come to believe, and as very cogent internal reasons urge, the *Comedy* was only now planned, it is hard to find in the records of literature an achievement comparable for the plenitude it implies of genius, intellect, moral passion, and will, with his. The works of Milton's blind old age alone approach it.

For, whatever the foreshadowings in the Latin *Monarchia* of its scheme and structure, the *Comedy* was built upon a fundamental change of purpose. The key to the whole is Virgil's offer, in the Prologue, when he finds Dante confronted by the three beasts, symbols of corrupt and incorrigible Church and State, to lead him out of that desperate *impasse* "by another way" to the ordered and righteous peace of Eden on earth, the "Sunlit Hill."

To an English Nonconformist, and one who had for years been following with deep sympathy the newly interpreted history of the religion of Israel, the temptation may well have been great to over-accentuate the lonely apartness of Dante's "other way," and the significance of the rejection of the guidance of the priest and of the civil ruler which it implied. Certainly he dismisses with incisive emphasis the attempts of some of the Catholic exponents to explain away the ecclesiastical interpretation of the obstructing evils from which Virgil offers to Dante, and through him to all men, the only available path to happiness in this life. Nor has any one drawn out more cogently than he the full bearings of this great moment, the close of the Prologue, as the key to the entire *Comedy*. But in Dante, we know, independence and discipleship, intellectual autonomy and reverent docility, were united as they have rarely been. Socrates, wisest of men, was accustomed to ascribe his wisdom to a divine voice or a divine woman; but he was the first and greatest master of "Irony"; and of this Greek quality, of which Dante, too, was a consummate master elsewhere, there is not a trace in his discipleship to Virgil and Beatrice. In other words, that intellectual autonomy of his, which permits him, as by a native right of sovereignty, to chastise emperors and popes with whips and scorpions, and to reshape as he pleases the Church's authentic traditions of Hell and Purgatory, makes him, no less, the submissive recipient of the authorities he recognizes, Philosophy and Theology themselves. The universe, it might be said without hyperbole, he "ruled as he thought fit." But what Dante "thought fit," was dictated, in the structure of the universe, as in his own poetry, by Love, whose splendour pervaded every part, and inspired his lady and her divine wisdom, as it moved "the sun and the other stars." He had made himself, by devoted and prolonged study, a proficient philosopher and theologian himself, and now he could offer to his countrymen, in language not technical but (so he fondly believed) such as any simple woman could understand, the means of reaching, as he had reached, the "Sunlit Hill" of earthly welfare and blessedness after death. It was now the *Comedy* which took the place of a corrupt Church and a decrepit State.

The lay temper of Dante's religion has been strikingly defined by Vossler: "There was nothing habitual or professional in Dante's piety . . . nothing priestly or ministerial, nothing of the virtuoso nor of the monk. A pious man but no saint." [1]

And thus in Philip Wicksteed's hands, a modern "layman" surely also in Vossler's sense, the *Comedy* could resume for thousands of English men and women something of the function for which Dante had designed it, a "banquet," far richer than his own *Convivio,* in the Bread of Angels, even the crumbs from which yield sustenance to the Spirit of Man.

He could not have done this, had there not been, in himself, some measure of that synthetic unity which Dante apparently without effort achieved, between autonomous personality and Catholic comprehensiveness. It was here that what was Greek in his mind, his profound sociality, his insight into the philosophy of the city state, of citizenship as the vitality of the citizen, of totality as the secret of individuality, found satisfaction and utterance, satisfying too, while yet controlling and guiding, the impetus of his "Norse" self-will.

X

If we sought to sum up in a single word the spirit of Wicksteed's Dante labours, it would be this vital synthesis of vision and citizenship, of apprehension of the things that endure and eager concern with the things that pass, to which Dante's writings and example so powerfully aided him. And such a word he found himself, in the great discourse on *The Religion of Time*

[1] K. Vossler, *Medieval Culture: an Introduction to Dante and his Times* (English translation), I, 82.

and The Religion of Eternity (1899), which may serve equally as an epilogue to this sketch of his work on Dante, and as an introduction to his study of Dante's relation to the principal scholastic source of his thought to which it will lead us. The discourse was delivered at Essex Hall, some two years after he had left London for a country home.

The doctrine that "eternity" is not time indefinitely prolonged, but the concentration of every "when" in one moment, as of every "where" in one point, was, of course, familiar to Wicksteed, as to many of his audience; for it is in Plato as in Boëthius. But it may well have been the overpowering sublimity of Dante's presentation of it which turned, for Wicksteed, what Newman called a "notional" into a "real" apprehension of it. The ordinary reader of the *Paradiso* is apt to be entirely bewildered when, after climbing with Dante and Beatrice through the successive planetary spheres, each revolving more rapidly than the last about its centre, the earth, he finds, in the Empyrean, that all his previous experience of space and time is illusory, and that every "where" and every "when" are embraced in that infinite point from which the universe depends, and which moves the sun and the other stars.

What Dante had done for Wicksteed, the Essex Hall discourse, through his powerful presentment, did for the majority of his hearers. And it did more. For Wicksteed, a staunch Liberal thinker and worker, a Protestant preacher, addressing an audience for the most part of the same mind, would have performed but a slight service had he merely expounded a medieval Catholic dogma with impressive power. But he showed how the medieval dogma was still for us potentially alive; how it was capable both of enriching our modernism, and of releasing us from some of its most attractive superstitions.

It was not difficult to show that the medieval conception of Eternity was no product of dogmatic ingenuity, or of visionary exaltation, but had a parallel in many kinds of intense experience familiar to the modern and to the secular mind. Psychological science and creative art concurred in describing it, and he quoted from William James the unconscious tribute of Mozart, when he declared of his own pieces: "All the invention and making goes on in me as in a beautiful strong dream. But the best of all is the hearing of it all at once." This "hearing all at once" was what Wordsworth calls "the awful and beautiful sense of coexisting completeness," experienced by one who follows the already familiar *Agamemnon* or *King Lear*. But from another side he found the germ of that religion of Eternity in the sublimity which, for Wordsworth, invested mathematical truth, a type of the Being which is beyond "melancholy space and doleful time, and hath the name of God."[1] We only "possess" the things which we call eternal if they exist for us complete in the moment in which we "realize" them. And we only "enjoy" completely and significantly when we thus possess.

It was thus that the medieval doctrine of "fruition" or enjoyment arose directly from the medieval con-

[1] It may be recorded here, as an example of Wicksteed's union of insight and scholarship, that, in a note to the published lecture (p. 12), he proposed to excise the comma before "God" in the 1850 text, which for the common reader improves, but for finer minds destroys, the sense. Mr. de Selincourt's reproduction of the original version confirms the excision.

ception of Eternity, and was the most vital expression of that religion. God "enjoys" the universe because "all existences exist in Him," and enjoyment as a divine attribute survived the Reformation and the austerity of Calvinism; for the Shorter Catechism bids the devout, not only to glorify God, but to "enjoy Him for ever."

Medieval religion had thus in its great doctrine of Eternity a compensation for the poverty of its conception of Time. Its Time, like its Space, was narrow and limited; no Copernicus had opened the prospect of a boundless universe, no doctrine of Progress had opened up infinite possibilities of future happiness on earth.

But precisely to our cherished faith in progress, which was also in the fullest degree his own, Wicksteed applies as a salutary caveat that medieval doctrine of fruition, and we may hear the voice of the man of abounding and glad vitality, as well as that of the student of Dante and Augustine, in the trenchant sentences in which he derides the ideal of progress as an end in itself, dismissing with humorous peremptoriness Lessing's famous preference of the eternal quest of Truth to its attainment, so often held up as the very acme of the idealistic temper.[1] Another great contemporary

[1] The repugnance to the postponement, whether of a satisfaction or of a debt, was deeply engrained in Wicksteed's mind, and determines his attitude in very varied regions of his thought. It was one of the sources of his contempt for the popular eschatology. "People seek refuge from all these questions in 'the future life,'" he had written some years before, to a brother; "but that seems to me to be a spendthrift philosophy, meeting all our present claims by recklessly drawing upon our 'expectations' instead of paying our way as we go along."—(To his brother Thomas Wicksteed, 1 January, 1886.) Wicksteed was all of one stuff; his religion and his economics were nourished at the same root. This was one reason why, as his friend Miss Knappert has acutely said, "he was always the same, and yet always a surprise."

poet, Robert Browning, had canonized that faith in scores of poems; that satisfaction is a lower state than aspiration is the central text of his ethical philosophy.[1] But, against this congenial doctrine, Wicksteed, as strenuous a Liberal as either Browning or Lessing, brings to bear the sharp corrective of St. Augustine; it is an example, he declares, of that perversity in which Augustine finds the source of every vice—an inversion of the proper rôle of "enjoyment" and "use." "We wish to enjoy what we ought to use, and to use what we ought to enjoy"; we seek, merely as a step to something beyond, what we ought to pursue for its own sake. And the moral struggle itself becomes self-contradictory if conceived merely as a struggle with evil, which if successful leaves us without a goal, a definite conception of good, to struggle for. The same solvent Wicksteed applies to more recent and more speculative examples of the fertility of the idea of "progress" in the modern mind: the heaven of "endless progress" towards perfection, which has replaced "the heaven of the landscape gardener, the lapidary, and the upholsterer"; a perfection, however, which, in the crucible of F. H. Bradley's analysis, turns out to be one which is realized only on condition that it is deferred, and ceases to exist when it is "enjoyed." Nor has Wicksteed any patience with the modern doctrine of a progressive *God*. "Our age demands a progressive Deity, capable of having his

[1] And yet another, whose idealism was more deeply grounded than Browning's, found himself in deep accord with Wicksteed here. "I have had your little book *Religion of Time and Religion of Eternity* beside me last week," wrote an old friend, after a bereavement, "and in my lectures on Progress as an ideal of action I quoted from it at length. Bless you for writing it!"

life enriched by successive experiences, a Christ who is an actual participant in the struggles of life, and has not won but is yet winning, his victories." And he reproaches his fellow Unitarians for allowing this anthropolatry to sap their faith in the divine Eternity. But far from discouraging their struggle for progress, that faith in divine fruition will only clarify and quicken it. "To conceive of love and knowledge as eternal fruition will surely throw us into our life of progress with a quickened realization of its significance, with the sense of its inherent contradiction banished, with its daily fragments of intercourse with God, with nature and with man deepened into continuity."

Such words make clear, if it were needed, the polar difference between the medievalism of Wicksteed and that of either the Oxford Movement, sixty years before, or of the Anglo-Catholics of his own day. The ritual of the Church of Rome, with its refined symbolism, its subtle appeal to the spirit through the senses, was beginning to exercise its solvent force upon Puritan tradition and habit, and it already had adherents among Unitarians. These might be supposed to welcome Wicksteed's attempt to call in the wisdom of the Catholic doctors of the Middle Ages as a corrective to Protestant infirmities. And, in fact, his later more explicit statements of his position, his *Dante and Aquinas* and the *Reactions*, were received nowhere with more understanding sympathy than by some Unitarians of Anglo-Catholic tendency. But it was clear from the first that the two kinds of approach to Catholicism were radically different in ultimate aim.

CHAPTER VIII

DANTE, AQUINAS, AND ARISTOTLE: THE LARGER SEQUENCE

PART I

DANTE AND AQUINAS

Wicksteed's Aquinas Studies—Individuality of Wicksteed's Thomism—Thomas's Problem—Exemplification: The Doctrine of the Soul—Hell to Purgatory in Aquinas and in Dante—The Doctrine of Eternity

I

WHEN Wicksteed, after completing his *Common Sense of Political Economy* in 1910, returned to the exploration of Dante, it was, he tells us, with relief. To make Economics generally accessible he held to be his most important duty to his generation; but to make Dante more widely accessible to it was, if a less imperative service, one more congenial to the prophet and the humanist in him. The study of Dante and Aquinas was originally delivered as a course of Jowett lectures at University Hall, in 1911; it was published as a volume under that title in 1913.

Wicksteed's first-hand acquaintance with the works of St. Thomas Aquinas was little more recent than his first-hand acquaintance with Dante. By 1911 he already merited better probably than any other non-Catholic Englishman the title which he modestly disclaims of "Thomist." At the outset of the lectures he gives his audience a notion of what competence in Thomism means. After reckoning the printed works of Aquinas to consist, apart from extraneous matter, of twenty double-columned folios of five hundred pages each—one volume a year for the whole of Thomas's literary career—he proceeds: "I am very far indeed from professing to have covered the whole of this stupendous mass of work"; but he does claim the "continuous and careful study of thousands of pages of it, and frequent consultations of the volumes up and down, during many years." [1]

That the exponent of Dante should become also an exponent of Thomas Aquinas, was for Wicksteed himself inevitable; but it was a step taken only at the inner urgency of the scholar, which nothing in his environment in any degree encouraged. The spiritual nourishment which the *Comedy* so richly yields could not be enhanced in intrinsic power and appeal, whatever it might gain in stringency of nexus, or in the ultimate refinements of scholastic dogma, when the same matter was drawn from the technical pages of Thomas. Still less, naturally, had the poetry anything to gain, whatever depths of implicit poetry might lurk in the sublime affirmations of his dogmatic creed. Least of all would Aquinas have allured him, had he been disposed, like the political Dantists of Gabriel Rossetti's type, to accentuate Dante's stern criticism of the policy of the papacy or his frequent denunciation of certain popes; for the work of Aquinas had been officially adopted as the authentic philosophy of the Church, while Dante's *Monarchia,* which stood in sharp opposition to the position of Thomas, though, as, Volkelt [2] has shown, largely influenced by his argument, was triumphantly brandished by the Reformers, had been publicly burned shortly after his death (1329).[3] That the

[1] *Dante and Aquinas,* p. 96.

[2] *Medieval Culture: an Introduction to Dante,* I, 286.

[3] It was put upon the Index only in 1554, in consequence of the damaging use of it made by the Reformers. It was removed thence only by the Liberal Pope Leo XIII.

modern Protestant world would dismiss Aquinas without question was the more a matter of course since modern philosophy had admittedly superseded his system with all others anterior to Descartes; and Milton's famous allusion was more often recalled because it put Aquinas below "our sage and serious Spenser," than as a sign of the general prestige implied in the very terms ("I dare be known") of that haughty preference. Protestant intolerance and philosophic disdain thus concurred in determining the attitude towards Aquinas normal outside the Catholic world when Wicksteed's Dante studies began. In the very year of the *Six Sermons* (1879) it was crucially exemplified. For in that year a papal encyclical (of Leo XIII) in effect canonized the entire work of St. Thomas. "I well remember," wrote Wicksteed thirty years later, "the amused contempt with which the papal prescription of Aquinas as the clue to the riddles of modern life was received in Protestant England."

Philip Wicksteed did not even then share that amused contempt. Yet a man bent solely on making Dante's moral inspiration and poetic sublimity a living influence in growing minds, might naturally and excusably leave Aquinas and his serried folios of medieval Latin alone. Such a severance was impossible for one in whom the scholar's passion for origins and the historian's passion for understanding how things came about, were no less living and potent than the educator's passion for teaching men how to live. And as Dante involved Aquinas, so Aquinas involved both his philosophical authority, Aristotle, and his own master, Albertus Magnus. In Albertus, as well as in Aquinas,

Wicksteed became probably better versed than any English non-Catholic scholar.[1]

II

That Dante's philosophical "sources" embraced a much wider field than these, Wicksteed was, of course, well aware. The brilliant and beautiful book of Ozanam, not to speak of Vossler's great Introduction, thus give a truer impression of the complex origins of Dante's thought than Wicksteed's powerful analysis and critical evaluation of his debt to Aquinas alone. Wicksteed was naturally well aware of this incompleteness, and it is interesting to learn from his correspondence that he contemplated investigating other aspects of those complex origins. "Many lines converge to make me see that Augustine must come next, or soon, in my course of study," he wrote in 1911, while still deep in the Aristotle-Aquinas sequence.[2]

But there were other reasons than the distraction of graver preoccupations why this larger plan remained in abeyance. For Wicksteed's Thomism had a very individual character, not easily paralleled among other adepts in that lore. Completely detached from his theology, so far as it rested on "Revelation," yet in deep sympathy with his religion, Wicksteed could delineate his genius with an objectivity difficult either to the sceptic or to the devotee. And this saves his account of the relation of Dante to Aquinas from the opposite flaws incident to those attitudes. The difficulty of the colossal task which Aquinas undertook—

[1] A friend relates that he once met Wicksteed coming out of the British Museum with a look of amusement on his face. "I have been reading," he explained, "a folio of Albertus Magnus; I found it unopened."

[2] To E. G. Gardner, 1 November, 1911.

the fusion of Aristotle's philosophy with orthodox Christian theology in a single harmonious body of doctrine—is common ground. It was not merely a question of picking out of Aristotle whatever could be profitably annexed by Christian tradition. Thomas was an Aristotelian as well as a Christian, a philosopher as well as a theologian, and though the latter province necessarily stood first in his allegiance, his problem was one of reconciliation, not merely of astute borrowing. He had, indeed, in the words of an eminent Catholic Thomist, "to Christianize Aristotle"; but that meant that Aristotle's philosophy "had to be so perfectly assimilated that it might, in that process, come to re-organize itself, as it were, of itself, in the sense of Christian thought." [1] And the problem thus defined he was held to have completely solved. "It is the honour of St. Thomas," adds M. Gilson, "to have undertaken this heavy task, and to have accomplished it."

On the other hand, the humanist, Alfred Vossler, first of living German Dantists, sees in Aquinas's work an attempt to combine incompatibles, an illusory compromise resting partly on clever accommodations, and plausible only because Thomas has no complete grasp of either his Christian authority (St. Augustine) or of Aristotle, and "only because he took neither of them seriously was able to come to an understanding with both."

Corresponding differences mark the conception of Dante's relation to Thomas. The Catholic Thomist, even one who, like Ozanam, is also a profound and reverent student of Dante, sees in Dante's presentment only an imperfect and distorted reflexion of a flawless

[1] Gilson, *The Philosophy of St. Thomas Aquinas* (tr. E. Bullough), p. 14.

original; of the four great series of philosophic ideas in St. Thomas's work, "Being, God, Spirit, and Man," Dante reproduces only the latter two, and these "broken and confused." [1] More recent Catholic-Thomists, discussing Dante's relation to Thomas, survey the *Comedy* in the spirit of learned specialists reviewing a book of popular philosophy, where subtleties are simplified, necessary grounds taken for granted, and argument not pursued to its last implications. The humanist Vossler, taking the view of Thomas above described, naturally regards Dante's divergences otherwise. A patchwork of incompatible systems was the only thing that Dante could learn from Thomas, "and most fortunately he learnt it very incompletely." "Thomas was to him a channel or a water-pipe—of lukewarm water, but no original source." [2] But Dante himself is for Vossler, as a philosopher a "dilettante," who had come to philosophy, by his own confession, as consolation for a lost love, not from a passion for truth.

Between these sharply contrasted standpoints Wicksteed's *Dante and Aquinas* holds, as has been said, a place of its own. It is not polemical, Wicksteed scarcely concerns himself with these antagonisms, but it bears throughout the impress of a mind enabled by its union of individual force with catholicity of sympathy, to enter with peculiar insight into many varied forms of strong personality in others; a mind, moreover, imbued alike with the passion of scholarship and the need to uplift men. He brings to Thomas, as he brings to Dante, a reverence which goes hand in hand with

[1] F. Ozanam, *Dante et la Philosophie Catholique* (1845), p. 229.

[2] Vossler, *u.s.*, p. 279. He gives as an example of Dante's feeble acceptance of Thomas's lead the argument by which he justified the admission of two heathens, Ripheus and Trajan, into Paradise.

criticism; recognizes even with awe the colossal achievement carried through by him in his short term of forty-six years, but does not pretend that his reconciliation of Aristotle and the Church is, for us, at all points successful; yet holds that Thomas's system, thus evolved, is for him impeccably consistent, and he willingly brings forward considerations which make them less complete than they appear. To Thomas's inner consistency, to the organic quality of his thinking, Wicksteed pays a tribute which the most devout Thomist would not better. His many years' reading, he records, has left him with "the vivid impression that in the whole of his output the cutting edge of Thomas's mind is never to be found blunted. His whole material is always under command. Whatever he says on any subject he says in relation to his thought on every other subject." [1]

On the other hand, he dismisses emphatically the view which ascribes Dante's divergences to the loose thinking of a dilettante, the random generalizations of a popular educator, or even to the pardonable licence of a great poet. He put aside peremptorily the very notion that Aquinas, or any one else was, in any significant sense, Dante's "source." "I am becoming deeply convinced," he wrote to Professor Gardner during the delivery of these lectures, "that Dante owes nothing to speak of to any one; . . . all the authors Dante read fed him, but his real roots were in the life and thought of his time . . . not in books; and that his own mind is so vigorous and so independent that he sweeps into the course of his creative evolution all that he reads or knows; but even when the actual words

[1] *Dante and Aquinas*, p. 96.

are preserved, the relation is nevertheless that of fire to fuel, or of food and tissue, rather even than that of bricks and beams to a house. . . . Aristotle, Augustine, Aquinas, and the rest, explain Dante only in the sense of a commentary explaining a text, they do not in any way explain him as a phenomenon." [1]

III

In Aquinas and Dante, then, Wicksteed saw, not the master and the disciple, but two men of immense but diverse genius using an instrument largely provided by the one for purposes, alike of no less immense significance, but determined by that diversity. Wicksteed puts the distinction between them, as he sees it, succinctly in the Preface: "I think it may be said, without undue sacrifice to the love of antithesis, that Aquinas regards the whole range of human experience and activities as the collecting ground for illustrations of Christian truth, and Dante regards Christian truth as the interpreting and inspiring force that makes all human life live." And still more explicitly, in the same preface, the spirit of the *Comedy* is contrasted with the purely doctrinal purpose of Aquinas. "It is both secular and sacred, owing its originality and intensity in no small measure to its vivid retention of earthly interests under the light of spiritual perception, and the consistently psychological and experiential interpretation of a sacramental and traditional religion."

It may be thought that these sentences emphasize over much the modernist—the "psychological and experiential"—point of view which admittedly drew Wicksteed so powerfully to Dante. But on the

[1] To E. G. Gardner, 11 November, 1911.

historical and philosophical side, Thomas had for him a hardly less powerful attraction. The man who had given his life to wrestling with a colossal problem fascinated his intellect. And then Thomas was the chief link between Dante and Aristotle, the Greek thinker who was for Wicksteed, as for them, supreme. What his chief contemporary exponent, Werner Jaeger, has described as Aristotle's "magnificent attempt to turn upon the mysteries of belief the light of critical comprehension" was in essence the aim of the two great medieval followers also. And in the humbler plane of their modern exponent, it was deeply congenial to the union of positive instincts with metaphysical aspirations in himself. They had all, with whatever differences, sought to make the "religion of eternity" accessible within the limits, and intelligible in terms, of the "religion of time"; and the closing pages of Wicksteed's book, to which we shall return, show how close is its affiliation with the discourse of ten years before.

What was most deeply attractive to Wicksteed in Aquinas, apart from his relation to Dante, was no doubt that imposing, if inevitably incomplete, synthesis which he attempted between philosophy and theology, between Greek thought and Christian tradition or "Revelation." There, in the heart of the Catholic world, Wicksteed found a powerful affirmer of the human principle of reason against obscurantism of every kind. And he had Aquinas and the whole spirit of Aquinas's system with him when he insisted, against some eminent Catholic interpreters, that Virgil, who guides Dante through Hell and Purgatory to the Earthly Paradise, stands for philosophy, a power subordinate and ancillary indeed, but entirely legitimate and authentic.

IV

While Wicksteed's book is meant, then, primarily, to explain the relation of Dante to Thomas, more than half of it is devoted to a summary account of the work of Aquinas himself, and his antecedents in Greek philosophy and medieval theology. It may be permissible to dwell for a moment upon the brilliant example of Wicksteed's method given in the sixth chapter, on Aquinas's doctrine of the soul. For the problem to be solved by the harmonizer of Aristotle and Christian tradition was here peculiarly critical and acute; nothing less than the doctrine of immortality being at stake. For the contradiction between Aristotle's doctrine that the soul is the "form" of the body, and the Christian doctrine that it is encased or imprisoned in it, until released by death, threatened a complete deadlock. Wicksteed shows, with the freedom facilitated by his detached standpoint, how Thomas, without relaxing his decisive grasp of the Christian doctrine, is yet able, in virtue of the ambiguous subtleties of the Aristotelian doctrine, to give his presentation an Aristotelian colouring, by making the individual Body prepared for the individual Soul.

From this preliminary study of Thomas we pass to the comparison with Dante which is the primary purpose of the book. The dominant interest of the comparison, for the student of Dante, lay in the characteristic union, in the poet's attitude to him, of reverence and independence. Here as elsewhere, as Vossler has said, Stoic pride and Franciscan humility were alike reflected in Dante. He was, in the first place, the disciple. Wicksteed shows, for instance, how even in the analyses of his own sonnets, so repellent to us, in the *Vita Nuova,* Dante is quaintly following the method of Aquinas's analysis of the arguments of Aristotle: how again, in the *Convivio,* he borrows the style of Aquinas's *Contra Gentiles,* addressed to the heathen opponents of Christianity, for his own refutation of the partisans of a worldly nobility. He shows, again, how often a question raised by the argument or narrative of the *Comedy* may be solved by a doctrinal deliverance of Aquinas. Thus it is with the question why Beatrice does not know of Dante's plight, and has to be urged by the Virgin to send Lucia to his aid. For "the dead," Aquinas tells us, "by their own natural state know nothing of the things that are being done in this world." Equally apposite is the commentary which the sublime but difficult doctrine (*Paradiso* i) that the movement of the universe carries every creature "over the great ocean of being to its proper haven," receives when set in the light of Aquinas's system; "the circling heavens being the ultimate instrument by which the divine power ripens and gathers in perfected human souls." [1]

The opening sentences of the seventh chapter explain very clearly Dante's attitude, as Wicksteed saw it, to Aquinas; they gain in intimacy and force, as has been already hinted, from the fact that it was in some sense analogous to his own attitude to Dante. Dante was not a professor officially expounding the text of a doctor of the Church, but an individual interpreter, "in the fullest Hebrew sense," as Wicksteed says,

[1] *Dante and Aquinas,* p. 143.

"a prophet," applying it to the issues of life. For those issues the Church of St. Thomas had shown itself insufficient, and the guide who escorts Dante by that "other way" to the Earthly Paradise is not St. Thomas, but Virgil. Hence, Dante often not only simplifies his original, but alters the character of its appeal. For the simplified argument allows, in effect, of different practical applications; also, by definitely altering the matter and course of the argument, he impresses upon it the mould of his own mind.

In the first *cantica*, the *Inferno*, Wicksteed had to deal with the part of the *Comedy* which is at once most celebrated as poetry, and apt to be the most repellent to the modern humanist who seeks in Dante the wisdom of a great ethical teacher.

In eternal punishment, Dante believed as unreservedly as St. Thomas. But Wicksteed shows how Dante's handling of the dogma has acquired, through an intensity of ethical insight outside Thomas's scope, perhaps beyond his power, a reconciling appeal to us.

Two things, it is necessary to recall, were vital for Dante in his handling of this matter. He had to preserve the belief in free will; for "men choosing good or evil by the exercise of free will" was, as he wrote to Can Grande, the *Comedy's* fundamental theme. He enforced that belief by appealing to our consciousness of power to choose and so to will. But he refrained from pushing the argument to that perplexing dilemma which awaits the theologian when he is asked whether or not God is responsible for our choice. Aquinas, on the other hand, pushes his analysis to the end . . . till he "analyses freedom away," thus making Hell, which punishes the evil choice, itself divine, and the pains of Hell good, though, as Wicksteed notes, "Aquinas with appalling candour adds that they are not good for those who suffer them." "Thomas thus pushes his explanation of hell so far as to carry it into the very being of God." But Dante, carrying his treatment of the freedom of the will (in *Purgatorio* xviii) "just to the point at which it removes the superficial objections and no further," and then dismissing logic in order to appeal to a man's consciousness of power to choose, emerges from the school in order to be truer to the great purpose of the *Comedy*.

V

But the second point involved a definite change of character, not merely a deliberate reticence. Thomas's Hell was purely penal, the creation of a vindictive God. Dante's Hell is, no less, a place of eternal torment, and the torments are described, as we know, with unflinching realism. Yet Dante has compelled us to feel in them a deeper and more lasting significance; the torments of the sinner are symbols of his sin, his pictures of the sinner in Hell show him not merely suffering for his sin but continuing in spirit to practise it, and in no case repenting of it or regretting it. His earthly mentality is prolonged; his "climate" is changed but (according to the proverb) not his character. He is there because he has so chosen, and he gets what he has chosen as well as what he deserves. And the choice which placed the sinners there is their own still; "they are at home and in their place." "Dante speaks, from time to time, of divine vengeance, but what he makes us feel is . . . the shame of that evil choice that makes a self-wrought hell for man." Wicksteed admits that this principle of congruity between crime and punishment is not consistently observed in the *Inferno*, and Dante's words are perhaps strained when the sinner's "choice" to do evil is identified with a "choice" to be punished for it. Nor did it lie in the plan of this book to notice, as he did abundantly in his lectures, the many passages in which the poet, the lover, the hero in Dante lift the *Inferno* into loveliness and grandeur at the cost of its ethical homogeneity.[1] But the contrast here drawn between Dante and Thomas springs from the heart of Wicksteed's nature; from his passionate horror of sin and his refusal to admit vindictiveness as a possible ingredient in the divine love.

Yet more radical contrasts come into view in the chapter on Purgatory. Here the paths of the Citizen and the Cleric, so long adjacent, decisively diverge. It is a small matter that Dante makes Purgatory a mountain rising in terraces from the sea-level, whereas the general notion current in the Church, if not dogmatically laid down, was that of a pit analogous to Hell. It meant vastly more that at the summit of the mountain, reached by the terraces, was the Earthly Paradise, where, the sinless state of the old Eden having been regained, the summit of happiness attainable on earth would be won. "Purgation" for sin is for Thomas simply a sacrament, significant primarily to the theologian and ecclesiastic; it is a condition of heavenly salvation, but not of earthly happiness. The linking

[1] Some of these intrusions of the poet's upon the moralist's ethic are noticed in the present writer's British Academy Warton Lecture: "Is there a Poetic View of the World?"

of the theological rite of purgation with his belief in an ideal state for man on earth, is justly held to be a significant example of Dante's synthesis of secular and spiritual things, of the intimate union of his ethics and his statesmanship; and it has nowhere been more luminously and eloquently expounded in English than by Wicksteed. Penitence being, then, for Dante not penal merely, but a step in the building up of a new life, the souls in Purgatory, therefore, do not abhor their pain but embrace and desire it. Hence the Earthly Paradise itself, to which Dante climbs through successive acts of purification, is no state of mere unsullied bliss. "Thus paradise is regained, and more than regained, for the souls are now not where Adam and Eve were before the Fall, but where they would have been had they borne the test." The sublime farewell in which Virgil leaves Dante "king and bishop" over himself is a charter of moralized will, not of arbitrary impulse. Wicksteed, interpreting Dante in the light at once of lofty citizenship and of spiritual religion, points out that that freedom to follow impulse was only the crown of a long and painful process—the difficult "other way" (*Inferno* I) in which "philosophy" or human reason was, indeed, man's "guide," but this "in obedient submission to revelation."

At no point was the "prophet" in Wicksteed more manifest, at no point did his Dante lectures become a more thrilling spiritual experience, at no point did they shoot a more disturbing ray into the fastnesses of Protestant and British prejudice, than when he was expounding Dante's transformation of the Catholic institution of Purgatory into a place where the penitents passionately desire their purifying pain, and where its end is not to exempt them from punishment, but to build up the higher life, where this upbuilding is a condition, not of future salvation only, but of ideal citizenship in this world.

Then he recalls the crowning example of that union in Dante of the theologian with the spiritual thinker and the ideal statesman, that "startlingly original and even audacious piece of unauthorized theology," as he calls it, by which in the seventh canto of the *Paradiso*, the exposition of the Atonement is entrusted to the representative of the Roman Empire, "and thus the temporal and spiritual orders were interlaced and blended together in the one supreme event of history."

VI

But the book closes on a note of deep accord. There was one aspect of Dante's ideal of spiritual secularity in which he reached both across to his great ecclesiastical teacher and to the Greek thinkers who were the masters of both. The doctrine of eternity and the eternal life was at the heart of the Dantesque and the Thomist conceptions of heaven and the heavenly fruition. But it had its roots in Plato's conception of a timeless reality, and what counted more directly for Aquinas and Dante, in Aristotle's kindred doctrine of the divine existence, the timeless and changeless One, the contemplation of which is the highest felicity of man, but also the supreme Actuality from which (as Aquinas and Dante said after him) "heaven and earth depend."

And Wicksteed himself, we know, in that memorable discourse of fourteen years before, had found in that conception of "eternity" which for Aquinas and Dante symbolized the divine existence, a key to the way of living most nearly divine for man. The "religion of eternity" man could not, under earth's limitations, make his own. But it could "transfigure" his "religion of time," subduing the agitations which belong to the pursuit of passing and partial aims, to give him the spiritual energy of minds which see life whole and are fixed on the things that endure.[1]

[1] That the medieval conception of Eternity was in some sense the key to Wicksteed's later thinking, and a clue in the nexus of his entire philosophical work, is apparent from a letter to an old friend, Mr. W. J. Jupp, of Croydon, written shortly after the publication of *Dante and Aquinas.* Mr. Jupp had written expressing deep interest in this aspect of the book, and enclosing an essay of his own (published in the *Inquirer*) suggested by Wicksteed's vivid rendering of this idea in the "passionate peace" of his Argument to the *Paradiso,* canto xxxi. Wicksteed replied from Childrey (6 September, 1913): "I had recognized the great fact or idea or whatever it is that makes Plato and Aristotle and Aquinas and Dante one—the conception of the energy of repose, that Peters in his translation of the *Ethics* says, quite seriously and without a hint of regret, has "become more unrealizable" to us, or some such phrase. . . . Well, I doubt whether the next translator of the *Ethics,* if he be a man of Peters' calibre, will say or think so. Perhaps we *have* lost touch with great things during the period your life and mine has covered, but most assuredly we have recovered touch with some. I am happy to think that my own attempt to present the greatest perhaps of all facts had some luminosity in it for you, my brother."

To the modern reader who may desire to follow, or to check, Wicksteed's exposition and criticism of Aquinas, some private counsels given by him to a beginner may not be unwelcome: "I think I should advise you to take out the three volumes of Part I (*Summa Theol.*) and judge for yourself which is most to your purpose. The extremely difficult and minute discussions of the doctrine of the Trinity, for example, would hardly repay the severity of the effort needed to follow them; and the section on the allegorical significance of the O.T. ceremonies . . . are dull and uninteresting. But I find him so interesting almost everywhere else that I can only recommend you to find your own place. Most people (and I share the experience) find the Angelology particularly fascinating, and his account of the State of Innocence is a perpetual delight to me. I give no references, for you will find your way about easily enough . . . the *Contra Gentiles* is a magnificent book, less well known than the *Summa,* but in some respects better worth knowing."—(Letter to Miss Z. Puxley, 1926.)

PART II

THE *REACTIONS*

The Aristotle-Aquinas Sequence — The Temper of the *Reactions*— Thomas's Doctrine of Reason and Revelation—The Nature of his Synthesis—His Doctrines of the Trinity and the Eucharist—Larger Bearings of Aquinian Thought: Mathematics—Poetry and Imagination in Aquinas—The Epilogue: Wicksteed's *Apologia*

I

THAT Wicksteed's pursuit of the historical antecedents of Dante's intellectual world was concentrated predominantly upon the path which led from Dante to Aquinas and from Aquinas to Aristotle, was not due solely to the fact that this was the path by which the most momentous determining philosophic influences had travelled. It answered, as already indicated, a psychological need in Wicksteed himself; the genius of Aquinas, Aristotle, and Dante alike realized, in varying degrees, the union of mastery of fact, logical thinking, and visionary contemplation which Wicksteed most whole-heartedly approved. An historian of another temper might have been drawn to an example of those "reactions" in which the attraction of passion and pathos is added to that of intellectual acumen and resource, St. Augustine; and have followed out that other line of evolution which leads to him, through St. Paul, from Plato. We know from the letter already quoted that at the time of *Dante and Aquinas,* Wicksteed recognized the need, in the sequence of his work, of a study of Augustine. Another letter of the same time shows more explicitly that Wicksteed once conceived the hope of tracing this evolution, only glanced at in his published work, before he died. But this never became a serious plan; and the same letter shows that there were not merely external reasons against it. Not only was Wicksteed of the mental type to which Plato appeals less than Aristotle, and Augustine than Aquinas; he was of those who feel the genius of Paul definitely alien. "Perhaps from Dante to Aquinas may take me from Aquinas to Augustine and from Augustine to Paul before I die. But up to now, though I have several times made a laborious attack on the epistles, and worked through them, line by line, they have never bitten." [1] And he could deliver a much more summary judgment upon Plato, some years later, in a letter to a son: "For reading I would not give Plato for twenty Aristotles; but as a thinker, Plato is not in it." The words serve to indicate the master current of Wicksteed's own mind, and to explain why he now, in the *Reactions,* took so decisively the course he did.

The book which Wicksteed entitled *Reactions between Dogma and Philosophy, illustrated from the work of St. Thomas Aquinas,* is described by its author, on one of the opening pages, as a "comparative" study; and it is dedicated the more appropriately on that account to the veteran friend who was also a master of the study of comparative religions, Estlin Carpenter.[2] Yet "comparison" does not touch the deeper gist of Wicksteed's book, or of the books of either man. It is, like his Dante books before and the Aristotle after, "an attempt to elucidate a mighty synthesis"; that organic

[1] To Lloyd Thomas, 21 September, 1911.

[2] The dedication is, like that of the *Dante and Aquinas* to Charles Hargrove, too beautiful to be omitted in his biography. It has been already quoted in another place (chapter iv, p. 138).

summing up of the vital knowledge, belief, and ideal goal of humanity, which Aquinas framed for his time as Aristotle and Dante for theirs. If Wicksteed himself had no pretensions to attempt the building of such a synthesis for our own time, the passion for synthetic thinking none the less gave an inner implicit nexus to the seemingly severed fragments of his rich culture; it was this that had drawn him so powerfully towards the colossal, if in part illusory, synthesis of Auguste Comte.

II

There were no doubt other sources of attraction. Wicksteed's reverence for the intellectual and spiritual genius of Aquinas was apparent in the previous book where he is primarily concerned with the gold into which Dante transmuted the less precious metal of his master. Here we are invited to watch the giant at work upon his problem of synthesis; and Wicksteed's sheer intellectual joy in problems mingles unmistakably with his sense of the magnitude of the issues involved; nay, we seem sometimes to be spectators of an actual game, and to hear his "checkmate" when at some crucial point the attempted synthesis breaks down. But this checkmate does not express only satisfaction at the vindicated rigour of the game. As little does it reflect merely the polemical triumph of a modern, or of the Protestant, at the collapse of a medieval Catholic claim; it is the voice of history, asserting above the pretensions of dogma the fidelity to fact and logic with which any lasting synthesis must comply.

The book opens with a vivid account of the conditions which made the solution of that problem no matter of theoretic satisfaction, but a crying need. The introduction in the thirteenth century, to the knowledge of educated Europe, of the great mass of the work of Aristotle, hitherto known only in fragments, created an *impasse*. A vast and coherent body of knowledge, covering immense regions of Nature and of Man on which Christian dogma had little to say, Aristotelianism exercised from the moment of its discovery a prestige which the most powerful intellects of Christendom were often the least disposed to resist. There were already, when Thomas began to write, not only Christian Aristotelians, but Aristotelians whose Christianity was suspect. Here was no heresy to be suppressed, pagan though its author was, but a philosophy standing over against Christian theology with an authority like its own. The Church had to avail herself of the external truth there provided, or suffer, if not intellectual impoverishment, material and personal defection. It perhaps required a historian at once completely detached from Catholicism yet profoundly religious, capable of spiritual as well as intellectual admiration for Thomas, and able to weigh his divided loyalties without bias, to describe adequately what he undertook. "Thomas knows perfectly well what he is doing, and he has not the least desire to conceal it. . . . What in other cases we have to conjecture or detect is, in his case, deliberately set out before us, and that, too, by an intelligence of which lucidity, order, and fearless integrity are no less characteristic than profundity. Aquinas arranges a formal alliance, as between two high contracting parties, in which frontiers are determined, principles laid down, relations defined, and rights safeguarded with admirable precision; but the whole is inspired by an *entente cordiale* in marked contrast with the lurking suspicions or repudiations with which, in many other cases, Christian teachers have attempted to fence or to disguise their indebtedness to ethnic thinkers or practices."

That the problem thus frankly faced by Thomas was in various ways more complicated than he knew, it again required the historian of religion to point out. Thomas himself could, for instance, only partially recognize how much Christian dogma itself owed to the pagan philosophy of Plato and Plotinus.

But such questions of origin did not affect the sharpness of the lines of demarcation drawn by Thomas between the two "powers." They divided the provinces of man's unaided "reason" and "Revelation," as determined by the Christian and Jewish scriptures. And the terms of the division showed the salutary effect upon Christian champions of controversy with Arabian and other "gentiles" who did not recognize the Christian "Revelation," but only Reason. For Reason received large, even dangerously large privileges. Revelation was to hold, no doubt, indefeasibly, the higher place, for she had to give assurance of some truths not accessible to Reason. But her truths must, over a large area, coincide with those of Reason, and in no case must they contradict them. Moreover, even his assertion of the necessity of a Revelation, Aquinas clinches by an appeal to Aristotle, that is to Reason. It may be said that the rest of the book is an examination in detail of Thomas's handling of his problem under conditions thus laid down.

III

Nowhere, perhaps, are the manifold strands of Wicksteed's intellect more apparent than in the exposition of the last of these theses, the necessity of a Revelation. For the very first step in that proof takes us at once to the Aristotelian teleology, expanded by Aquinas in the doctrine that all things have a divinely appointed "end," which is their good. And their supreme good is that "vision of God" in which the Christian benediction and the philosophic ideal concur, while Thomas's interpretation of it, as of the intellectual love of God which leads to it, is saturated with his Hellenic thinking. And for Philip Wicksteed, too, that sublime conception is a focus of inexhaustible spiritual suggestion, a *point de repère* upon which many avenues of his experience and reflection converge. No hearer of his Dante lectures will forget the rapt tension which would hold his audience as he described the transcendent moment in the last canto of the *Paradiso* in which Dante attains that vision. And he turns for illustrative analogies to modern poets and thinkers, to Faust in his study baffled of such vision, to Wordsworth's great moments of ecstatic communion with "the heart of things," and then, as Wordsworth had turned before him, to the direct knowledge of permanent existences afforded by mathematics. The assertion of that mystic vision by Plato and Plotinus as attainable by man had entered since Augustine into the heart of Christian theology. And Aquinas shares the belief. But he also shared Aristotle's psychology, which denied to the natural man a mystic sense, a power of himself achieving that which Aristotle yet recognized as his supreme good. It will be well, at this crucial point of Wicksteed's argument, to quote his own words (pp. 158–9):

"With Plotinus (Aquinas) accepts the 'goal' as nothing short of the complete and conclusive acquisition of a mystic sense which will unite us with God; but he also accepts the psychology of Aristotle which will allow us no such mystic sense at all. . . . To take our account of man's goal from the Neoplatonist, therefore, and our account of his constitution from Aristotle, leaves us with a huge gap in our theory. But this gap is exactly what Aquinas wants." For it answered to his need of a Christian revelation. "The Christian revelation and its promises . . . exactly fitted into the gap that he had made for them by his Platonic mysticism united with his Aristotelian ejection of the mystic sense." So put, the argument has an air of clever juggling too familiar in Christian and other apologetics, but equally untrue to the intention of Wicksteed and to the mind of Aquinas. Only a hasty reader will imagine that Thomas's mysticism and his psychology were the carefully prepared piers of a doctrinal arch, between which, at the appropriate moment, he inserted his Christian faith, as the keystone which "exactly fitted the gap he had made." Thomas was a controversialist of immense power and resource; but forensic skill was only one of the instruments of a mind which, before beating down the opposition of heathen and heretics, had to reckon with the competing urgencies of its own catholicity. If his Christian faith was vital to him, his scientific intelligence was no less intimately wedded to Aristotle, and his idealism to the mystic ecstasy of Plato. It is by unconscious adjustments that he reaches a way out which has the air of a clever solution of a puzzle.

Thus, as Wicksteed in less equivocal terms puts it, Thomas's belief in a miraculous revelation unifies the whole complex of his new enthusiasms and his old organic loyalties and loves, and is, in fact, dictated by them, while it appears to himself to emerge in strict obedience to the claims of the naked intelligence. And he adds a significant comment on the superiority, even for controversy, of prophetic conviction to forensic acumen: "Not consciously looking for a defensive line on which to protect a foregone conclusion, but forging, in complete good faith, what he conceives to be the adamantine links which bind all truth into a coherent whole . . . (Thomas) has performed a feat of constructive apologetics which no adroitness of a conscious advocate could rival"—a tribute which the modern humanist, whose withers are unwrung by Thomas's pleadings, can afford to pay with a whole heart, but which it seldom occurs to him to offer.

But there remained, for Aquinas, one first step, superfluous indeed, so long as he was addressing his fellow-Christians, but vital when he had, as in the treatise *Contra Gentiles,* to do with pagans and infidels. He had to prove that his necessary "Revelation" was to be found in the Old and New Testaments. With this contention Wicksteed is not here concerned, but only with Thomas's argument as tried by the "philosophical" canon of logic which he himself and Thomas alike accept; and he is strictly within the compass of his chosen theme when he finds that Aquinas, basing the authority of Scripture on that of the Church, and the authority of the Church on that of Scripture, has inadvertently reasoned in a circle. But the fallacy is announced with the consideration due to a great master found in error, and the fullest recognition of the historical conditions which made such assumptions as the truth of miracles then appear of axiomatic security.

But the modern is not allowed to congratulate himself on the scientific criticism which exempts him from that illusion. On the contrary he is bidden to read a warning in Thomas's errors against the illusions to which all belief is exposed. In a significant passage (p. 173) he repels the suspicion that he is trying to "pick holes in Thomas's logic, or to replough the barren sands of obsolete polemics. My purpose is very different. It is to throw light on the general psychology of conviction and to draw lessons of universal application. *De nobis* be sure (whoever we are) *fabula narratur*."

But he does not stop there. Aquinas furthers that purpose otherwise than by failures in logic. How does it come, Wicksteed presses the question home, that a reasoner so powerful and so absolutely sincere, falls into that error? And this brings into view a "reaction" in which the Christian element of his thought quietly supersedes the Aristotelian. "Faith" is in the last resort for him above logic, and in faith will has its legitimate place, and divine grace as a vouchsafed source of will. The long and subtle discussion brings into view the great medieval Catholic's points of contact with both the modern psychology of the "will to believe," and the Protestant doctrines of "private judgments" and the "inner light."

IV

The ground has now been prepared for the examination of Thomas's procedure in his momentous synthesis of "philosophy" and "dogma," of Natural and Revealed Religion. The nature and credentials of the two powers are known, and the conditions of the "treaty" between them agreed upon; what precisely was the character of the "treaty" itself, as drawn up by the master-diplomat, Aquinas, and accepted by his Church? Wicksteed, whose bias did not lie on the side of ecclesiasticism, but whose historical temper did not allow him to be easily unjust to the Catholic Church, does not disguise his sense of the debt of the Church to Aristotle, even in providing grounds for dogmas which, like the existence of God, they held in common. And when Thomas is engaged in wrestling with the problem of reconciling of "evil" with the goodness of God, imposed by Christian theology, and wins a dubious triumph over the intellectual perils incident to that encounter, Wicksteed cannot suppress an outburst of impatience, as he turns "with relief from the atmosphere of sophistry and of moral confusions and contradictions into the wholesome objectivism of Aristotle, where the 'problem of evil' that absorbs our attention is the problem of how to control and eliminate it, rather than how to explain it away."

"Evil," moreover, for Thomas, included, as it has ceased to do for the modern world, the tortures of an eternal material Hell inflicted by the goodness of God upon all who have not received the sacraments of the Church. The late Poet Laureate has recently pointed to his adoption of "the divine fiasco" as a grave blot in the philosophy of the great Thomas. Wicksteed, too, finds Aquinas here "at his worst." His reason, however, is characteristic. Had Aquinas sought shelter in mystery, and explained the "goodness" of Hell in some sense beyond our human understanding, it could have been condoned. "But Aquinas will have none of it"; Hell must be "good" by our standards of goodness. But Wicksteed sees that this stultifies our human struggle with the evil of the world; and it is the passion of the reformer, not the animus of the liberal theologian, which kindles his comment: "If God is the universal cause . . . the attempt to 'justify His ways' at the bar of our derivative sense of justice and love can only result in eviscerating our philosophical conception of the source, or polluting the stream that flows from it into our hearts. St. Thomas's defence of hell as an element in God's goodness, in a sense intelligible to us, is an appalling example and illustration of this" (p. 252).

A hostile exponent, with a brief against the Catholic Church, might not have contented himself with this dignified expression of indignation. He might have asked us to observe that Thomas's argument only led him to a moral catastrophe such as this, when it was based solely upon Catholic dogma, and beyond the reach of any other "reaction" of philosophy than that, here not salutary but deadly, of its inexorable logic. But Wicksteed, as we know, is engaged in pursuing an intricate psychological inquiry, not in pleading a cause; and the situations which most fascinate and rivet him are not those in which dogma is beyond the scope of philosophy, and "reaction" therefore impossible, but those in which "reaction" works as a fertile and significant influence. And so he goes on to explain, with obvious delight, Thomas's "consummately skilful conduct of his account of 'Natural Theology' in the *Contra Gentiles*"; a work he pronounces, when all reserves have been made, to be "in the majesty of its progress, in the continuity of its structure, in its sustained fervour, and construction, the outstanding example, to the disinterested student of philosophy and literature, of what scholasticism at its highest could achieve" (p. 257). It is on that last division of this treatise that the modern student's interest concentrates itself. For Thomas the theologian is here explaining those doctrines of Revealed Religion which transcended reason, but which Thomas the philosopher required him to show, did not contradict it. These are the Trinity, the Incarnation, the Sacraments, and the Eternal Life. The modern believer may shrink from Thomas's confident appeal even thus far, to reason in the decision of these "mysteries," and some modern historians may call in other explanations of the growth and "development" of dogma than Thomas could foresee; other even than his present exponent appears to recognize. But that is irrelevant to the present argument. The theologian Thomas has appealed in the last resort to reason, and it is the philosopher Thomas, not the sceptic or the unbeliever, who condemns the dogma which transgresses it.

V

It is impossible to do more here than call attention to the brilliant pages, alive with dramatic, no less than with dialectic interest, in which Wicksteed allows us to watch the demeanour of the mighty Thomas as he faces, with imperturbable assurance and inexhaustible resource, what the spectators hold to be the intractable *impasse*, the insoluble dilemma, of a Christian Trinity. The encounter has for us some of the elements of tragedy, and provokes a touch of what resembles tragic pity.

"Whoever desires to enter with sympathy into the supreme effort of this great man's mind must school himself to a potential respect for 'a distinction without a difference.' The doctrine requires the persons of the Trinity to be 'distinct,' but forbids them to be 'different.' Reason obediently tries by every device to reconcile the propositions, but 'contradiction is always there at one remove.' The mystic may impatiently refuse to recognize all competence of reason in these high matters. But Thomas has expressly made reason, in the last resort, the test. He has appealed to Cæsar. And we are 'forced to admit that if reason . . . is required to hold [two contradictory propositions] at once, and not to draw either of the two mutually destructive conclusions, its submission has been pushed to the point of flat contradiction to its own nature.'"

With no less interest, nay, excitement and suspense, the student of "reactions" under Wicksteed's guidance watches when Thomas, explaining the Eucharist, saves himself from the frustrating logic of a contradiction in terms only by embracing an un-Aristotelian heresy.[1]

The reader of the *Reactions* may, perhaps, at such

[1] By affirming, contrary to his Aristotelian orthodoxy, that the "accident" of the bread and wine (their appearance, taste, etc.) can persist when their "substance" is gone (p. 359).

passages in the argument, turn away with impatient wonder and regret that Wicksteed should devote so much labour and learning to showing how a Catholic dogmatist reconciled it with his spiritual intellect, "to see God made and eaten all day long," and not merely, like Browning's bishop, with his prospective satisfaction in the after-world. But our business in this book is with the mind of Philip Wicksteed, not with the practical urgency of the problems on which he engaged it; and in that mind the scholar's inexhaustible patience in pursuing questions of only theoretic or historical moment to the utmost attainable end was as fundamental as its alert and energetic response to the call of practical urgency whenever and whencesoever it came. At a step he could pass from the cloister to the field, from the field to the cloister; a true crusader, with a scholar's gown over his coat of mail.

But the course of the argument leads him now to a problem which was not only the central crux of Thomas's task, but, in a different context, and expressed in other terms, still confronts the modern mind no less: the problem of "Soul and Body," of "Matter and Mind." The case had been presented in succinct and lucid outline in the *Dante and Aquinas*, as we know; and it is needless to dwell upon the more elaborately articulated argument of the present course (Lect. V and VI). Enough that he is still convinced, both that Thomas sincerely believed in his own solution and that his solution is impossible. Aristotle's "soul" (life), inseparable from the body, had to be reconciled with the soul of Platonized Christian dogma, which is liberated at death from the body, its "prison." But he points out, with a touch of amusement, how some help came to Thomas from a quarter we should least expect, the Christian doctrine of the resurrection of the body tending to support the view that "body" and "soul" are organically connected. And in the end it is the Platonic aspect of his thought which predominates. The "soul," he is clear, however it be conditioned, during life, by the body, is not evolved by it, but is an entity, created anew by the divine act.

VI

In the significant closing pages of the sixth lecture Wicksteed attempts to "relate the system of Aquinas to a wider and deeper strain of thought and experience." Not, however, by dwelling, as the polemical scientist or philosopher so easily might, upon its shortcomings, but by showing how the principles which strove for mastery in the mind of Aquinas foreshadow those which stand in still incompletely resolved disaccord to-day. The evolutionary history of man on the physical side stands fast for us as it would have done for Aristotle, but the dawn of consciousness and of mind remains mysterious. And the physicist who confidently resolves mind too into physical elements encounters affirmations as assured, if less vocal than those of theology, that mind, however evolved in man, finds symptoms of itself in the universe; symptoms which it does not create but discovers, in a universe where it consequently "feels at home." Aristotle and Aquinas had found in the axioms of mathematics and logic a clue to something which is both first to us and first in nature, to laws fundamental to the inmost constitution of nature as well as for our thought. And it is in the immediate knowledge we seem to have of mathematical truth that their interpreter finds his own most satisfying assurance of the mind in the universe analogous to our minds. And since the mind of Philip Wicksteed is here our subject, it is pardonable to linger over these pages in which he describes, with an awed emotion like theirs, the "rapture of Pythagoras, Plato, Kepler, Wordsworth, Auguste Comte, in the discovery or contemplation of mathematical truths." Wicksteed has in full measure the "positive" trait, the demand for a basis of unassailable fact, which underlay or conditioned the soaring speculative or imaginative constructions of all these great men; it was one of the links, not the less real because for the most part unconfessed and even unconscious, which bound the student of Wordsworth and Comte, Aquinas and Aristotle, *in uno volumine* with the Jevonian economist, the dispenser of Dante's bread of angels with the enthusiastic exponent of differential coefficients.

To the analyst of the "reactions" between Christian and Aristotelian thought, ethics was a not less alluring topic than psychology. Aristotle left a mark upon western civilization which Christianity at the height of its dominance could only supplement, not overpower. For the "virtue" recognized by Aristotle expressed the kind of excellence which a great citizen of the community in which civic life was first clearly understood and proximately realized, held to be the basis of its private life; while his doctrine of the "mean" reflected a temper of cool sagacious common sense as little consonant with the Christian "love" which "knows no measure, but strives beyond all measure," as with the Christian awareness of "sin," the legend of "the

Fall," and the theological apparatus of rewards and punishments. Wicksteed shows in an interesting way how Aquinas's treatment of the Christian virtues is permeated by the Aristotelian psychology, and how the Aristotelian virtues in his hands are suffused with the ardour of the Christian spirit; the "justice" which "gives every man his due" being quickened into the "righteousness" for which men hunger and thirst. And he points out how the Christian ethic of love, so alien in origin from social or political interest, yet contributed to enlarge that Greek ideal of citizenship itself, by dissolving the limitation—slavery—which Aristotle had accepted. It was to Aquinas and his fellow scholastics, he recalls, that Comte ascribed the main share in the modern conception of humanity.

VII

The closing section of the *Reactions* moves in a sphere remote at first sight from Aquinas, if not from Aristotle. Wicksteed's eloquent exposition of the "poetry and imagination" of Aquinas may surprise the modern reader who expects in him only "arid intellectualism," as it may offend the devout Catholic who refuses to apply these profane rubrics to the presentment of theological mysteries. But his interpreter easily justifies his attempt to tread the narrow and little frequented path of æsthetic appraisement which lies between these two opposed lines of approach. It was not difficult, indeed, to call attention to the "magnificent hymns" of the Roman breviary, reminiscent in their exultant fervour, as in their resonant and leaping metre, of the great Spring Love-song of the late-Roman pagan poet.

Aquinas's hymns all occur in the office of Corpus Christi, and are inspired by that very dogma of Transubstantiation his defence of which had occasioned his gravest lapse from "philosophy," and his interpreter's severest comment upon his procedure. And an outsider, who knew Wicksteed only as a left-wing Protestant, might have heard with surprise the whole-hearted tribute of this descendant of Puritan martyrs to the transcendent spiritual qualities enshrined in the Mass; and, in particular, to this office of "Christ's Body"—"the highest point of devotional fervour and of the interpenetration of dogma and mystic rapture that the ritual of the Mass has ever attained." Such a recognition implied, of course, no abnegation of historical criticism; and Wicksteed can point out, not without amusement, how the maker of that "office" had fortified it by a sort of cento of "prophetic" allusions to Bread and Wine in the Old Testament from Melchizedek to Job; just as he can recognize in the Eucharist itself the influence of pagan cults of initiation. But all this pseudo-historical farrago contributed, none the less, to the imaginative richness of the Roman Mass, "attenuated rivulets from which alone trickle through the rituals of Protestant Christendom." Here was for Wicksteed no paradox. That rich material could become the language of the religious spirit, no less than the simplicity which strips away every material association, just as the complexities of figure and symbol, no less than bare simplicity, may convey poetry and passion. In this sense he can equate the polar differences (within Catholicism) between Thomas Aquinas and Thomas à Kempis. "They represent almost the extreme limits of the cultivation or neglect of pure intellectualism, yet they are alike in finding their supreme inspiration just in that sacrament which has retained at its very heart, undisguised and yet transfigured, the clearest notes of its historic relation to the weird imaginings of primitive man." And similarly he recalls how, "within the New Testament itself, that Gospel which expresses the conception of eating the flesh and drinking the blood of the divine being in the crudest form, and in complete detachment from any record of the institution of the rite, is also the one that utters the declaration, 'God is spirit, and they that worship him must worship him in spirit and in truth.'"

Such passages reflect with unusual distinctness the synthetic apprehension of things remote or incompatible to common sense, which, if not inborn with Philip Wicksteed, had by now established itself deeply in his mental nature, and was one of the sources both of the rich texture of his intellect and of the many-sided humanity of his life. A mystic "transubstantiation" of bread and wine into a corporal divinity was for him a superstitious as well as a materialist belief. But deeper than the dogmatic paradox which he dismissed without appeal, lay subtle threads of unapparent, perhaps unconscious, affiliation. The "bread and wine" that could not be "sanctified" were needed to support the saint. It was not only a taste for economic theory or delight in mathematics (though both of these concurred) which made him devote years of strenuous thought to clarifying the budget of the cottage. And "common things," without any transformation to look for, were yet at every point needful to the plenitude of the human spirit. It was one of the springs, in him, of the "pity that renneth sone in gentil herte," of the genius for fellowship, in all its articulations, which made him abhor the torture of animals not merely as cruelty, but as a kind of treason; and which taught him that tender insight into the ways and possibilities of simple souls that enabled him to enthral village audiences with the mysteries of the Empyrean.

VIII

The epilogue which closes the *Reactions* is also in some sense an epilogue to that *Apologia* of his own life-faith which, save in fragments, he never wrote. Its few pages of close-knit eloquence sum up the lasting significance as he sees it, of the Angelic Doctor, and of the mighty synthesis of theology and philosophy to which he gave his life. They will leave no reader under the illusion that Wicksteed's long and devoted study of Aquinas signified any approximation to medieval dogma or ways of thought, any disposition to take part in what an English Thomist, soon after these lectures were published, described as the "homeward march of the intellect of Europe." [1] Still less was he allured by the spectacle of the thousands, in England and elsewhere, who were going, or seeking to go, that way

[1] Dr. T. McNabb, preface to Gilson's *St. Thomas Aquinas*, translated by E. Bullough, 1924. In his review of the *Reactions* in the *Blackfriars Review* (January, 1921), Dr. McNabb welcomed this "significant and perhaps astounding book" by a convinced Unitarian, and confessed that "a life-long Thomist" had been able to find "at first sight and on a cursory examination no grave misunderstanding of St. Thomas's thought." A reviewer in the *Church Times* (30 September, 1921) more naïvely suggested that Wicksteed had expounded Aquinas with the subconscious thought: "Almost thou persuadest me to be a Christian!" Wicksteed's position was explained with insight and power by his reviewer, Rev. J. H. Weatherall, in the *Inquirer* (19 and 26 March, 1921).

"home," and by easier routes than through the folios of Aquinas. His book rather made clear that the "home" to which Aquinas so brilliantly led the intellect of his day, was not and could not be a home for it in ours. And he did this with a hand as incisive as it was reverent, as uncompromising as it was devout. Thomas's doctrinal edifice, seemingly firm as a pyramid on its base, was a pyramid balanced on its apex. And not Thomas's pyramid only, but that of all dogmatic theology. To modern thought there is no science of theology, in the sense of "a body of ascertained, approved, and accurately defined truth." Thomas's magnificent confidence in the stability of his inverted pyramid can no longer be justified, and Wicksteed contrasts with it, to their discredit, the half-hearted attempts of modern apologists to argue the stability of "pyramids" in no better case than his, "by showing not how firmly they stand, but how little weight they are called upon to bear"; for they have become historical documents only—alluring pictures of pyramids that *once* stood firm.

But to take part in the demonstration of the instability of the Roman "pyramid" was not Wicksteed's purpose. The *Reactions* is not a polemical pamphlet, a Protestant or Unitarian tract. It may, with far more justice, be held to be an attempt to make clear to Protestant eyes the solidity which Thomas had given, by the help of the Hellenic mortar of Aristotle, to the fabric of Catholic faith. But it was consonant with that attempt to show also how at certain points the process failed, not because the mortar was less good but because Aquinas was unwittingly using an illusory "substitute." And it happened that these points touched the very core of Catholic Christianity—the doctrines of the Trinity and of the Eucharist. Christology had never been a part of Wicksteed's religion, but he knew well that its potent and even growing appeal, precisely in the present century, had other and more intimate sources than any which history and logic can either justify or annul.

But this would not suffice to answer the question why then Wicksteed devoted half a lifetime to the exposition of the heroic builder of an impossible creed. And it becomes clear that he recognizes in Thomas's thinking an element of creative and enduring principle, which survives, with unexhausted virtue, amid the debris of the Catholic system. His "alliance between Reason and Revelation," which rejected the claims of man's reason to be its own "revelation," dismissed no less the pretension of "revelation" to override reason. And "revelation," indispensable though it was, came only as a potentiality which it remained for the organism of the human spirit in which it was received, to make actual. Aquinas's doctrine taught that the "supernatural" virtues of hope, faith, and love, first formulated by Christianity, did not supersede or replace the qualities of the natural man, but entered, as it were, the matrix of the human spirit, blending with and transmuting the natural virtues, and prepared the way for the religion which recognizes no frontier between the human and the divine because the divine is a spirit which humanity makes human when it lives its own apprehension of goodness, beauty, and truth. And Wicksteed was one of those who would go much further, and look for a clearer vision of what is, indeed, divine, when it is liberated from the integument of incredible dogma and miraculous ritual, and committed to the "magic" of that apprehension alone.

The apprehension of beauty, goodness, and truth, was not in all its aspects among Wicksteed's more signal and individual gifts. His Puritan ancestry, outlived as doctrine, persisted in a certain obtuseness to the finest sensibilities of the artist and the poet, and placed artistic and poetic creation of any kind beyond his reach. But he had early won a liberation from the integument of dogma as complete as it was rare. Hence his vision of beauty, far from extraordinarily acute or subtle as it was, responded with rapturous freedom to the glorious creations of Catholicism, so long seen askance by the Protestant world. The wonders of the Gothic cathedrals had indeed long been a familiar, if an imperfectly comprehended story. Goethe had uttered his ecstatic song over Strassburg minster a century, and Pugin and Barry stammered their halting Gothic echoes fifty years, before Wicksteed made his first pilgrimage to Chartres and Orvieto. Dante, too, the most complete representative of Catholicism who ever lived, it had not been left to Philip Wicksteed to discover. But it is probable that Wicksteed was the first Englishman who taught us to glory in Dante, not as an armoury of weapons against the papacy, or of arguments either for or against the Catholic faith, or simply as a supreme master of poetic craftsmanship, but as a sublime poet-prophet, whose mighty Catholic hymn, rightly heard, is vocal to the whole of humanity. But this great Catholic had sternly castigated his Church; that Catholic hymn itself had been chanted by him as he sought earthly salvation by "another way" than hers. It meant yet more, when the tried interpreter of Dante presses home to the heart of Catholic ritual and worship—that Mass which he had lately found so gravely wanting in the crucible of logical analysis. "Is it vain to hope that when the ecclesiastical tradition, alike in its Roman wealth and in its attenuated derivative streams, no longer has to carry the weight of unbelievable dogmas and sanctions that will bear no scrutiny, its true power will be felt in wider circles? Will the gathered wealth of the Breviary (little rills from which have already trickled out into a larger world), will the splendours of the *Rituale* and the *Pontificale* take the place that is their own in the literature and the devotions of the world, when they have ceased to be the prescribed exercises of a spiritual aristocracy, or the professional instruments of an order of wonder-workers?"[1] Not every reader can adapt his focus to what he takes to be the abrupt change of perspective, when he sees Catholicism a pyramid perilously poised upon its apex in the realm of dogma suddenly become a pyramid eternally secure in the realm of poetry and religion, and the pure worship of an enlightened theism an attenuated rill trickling down from the great mother stream of the Roman faith. But such seeming inconsistencies are but the inevitable paradoxes incidental to the attempt to give articulate expression to a religion simple with simplicity of spirit, which yet holds Humanity and Nature, Time and Eternity, in its embrace.

[1] *Reactions*, p. 561 f.

PART III

THE *PHYSICS* OF ARISTOTLE

The Modern Significance of the *Physics*—Physics and Metaphysics—Conclusion: Wicksteed the Interpreter

I

THAT Philip Wicksteed, in his later seventies, should decide to devote himself to such a task as a translation, with commentary, of the *Physics* of Aristotle requires, at first sight, some explanation.[1] The *Physics* is not one of the works by which Aristotle ranks as "the master of those who know," or as a propounder of the happy guesses that foreshadow knowledge. In Ethics, Politics, Poetics, Metaphysics, Psychology, he is a builder of the first rank. But in the study of inanimate nature, which, roughly speaking, he called Physics, his value is less easily, as well as less generally, recognized; and in some cases, as when he is dealing with the guesses of the earlier scientists, he has often, as Wicksteed admits, merely excellent reasons for taking the wrong side.[2]

He is, moreover, in the *Physics*, occupied, in the main,

[1] How far his aim was successful, even when supplemented and reinforced by the skill and insight of his co-editor and the co-operation of other devoted helpers, this is not the place, nor is it within the province of the present writer, to decide. In Wicksteed's scholarly apparatus, rich as it was, there were some lacunæ. In choosing paraphrase, too, as the only alternative to a "literal version," he perhaps undervalued the power of the English language, handled with full command of its resources, to reach a fidelity unattainable by either. To paraphrase a difficult writer is to increase indefinitely the danger of error, and the occasions and opportunities of criticism. Let it be remembered that Wicksteed deliberately incurred these risks in order, if he could, to make Aristotle lucid to the plain man.

[2] *Physics*, Introduction, p. xviii.

with questions which the positive spirit of modern science dismisses, or till lately dismissed, as irrelevant or idle. Since Galileo and Descartes, the experimenter investigates the rate of a given motion, or the conditions of a particular change, but he is not troubled by Zeno's denial that change and motion exist, or interested in Aristotle's refutation of Zeno, or in his patient inquiry what, then, change and motion actually are. These questions belonged at best to metaphysics, not to science, and the metaphysician, with the old *Naturphilosophie* his creation, was long since excluded from the laboratory.

Yet, in our own day, the metaphysician, in person or in a very specious disguise, has re-entered those closed doors as a welcome, even an invited, guest. Bergson in 1889 opened his classical treatise on *durée* by a rehabilitation of the paradox of Zeno, and within a few years Einstein and his followers were compelling a reconstitution of the very nature of Space and Time. Of a return to Aristotle's ideas, as to his data, there could seldom be a question; but there was a real return to a state of knowledge and of thought in which Aristotle's ideas were no longer irrelevant, were even of grave importance. This was a principal consideration with Wicksteed in undertaking this work.

"The present translation," he writes, "has been inspired by a conviction that contemporary philosophical thought and discussion is seriously handicapped by the fact that Aristotle's *Physics* is practically unread, and without such help as is here attempted, must remain unreadable except to a few special students."[1] For, he adds, more explicitly, the book

[1] Introduction, p. xix.

contained, besides much matter of interest and value on other grounds, "much that is of vital significance in relation to that borderland between physical and metaphysical thought, where mathematics and philosophy meet." [1]

It is easy to see that thought which moved in this "borderland," even if it had to be disengaged from obsolete terms, could become of more than merely antiquarian interest for the student. It is easy, too, to understand the attraction of Wicksteed himself to a book in which "mathematics and philosophy meet." [2] His own mathematical aptitude lay less in the solution of strictly mathematical problems, than in applying mathematical methods in other provinces of thought commonly regarded as beyond their scope. His fruitful career in economics began when he learnt from Stanley Jevons to apply a mathematical calculus to the "philosophy" of human relations. But mathematics was for him something more than a potent key, an "alphabet" by aid of which the words of a difficult speech could be spelt. Some aspects of it were capable of exciting in Wicksteed's positive intellect a kind of mystic awe. The so-called "imaginary" quantities (like $\sqrt{-1}$), which can neither be imagined nor conceived, but which, treated as if they were real,

[1] It is to be borne in mind that Aristotle's conception of these studies and their mutual relations was not wholly consonant with ours. Physics was for him the study of bodies capable of change; mathematics of unchangeable things without separate existence (the formal aspect of bodies), metaphysics of unchangeable but immaterial substances. Cf. Ross, *Aristotle*, chapter iii.

[2] In a letter to Miss Knappert (April 1923) he describes himself as finding his "play" in "an attempt to disentangle the metaphysics from the mathematics in the fourth dimensioners and Einsteiners, and so clear up the apparent paradoxes in the attempted expositions of them."

carry us infallibly from one real and intelligible equation to another, gave for him a kind of warrant that mathematical truth expressed something inherent in the structure of the universe.[1] And we know how the Pythagorean religion of Number, even Zeno's illusory but fascinating paradox, and Wordsworth's association of the permanent proportions of geometry with the universal timeless and passionless Life of God,[2] were recurring topics of his talk and lecturing.[3]

To a mind of this temper, breathing an air electrified by the recent achievements of mathematical physics, Aristotle's elementary yet pregnant glimpses into that "borderland" naturally appeared both relevant and fascinating.

II

But the forces which drew Wicksteed in his old age to this sustained labour were not confined to these. Aristotle was, for Wicksteed, not merely the philosophic

[1] The thought had been finely expressed in the *Reactions* (p. 445 f.): [At the close of an operation involving imaginary qualities] "the solid fact will be there to receive the traveller, who has lost sight of all fact in his weird voyage, but has been true to the compass of his thought. That thought, for a time, had no factual or conceptual content to steady it, but was guided by the spirit of its own form alone. I confess that such reflections have given a new meaning for me to the word that "man is the child of God," and have taught me to think of the mind as reflecting far more explicitly than the senses ever can do the inner meaning and constitution of the universe, and as giving us a directer as well as a deeper access to reality than the composition of our animal frame from the elements can open up to us."

[2] *Prelude*, vi, 140 f. (130 f.).

[3] In the case of Zeno his interest was wholly polemical. He regarded the attempts to rehabilitate Zeno's paradox as the basis of a new mathematics as wholly mistaken, and was occupied at the very close of his life with a paper, left incomplete, on Bergson's renewed discussion of Zeno.

fountain-head of Aquinas and Dante; he appealed to him by traits of profound affinity, under whatever diversity, to both, and to that in them which had found most complete response in himself. The *Physics* was a link, and not one of the least essential, in the vast synthesis which it had been the life-work of Aristotle to effect for the Hellenic world, as it was to be the life work of Aquinas and of Dante to effect a synthesis of that part of the medieval Christian universe which lay within their ken. The popular antithesis between Aristotle and Plato disguises the fact that Aristotle's synthesis embraced vital elements of the thought of Plato himself. He grappled, as he taught Aquinas and Dante to grapple, with the problem of thinking a religion in terms of science. One of the first Aristotelians of our day, Werner Jaeger, has expressed this in a salient passage of his monograph: [1]

"Aristotle's is the first Metaphysic begotten of the conflict between the religious convictions due to Plato and the analytic reflexion of science. This conflict is not yet found in Plato himself. It arose from the rupture of the (apparently) scientific form which Plato had found for the new Reality of his supersensuous world. . . . The dissolution of Plato's system left Aristotle, however, with the immovable conviction that the deepest core of his early Platonic faith must, after all, be true. His *Metaphysics* is the grandiose attempt to make this Something which transcended the limits of human experience accessible to human reason. It was by this hitherto misunderstood identity of his problem with that of the philosophic dogmatists of the Christian, Jewish, and Mohammedan faiths, and

[1] W. Jaeger, *Aristoteles* (Berlin, 1923), p. 404.

not by the mere accident of transmission, that Aristotle became the intellectual guide of the post-Augustinian centuries, whose inner world had been expanded by the tension of Faith and Knowledge far beyond the limits of the Hellenic soul. The history of his development shows that his metaphysic already rests, like theirs, upon a *credo ut intelligam*." This view, though less explicitly expressed, permeates Wicksteed's Introduction.

And if it is the task of the *Metaphysics* to effect this synthesis, the *Physics* presupposes it. Its philosophy of "Nature" does not cross the frontier into a super-sensuous world, but it implies that such a world exists. The material universe and the processes of Nature, with the description of which it is engaged, are real and everlasting; but they point beyond themselves to an immaterial existence on which they depend for all their functions.

But the centre and basis of Aristotle's synthesis is yet of the material world. If his scientific interpretation of Plato anticipated the attempts of Aquinas and Dante to give articulate expression to transcendental theology, his fundamental acceptance of the world in which we live provided an enduring basis, no less, for that which made the Angelic Doctor a herculean worker for the instruction and defence of the Church upon earth, and made the devoted lover of Beatrice a great citizen, whose unique poem about her was designed to enable men, while they live, to transform their earthly city into a City of God.

III

It was upon these three great transcendental realists, if one may venture the phrase, that Philip Wicksteed concentrated the labour of the eighth, and of most of three earlier decades, of a life that never knew senility. Is it extravagant to find there a clue to the final interpretation of the interpreter? He, too, was of those who possess at once the eye which seizes with eager precision the tangible things and facts about them, and that which sweeps by instinctive impetus beyond the chartered limits of their country, their generation, and of the material world itself. He spent his strength lavishly in fathoming and expounding the common sense of our daily "getting and spending"; but he is no less himself when he is reaching across the ages to the masters of wisdom, conveyed perhaps through impossible dogma or obsolete science, which had for him, too, no other end than to prepare the way for a nobler and completer citizenship. The religion of Eternity neither effaced in him, nor succumbed to, but only fortified, illuminated and enriched, the religion of Time.

And the twofold range and reach of power was aided in him, as in his other master Wordsworth, by something elemental and homely in his own nature. There was in him, as in Wordsworth, as in Burns, a kind of provinciality, which enabled him, as it enabled them, to evade many of the provincialisms of his environment, and exempted him from some limitations to which more academic or cosmopolitan natures succumb.

It also led him easily and naturally to another point

of contact with those earlier, as well as with the later masters, that regard for the common mind which was instinctive in Wordsworth, but to which Aristotle and Dante in their most transcendental flights had never been untrue. Neither Dante, who told of the Beatific Vision in speech fitted for the understanding of simple womanhood, nor Aristotle, whose philosophy is, finally, sifted and sublimated common sense, would have disdained the fellowship of the man who spent so large a part of a long life, even to his last breath, in making them the living possession of his unlearned countrymen.

APPENDICES

APPENDIX I

The following detailed lists of Wicksteed's University Extension courses for the Oxford, Cambridge, London, Liverpool, and Manchester centres have been kindly supplied by the Registrars for the Extension Boards of those Universities. It does not include other courses of lectures.

OXFORD UNIVERSITY

Term and Year	*Centre*	*Subject*
Michaelmas 1895	Halifax	Dante
Michaelmas 1895	Halifax	Wordsworth
	Harrogate	Dante
	Ilkley	Dante
	Ripon	Dante
Michaelmas 1896	Dover	Dante
Trinity 1897	Dover	Dante (continued)
	Brighton	Dante's *Purgatorio*
Trinity 1900	Bradford	Dante
Trinity 1901	Tunbridge Wells	Dante
Trinity 1902	Tunbridge Wells	Dante's *Purgatorio*
Michaelmas 1902	Hoddesdon	Dante
Trinity 1903	Birmingham	Gaining and Spending
	Edgbaston	Dante
	Tunbridge Wells	Dante's *Paradiso*
Michaelmas 1903	Rochdale	Dante
Michaelmas 1904	Hove	Dante
	Winchester	Dante
Trinity 1905	Edgbaston	Dante's *Purgatorio*
	Tunbridge Wells	Wordsworth
Michaelmas 1905	Canterbury	Dante
	East Grinstead	Dante
	Limpsfield	Dante
	Reading	Dante
Trinity 1906	Eastbourne	Dante's *Purgatorio*
	Edgbaston	Dante's *Paradiso*
	Winchester	Dante's *Purgatorio*
Michaelmas 1906 and Trinity 1907	Canterbury	Dante's *Purgatorio*
Michaelmas 1906	East Grinstead	Dante's *Purgatorio*
Michaelmas 1906 and Trinity 1907	Hove	Poems of Revolt and Reconciliation

Term and Year	*Centre*	*Subject*
Michaelmas 1906 and Trinity 1907	Ilkley	Dante
Michaelmas 1906	Reigate	Dante
Trinity 1907	Reading	Dante
Michaelmas 1907	Haslemere	Dante
	Westgate	Dante
Trinity 1908	East Grinstead	Dante's *Paradiso*
Michaelmas 1908	Bedford	Dante
Michaelmas 1908 and Trinity 1909	Bournemouth	Dante
Michaelmas 1908	Bournemouth (Pokesdowne)	Getting and Spending
	Bournemouth (Winton)	Getting and Spending
Michaelmas 1908 and Trinity 1909	Haslemere	Dante's *Purgatorio*
Michaelmas 1908 and Trinity 1909	Ryde	Dante
	Shanklin	Dante
	Surbiton	Dante
Trinity 1909	Bournemouth (Pokesdowne)	Wordsworth
	Ilkley	Poems of Revolt and Reconciliation
Michaelmas 1909	Ramsgate	Dante
	Westgate	Wordsworth
Michaelmas 1910	Cheltenham	Dante
	Haslemere	Dante's *Paradiso*
Trinity 1911	Ilkley	Getting and Spending
Michaelmas 1911	Canterbury	Dante's *Paradiso*
	Ramsgate	Dante's *Purgatorio*
Trinity 1912	Bolton	Dante
	Bolton	Wordsworth
Michaelmas 1912	Windsor	Dante
Trinity 1913	Caterham Valley	Dante
	Parkstone	Dante
	Parkstone (Miss Rudd)	Dante
Michaelmas 1913	East Grinstead	Greek Drama
	Kingswood	Dante
	Tunbridge Wells	Dante
Trinity 1914	Parkstone	Dante
Michaelmas 1914 and Trinity 1915	Parkstone (Miss Rudd)	Greek Tragedy

Term and Year	Centre	Subject
Trinity 1914	Parkstone (Miss Rudd)	Wordsworth
Trinity 1915	Tunbridge Wells	Greek Tragedians
Michaelmas 1915	Wantage	Æschylus and Sophocles
	Canford Cliffs	Dante
	Stoke	Dante
	Tolmers Park	Dante
Trinity 1916	Leighton Park	The Roots of Economy
Michaelmas 1916	Canford Cliffs	Influence of Greek Philosophy on Medieval and Modern Thought
Michaelmas 1917 and Trinity 1918	Canford Cliffs	Wordsworth

CAMBRIDGE UNIVERSITY

Term and Year	Centre	Subject
Michaelmas 1896	Leicester	Dante
Michaelmas 1897	Colchester	Dante
	Cambridge	Dante
Lent 1898	Leicester	Dante
Michaelmas 1898	Colchester	Italian Literature (Dante)
	Norwich	Italian Literature (Dante)
Lent 1899	Norwich	Italian Literature (Dante's *Purgatorio*)
Michaelmas 1899	Exeter	Italian Literature (Dante)
	Torquay	Dante
	Plymouth	Dante
Lent 1900	Exeter	Dante's *Purgatorio*
	Brighton	Dante's *Paradiso*
Michaelmas 1900	Scarborough	Dante
	York	Dante
	Hull	Dante
	Sunderland	Dante
	Newcastle	Dante
	Leeds	Wordsworth
	Darlington	Dante
Lent 1901	Exeter	Dante's *Paradiso*
	Torquay	Poems of Revolt and Reconciliation
	Leicester	Dante's *Paradiso*, Principles of Human Conduct
Michaelmas 1901	Hull	Dante's *Purgatorio*
	Scarborough	Poems of Revolt and Reconciliation
	Darlington	Dante

Term and Year	*Centre*	*Subject*
Michaelmas 1901	Northallerton	Earning and Spending
Lent 1902	Hurstpierpoint	Dante
Michaelmas 1902	Newcastle	Dante's *Purgatorio*
	York	Dante's *Purgatorio*, Getting and Spending
Lent 1903	Hull	Dante's *Paradiso*
	Eastbourne	Dante
Lent 1904	Hurstpierpoint	Dante's *Purgatorio*
Michaelmas 1904	Nottingham	Dante
	Ipswich	Dante
Michaelmas 1905	Nottingham	Dante
	Hastings	Dante
	Hull	Aristotle and Medieval Thought
Lent 1906	Nottingham	Dante's *Purgatorio*
	Middlesbrough	Dante
	Grantham	Dante
Michaelmas 1906	Darlington	Earning and Spending
	West Hartlepool	Dante
	Nottingham	Dante's *Paradiso*
Lent 1907	Hull	Earning and Spending
Michaelmas 1907	Hastings	Poems of Revolt and Reconciliation
Lent 1908	Hull	Wordsworth
	Nottingham	Aristotle and Medieval Thought
Lent 1909	Scarborough	Dante's *Purgatorio*
	Southport	Dante
Michaelmas 1909	Derby	Dante
	Worthing	Dante
Lent 1910	Leicester	Dante
	Northampton	Dante
	Hull	Dante
	Hull	Poems of Revolt and Reconciliation
Michaelmas 1910	Southport	Dante's *Purgatorio*
Lent 1911	Hull	Dante's *Purgatorio*
	Letchworth	Dante
Lent 1912	Hull	Dante's *Paradiso*
Michaelmas 1912	Hastings	Dante's *Purgatorio*
Lent 1913	Cambridge	Dante
	Middlesbrough	Poems of Revolt and Reconciliation
Michaelmas 1913	Hastings	Dante's *Paradiso*
Lent 1914	Worthing	Dante's *Purgatorio*
Michaelmas 1916	Scarborough	The Greek Drama
	Hull	The Greek Drama

LONDON UNIVERSITY

S—Sessional Course of twenty-four University Extension Lectures.
T—Terminal Course of ten or twelve University Extension Lectures.
Short—Short Course of five or six University Extension Lectures.

		1887–1888
T	Wimbledon	Dante
		1888–1889
T	Essex Hall	Elements of Sociology
T	Harrow	Parallels from English and Italian Literature
T	Wimbledon	English and Italian Literature
		1889–1890
T	Essex Hall	Making and Sharing
T	South Lambeth	Dante
T	Whitechapel	Sociology
Short	Chelsea	Dante
Short	South Lambeth	Dante
		1890–1891
T	Chelsea	Dante's *Inferno*
T	Kew and Richmond	Dante
T	South Lambeth	Dante's *Inferno*
T	Whitechapel	Dante
T	Chelsea	Dante's *Purgatorio*
T	University Hall	Life and Structure of Human Societies
T	Whitechapel	Dante's *Inferno*
		1891–1892
T	University Hall	Dante (2 courses)
T	,,	Elements of Political Economy
T	Chelsea	Dante's *Paradiso*
T	University Hall	Theory of Exchange, Hire and Interest
T	,,	Dante's *Inferno* (2 courses)
Short	,,	Dante's *Purgatorio*
		1892–1893
S	,,	Dante: *Purgatorio, Paradiso* (2 courses)
		1893–1894
T	Bromley	Dante and *Inferno* (3 courses)
T	Essex Hall	The Theory of Sharing
2 Ts	Central Course	Dante
2 Ts	Notting Hill	Dante and *Inferno*

1893–1894 (*continued*)

2 Ts	University Hall	Theory of Sharing (2 courses)
Short	,,	Foreign Trade and Population
Short	,,	Dante's Historical and Philosophical Conceptions

1894–1895

2 Ts	Croydon	Dante and *Inferno*
T	Morley College	Life and Structure of Human Societies
T	,,	Theory of Earning and Spending
T	North Hackney	Dante
2 Ts	Notting Hill	Dante's *Purgatorio* and *Paradiso*
S	Streatham	Dante and *Inferno*
T	University Hall	Wordsworth
S	,,	Theory of Production. Theory of Earning and Spending. First Principles of Currency

1894–1895

T	University Hall	Theory of Earning and Spending (afternoon course)

1895–1896

S	Streatham	Dante's *Purgatorio, Paradiso,* Scholastic Philosophy
S	Toynbee	Wordsworth. Poems of Revolt and Reconciliation. Wordsworth and his Circle
S	University Hall	Theory of Earning and Spending. Currency and Finance, Taxation
T	Bushey Heath	Dante
T	Camberwell	Theory of Earning and Spending
T	University Hall	Poems of Revolt and Reconciliation
Short	,,	Wordsworth and his Circle

1896–1897

T	Bloomsbury	Theory of Earning and Spending
T	Chelsea	Wordsworth
T & Sh.	,,	Dante, and Dante's *Convito*
S	Croydon	Theory of Earning and Spending. Currency and Finance
S	Regent St. Poly.	Dante, and Dante's *Convito*
T	Bushey Heath	Wordsworth
T	Chislehurst	Dante (Part II.)
Short	Woolwich	Money (part course)

		1897–1898
S	Chelsea	Dante, *Purgatorio, Paradiso, Canzoni*
T	Chislehurst	Dante's *Paradiso*
S	Greenwich	Dante, Dante's *Purgatorio, Convito*
2 Ts	Pass. Edwards	Dante. Dante's *Purgatorio*
T	Regent St. Poly.	Dante's *Paradiso*
T	Weybridge	Dante
T	Pass. Edwards	Dante. Life, Character, and Studies
T	Regent St. Poly.	Dante. Life, Character, and Studies
		1898–1899
T	Greenwich	Dante's *Paradiso*
T	,,	Poems of Revolt and Reconciliation
2 Ts	Hammersmith	Dante, Dante's *Purgatorio*
T	Notting Hill	Poems of Revolt and Reconciliation
S	Westbourne Park	Dante, Dante's *Purgatorio, Paradiso*
T	Woolwich	Dante
T	Finchley	Dante
		1899–1900
T	Chislehurst	Wordsworth
T	Croydon	Wordsworth
T	Harrow	Dante
T	Croydon	Poems of Revolt and Reconciliation
T	Finchley	Dante with special reference to *Purgatorio*
		1901–1902
S	Canning Town	Theory of Earning and Spending
T	Harrow	Dante with special reference to *Purgatorio*
S	Regent St. Poly.	Dante (2 courses)
2 Ts	Sidcup	Dante
S	Westbourne Park	Dante
T	Chislehurst	Poems of Revolt and Reconciliation
		1902–1903
T	Greenwich	Wordsworth
S	Richmond	Dante
T	Sutton	Dante
2 Ts	Toynbee	Dante
T	Westbourne Park	Wordsworth
2 Ts	Wimbledon	Dante
T	Sutton	Theory of Earning and Spending
T & Sh.	Westbourne Park	Poems of Revolt and Reconciliation
		1903–1904
2 Ts	Epsom	Dante
T	Hampstead	Dante

1903–1904 (*continued*)

2 Ts	Regent St. Poly.	Dante
2 Ts	Upper Holloway	Dante
T	Wimbledon	Dante's *Paradiso*
T	Chislehurst	Getting and Spending
Short	Upper Holloway	Studies in Medieval Thought

1904–1905

T	Barnet	Dante
2 Ts	City of London Coll.	Dante
2 Ts	Hampstead	Dante
T	Upper Holloway	Dante's *Paradiso*
Short	Central Course	Dante's *Commedia*

1906–1907

2 Ts	Greenwich	Dante
T	Epsom	Dante's *Paradiso*

1907–1908

Short	Putney	Dante
Short	St. John's Wood	Wordsworth

1908–1909

T	Upper Holloway	Some Poets of the Nineteenth Century

1910–1911

S	Central Course	Dante, and Dante with special reference to *Purgatorio*
S	Richmond	Dante's *Purgatorio* and *Paradiso*

1911–1912

S	Central Course	Dante's *Paradiso*, and Some Aspects of the Influence of Greek Philosophy on Medieval and Modern Thought

1913–1914

Part	City of London Coll.	Development of Literatures (Part I, Ancient and Early Renaissance)
T	Wimbledon	Dante

1914–1915

T	Chelsea	Dante
T	Walworth Road	Dante
T	Wimbledon	Greek Tragedy
Short	Greenwich	The Greek Drama

1915–1916

S	Morley College	Dante
T	Ashtead	The Greek Drama

LIVERPOOL UNIVERSITY

Term and Year	*Centre*	*Subject*
Michaelmas 1903	Liverpool	Dante
	Neston	Dante
Lent 1903	Liverpool	Dante's *Purgatorio*
Michaelmas 1904	Liverpool	Dante's *Paradiso*
	New Brighton	Getting and Spending
Michaelmas 1910	Royal Institute	Dante
Michaelmas 1914	Liverpool	Dante's *Purgatorio*
Lent 1915	Liverpool	The Greek Tragedians
Michaelmas 1915	Liverpool	Æschylus and Sophocles
Lent 1916	Liverpool	Wordsworth

MANCHESTER UNIVERSITY

Session	*Centre*	*Subject*
1895–6	Leeds (Yorkshire Ladies' Council of Education)	Dante
1896–7	Leeds (Yorkshire Ladies' Council of Education)	Dante
1903–4	Altrincham and Bowdon	Dante
	Ancoats	Poems of Revolt and Reconciliation
	Warrington	Dante
	Withington	Dante
1904–5	University	Dante
1912–13	Warburton Lecture at the University	The Implications of Taxation, Imperial and Municipal

APPENDIX II

Wicksteed's Review of Marx's *Das Kapital* in *To-Day*, October 1884, with reply by G. Bernard Shaw and Wicksteed's rejoinder.

A.—WICKSTEED'S REVIEW OF DAS KAPITAL

I have long wished to lay before the disciples of Karl Marx certain theoretical objections to the more abstract portions of *Das Kapital* which suggested themselves to me on my first reading of that great work, and which a patient and repeated study of it have failed to remove.

The editors of *To-Day*, with equal candour and courtesy, have given me the opportunity I sought; and my first duty is to thank them for opening the pages of their review to a critical analysis of the teaching of the great Socialist thinker. The sense of obligation will be more than doubled if any student of Marx should think my criticisms deserving of a reply; for while making no illusions to myself as to the probability of serious and matured convictions being shaken, on either side, by such a controversy, I am none the less persuaded that in studying so profound and abstruse a work as *Das Kapital*, neither disciples nor opponents can afford to neglect the sidelights that may be thrown upon the subject by any earnest and intelligent attempt to analyse and discuss it from a point of view differing from their own.

As a challenge, then, to a renewed study of the theoretical basis of *Das Kapital* the following remarks may perhaps be regarded as not altogether out of place in *To-Day*, even by those Socialists who are most convinced that a vigorous propaganda, rather than a discussion of first principles, is the specific work to which the Socialist press is now called.

It has been held by Economists of the most widely divergent schools that the wages of manual labour normally tend, under existing conditions, to sink to a point at which they barely suffice to support existence and allow of reproduction; and that the only means (always under existing conditions) by which wages could be permanently raised would be a collective refusal on the part of the working-classes to live and propagate on the terms at present granted—i.e. a raising of the standard of minimum comfort. This position—which I do not stay to examine—is accepted by Marx (*Das Kapital*, pp. 155-163 [73–5]).[1]

But if his results coincide, in this respect, with those of the old school of

---

[1] I cite from the second German edition (1872), which is probably the one in the hands of most of my readers. References to the French translation are added in square brackets.

Economics, the grounds on which he rests them are, of course, entirely different.

In the Malthusian philosophy the reason why wages steadily tend to the minimum allowed by the "standard of comfort" (*aliter dictum*—to starvation point) is sufficiently obvious. It is a law not of society but of nature. The point of "diminishing returns" has been reached and passed, and every additional labourer whom the increase of population throws upon the field reduces the average productiveness of labour, so that there really is less wealth per head to be consumed, and each labourer, of course, gets less for himself. This is supposed to go on until the labourers refuse to add to their numbers (standard of comfort check) or are unable to do so because their children cannot live (starvation check).

On the monstrous assumptions of Malthusianism all this is obvious enough; but it need hardly be said that Marx does not grant these assumptions, and must, therefore, find some other explanation of the phenomenon they are called on to account for. It is not in the material environment of humanity, but in the social and industrial organization of capitalistic societies that we must look, according to Marx, for the reasons that force men to accept starvation wages.

What is it, then, in the conditions of modern industrialism that compels the producers of all wealth to make such hard terms with the non-producers? What is it that constantly fills the markets with men willing and anxious to sell their "labour force" for the wages of bare subsistence?

As far as I can see, Karl Marx gives two distinct and disconnected answers to this question. In the later portion of *Das Kapital* (I speak, of course, of the single volume published), he shows how the alternate expansions and contractions of the several branches of industry, aggravated by the disturbances caused by the introduction of "labour-saving" machinery and so forth, tend constantly to throw upon the market a number of unemployed labourers, who will offer their "labour-force" to the purchaser at prices barely adequate to support existence. All this seems to me worthy of the most earnest attention; but it is not my present purpose to dwell upon it further; for according to Marx there is a deeper cause of the phenomenon we are examining, immanent in the very fact of the purchase of "labour-force" in the market at all, and essentially independent of any such influences as I have just referred to which may depress or disturb that market when once established. It is to this alleged inherent necessity of "capitalistic"[1] production that I wish to direct attention.

---

[1] Throughout his argument in the published volume of *Das Kapital* Marx deals with the "capitalist" simply as an employer of labour, reserving for future treatment not only the merchant, but the possessor and investor of money who draws interest from it without personally engaging in any industrial or commercial pursuit (pp. 148, 149, [69*b*, 70*a*]). Now it is the investor of money, as such, whom recent English-writing economists, such as Sidgwick and Walker, have agreed (as it seems to me with good

I must ask leave to restate the main positions which lead up to Marx's conclusions in the order which will be most convenient for subsequent analysis. According to Marx, then, the (exchange) value of wares is determined by the amount of labour necessary on the average to produce them, and in the last resort their average selling price depends upon their value (pp. 52, 81, 151 *note* 37, etc. [30*a*, 42*a*, 70*b* *note*, etc.]), so that in

---

reason) to call the "capitalist," in contradistinction to the employer of labour, or the trader, who may or may not be his own capitalist. On this, however, I do not insist. Marx is justified, from his point of view, in using the term as he does, for he regards the function of the employer of labour, i.e. the purchase of labour-force and the employment of it in producing "utilities," "commodities," or "wares" (*vide infra*), as the sole normal source of that "surplus value" which is subsequently divided up into rent, interest, and profit (pp. 204, 205, 210, cf. 195 *note* [92*b*, 94*b*, cf. 88*a*, *note*]). According to him, therefore, the function of the "rentier" or receiver of interest is merely a derived form of the function of the "entrepreneur" or employer of labour, and it is this latter who is the "capitalist," *par excellence*, the prime recipient or extractor of all the wealth which labour creates, but which the labourer does not receive. Marx is perfectly aware, though I am not sure that his disciples always remember it, that this view of the origin of all "surplus value" appears to stand in glaring contradiction to experience and to the historical order in which the successive forms of capital have been evolved, and that this apparent contradiction can only be removed by a long chain of reasoning which is *not* given in the published volume of *Das Kapital*, though it seems to be promised in a future portion of the work (pp. 312, cf. 148, 149, 203 [133*a*, cf. 69*b*, 70*a*, 92*b*]); but again I have no intention of insisting upon this, as my purpose is not to inquire whether Marx's explanation of the phenomena of capitalistic industry is adequate, but whether the fundamental analysis upon which it rests is sound.

With reference to the terms "commodity" and "ware," which will frequently occur in this article, it may be noticed that Marx's use of the word *Gebrauchswerth* for concrete objects exactly corresponds to Jevons's definition of a *commodity*: "By *commodity* we shall understand any object, substance, action or service, which can afford pleasure or ward off pain" (*Theory of Pol. Ec.*, p. 41), except that Marx would substitute "labour-force, etc." for "action or service." It seems a pity that "utilities" as a designation of concrete objects is not sanctioned by English usage. Marx uses *Waare* to signify a commodity or "utility" *which was made expressly with the view of exchanging it*, not of using it directly (p. 15). It seems to me that *ware* is the proper English for this, though there are indications that Marx himself might perhaps have translated it "commodity," a term which in English writers certainly does not carry the *differentia* of his *Waare*. Passages bearing on the correct translation of *Waare* will be found on pp. 15, 17, 55, 61, 63, 111, 137, etc. of *Das Kapital*.

dealing with normal relations we must always assume that whatever is sold or purchased, is sold or purchased at its full value and no more.

The manufacturer, then, must be supposed to sell his product at its value, which is as good as to say that he receives a sum of money for it representing the number of days of labour required to produce it. But he must also be supposed to have purchased all the machines, raw material, labour-force, etc. necessary to production at their value, i.e. he must have given as much money for them as represents the number of days of labour needed to produce them. Now if we take any one of these necessaries of production, such as the coal needed to work the engines, and inquire into the relation in which it stands to the value of the product, the problem seems to be a very simple one. Inasmuch as a certain amount of coal must be burned before so much cotton cloth can be produced, the labour expended in getting the coal is in reality a part of the labour expended in producing the cotton cloth, and in estimating the value of the cotton cloth, we must reckon in so many days' labour expended in getting coal. The cloth, then, is more valuable than it would have been had the coal been unnecessary to its production by the precise amount of labour needed to produce the coal; but by hypothesis this is exactly represented by the money paid for the coal, so that the price of the coal (if purchased at its value) will reappear in the price of the cloth (if sold at its value)—so much *and no more.* The same reasoning will apply to the machinery, raw cotton, and so forth. The labour needed to produce each of these is labour needed to produce the cotton, and the fact that they are all necessary to the production of cotton enhances the value of cotton by precisely the amount of their own value—so much *and no more.* But when we come to labour-force, the case is different. Labour-force, like every other ware, has its value determined by the amount of labour needed to produce it. Now the amount of labour needed to produce, say, a day's labour-force, is the amount of labour needed to produce food, clothing, etc. adequate to maintaining the labourer in working condition for one day, allowance being made for the support of a number of children adequate to keeping up the supply of labourers, and so forth. Our capitalist then goes into the market and purchases labour-force *at its value.*[1] We may suppose, for the sake of argument, that this value represents six hours' work, i.e. that it would need so much work to provide the labourer with all things needful to keep him in working condition for one day. The capitalist, then, by expending a sum of money representing six hours' work has purchased at its value, and becomes the possessor of, a day's labour-force. It is now at his absolute disposal, and on the supposition that a man can work eight or ten hours a

---

[1] He may, and often does, purchase it below its value, but the abstract argument assumes the contrary as the normal condition of things. It is essential that this should be quite clearly understood. (Cf. pp. 150, 151, 207. Da der Werth des variablen Kapitals—Werth der von ihm gekauften Arbeitskraft) and [70 and 93 *b*] *passim.*)

day without any undue strain upon his system (so that the labour-force, the value of which the capitalist has paid, is labour-force capable of being applied over eight or ten hours), it is obvious that the capitalist will realize a gain of two or four hours' work. He (virtually) puts into the labourer (in the shape of food, clothing, etc.) a value representing six hours' work, and in virtue of this transaction, he causes the labourer to put eight or ten hours' work into the cotton. Hence the result that, though he buys all the things needful to the production of the cotton (including labour-force) *at their value,* and sells his cotton *at its value,* yet *more value comes out than goes in.* This "more" is the "surplus value" to secure which is the capitalist's aim, and from which interest, rent and profit are ultimately cut out as so many slices.

The production and appropriation of this surplus value is, according to Marx, the immanent law of capitalistic production, and no mere incidental development of it. If the extraction of surplus value from the application of labour-force were rendered impossible, the capitalist would lose his sole motive for engaging in his peculiar form of production at all.

I believe this is a fair summary of Marx's argument, and if so, its essential positions are as follows:

First. The (exchange) value of a ware is determined by the amount of labour needed on the average to produce it.

Second. There is such a degree of correspondence between the value of a ware and its average selling price, that for theoretical purposes we must assume that nominally wares are bought and sold at their values.

Third. Labour-force is (in our industrial societies) a ware subject to the same laws and conditions of value and exchange as other wares.

Whether Marx's conclusions can be logically deduced from these positions or not is a question which I will not attempt to answer now, for I am concerned with the positions themselves. Against the second (when a correct definition of value has been reached) I have nothing to urge. It is the first and third that I wish to test.

With reference to the theory of value, it will be convenient to follow Marx in his fundamental analysis of the process of exchange.

He begins by pointing out that the fact of two wares being exchangeable (no matter in what proportion) implies of necessity, both *Verschiedenheit* and *Gleichheit*; i.e. that they are *not identical* (else the exchange would leave things exactly where it found them), and that they are different manifestations or forms of *a common something* (else they could not be equated against each other). In other words, things which are exchangeable must be *dissimilar in quality,* but yet they must have some common measure, by reduction to which the equivalent portions of each will be seen to be *identical in quantity.*

Now with regard to the qualitative dissimilarity, I do not see that there is any room for difference of opinion. It consists in the divergent nature of the services rendered by the respective wares. Cast-iron nails and new-laid eggs differ in respect to their "value in use." They serve different purposes. Even a red and a blue ribbon, though they both serve purposes of adornment, are capable each of rendering some particular services of adornment under circumstances which would make the other a mere disfigurement. I agree with Marx, then, that the *Verschiedenheit* of the wares is to be found in the respective *Gebrauchswerth* of each, or, as I should express it, *commodities differ one from another in their specific utilities.*

But in what does the *Gleichheit* consist? What is the *common something* of which each ware is a more or less? Marx replies that to get at this something, whatever it is, we must obviously set on one side all geometrical, physical, chemical, and other natural properties of the several wares, for it is precisely in these that they differ from one another, and we are seeking that in which they are all identical. Now in setting aside all these natural properties, we are setting aside all that gives the wares a value in use, and there is nothing left them but the single property of being *products of labour.* But the wares, as they stand, are the products of many *different kinds* of labour, each of which was engaged in conferring upon them the special physical properties in virtue of which they possess specific utilities. Now to get at that in which all wares are identical we have been obliged to strip off all these physical properties in which they differ, so that if we still regard them as products of labour, it must be labour that has no specific character or direction, mere "abstract and indifferent human labour," the expenditure of so much human brain and muscle, etc. The *Gleichheit,* then, of the several wares consists in the fact that they are all products of abstract human labour, and the equation x of ware A $=y$ of ware B, holds in virtue of the fact that it requires the same amount of abstract human labour to produce x of ware A or y of ware B (pp. 12, 13, cf. 19, 23, seq. [14*b*, 15*a*, cf. 17*a*, 19 seq.]).

Now the leap by which this reasoning lands us in labour as the sole constituent element of value appears to me so surprising that I am prepared to learn that the yet unpublished portions of *Das Kapital* contain supplementary or elucidatory matter which may set it in a new light. Meanwhile the analysis appears to be given as complete and adequate, so far as it goes, and I can, therefore, only take it as I find it and try to test its validity. But instead of directly confronting it with what seems to be the true analysis of the phenomenon of exchange, I will follow it out a little further, and we shall see that Marx himself introduces a modification into his result (or develops a half-latent implication in it), in such a way as to vitiate the very analysis on which that result is founded, and to lead us, if we work it out, to what I regard as the true solution of the problem.

A few pages, then, after we have been told that wares regarded as "valuables" must be stripped of all their physical attributes, i.e. of everything that gives them their value in use, and reduced to one identical spectral objectivity, as mere jellies of undistinguishable abstract human labour, and that it is this abstract human labour which constitutes them valuables, we find the important statement that *the labour does not count unless it is useful* (pp. 15, 16, 64 [16*a*, 35*a*]). Simple and obvious as this seems, it in reality surrenders the whole of the previous analysis, for if it is only useful labour that counts, then in stripping the wares of all the specific properties conferred upon them by specific kinds of useful work, we must not be supposed to have stripped them of the abstract utility, conferred upon them by abstractly useful work. If only useful labour counts then when the wares are reduced to mere indifferent products of such labour in the abstract, they are still *useful* in the abstract, and therefore it is not true that "nothing remains to them but the one attribute of being products of labour (p. 12 [14*b*]), for the attribute of being useful also remains to them. In this all wares are alike.

Armed with this result let us return to the fundamental analysis of the phenomenon of exchange.

The exchange of two wares implies a heterogeneity (Verschiedenheit) and a homogeneity (Gleichheit). *This is implied in the fact that they are exchangeable.* And here I must challenge the attention of students of *Das Kapital* to the fact that the analysis by which "labour" is reached as the ultimate constituent element of (exchange) value, starts from the naked fact of exchangeability and is said to be involved in that fact. It is true that in the instances given by Marx the articles exchanged are wares (i.e. commodities which have been produced for the express purpose of exchange), and moreover wares which can practically be produced in almost unlimited quantities. It is true also that Marx elsewhere virtually *defines* value so as to make it essentially dependent upon human labour (p. 81 [43*a*]). But for all that his analysis is based on the bare fact of exchangeability. This fact alone establishes *Verschiedenheit* and *Gleichheit,* heterogeneity and homogeneity. Any two things which normally exchange for each other, whether products of labour or not, whether they have, or have not, what we choose to *call* value, must have that "common something" in virtue of which things exchange and can be equated with each other; and all legitimate inferences as to wares which are drawn from the bare fact of exchange must be equally legitimate when applied to other exchangeable things.

Now the "common something," which all exchangeable things contain, is neither more nor less than abstract *utility,* i.e. power of satisfying human desires. The exchanged articles differ from each other in the *specific desires* which they satisfy, they resemble each other in the *degree of satisfaction* which they confer. The *Verschiedenheit* is qualitative, the *Gleichheit* is quantitative.

It cannot be urged that there is no common measure to which we can reduce the satisfaction derived from such different articles as Bibles and brandy, for instance (to take an illustration suggested by Marx), for as a matter of fact we are all of us making such reductions every day. If I am willing to give the same sum of money for a family Bible and for a dozen of brandy, it is because I have reduced the respective satisfactions their possession will afford me to a common measure, and have found them equivalent. In economic phrase, the two things have equal abstract utility for me. In popular (and highly significant) phrase, each of the two things is *worth* as much to me as the other.

Marx is, therefore, wrong in saying that when we pass from that in which the exchangeable wares differ (value in use) to that in which they are identical (value in exchange), we must put their utility out of consideration, leaving only jellies of abstract labour. What we really have to do is to put out of consideration the concrete and specific qualitative utilities in which they differ, leaving only the abstract and general quantitative utility in which they are identical.

This formula applies to all exchangeable commodities, whether producible in indefinite quantities, like family Bibles and brandy, or strictly limited in quantity, like the "Raphaels," one of which has just been purchased for the nation. The equation which always holds in the case of a normal exchange is an equation not of labour, but of abstract utility, significantly called *worth*. The precise nature of this equation we shall presently examine; but let it be observed, meanwhile, that "labour" is indeed one of the sources (not the only one) alike of value in use (specific utility) and value in exchange (abstract utility), but in no case is it a constituent *element* of the latter any more than of the former. A coat is *made* specifically useful by the tailor's work, but it *is* specifically useful (has a value in use) because it protects us. In the same way, it is *made* valuable by abstractly useful work, but it *is* valuable because it has abstract utility. Labour, in its two-fold capacity of specifically useful work (tailoring, joinery, etc.) and abstractly useful work, *confers* upon suitable substances both *Gebrauchswerth* (value in use) and *Tauschwerth* (value in exchange), but it is not an element of either.

I venture to think that if any student of Marx will candidly re-peruse the opening portion of *Das Kapital*, and especially the remarkable section on "the two-fold character of the labour represented in wares" (pp. 16–21 [16–18]), he will be compelled to admit that the great logician has at any rate fallen into formal (if not, as I believe to be the case, into substantial) error, has passed unwarrantably and without warning, from one category into another, when he makes the great leap from specific utilities into objectivized abstract labour (p. 12 [14*b*]), and has given us an argument which can only become formally correct when so modified and supplemented as to accept *abstract utility* as the measure of value.

But to many of my readers this will appear to be an absurd and contradictory conclusion. "When all is said and done," they will think, "we know that as a matter of fact the exchange value of all ordinary articles *is* fixed by the amount of labour required to produce them. It may be true that *I am willing to give* equal sums for A and B because they will gratify equally intense or imperious desires, but, for all that, the reason why *I have to give* equal sums for them, and why *I can get them* for equal sums is that it took equal amounts of labour to produce them; and the proof is that if owing to some new invention A could be made henceforth with half the labour that it requires to make B it would still perform the same service for me as it did before, and would therefore be equally useful *but its exchange value would be less.*"

It is the complete and definitive solution of the problem thus presented which will immortalize the name of Stanley Jevons, and all that I have attempted or shall attempt in this article is to bring the potent instrument of investigation which he has placed in our hands to bear upon the problems under discussion. Under his guidance we shall be able to account for the *coincidence,* in the case of ordinary manufactured articles, between "exchange value" and "amount of labour contained," while clearly perceiving that exchange value itself is always immediately dependent, not upon "amount of labour," but upon abstract utility.

The clue to the investigation we are now to enter on is furnished by the combined effects of "the law of indifference" and "the law of the variation of utility" (See Jevons's *Theory of Political Economy*, pp. 49 and 98). By the former of these laws "when a commodity is perfectly uniform or homogeneous in quality, any portion may be indifferently used in place of an equal portion; hence, in the same market, and at the same moment, all portions must be exchanged at the same ratio"; and by the latter, each successive increment of any given commodity (at any rate after a certain point has been reached) satisfies a less urgent desire or need, and has, therefore, a less utility than the previous increment had. For example, one coat possessed by each member of a community would satisfy the urgent needs of protection and decency; whereas a second coat possessed by each member would serve chiefly to satisfy the less urgent needs of convenience, taste, luxury, etc. Now in a community every member of which possessed two coats already, a further increment of coats would (*ceteris paribus*) satisfy a less urgent need, possess a less utility, and therefore have a lower exchange value than would be the case in a community each member of which possessed only one coat; and, by the "law of indifference," all coats (of identical quality) would exchange with other goods at this lower ratio. Thus the abstract utility of the last available increment of any commodity determines the ratio of exchange of the whole of it. The importance of these facts in their bearing on our problem, I must endeavour briefly to indicate, while referring to Jevons for their full elaboration.

Exchange value is a phenomenal manifestation (conditioned by our present social and industrial organization) of *equivalence of utility*, which equivalence of utility would, and does, exist even under industrial conditions which render its manifestation in the particular form of exchange value impossible. Let us, then, try to track it down on ground where it is less surrounded by complications and prejudices than it is at home. "All the mystery," says Marx, "of the world of wares, all the false lights and magic which play about the creations of labour when produced as wares, disappear at once when we have recourse to other forms of production. And since Political Economy delights in Robinsoniads, let us begin with Robinson on his island" (p. 53 [30]). I accept this invitation, and proceed to make my own observations on what I see.

Robinson, then, has to perform various kinds of useful work, such as making tools or furniture, taming goats, fishing, hunting, etc.; and although he does not ever exchange things against each other, having no one with whom to exchange, yet he is perfectly conscious of the equivalence of utility existing between certain products of his labour, and as he is at liberty to distribute that labour as he likes, he will always apply it where it can produce the greatest utility in a given time. The need of food being the most urgent of all needs, his first hours (if we suppose him to start with nothing) will be devoted to procuring food, but when he has got some little food, a further increment of it, however acceptable it would be, is not so necessary as the first instalment was, and will, therefore, not be so useful. By devoting a few hours to the search for, or construction of, some rude shelter he will now be producing a greater utility than he could produce in the same time by obtaining more food; and thus he continues always producing so much of what he wants most that the next increment would have a less utility than some other thing which it would take the same time to secure. He has arrived at a state of equilibrium, so to speak, when his stock of each product is such that his desire for a further increment of it is proportional to the time it would take to produce it, for when this state of things is realized, equal expenditures of labour, wherever applied, would result in equal utilities.

Let us now take the case of an industrial community the labour of which is directed to the immediate supply of the wants of its own members, without the intervention of any system of exchange, and let us suppose, for instance, that it takes a working member of such a community four days to make a coat and half a day to make a hat. We will put all other branches of industry out of consideration, we will suppose that at a given moment the members of the community are, owing to some special cause, equally ill-provided with coats and hats, and that under the climatic and other conditions to which they are subject, it would cause them equal discomfort to go without coats or without hats. A hat is therefore, at the present moment, as useful as a coat, and it only takes one-eighth of the time to make it. Labour will, therefore, be directed to hat-making rather than to coat-making; for why should I spend four days in producing a certain utility when I could produce another utility exactly equivalent to it in half a day? But when a certain number of hats have been made the inconvenience caused by the insufficient supply becomes less acute, whereas the want of coats is as great as ever. Additional hats, therefore, would no longer be as useful as the same number of additional coats, but would be, say, half as useful. But since a man can produce eight hats in the time it would take him to make one coat, and since each hat is worth half as much (i.e. is half as useful) as a coat, he can still produce four times the utility by making hats which he could produce in the same time by making coats. He therefore goes on making hats. But the need of hats is now rapidly diminishing, and the time soon arrives when additional hats would be only *one-eighth* as useful as the same number of additional coats. A man can now produce equal utilities in a given time whether he works at coats or hats, for though it will take him eight times as long to make a coat as to make a hat, yet this coat when made will be as useful as eight hats, it will be *worth* eight hats to the community. Equilibrium will now be established, because the stock of coats and hats is such that the utility of more coats would be to the utility of more hats as the time it takes to make a coat to the time it takes to make a hat. But observe a coat is not worth eight times as much as a hat to this community, because it takes eight times as long to make it (that it always did, even when *one* hat was worth as much to the community as a coat)—but the community is willing to devote eight times as long to the making of a coat, because when made it will be worth eight times as much to it.

The transition to the industrial conditions under which we actually live is easy. Indeed it is already contained in the word "worth." The popular instinct has appropriated this word to the "common something" which all exchangeable commodities embody, irrespective of the industrial conditions of their production and of the commercial conditions of their circulation and consumption. From my own individual standpoint I may say that A is worth as much to me as B, i.e. that there is to me an *equivalence of utility* between A and B, though their specific utilities may be wholly unlike. From the standpoint of communistic or patriarchal economics, I might use the same language with the same meaning. A is worth as much to the community as B, i.e. there is an equivalence of utility to the community between A and B. Lastly, from the point of view of a commercially organized society in which no man's wants are reckoned unless he can give something for their gratification (the ordinary point of view) we may say "A and B are *worth* the same," ="there is an equivalence of utility to "the purchaser" between A and B," ="there are persons who want more A and persons who want more B; and the desire for more A on the part of the former (as measured against their desire for other commodities), is equivalent to the desire for more B on the part of the latter, measured in the same way" ="the (exchange) values of A and B are equal."

One point remains to be cleared up. In the case of manufactured articles, such as hats and coats, for instance, there is always a certain stream of supply flowing, and when we speak of "the desire for more hats," we must be understood to mean, not the desire on behalf of purchasers for more hats *than they have*, but their desire for more hats *than are being supplied*, i.e. the pressure (or rather suction) which seeks to widen supply. By the "law of indifference" it is the force of demand *at the margin* of supply which determines the exchange value of the whole. For example, a watch of a certain quality is *worth* £15 to me, i.e. it would have as great a utility to me as anything else which I have not got, and which I could obtain for £15. But watches of the quality in question are now being supplied to the commercial society of which I am a member at the rate of fifty *per diem*, and the ranks of the men to whom such watches are worth £15, are only recruited at the rate of ten *per diem*. The ranks of those to whom they are worth at least £10 are, however, recruited at the rate of fifty *per diem*, i.e. the worth or utility of watches of such and such a quality, supplied at the rate of fifty *per diem,* is, at the margin of supply, £10, and, therefore, by the "law of indifference" all the watches exchange at that same rate. A desire for *all* the watches that are available (theoretically identical with the desire for an infinitesimal increment of watches *beyond* what are available) is felt by persons to whom each watch has a utility represented by at least £10. A desire for *some* of the watches (but not all) is felt by persons to whom each watch would have a utility represented by some larger amount, in some cases perhaps £15 or even more, but this high utility of watches to *some* people does not affect their utility at the margin of supply, and therefore does not affect their exchange value. Thus, while value in exchange is rigidly determined by value in use, yet it may happen that any number of persons short of the whole body of purchasers, may obtain for £10 each, watches which have a utility *for them* represented by something more than £10. It is needless to add that the "margin of supply" may be fixed by the holding back from the market of a certain part of the commodities in question by the traders, or by the deliberate limitation of the production by the manufacturers, or by the physical limits imposed on the manufacture, or perhaps by other causes. This does not affect the matter.

Let us now take up the problem from the other side. Watches are being produced at the rate of fifty *per diem,* and they are worth £10 each when produced. It requires, say, twelve days' labour to produce a watch, and (due allowance being made for the quality of the labour (cf. *Das Kapital,* p. 19 [17*a*]) we will suppose there is no other direction which could be given to this labour by which in the same time it would produce anything worth more than £10, i.e. having a greater utility at the margin of supply than the watch has.

Now suppose an improvement in the manufacture of watches to be made which saves twenty-five per cent of the labour. This does not, in itself, affect the utility of watches, and therefore, nine days' labour applied to watch-making will now produce as great a utility as twelve days applied to any other industry. Any one who has the free disposal of labour will of course, now apply it to watch-making, but the watches he makes *will no longer be as useful* as watches have been hitherto, and for the following reason. There are more watches available now than there were formerly. If they are all to be bought (or indeed used) they must, some of them, be bought (or used) by persons to whom (in comparison with other things) they are *less useful* than the watches formerly sold were to their purchasers. All the persons to whom a watch was as useful as 200 lb. of beef (supposing beef to be a shilling a pound), or anything else they would get for £10, are already supplied (or are being continuously supplied as they continuously appear), and if more watches are sold it must be to persons to whom they are only as useful as, say, 180 lb. of beef would be. A man to whom *one* watch was as useful as 200 lb. of beef, but to whom a second watch in the family (though a great convenience) was not so imperiously required as the first, will now determine to buy a second watch which *will be less useful* than the first, but still as useful as 180 lb. of beef. Others to whom even a single watch would not have been as useful as the greater amount of food, purchase one now because it is as useful as the smaller amount. The usefulness of a watch at the margin of supply is now represented by £9. The value of watches has fallen, *not because they contain less labour*, but because the recent increments have been *less useful*, and by the "law of indifference" the utility of the last increment determines the value of the whole.

Still, however, there is an advantage in making watches. Nine days' labour applied in any other direction would only produce a utility represented by £7 10s., whereas if applied to watch-making it will produce a utility represented by £9. Labour free to take any direction will still be directed to watch-making, and by increasing still further the number of watches available, will again lower their *usefulness* (measured by its ratio to the usefulness of other things) at the margin of supply, till at last there are so many watches already in the possession of those to whom they are useful, or in the normal stream of supply, that any further increment of watches would not be more useful to any one than 150 lb. of beef or a dress suit, or a sofa, or new clothes for the children, or something else which he wants, which he has not got, and which he can get for £7 10s. When this point is reached equilibrium is restored. Nine days' labour produces a utility represented by £7 10s., whether devoted to watch-making or anything else. The value of the watch now coincides with the amount of labour it contains, yet it is not worth £7 10s., neither more nor less, because it contains nine days of a certain quality of labour, but men are willing to put nine days and no more of such labour into it, because when made it will be worth £7 10s., and it will be worth that sum in virtue of its utility at the margin of supply which, by the "law of indifference" determines its exchange value.

The correctness of this theory of value may be tested in another way. Utility arises from the power possessed by certain things of gratifying human desires. We have seen that as these things are multiplied, the desires to which each successive increment ministers, become relatively less intense, by which their utility at the margin of supply (called by Jevons their "final utility") is lowered. We have seen that this "law of variation of utility" fully accounts for all the phenomena of supply and demand and for the coincidence, in the case of articles that can be indefinitely multiplied, between the relative amounts of labour they contain and their relative values. But if utility is the real constituent element of value, there must be another aspect of the question. Utility rising out of a relation between human desires and certain *things* (whether material or immaterial), must be affected by any modification either in the things or in the desires. We have seen that in many cases labour can indefinitely modify the number of the things, and by so doing can modify their (final) utility, and so affect their value. But there are other things which are normally exchanged (and which we must, therefore, regard as containing that "common something" which is implied in every equation of exchange, and to which it is the height of arbitrariness to refuse the name of "value"), the number and quality of which labour is powerless to affect; and yet they, too, rise and fall in value. Such are specimens of old china, pictures by deceased masters, and to a greater or less degree, the yield of all natural or artificial monopolies. The value of these things changes because their utility changes. And their utility changes, not because of any change in their own number or quality, but because of a change in the desires to which they minister. I cannot see how any analysis of the act of exchange, which reduces the "common something" implied in that act to *labour* can possibly be applied to this class of phenomena.

We have now a theory of value which is equally applicable to things that can, and things that can not, be multiplied by labour, which is equally applicable to market and to normal values, which moves with perfect ease amongst the "bourgeois categories" that have been prominent in the latter part of our argument, and fits all the complicated phenomena of our commercial societies like a glove, and yet all the while shows that these phenomena are but the specially conditioned manifestations of the ultimate and universal facts of industry, and find their analogues in the economy of a self-supplying patriarchal community or of Robinson Crusoe's island.

It only remains to apply our results to Marx's theory of surplus value. The keystone of the argument by which that theory is supported is, as we have seen, the proposition that the value of labour-force is fixed by the amount of labour needed to produce it, whereas in its expenditure that same labour-force liquefies into a greater amount of labour than it took to produce it, so that if a man purchases labour-force at its value, he will be able to draw out at one end of his bargain more labour (and therefore more value) than he puts in at the other.

We have now learned, however, that value does not depend upon "amount of labour contained," and does not always coincide with it. Under what conditions does it so coincide? And does labour-force comply with those conditions? Whenever labour can be freely directed to the production of A or B optionally, so that x days of labour can be converted at will into y units of A, or z units of B, then, but then only, will labour be directed to the production of one or the other until the relative abundance or scarcity of A and B is such that y units of A are as useful at the margin of supply as z units of B. Equilibrium will then be reached.

But if there is any commodity C, to the production of which a man who has labour at his disposal can *not* direct that labour at his will, then there is no reason whatever to suppose that the value of C will stand in any relation to the amount of labour which it contains, for its value is determined by its utility at the margin of supply, and by hypothesis it is out of the power of labour to raise or lower that margin.

Now this is the case with labour-force in every country in which the labourer is not personally a slave. If I have obtained by purchase or otherwise the right to apply a certain amount of labour to any purpose I choose, I cannot direct it at my option to the production of hats (for instance) *or to the production of labour-force,* unless I live in a country where slave-breeding is possible; and, therefore, there is no economic law the action of which will bring the value of labour-force, and the value of other commodities, into the ratio of the amounts of labour respectively embodied in them.

It appears to me, therefore, that Marx has failed to indicate any immanent law of capitalistic production by which a man who purchases labour-force at its value will extract from its consumption a surplus value. We are simply thrown back upon the fact that a man can purchase (not produce) as much labour-force as he likes at the price of bare subsistence. But this fact is the problem we are to investigate, not the solution of the problem.

The object of this paper is purely critical, and my task is, therefore, for the present, completed. Only let me repeat that in the latter portion of the published volume of *Das Kapital* Marx appears to me to have made contributions of extreme importance to the solution of the great problem, though I cannot see that they stand in any logical connection with the abstract reasoning of his early chapters.

PHILIP H. WICKSTEED.

October 1884.

B.—REPLY BY BERNARD SHAW

(*Printed here by kind permission of Mr. Bernard Shaw*)

The October number of *To-Day* is memorable for containing an attack by a Socialist on the theory of value held by the late Karl Marx. A Roman Catholic impugning the infallibility of the Pope could have created no greater scandal. Sentence of excommunication was pronounced by *Justice. The Inquirer* and other papers well affected to the cause demanded impatiently, as the months passed, why the heretic remained unanswered. That he can easily be answered, refuted, exposed, smashed, pulverized, and economically annihilated, appears to be patent to many able Socialists. Without adding such an atrocious comment as that I am glad to hear it, I do not mind admitting that a certain weight will be removed from my mind when the attack is repulsed, and the formerly pellucid stream of the Ricardian labour value theory has deposited the mud which the late Stanley Jevons stirred up in quantities which, though expressed by differentials, were anything but infinitely small. Mr. P. H. Wicksteed, the assailant of Marx, has adopted the Jevonian theory. He is known as an accomplished Scriptural critic, and was perhaps in search of fresh Bibles to criticize when *Das Kapital*, the Bible of Socialism, came under his notice and struck him as being vulnerable to Jevonian equations of utility. Socialists often dogmatize intolerably on the subject of what Marx taught, or what they suppose him to have taught, on the subject of value; and Mr. Wicksteed, being a sworn enemy of dogma, has in my opinion acted wisely as well as written ably in leading the assault which must have been made sooner or later upon the economic citadel of Collectivism. An odd effect of this assault is the appearance of Marx, for the first time since he defended Ricardo against Proudhon nearly forty years ago, in the ranks of the orthodox economists. As against Cournot, Jevons, Walras, Professor Marshall, and Mr. J. Y. Edgeworth, Marx is undoubtedly on the side of the standard English school of Adam Smith, Ricardo, Mill, and Cairnes. His disciples are still a little bewildered at being no longer scouted as the dupes of a revolutionist and incendiary, but patronized as the old-fashioned followers of an excellent writer of the past generation, whose ideas, all very well in their day, are now quite obsolete.

I have not the slightest intention here of defending Karl Marx against Mr. Wicksteed. It is impossible, in the face of the *Misère de la Philosophie,* and several passages in *Capital,* to suspect Marx of having lost sight of the supply-and-demand phenomena which make the actual world so different from the sphere of "catallactic atoms" with which he deals in the opening chapters of his great work. On the other hand it is equally impossible, without access to the unpublished volumes of that work, to answer for the way in which so subtle a reasoner may have reconciled these contradictions, or even to feel sure that Jevons might not, had he lived, have found himself anticipated in the very quarter from which he expected the most determined opposition. I write partly to draw further attention to a controversy which seems to me of great interest because it is one on which Socialists, without at all ceasing to be Socialists, are sure to divide very soon; and partly because I wish to have a word with Mr. Wicksteed as to my own perplexities concerning "final utility" before some more competent hand deals him the *coup de grâce* to which I have already alluded. Even were I economist enough to do that myself, I am not mathematician enough to confute Mr. Wicksteed by the Jevonian method. I somewhat mistrust mathematical symbols. I remember at school a plausible boy who used to prove to me by algebra that one equals two. He always began by saying, "Let x equal a." I saw no great harm in admitting that; and the proof followed with rigorous exactness. The effect was not to make me proceed habitually on the assumption that one equals two, but to impress upon me that there was a screw loose somewhere in the algebraic art, and a chance for me to set it right some day when I had time to look into the subject. And I feel bound to make the perhaps puerile confession that when I read Jevons's *Theory of Political Economy,* I no sooner glanced at the words "let x signify the quantity of commodity," than I thought of the plausible boy, and prepared myself for a theory of value based on algebraic proof that two and two make five. But as it turned out, Mr. Jevons, less ingenious or more ingenuous than my schoolfellow, arrived at no more remarkable conclusion than that if x equalled y, y equalled x, which I should have granted freely without the aid of algebra. And I was much relieved subsequently to find that the late Professor Cairnes regarded these equations as identical propositions.

Says Mr. Wicksteed: "The clue to the investigation we are now to enter on is furnished by the combined effects of the 'law of indifference' and 'the law of the variation of utility.'" Let us take an example of the law of the variation of utility. To a hungry man the utility of beef is high. The first few mouthfuls, which save him from actual starvation, are of very great utility to him indeed. But as he gets his fill, every successive mouthful has less and less utility, until finally he can eat no more, and the remainder of the beef is useless to him. Here the utility has varied constantly. Now by the law of indifference, which is that there cannot be two prices for like commodities at one time in one market, the last mouthful of beef costs just as much as the first. Consequently the man has not to pay more for the first mouthful than for the twentieth, though it is infinitely more useful to him, nor, when he has eaten so much that he can eat no more, could he buy another mouthful more cheaply than the first, useless as the beef has become to him. The value has not varied at all, whilst the direct utility has varied from infinity to zero. But the beef which is thus bereft of its direct utility may possess acquired utility; that is, its satiated possessor may have a hungry neighbour willing to pay him for it. Suppose, however, the man to be a member of a wholly improvident community, every member of which has just, like himself, had a sufficient dinner. The utility of his beef will then be at zero; the choicest undercut will be as valueless as it is in heaven, no matter how much labour its production may have cost. Utility, then, is evidently a condition of value. But let six hours elapse. In that space Nature produces "negative utilities" in the form of appetite: the universal discommodity. The utility of beef, useless and valueless six hours before, rises to the utility of human life itself: from nothing to everything. Will the exchange value rise equally? By no means: it will rise to the cost of catching, killing, and cooking a cow: not a farthing higher. If a man demand a greater price from another, obviously that other will, in the last resort, catch, kill, and cook for himself, and so save the excess demanded from him. If the labour necessary to produce the beef be halved or doubled, neither the mass nor the final degree of utility in the beef will be altered one jot; and yet the value will be halved or doubled. Evidently, then, the utility does not determine the value. The utility of water to a thirsty man is exactly the same at Aldgate Pump as in the middle of the Sahara, yet he will give nothing at Aldgate for a gallon, whereas in the Sahara he may give all he possesses for a thimbleful. Even in the latter extreme instance of a monopolist demanding an outrageous bribe for a share of the means of subsistence, the price of the water would vary without the least regard to the utility. To half a dozen travellers dying of thirst, but having unequal possessions, half a dozen draughts of water would possess equal utility; yet a Jevonian sheikh with command of the water would receive different quantities of commodity for each draught. And if the parties were in the same position a few hours later, the desperate necessity of the travellers would recur; the sheikh would still have command of the water, the final utility of which would again be infinite; yet the price of the water would be a mortgage on their future labour as slaves; the travellers having nothing else to give. I use this illustration because it shows that even a monopoly value is not determined by the final utility any more than a market value (such as that of beef), and because it directly illustrates the ordinary economist's habit of regarding the value of a thing as the maximum of blackmail which its possessor can extort from the person who desires to consume it. To the end of time a monopolist who cannot be expropriated by force will be able to force other men to do more labour for him than he does for them in return. If he be at once base and acute enough to extort the utmost his victims will give, then, in a community of infinitely rich men, the prices obtained by him might be said to be determined by the final utility of his commodity to the purchasers; but each of them would pay a different price, and would, therefore, have to be presupposed incapable of exchanging the commodity one with another after purchasing. Otherwise they would defeat the operation of final utility, precisely as rich people defeat it now when they borrow their servants' clothes and obtain gratuitous medical advice at hospitals.

"If I am willing," says Mr. Wicksteed, "to give the same sum of money for a family Bible and for a dozen of brandy, it is because I have reduced the respective satisfactions their possession will afford me to a common measure, and have found them equivalent." This may be so; but it does not at all follow that Mr. Wicksteed will find Bibles and brandy exchanging in that ratio. The price of neither would be raised or lowered by one farthing if Mr. Wicksteed suddenly got tired of the Bible and became a dipsomaniac. Apart from that, his nearest teetotal neighbour would probably give more money for a Bible than for a dozen hogsheads of brandy; whilst the nearest drunkard would eagerly offer a dozen Bibles for a single bottle of brandy, if the ratio of exchange were determined by the utility of the commodities. But as the rain falls alike on the just and the unjust, so is the price of Bibles and brandy the same to Mr. Wicksteed and his neighbours, though the utility differs in each of their cases. And even were it possible to determine an average ratio of utility between brandy and Bibles, the fact that this would remain the same although the ratio of the labour necessary to produce them should vary, and that the ratio of exchange would nevertheless immediately alter, shows that the ratio of exchange does not depend on utility. Mr. Wicksteed insists on "abstract" utility; but what he has really abstracted is not utility but value. He has accused Marx of having leaped from one category to another, because, as it seems to me, he has mistaken the category to which his own abstraction belongs.

Every appreciative reader of Mr. Wicksteed's article will at once conclude that these considerations are as obvious to him as they are to me, and that his theory must in some way explain them. "For example," he says, "a watch of a certain quality is *worth* £15 to me: i.e. it would have as great a utility to me as anything else which I have not got, and which I could obtain for £15." But again it does not follow that the watch will therefore cost Mr. Wicksteed £15. It may cost him only £5. All that does follow from the conditions laid down is that, if necessary, he will go as high as £15 for the watch, but that if the price rises to fifteen guineas he will go without a watch. That does not mean that the utility of the watch to him will fall to zero the moment the odd shillings are added to the price. It simply means that though the utility remains the same, he will not be able to afford the price, or will think that he might spend fifteen guineas to better advantage on a writing-table than on a watch. The comparison of utility which he has made between them does not change the value of either. The order in which desires arise does not affect the cost of satisfying them, which is always ultimately a cost of labour. On the contrary, the labour cost of satisfying our desires generally determines the order of them. A child sometimes quarrels with its bread-and-milk and cries for the moon; but eventually it succumbs to economic conditions and puts off thinking about the moon until its bread-and-butter is secured.

Mr. Wicksteed maintains that if twenty-five per cent of the labour necessary to make a watch be saved by an improvement in manufacture, the value of watches will fall "not because they contain less labour, but because the recent increments have been less useful." By this he appears to mean, not that a watch is less useful to a workman with a pound a week than to a lord with a hundred pounds a day, which is obviously not the case, but that the workman can now afford to buy a watch whereas he could not do so before. If the determination of the ratio of exchange (or the measure of exchange value) by duration of labour be founded on the fact that if two "catallactic atoms" A and B produce and exchange commodities, A cannot afford to give more than the product of an hour of his labour to B in exchange for the product of an hour of B's labour, and that B cannot afford to take less, it is not clear to me that Mr. Wicksteed advances the matter by calling exchange value "utility at the margin of supply." He certainly does not simplify it to the Socialist proletary who, face to face with the monopolist, does not achieve quite so fair a bargain as a couple of "catallactic atoms" might strike on Marx's principles.

I regret that the utility of space at the margin of supply, the obscurity of the Jevonese language, and the extreme unpopularity of our subject, have compelled me to put forward a counterblast to Mr. Wicksteed rather than a thorough analysis and discussion of his interesting contribution. Some considerations which arise from his paper are important from a domestic point of view. At present a middle-class man, when his immediate needs are satisfied, furnishes himself with commodities in a certain order, as, for instance, wife, house, furniture, pianoforte, horse and trap. The satisfaction of each desire leaves the mind free to entertain the next, so that you actually make a man feel the want of a horse by giving him a pianoforte. Let the cost of a pianoforte suddenly rise to a figure exceeding that of a horse and trap; and the conventional order of furnishing will be altered: the horse and trap will be bought before the family ventures on the extravagance of a pianoforte. A collectivist administration, bound to preserve the catallactic atomicity of the markets by adjusting supply to demand, may yet find themselves compelled by the operation of purely subjective notions of utility to admit that Jevons was on the right track when he broke away from economics into psychology, and that the comparative utilities of things are of far greater moment to the community than their ratio of exchange, to which our social system has given a factitious importance. Marx saw this when, many years ago, he compared the utility of the capitalist commodities, potatoes and cotton stuffs, with that of the pre-capitalist commodities, wheat and woollens. My own hopes centre in a Socialist state in which Mr. Wicksteed and I, as perfect and regenerate catallactic atoms, shall dispute about utilities alone, forgetful of the very existence of a ratio of exchange.

BERNARD SHAW.

January 1885.

C.—REJOINDER BY P. H. WICKSTEED

Mr. Bernard Shaw's brilliant but good-natured "comments" on my article on the theory of value seem to invite a few words of reply from me. I will, however, make them very short. After admirably illustrating the fact that to each individual the utility of beef runs daily and weekly through enormous variations, Mr. Shaw declares that this does not affect the exchange value of the article. No more it does, if the variations counteract each other. If they are all in the same direction at the same time they do affect the exchange value—as Mr. Shaw would know were he a butcher or a housekeeper. But at any rate, says Mr. Shaw, the exchange value cannot rise above the "cost of catching, killing and cooking a cow." Had I Mr. Shaw's pen in my fingers I could give my readers a delectable picture of the indignant housekeeper defeating the extortionate butcher by sallying forth to catch, kill and cook "a cow" for dinner, but I will not enter upon an unequal combat in badinage with Mr. Shaw. I presume he means that the price of beef cannot rise above the cost of bringing it into the market. No more it can, permanently. Temporarily it can, and often does. The only reason why it cannot do so permanently is because as long as labour can produce a higher average utility by bringing beef into the market than by taking any other direction it will put itself to that special task by preference and so will *reduce the final utility of beef* by supplying the want of it down to a lower point.

I am quite at a loss to know what Mr. Shaw means by saying that "If the labour necessary to produce the beef be halved or doubled, neither the mass nor the final degree of utility in the beef will be altered one jot; and yet the value will be halved or doubled." Unless and until both the total and the final utilities *are* altered the exchange value will remain exactly the same. It is only by producing more beef, and thus at the same time increasing its total and lowering its final utility, that the increased facilities of beef-making can produce any effect on the price whatever.

As for Mr. Shaw's extortionate sheikh, he simply illustrates my contention that *some* of the consumers always get the whole, and every consumer may sometimes get a part of the commodity he consumes at something less than it is worth to him (the first mouthful of beef costs no more than the twentieth), but that all pay the price represented by the minimum or final utility of the last increment to that one of the consumers, to whom it has, relatively to other commodities, the least utility.

Similar remarks apply to Mr. Shaw's remaining criticisms; but I should like to say a word in elucidation of my statement that when the supply of any commodity is increased the successive increments meet an ever less urgent want, and are, in fact, less and less useful. I admit that in a certain sense this language is misleading, for if we are speaking of *absolute* utilities the presumption is that if the supply of beef is increased till it falls to sixpence a pound, the final increments which get into the workman's alimentary canal are more useful than previous ones, the fate of which we need not pursue beyond the servants' hall. But I never compare absolute utilities, and I do not see how such a comparison could be instituted on any scientific basis. All I contend for is that if yesterday no one had a watch except those to whom a watch was as useful as anything that could be got for £15, and if to-day a number of men possess watches to whom they are only as useful as other things which could be got for £10, the new watches are *relatively to other things* less useful than the former ones were.

Mr. Shaw's youthful experiences about x and a are so highly instructive that I cannot refrain from dwelling upon them for a moment. His friend induced him to "let $x=a$," and Mr. Shaw—not expecting that x would take any mean advantage of the permission—granted the request. But he did not understand that in letting $x=a$ he was also letting $x-a=0$, and the proof (of the proposition, $2=1$) that "followed with rigorous exactness," assumed that $x-a$ did *not* equal 0.

Mr. Shaw arrived at the sapient conclusion that there was "a screw loose somewhere"—not in his own reasoning powers, but—"in the algebraic art"; and thenceforth renounced mathematical reasoning in favour of the literary method which enables a clever man to follow equally fallacious arguments to equally absurd conclusions *without seeing that they are absurd.* This is the exact difference between the mathematical and literary treatment of the pure theory of political economy.

Only a single word, in conclusion, on the importance of this controversy. It is not a mere question of abstract reasoning (although, if it were, that could hardly be urged in its disparagement by an admirer of Marx). It affects the whole system of economics, and more particularly Marx's economics. In admitted contradiction to apparent facts, and without (at present) any attempt to remove the apparent contradiction, Marx by sheer logic attempted to force us into the admission that "profits," "interest," and "rent," *must* have their origin in the "surplus-value" that results from purchasing "labour-force" at its value, and selling wares at their value. The keystone of the arch is the theory of value adopted by Marx, and I have tried to show that it is not sound. In doing so, I have found an unexpected but powerful ally in Mr. John Carruthers, whose elaborate and thoughtful essay on "The Industrial Mechanism of a Socialist Society," shows the phenomena of "profits" reappearing, in a modified form, in communal industry. My own rather clumsy illustrations of the varying utilities and values of "coats and hats," etc. laboured under the disadvantage of requiring my readers to imagine the wants of society in part at least supplied successively, not contemporaneously. Mr. Carruthers escapes this, and shows how, in a communal industry, the price (though he would not say the "exchange" value) of each article depends on its final utility, and that it is only when, *as a consequence* of the indications thus afforded, labour has been properly apportioned amongst the industries, that prices are apportioned to labour cost.

PHILIP H. WICKSTEED.

April 1885.

BIBLIOGRAPHY

BIBLIOGRAPHY

The following may claim to be a reasonably comprehensive list of Dr. Wicksteed's published writings, though it is not unlikely that some reviews and articles in periodicals have been overlooked. An attempt has been made to provide a complete list of contributions to the *Inquirer*; these afford a good illustration over a long period of years of the width of Dr. Wicksteed's interests. Except in one or two cases, contributions to the *Inquirer* are *not* included in the general classified bibliography which precedes. The main bibliography is divided into five sections: Religion and Philosophy; Dante and the Middle Ages; Economics and Sociology; Memorial and Obituary; Miscellaneous.

RELIGION AND PHILOSOPHY

"Roskoff's History of the Devil." *Theol. Rev.* viii, 30–52 (Jan. 1871).

Notices of books—"Recent Dutch Theology." *Theol. Rev.* ix, 410–17 (July 1872).

The Sunday School Teacher's Manual. Vols. i–iii. Edited by P. H. Wicksteed and J. Reynolds. Manchester, 1872–4.

"Lessons on the History of Israel." *The Sunday School Teacher's Manual.* Vols. i–iv (1872–5).

The Bible for Young People. By H. Oort and I. Hooykas. Translated from the Dutch by Philip H. Wicksteed. 6 vols. London: Williams & Norgate, 1873–9. Republished under title: *The Bible for Learners.* 3 vols. Boston, U.S.A. 1878–9.

Notices of books—"Dutch Theology." *Theol. Rev.* xi, 264–70 (Apr. 1874).

The Ecclesiastical Institutions of Holland, treated with special reference to the Position and Prospects of the Modern School of Theology. A report presented to the Hibbert Trustees (pp. 61). London: Williams & Norgate, 1875.

Notices of books. *Theol. Rev.* xii, 310–15 (Apr. 1875).

"Hilgenfeld's Introduction to the New Testament." *Theol. Rev.* xii, 515–32 (Oct. 1875), xiii, 1–16 (Jan. 1876).

Going Through and Getting Over. A discourse delivered at South Place Chapel, Finsbury, Sunday, Jan. 30, 1876 (pp. 16).

Address delivered to the Congregation of Little Portland Sireet Chapel, on Sunday, the 30th March, 1879, on the subject of the Prayer Book now in use in the Chapel. Printed for private circulation (pp. 14). London: C. Roworth, 1879.

"Histories of the Devil." *Theol. Rev.* xvi, 398–415 (July 1879).

"The Miracles of the New Testament." *Mod. Rev.* i, 147–65, 375–87 (Jan.–Apr. 1880).

Be Not Overcome of Evil. Sermon preached on occasion of the assassination of the Emperor of Russia (pp. 8). Printed for private circulation. 1881.

"The Place of the Israelites in History." *Mod. Rev.* ii, 548–64 (July 1881).

The Mission of our Churches. A discourse delivered at the anniversary meeting of the Scottish Unitarian Christian Association, on Sunday morning, Oct. 15, 1882 (pp. 10).

"A Controversy on the Talmud." *Mod. Rev.* iii, 168–72 (Jan. 1882).

National Religions and Universal Religions. By A. Kuenen. Translated by P. H. Wicksteed. Hibbert Lectures, 1882.

"The Kingdom of God." A sermon. No. 14 in *Modern Sermons.* Manchester: Johnson & Rawson, 1883, etc.

"The Literature of Israel." *Mod. Rev.* iv, 1–23 (Jan. 1883).

Christianity and the Personal Life. Christianity and Social Life. Christianity and Trade. Christianity and Politics. Elimination or Redemption? Being an attempt to answer the question, Is Christianity Practical? Five sermons (pp. 40). London: W. Reeves, 1884. Reprinted with title: *Is Christianity Practical?* (pp. 96). London: Lindsey Press 1920.

Lectures on the Origin and Growth of Religion as Illustrated by Mexico and Peru. By A. Réville. Translated by Philip H. Wicksteed. Hibbert Lectures, 1884.

Our Prayers and Our Politics. Three sermons (pp. 23). London: Swan Sonnenschein, 1885.

"On the Age of the 'Ten Words' (Ten Commandments)." *Christian Reformer*, i, 307–13 (May 1886).

"Evolution and the Existence of Satan." *Chr. Ref.* ii, 1–8 (July 1886).

"The Gospel and the Gospels." *Chr. Ref.* ii, 75–82 (Aug. 1886).

"The Place of Jesus in Religion." *Chr. Ref.* ii, 148–58 (Sept. 1886).

"Echoes of Truth." Review of sermons by E. M. Geldart. *Chr. Ref.* ii, 321–7 (Dec. 1886).

An Historico-critical Inquiry into the Origin and Composition of the Hexateuch. By A. Kuenen. Translated from the Dutch by Philip H. Wicksteed. 1886.

"The Place of Jesus in History." *Chr. Ref.* iii, 23–30 (Jan. 1887). Reprinted in *Studies in Theology*, 1903.

"An Ecclesiastical Storm in Holland." *Chr. Ref.* iii, 308–16 (May 1887).

"The Year of Jubilee." *Chr. Ref.* iv, 65–75 (Aug. 1887).

Lessons on the Growth of Moral and Spiritual Ideas. Lesson notes for teachers (pp. 56). London: Sunday School Association, 1888.

The Place of Sociology in the Circle of Theological Studies. An address to the students of Manchester New College inaugurating the session 1888–9 (pp. 21). Manchester: H. Rawson, 1888. Reprinted in *Studies in Theology*, 1903.

"The Relation of the Churches to the Social Movements of the Times." Address at National Conference of Unitarian and Free Christian

Churches, Fourth Triennial Meeting, London, Apr. 1891. *Inquirer*, Apr. 25, 1891, and May 2, 1891 (Suppl.).

"Religion and Society." In *Religion and Life*. Eight essays by various writers. Edited by Richard Bartram. London: British and Foreign Unitarian Assoc., 1891. Reprinted in *Studies in Theology*, 1903.

"The Battle with Materialism." Sermon preached Oct. 21, 1891, before the Provincial Assembly of London and S.E. Counties. *Inquirer*, Oct. 31, 1891.

Lectures on the Origin and Growth of the Conception of God. By Count Goblet d'Alviella. Hibbert Lectures, 1891. Translated by P. H. Wicksteed, 1892.

The Significance of Unitarianism as a Theology. A sermon preached at the annual meeting of the British and Foreign Unitarian Association, June 8, 1892 (pp. 16). London: Brit. and For. Unit. Assoc., 1892. Reprinted in *Studies in Theology*, 1903.

Old and New Conceptions of the Structure and Chronology of the Old Testament. McQuaker Lecture, 1892 (pp. 27). London: Brit. and For. Unit. Assoc., 1892. 2nd ed. (pp. 26) London: P. Green, 1897.

"Worship." Sermon preached in Mill Hill Chapel, Leeds, on the fiftieth anniversary of the opening of the new chapel (Dec. 27, 1898). *Inquirer*, Dec. 31, 1898.

The Religion of Time and the Religion of Eternity: being a study of certain relations between mediaeval and modern thought. Essex Hall Lecture, 1899 (pp. 108). London: P. Green, 1899. Reprinted in *Studies in Theology*, 1903.

"The Fear of God and the Sense of Sin." Read at the meeting of the National Conference at Leicester, Apr. 5, 1900. *Inquirer*, Apr. 14, 1900. Reprinted in *Studies in Theology*, 1903.

Studies in Theology. By J. Estlin Carpenter and P. H. Wicksteed (pp. 343). London: J. M. Dent, 1903. The following are by P. H. W.:

I. "The Religion of Time and the Religion of Eternity."
III. "The Significance of Unitarianism as a Theology."
V. "The Fear of God and the Sense of Sin."
X. "The Place of Jesus in History."
XI. "Sociology and Theology.
XIII. "Religion and Society."

On the Scholarly Habit of Mind. An address on the occasion of the closing of the 119th session, June 29, 1905. Manchester College, Oxford (pp. 15). Manchester, 1905.

Foreign Policy and Christian Ethics. 1912.

"Theology and Philosophy." Lindsey Hall Lecture, Jan. 16, 1913 (pp. 8). *The Modern Pulpit*, No. 111. Suppl. to *Christian Commonwealth*, Jan. 22, 1913.

"Belief and Experience." In *Ethical and Religious Problems of the War*. Ed. J. Estlin Carpenter, 1916.

The Reactions between Dogma and Philosophy, illustrated from the Works of S. Thomas Aquinas. Hibbert Lectures, 1916 (pp. xxvi, 669). London: Williams & Norgate, 1920.

Miscellaneous sermons (undated), preached in Little Portland Street Chapel, and printed for private circulation.—*Naomi: Gratitude and Love* (pp. 7). London: C. Green. *Conditional Immortality* (pp. 8). London: C. Green. *The Power of Ideals* (pp. 8). London: C. Green. *On Holidays* (pp. 7). London: C. Green. *Salvation* (pp. 8). London: C. Green. *The Sleep of Jonah and the Sleep of Jesus* (pp. 8). *The Survival of the Fittest.* Preached on behalf of the London Domestic Mission (pp. 7). London: C. Green.

Aristotle: the Physics, with an English translation by Philip H. Wicksteed and Francis M. Cornford. Loeb Classical Library. London: Heinemann. Vol. I, 1929. Vol. II, *in the press.*

DANTE AND THE MIDDLE AGES

Dante. Six sermons (pp. vii, 158). London: Kegan Paul, 1879. 2nd ed. (pp. 122), Elkin Mathews, 1890. 3rd ed., ditto, 1892, and subsequent unaltered reprints.

Dante. The De Monarchia. Books I–III. Translated into English and annotated. Three parts (pp. 32, 37, 39). Hull: printed for the translator, 1896. Revised edition in *Latin Works,* 1904.

Selections from the first nine books of the Croniche Fiorentine of Giovanni Villani. Translated for the use of students of Dante and others by Rose E. Selfe. Edited by Philip H. Wicksteed (pp. xlviii, 461). Westminster: Constable, 1896. 2nd ed., carefully revised, with title: *Villani's Chronicle: being selections, etc.* (pp. xlviii, 461). Constable, 1906.

Essays on Dante by Dr. Karl Witte. Selected, translated, and edited with introduction, notes, and appendices by C. Mabel Lawrence and Philip H. Wicksteed (pp. xxiii, 448). London: Duckworth, 1898.

A Provisional Translation of the Early Lives of Dante, and of his Poetical Correspondence with Giovanni del Virgilio. Philip H. Wicksteed (pp. 112). Hull: printed for the translator, 1898. Revised edition in *Dante and del Virgilio,* 1902, and *Early lives of Dante,* 1904.

A Provisional Translation of Dante's Political Letters. By Philip H. Wicksteed. To which is added the section of the *Convito* that concerns the Roman Empire (pp. 41). Hull: printed for the translator, 1898. Revised edition in *Convivio,* 1903, and *Latin Works,* 1904.

The Paradiso of Dante Alighieri. Temple Classics. London: J. M. Dent, 1899, and frequent reprints. Translation and arguments by P. H. W.

The Inferno of Dante Alighieri. Temple Classics. London: J. M. Dent, 1900, and frequent reprints. Special notes by P. H. W.

The Purgatorio of Dante Alighieri. Temple Classics. London: J. M. Dent, 1901, and frequent reprints. Arguments and special notes by P. H. W.

Dante and Giovanni del Virgilio. Including a critical edition of the text of Dante's "Eclogae Latinae" and of the poetic remains of Giovanni del Virgilio. By Philip H. Wicksteed and Edmund G. Gardner (pp. xi, 340). Westminster: Constable, 1902.

"Recent Dante literature" (reviews). *Hibbert Journal*, i, 624–30 (Apr. 1903).

The Convivio of Dante Alighieri. Temple Classics. London: J. M. Dent, 1903. Translation and notes by P. H. W.

"The Revived Interest in Mediaeval Religion." In *Religion and Liberty.* Addresses and papers at the Second International Unitarian Council, Amsterdam, Sept. 1903. Ed. P. H. Hugenholtz Jr. Leyden, 1904.

The early lives of Dante. Translated by Philip H. Wicksteed. The King's Classics (pp. xxi, 159). London: Alex. Moring, 1904.

Life of Dante. Written by Giovanni Boccaccio, and now translated from the Italian by Philip Henry Wicksteed. Folio (pp. 74). Cambridge, Mass.: Riverside Press, 1904. 265 copies, printed for Houghton Mifflin & Co. Reprinted from *Early Lives.*

A Translation of the Latin Works of Dante Alighieri. Temple Classics. London: J. M. Dent, 1904. All by P. H. W. except "De Vulgari Eloquentia."

"Treachery of ciphers" (review of Moore's *Studies in Dante,* 3rd series). *Hibbert Journal,* ii, 634–6 (July 1904).

The Vita Nuova and Canzoniere of Dante Alighieri. Temple Classics. London: J. M. Dent, 1906. Translation of "Canzoni" only by P. H. W.

"La Vita Nuova . . . per cura di Michele Barbi" (review). *Mod. Lang. Rev.* iii, 183–6 (Jan. 1908).

"La Quaestio de Aqua et Terra . . . da Vincenzo Biagi" (review). *Mod. Lang. Rev.* iv, 254–8 (Jan. 1909).

"Dante: Quaestio de Aqua et Terra." Ed. and trans. C. L. Shadwell (review). *Mod. Lang. Rev.* v, 255–6 (Apr. 1910).

"The Mediaeval Mind" (review of H. O. Taylor's book). *Sociol. Rev.* iv, 345–8 (Oct. 1911).

Dante and Aquinas. Being the substance of the Jowett Lectures of 1911 (pp. xii, 271). London: J. M. Dent, 1913.

"On the Disputed Reading in Dante's Epist. V, 129–30." *Mod. Lang. Rev.* xi, 69–72 (Jan. 1916).

"Dante." *Contemp. Rev.* cxix, 590–9 (May 1921).

"Dante and the Latin poets." In *Dante. Essays in commemoration.* London: Univ. Press, 1921.

"The Ethical System of the 'Inferno.'" *Mod. Lang. Rev.* xvi, 265–80 (July–Oct. 1921).

From Vita Nuova to Paradiso. Two essays on the vital relations between Dante's successive works. Publ. of Univ. of Manchester, No. cli (pp. xv, 152). Manchester Univ. Press, 1922.

ECONOMICS AND SOCIOLOGY

"Das Kapital." *To-Day*, ii, 388–409 (Oct. 1884).

"The Jevonian Criticism of Marx" (reply to G. B. Shaw's criticism of 'Das Kapital,' in *To-Day*, Jan. 1885). *To-Day*, iii, 177–9 (Apr. 1885).

The Alphabet of Economic Science (pp. xv, 142). London: Macmillan, 1888.

Articles (on Stanley Jevons, etc.) in Palgrave's *Dictionary of Political Economy.* London: Macmillan, 1894, etc.

Getting and Spending (pp. 36). London, 1888. Reprint of twelve special articles entitled "Money," in *Inquirer*, May 19–Sept. 29, 1888. Further unaltered reprint (pp. 52), 1897.

"On certain passages in Jevons's 'Theory of Political Economy.'" *Quarterly Journal of Economics*, iii, 293–314 (Apr. 1889).

What does the Labour Church stand for? 1892.

An Essay on the Co-ordination of the Laws of Distribution (pp. 56). London: Macmillan, 1894.

"The Advent of the People." In *The New Party, described by some of its Members.* 1894.

A Symposium of Value. Ed. J. H. Levy. London: P. S. King & Son, and the Personal Rights Association, 1895. No. VI by Philip H. Wicksteed (pp. 38–40).

"Land Nationalization." *Transactions of the National Liberal Club Political and Economic Circle*, iii, 214–38 (1901).

"Note on Jevons's economic work." *Economic Journal*, xv, 432–6 (Sept. 1905).

Review of H. Stanley Jevons's "Essays on Economics." *Econ. Journ.* xv, 570–3 (Dec. 1905).

Review of Prof. V. Pareto's "Manuale di Economia Politica." *Econ. Journ.* xvi, 553–7 (Dec. 1906).

'The Social Ideals and Economic Doctrines of Socialism." An address . . . given at Nottingham, under the auspices of the National Conference Union for Social Service. *Inquirer*, Nov. 28, 1908; reprinted by the Union (pp. 16).

The Common Sense of Political Economy, including a Study of the Human Basis of Economic Law (pp. xiv, 702). London: Macmillan, 1910.

Review of S. J. Chapman's "Political Economy." *Econ. Journ.* xxiii, 72–5 (Mar. 1913).

"The Distinction between Earnings and Income, and between a Minimum Wage and a Decent Maintenance: a Challenge." In *The Industrial Unrest and the Living Wage.* Converging Views of Social Reform. No. 2. Being a series of lectures . . . given at the Inter-Denominational Summer School at Swanwick, 1913. London: The Collegium, 1913.

"The Scope and Method of Political Economy in the Light of the 'Marginal' Theory of Distribution." Presidential Address to Section F of the British Association. In *Report of the British Association for the Advancement of Science*, 1913, 560–73. Also in revised form with diagrams, *Econ. Journ.* xxiv, 1–23 (Mar. 1914).

Review of H. J. Davenport's "Economics of Enterprise." *Econ. Journ.* xxiv, 421–5 (Sept. 1914).

"The Mission of the Churches in War Time." In *International relationships in the light of Christianity.* Lectures at the Inter-Denominational Summer School at Swanwick, 1915.

"Who said 'Barren Metal'?" A Symposium by Prof. E. Cannan, W. D. Ross, Dr. J. Bonar, and Dr. P. H. Wicksteed. *Economica*, ii, 105–11 (June 1922).

"Church and State in Conflict." By Romolo Murri; trans. P. H. Wicksteed. *Hibbert Journal*, xx, 643–56 (July 1922).

MEMORIAL AND OBITUARY

"John William Colenso." *Mod. Rev.* iv, 697–727 (Oct. 1883).

Two Discourses in Memory of Edmund Martin Geldart. . . . Evening Discourse by Philip H. Wicksteed. London: Swan Sonnenschein, 1885.

Memorials of the Rev. Charles Wicksteed, B.A. Edited by his son Philip Henry (pp. viii, 358). London: Williams & Norgate, 1886.

Controversial Lectures by the Rev. Charles Wicksteed, B.A. Edited by the Rev. Philip Henry Wicksteed, M.A. London: Brit. and For. Unit. Assoc., 1887.

"William Shaen: with special reference to his Labours for Social Purity." *Chr. Ref.* iii, 223–9 (Apr. 1887).

"Abraham Kuenen." *Jewish Quarterly Rev.* iv, 571–605 (July 1892).

"Personal Impressions of Dr. Martineau." *Contemp. Rev.* lxxvii, 187-93 (Feb. 1900).

"Brooke Herford." Biographical sketch in *Anchors of the Soul.* Sermons by Brooke Herford. 1904.

"R. A. Armstrong." Introductory letter in *Richard Acland Armstrong.* A memoir by his son, George G. Armstrong. 1906.

"Herbert and Alice Rix." An appreciation in *Sermons, Addresses, and Essays.* By Herbert Rix. 1907.

"Charles Herbert Frogley." Introduction to *A Voice From the Trees, and other Poems.* By C. H. Frogley. 1915.

See also below: Contributions to *Inquirer.*

MISCELLANEOUS

"Henrik Ibsen's poems." *Contemp. Rev.* lx, 333–46 (Sept. 1891).

Henrik Ibsen: four Lectures, dealing chiefly with his Metrical Works (pp. xiv, 112). London: Swan Sonnenschein, 1892.

Our Lady's Tumbler: a Twelfth Century Legend. Transcribed for Lady Day, mdcccxciv (pp. 42). London: J. M. Dent, 1894, and subsequent reprints.

"Literature and life," and various other contributions to the *University Extension Journal*, 1895–1907.

"Wordsworth's Ideals and the Nineteenth Century." In *Liberal Religious Thought at the Beginning of the Twentieth Century.* Addresses and papers at the International Council of Unitarian and other liberal religious thinkers and workers, London, 1901. Ed. W. Copeland Bowie. London: P. Green, 1901.

"The Secret of the Universe, and other Essays" (review). *Hibbert Journ.* ii, 419–20 (Jan. 1904).

"Robert Browning." *Contemp. Rev.* lxxxiii, 86–99 (Jan. 1903).

"'Magic'—a contribution to the study of Goethe's Faust" *Hibbert Journ.* ix, 754–64 (July 1911).

Lyrics and Poems from Ibsen. Translated by F. E. Garrett. With an introduction by Philip H. Wicksteed. 1912.

Ernesto Buonaiuti and his Recent Excommunication. By Romolo Murri. Translated from the Italian by P. H. Wicksteed. *Hibbert Journ.* xxiv, 660–73 (July 1926).

Various contributions to anti-vivisection publications.

CONTRIBUTIONS TO THE "INQUIRER"

1872

Sept. 14. "Hymns for the Christian Church and Home" (letter).

1873

Mar. 22. "Talmudical" (letter). Apr. 5. "The Jewish Character" (letter). May 3. "Scholten and Strauss" (letter). Nov. 15–Dec. 20. "Dr. J. C. Matthes on the Miracles." Translated by the Rev. Philip H. Wicksteed (articles).

1874

Jan. 17. "The Miracles" (letter). Apr. 25. "Protestanten-Bibel Neuen Testaments" (review). July 18. "Kuenen: Religion of Israel" (review). Oct. 3. "Hoekstra: Bronnen en Grondslagen van het Godsdienstig Geloof" (review). Nov. 28. "England and the Inferior Civilisations" (article).

1875

Feb. 20. "Oosterzee: Image of Christ as presented in Scripture" (review). Mar. 6. "Saturn and the Sabbath of the Jews" (article). Mar. 13. "Greg: Creed of Christendom" (review). Apr. 3. "S. Baring-Gould: Lost and Hostile Gospels" (review). Apr. 10. "Ed. Reuss: La Bible" (review). May 22. "Comte: System of Positive Polity" (review).

1876

Jan. 22. "F. Harrison: Order and progress" (review). Dec. 23. "G. B. Airey: Notes on Earlier Hebrew Scriptures" (review).

1877

Jan. 27. "Ewald: Antiquities of Israel" (review). May 19. "H. B. Hackett: Commentary on the Original Text of Acts" (review). Dec. 15. "The Limits of our Freedom in Teaching Theology" (article).

1879

Apr. 5–May 10. "Lectures on Dante." Reports of six lectures, reprinted from the *Croydon Chronicle*. Aug. 2. "Duns Scotus and Erigena" (letter).

1880

Apr. 10. "Prof. Huxley: Science Primers" (review). May 8. "Pfleiderer: Paulinism" (review). June 12. "The Government and the Opium Traffic" (article).

1881

Jan. 8. "The Rising in the Transvaal and Public Opinion in Holland" (article). Apr. 2, 9, 16, 30, May 7. "The Opium Traffic" (letters and articles). June 11. "First impressions of the Revised New Testament" (article).

1882

Mar. 11, Apr. 8. "The Opium Trade" (letters). Sept. 23. "The Egyptian Question" (letter). Oct. 14. "J. Seymour Keay: Spoiling the Egyptians" (review). Dec. 30. "Progress and Poverty" (article).

1883

Apr. 21, May 5, 12. "Mr. Toynbee's Lectures on Progress and Poverty" (3 articles). June 23. "Progress and Poverty" (letter); "The Death of Bishop Colenso" (article).

1884

Feb. 2. "Mr. Wicksteed and Mr. George" (letter). Feb. 16. "The Nationalisation of Land" (letter).

1885

Aug. 22. "The late Rev. Charles Wicksteed, B.A." (letter).

1887

Dec. 10. "Plumptre: Commedia and Canzoniere of Dante" (review).

1888

May 19–Sept. 29. "Money." Twelve special articles; reprinted with title: *Getting and Spending*.

1890

Aug. 16. "Fabian Essays in Socialism" (review).

1891

Apr. 25, May 2, Suppl. "Church and Social Questions" (address to National Conference). Oct. 31. "The Battle with Materialism" (Provincial Assembly sermon). Dec. 26. "The late Professor Kuenen" (obituary).

1892

July 2. "Mr. Wicksteed and the Labour Churches" (letter). Sept. 10. "Denominational Papers" (article).

1893

July 29. "R. L. Carpenter: Sermons and Addresses" (review).

1895

June 22. "P. Villari: Two First Centuries of Florentine History" (review).

1896

Mar. 21. "P. Villari: Two First Centuries, etc.," vol. ii (review). Apr. 18, June 13. "Knight's Wordsworth" (review).

1897

May 15. "Knight: Prose works of Wordsworth" (review). July 17, 31, Aug. 7, 14. "The Armenian Question" (letters).

1898

June 18. "Edm. Gardner: Dante's Ten Heavens" (review). Aug. 13. "Mr. John Bridge" (obituary). Oct. 22, 29. "Anselm's 'Cur Deus Homo'" (2 articles). Nov. 5. "Among the Labour Churches" (article). Dec. 24. "Russell Martineau" (obituary). Dec. 31. "Worship" (a sermon in Mill Hill Chapel, Leeds).

1899

May 20, June 17. "The Atonement" (2 letters). Sept. 16. "Paget Toynbee: Dante Dictionary" (review); "Edw. Moore: Studies in Dante, 2nd series" (review). Nov. 11. "Anna Swanwick" (obituary). Dec. 16. "Bryce: Impressions of South Africa" (review).

1900

Apr. 14. "The Fear of God and the Sense of Sin" (report of address to National Conference at Leicester). July 7. "Our Differences: Political and Religious" (report of address to Provincial Assembly of Lancashire and Cheshire).

1901

Jan. 19. "Miss Barmby's Poems" (article). Jan. 26, Feb. 1. "The Hexateuch" (2 articles). Apr. 13. "Froebel" (report of address to Manchester District Sunday School Assoc.). Apr. 20. "Mrs. Brooke Herford" (obituary). July 13. "Wordsworth's ideals and 19th cent." (report of address to International Council). Sept. 14.

"Alfred the Great" (article). Oct. 26. "For the magnanimity of England" (letter).

1902

May 10. "C. A. Dinsmore: The Teachings of Dante" (review). Sept. 6. "The Natives of the Transvaal" (letter); "In Praise of Wheels" (article).

1903

Jan. 3. "J. E. Carpenter: The Hexateuch" (review). Jan. 10. "The Friendship of St. Francis and St. Dominic" (letter). Jan. 31. "H. R. Fox: Civilisation in Congoland" (review); "James Bryce: Relations of Advanced and Backward Races of Mankind" (review). Aug. 1. "Social and Family Ethics" (letter). Aug. 8. Note on above letter. Aug. 29. "My First Visit to Holland" (article). Nov. 21. "Beatrice Barmby's Verse and Prose" (review).

1904

Jan. 2. "Funeral Address for Dr. Brooke Herford" (obituary). Jan. 23. "For the Healing of the Nations" (review of books on the Boer War). Feb. 27. "Marcus Dods: Forerunners of Dante" (review); "J. S. Carroll: Exiles of Eternity" (review). Aug. 13. "Edw. Moore: Studies in Dante, 3rd series" (review). Nov. 12. "Edw. Moore: Tutte le Opere di Dante Alighieri" (review). Dec. 10. "W. P. Ker: The Dark Ages" (review).

1905

Feb. 25. "Address at Memorial Service to Dr. and Mrs. Brooke Herford" (obituary). Apr. 22. "Dr. Martineau and John James Tayler" (article). May 27. "Janet Case: The Prometheus Bound of Aeschylus" (review).

1906

June 2. "Henrik Ibsen" (article). Oct. 20. "Herbert and Alice Rix" (obituary).

1908

May 9. "Licensing reform" (letter). June 6, Aug. 15. "W. Knight: Letters of the Wordsworth Family" (review). Nov. 28. "The Social Ideals and Economic Doctrines of Socialism" (address). Dec. 5. "Passages from Vondel done into Miltonic Verse"; "Milton's Satan" (article).

1909

Nov. 6. "Lady Schwann's Appeal for Miss Colenso" (letter). Nov. 13. "The Congo" (article). Nov. 27. "M. F. Jerrold: Francesco Petrarca" (review).

1910

Feb. 26. "The Genius of the Earthly Paradise" (article). July 30. "Street Trading by Children" (letter). Dec. 10. "R. Storr: Concordance to 'De Imitatione Christi'" (review).

1912

Mar. 23. "Report of the Royal Commission on Vivisection" (letter). May 18. Ditto (article). Sept. 7. "The Churches and Industrial and Social Unrest" (article). Oct. 19. "Foreign Policy and Christian Ethics" (letter). Nov. 16. "J. H. Harris: Dawn in Darkest Africa" (review).

1913

Jan. 11. Address at Unveiling of Coleridge Memorial at Shrewsbury. July 26. "H. S. Perris: Pax Britannica" (review); "Norman Angell: War and Essential Realities" (review). Aug. 9. "A Plea for Dogs" (letter).

1914

July 25. "Graham Wallas: The Great Society" (review).

1915

June 5. "Gas as a Weapon" (letter). July 17. "Edward Spenser Beesly" (obituary).

1918

June 15. "Dante's Vision of Peace" (article). Aug. 17. "W. J. Jupp: Wayfarings" (review).

1920

Nov. 13, Dec. 11. "Professor Murray's Agamemnon" (2 reviews).

1921

Aug. 27. "The Founder of the 'Poor Clares'" (article).

1923

June 9. "Mrs. Geldart" (obituary). July 21. "Professor Murray's Choephoroe" (review). Nov. 3. "H. W. Garrod: Wordsworth" (review).

INDEX

INDEX

NOTE. In this index the initials P. H. W. are used to indicate Philip Henry Wicksteed.

S